FRAUENLOB'S SONG OF SONGS

A MEDIEVAL GERMAN POET AND HIS MASTERPIECE

Frauenlob's
SONG OF SONGS

BARBARA NEWMAN

with the CRITICAL TEXT OF KARL STACKMANN

AND A MUSICAL PERFORMANCE ON CD
by the ENSEMBLE SEQUENTIA

directed by BARBARA THORNTON AND BENJAMIN BAGBY

The Pennsylvania State University Press
University Park, Pennsylvania

Library of Congress
Cataloging-in-Publication Data

Frauenlob, d. 1318.
[Marienleich. English & German (Middle High German)]
Frauenlob's Song of songs : a medieval German poet and his masterpiece / Barbara
Newman ; with the critical text of Karl Stackmann ; and a musical performance on CD
by the Ensemble Sequentia directed by Barbara Thornton and Benjamin Bagby.
p.   cm.
Includes bibliographical references and index.
ISBN 0-271-02925-0 (pbk. : alk. paper)
1. Frauenlob, d. 1318. Marienleich.
2. Frauenlob, d. 1318—Criticism and interpretation.
3. German poetry—Middle High German, 1050–1500—
History and criticism.
I. Newman, Barbara.
II. Stackmann, Karl.
III. Title.

PT1519.F7A66 2006
831'.22—dc22
2006016920

The Pennsylvania State University Press
is a member of the Association of American University Presses.

It is the policy of The Pennsylvania State University Press to use acid-free paper.
This book is printed on paper containing 50% post-consumer waste,
and meets the minimum requirements of
American National Standard for Information Sciences—Permanence of Paper for
Printed Library Material, ANSI Z39.48–1992.

CONTENTS

LIST OF ILLUSTRATIONS

IN MEMORIAM
Barbara Thornton

PREFACE

The poet Frauenlob, whose stage name means either "praise of ladies" or "praise of Our Lady," was born between 1250 and 1260 in Meissen, Saxony, near the Bohemian border, and died in Mainz on November 29, 1318.[1] Manuscripts refer to him as Heinrich von Meissen, after his birthplace, or, more often, Meister Heinrich Vrouwenlop, after his art. From the mid-1270s until his death, Frauenlob pursued the life of a traveling minstrel, composing and performing topical poems, religious verse, and the occasional love song at the courts of noble patrons ranging from the kings of Bohemia and Denmark to the archbishops of Bremen and Mainz. Admired equally for his gifts as musician and poet, he became the acknowledged master of the *geblümter Stil*, or "flowery style." By the time of his death, he was a highly acclaimed and much imitated though controversial figure whose talents and connections merited the privilege of burial in Mainz Cathedral. The poet's star remained in the ascendant for three centuries afterward: the meistersingers regarded Frauenlob as the greatest of the twelve old masters they revered as precursors, even claiming that he had founded the first singing school in Mainz. In their own schools, aspiring poets continued to compose new lyrics for his melodies and rhyme schemes up to the eighteenth century.

Thereafter, Frauenlob's fame suffered a swift and near-total eclipse. Although a few of the Romantics appreciated him, most critics had little use for his hermetic and immensely learned poems, which in their view savored too much of the intellect and too little of the heart. Protestants tended to find his fervent Marian piety blasphemous, and rationalist scholars even questioned his sanity. Despite the publication of Frauenlob's collected works by Ludwig Ettmüller in 1843,[2] the poet attracted virtually no further attention until 1913, when Ludwig Pfannmüller

---

1. For a general introduction, see Karl Stackmann, "Frauenlob," *Die deutsche Literatur des Mittelalters: Verfasserlexikon*, 2nd ed. (Berlin: Walter de Gruyter, 1980), 2:865–77.

2. Frauenlob (Heinrich von Meissen), *Heinrichs von Meissen des Frauenlobes Leiche, Sprüche, Streitgedichte und Lieder*, ed. Ludwig Ettmüller (Leipzig: G. Basse, 1843).

produced a new edition of his masterpiece, which he titled the *Marienleich*. But Pfannmüller, for all the erudition he lavished on Frauenlob's text, was hardly an admirer of the poet. In fact, he devoted much of his introduction to diagnosing "inadequacies of the style and the man," whom he branded a *Strudelkopf* ("noodlehead").[3] Thus ill-served by his editor, Frauenlob continued to languish in obscurity until 1972, when Karl Stackmann paved the way for a new critical edition with an essay arguing the radical thesis that Frauenlob's poems were, and were meant to be, comprehensible: neither the ravings of a madman, nor empty rhetoric composed merely "to please the ear and intoxicate the senses," nor oracles whose interpretive key is lost beyond recovery.[4] Thanks to the tireless efforts of Stackmann, his colleagues, and his students, Frauenlob is slowly beginning to regain his rightful place in the history of German poetry. But anglophone scholarship on this master is nonexistent, although he merits comparison with such luminaries as the *Pearl* poet in English and Guido Cavalcanti in Italian.[5]

To remedy this lack, I am pleased to present a new poetic translation of the *Marienleich*, together with Stackmann's critical text on facing pages,[6] a detailed commentary on the poem, and an introduction to Frauenlob's life and works. This book also includes a musical performance on CD by the ensemble Sequentia, recorded in 1990 under the direction of Benjamin Bagby and the late Barbara Thornton but now released for the first time in North America. In Chapters 1 through 5, readers will find a discussion of Frauenlob's oeuvre and social context and his philosophical ideas, sources, language and prosody, music, and influence. The commentary presents a strophe-by-strophe analysis of the text, identifying allusions, elucidating cruces, and highlighting the poet's rich and often difficult imagery. In the remainder of this preface, I sketch the broad outlines of the poem and present an interpretation in bold strokes.

To understand the *Marienleich,* one of the most astonishing poems the European Middle Ages produced, we must first remember and then forget everything we thought we knew about the medieval cult of the Virgin, for the poem is at once the brilliant consummation of a preexisting genre, the *Marienlob* (or "Marian praise"), and a theological and philosophical statement that goes far beyond anything that mainstream devotion, or indeed orthodox theology, had yet conceived. To begin with its title, which is based on editorial custom rather than manuscript evidence, the *leich* is a demanding, virtuosic genre akin to the Latin sequence. It can be loosely translated as "lay," but that is misleading if it suggests a parallel with the French *lais* of Marie de France or with such medieval English lays as *Sir Orfeo*. The Old French and Middle English

---

3. *Frauenlobs Marienleich*, ed. Ludwig Pfannmüller (Strassburg: Karl Trübner, 1913), 13–18. Pfannmüller deplores Frauenlob's "eccentricity and *Strudelköpfigkeit,* his inability for once to think and say something totally comprehensible" (17).

4. Karl Stackmann, "Bild und Bedeutung bei Frauenlob," *Frühmittelalterliche Studien* 6 (1972): 441–60, citing Otto Mordhorst, *Egen von Bamberg und "die geblümte Rede"* (Berlin: Ebering, 1911), 87, on the emptiness of the *geblümter Stil*.

5. Harald Bühler, "Zur Gestaltung des lyrischen Ichs bei Cavalcanti und Frauenlob," in Werner Schröder, ed., *Wolfram-Studien* 10: *Cambridger "Frauenlob" Kolloquium 1986* (Berlin: Erich Schmidt, 1988), 179–89; Barbara Newman, "The Artifice of Eternity: Speaking of Heaven in Three Medieval Poems," *Religion and Literature* 37 (2005): 1–24.

6. The text and all citations are from Frauenlob (Heinrich von Meissen), *Leichs, Sangsprüche, Lieder,* ed. Karl Stackmann and Karl Bertau, 2 vols. (Göttingen: Vandenhoeck & Ruprecht, 1981).

narrative lay is a popular form—a brief romance in rhyming couplets easily grasped by a listening audience. The Middle High German *leich*, on the other hand, is a learned form that employs difficult rhyme schemes and cannot be fully understood without reading as well as hearing.[7] As Patrick Diehl notes, only the most famous poets are known to have written *leichs*, and very few composed more than one.[8] Frauenlob, exceptional in this as in so many ways, produced three.

Even the first half of the title *Marienleich* is hard to translate, for in this poem of more than five hundred lines, the name "Maria" never occurs, nor does "Jesus." This omission is deliberate, for the "I" who speaks more than two-thirds of the poem both subsumes and transcends the woman who gave birth to Jesus. Although she is the earthly mother of Christ, she is also the eternal partner of the Trinity and the life-giving principle of Nature.[9] With good reason, the ensemble Sequentia gave their original performance of this piece the title "Celestial Woman." Like Jesus himself, Frauenlob's Mary is dual-natured, as she reveals in the last, climactic strophe: "Ich menschlich gotlich wart, / ja gotlich menschlich" ("Human, I became divine—divine and human"; 20.30–31). In Frauenlob's profoundly gendered cosmology, the divine Word and the creative Wisdom of God are everlasting lovers, Bridegroom and Bride, who become manifest to mortals through their earthly existence as Mary and Jesus, Mother and Son. In deference to orthodoxy, however, there is one key difference between them: Jesus is God-made-man, an immortal who assumed our humanity at the Incarnation, while Mary is woman-made-goddess, a mortal who was lifted into her divinity at the Annunciation. Of course, these two moments are the same moment—the instant when Mary responds to the angel's greeting with her *Fiat mihi* and conceives the Word made flesh. For Frauenlob, this moment of total bodily union is the consummation of an eternal love affair in human flesh and blood. His poem circles back to it time and again, visiting it from multiple angles with an inexhaustible array of images, some vividly erotic, some philosophical. The moment of consummated love is also the pivot of salvation: from that instant, human and divine are one, never again to be parted.

Although this doctrine rings strangely to Protestant and even Catholic ears today, Frauenlob would have considered it fully scriptural. This is because the medieval church, through its liturgy, drew far more of its Mariology from the Old Testament than the New, first choosing Old Testament readings for Marian feasts, then developing an exegetical theology to account for them.[10] So, in accord with one of the poet's favorite metaphors, the *Marienleich* can be approached as a braid woven from three biblical strands: the Song of Songs, the Apocalypse,

7. On the *leich* and cognate forms in Latin and Romance languages, see Olive Sayce, *The Medieval German Lyric, 1150–1300: The Development of Its Themes and Forms in Their European Context* (Oxford: Clarendon, 1982), 346–407.

8. Patrick Diehl, *The Medieval European Religious Lyric: An Ars Poetica* (Berkeley and Los Angeles: University of California Press, 1985), 97.

9. For Natura, Minne, Sapientia, and Mary herself as medieval goddesses, see my *God and the Goddesses: Vision, Poetry, and Belief in the Middle Ages* (Philadelphia: University of Pennsylvania Press, 2002). Chapters 2, 4, 5, and 6 of that book explore several traditions on which Frauenlob drew.

10. Rachel Fulton, "Mimetic Devotion, Marian Exegesis, and the Historical Sense of the Song of Songs," *Viator* 27 (1996): 85–116; Fulton, *From Judgment to Passion: Devotion to Christ and the Virgin Mary, 800–1200* (New York: Columbia University Press, 2002), part 2.

and the wisdom books (Proverbs, Ecclesiasticus, and the Wisdom of Solomon). The Song of Songs is the most obvious, shaping the pervasive erotic mood of the poem and many of its details. In fact, several manuscripts give it the title *Cantica canticorum,* or, in one case, "der guldin flügel ʒu latin Cantica canticorum" ("the golden wing on the Latin Song of Songs").[11] When Mary speaks as the Bride, it is her "human" voice that we hear—sometimes as mature sexual partner, sometimes as innocent maiden, sometimes as the mother who gazes on her "ancient lover" and makes him young. Christ is both her bridegroom and her son, though at several points she presents herself as bride of the whole Trinity, most stunningly when she proclaims, "Ich slief bi drin" ("I slept with Three," 11.8). Frauenlob knew the Song of Songs as mediated through both the liturgy and the exegetical tradition, especially the Song commentary of Alan of Lille.[12] Twelfth-century exegetes such as Alan and Rupert of Deutz, as Ann Astell remarks, present Mary as sexually innocent yet experiencing deep and inexpressible joy at the moment of her intimate union with the Beloved. Her virginity "intensifies, rather than diminishes, the strength of her emotional responses" and thus "allows her to have a 'sexual' experience of God—that is, a surpassing sense of personal completion by him in body and soul"—without losing her physical purity.[13] The same could be said of Frauenlob's Mary. Though the poet's metaphors are audacious, they are not meant to be blasphemous. He viewed both human and cosmic sexuality in an extremely positive light, so his Virgin is no less holy for being highly sexed. In fact, she may be more so, in the long lineage of ancient fertility goddesses—although these would have been known to the poet only through their Latin avatars, Venus and Natura.

The "divine" Mary speaks through Frauenlob's other biblical fonts, the Apocalypse and the wisdom books. Although the last twelve strophes of the *leich* are voiced by the Virgin herself, the first eight are uttered in the person of a seer modeled on Saint John the Divine, whose vision of the Woman clothed with the sun (Apoc. 12:1) opens the poem. In addition to this prophetic figure, Mary is identified with the Bride of the Lamb (Apoc. 21:9) and the new Jerusalem (Apoc. 21:2)—two overlapping symbols that were normally interpreted as figures of the church. Although the Virgin sometimes appears as a synecdoche for the church, as when she declares, "Ich binz die groʒe gotes stat" ("I am the great city of God," 15.3), this sense is not much to the fore. More often, Frauenlob uses the apocalyptic imagery to heighten the cosmic resonance of his Mary. "The moon has laid itself down at [her] feet" (10.12–13) for much the same reason that it adorns the headdress of Isis: like Isis, Mary is a celestial goddess who arranges the stars in the firmament and sets the spheres on their axis (strophe 17b). This role falls to Mary as the embodiment of Sapientia or eternal Wisdom, the daughter-bride of God, who speaks forcefully of her

11. These are manuscripts E, t, and W. For a discussion of the manuscripts, see below, Chapter 5, pp. 140–47.

12. Gerhard M. Schäfer, *Untersuchungen zur deutschsprachigen Marienlyrik des 12. und 13. Jahrhunderts* (Göppingen: Kümmerle, 1971), chap. 4.

13. Ann Astell, *The Song of Songs in the Middle Ages* (Ithaca: Cornell University Press, 1990), 62–63.

creative work and her intimacy with the Holy One in Proverbs 8–9 and Ecclesiasticus 24. These biblical books furnished readings for the Marian feasts of the Assumption (August 15) and the Nativity (September 8). In the antiphons and responsories for those feasts, the wisdom texts are already so intertwined with the Song of Songs as to be inextricable. Thus Frauenlob would have inherited many of his biblical linkages directly from the liturgy.[14] Still more important, the sapiential books provided him with a model for the first-person speech of his Virgin, which is not at all typical of hymnody or prayer. Rather, it is an ancient Near Eastern mode of divine self-revelation, the appropriate style for a deity proclaiming his or her own praise. Wisdom in particular speaks of her eternal preexistence in this mode: "I was ordained from eternity and from of old, before the earth was made" (Prov. 8:23); "when he laid the foundations of the earth, I was with him, fashioning all things" (Prov. 8:30); "I came forth from the mouth of the Most High, the firstborn before all creation" (Ecclus. 24:5); "I am the mother of fair love and of fear, of knowledge and of holy hope" (Ecclus. 24:24).[15] This kind of language is rare in the Bible; aside from the wisdom books, it appears only in the "I am" sayings of the Johannine Jesus. So in choosing this semantic register, Frauenlob was deliberately heightening the divinity of his Virgin through her identification with Sapientia.

The braiding of these scriptural sources gives the poem a strange iridescence. Mary's earthly and heavenly aspects are interwoven as thoroughly as are the biblical texts from which her speech is crafted, so that she appears now woman and now goddess, now mistress and now mother, now innocent girl and now timeless principle. The mystery of her double nature unfolds gradually, though it is fair to say that erotic passion dominates the first part of the poem, while eternal divinity governs the second. But in addition to these biblical sources, Frauenlob drew extensively on secular literature. He structures much of the poem around the seven liberal arts and the ten categories of Aristotelian logic, not to mention riddling allusions to alchemy, the legend of the Holy Grail, and the allegorical beasts of the *Physiologus* tradition. With each new frame of reference, Mary gains another dimension and wins preeminence in another sphere, until she comes more and more to seem all in all.

By far the most important of these secular traditions is *hohe Minne* ("courtly love"), for Frauenlob himself was a minnesinger as well as a religious poet. At several points in the *leich*, the eroticism of the Song of Songs is overlaid with that of vernacular romance, which speaks a very different idiom. To choose just one example, after her amorous tryst with God, the Virgin asks the same seemingly innocent question as Isolde asked after drinking the fatal love potion with Tristan.[16] Later, in strophe 15a, the love affair of Christ and Mary is cast in the unexpected terms of

14. Kurt Gärtner, "Das Hohelied in Frauenlobs Marienleich," in Schröder, ed., *Wolfram-Studien* 10:105–16.

15. All biblical citations in this book are from the Latin Vulgate. Translations are my own, though I have remained as close as possible to the wording of the Revised Standard Version.

16. See Commentary on the *Marienleich*, below, strophe 9, p. 186.

a romance plot: a young prince is caught with a beautiful maiden, denounced to his father, and disinherited. Forced into exile, he bears his sufferings patiently but fights and ultimately succeeds in regaining his kingdom. So how fortunate it is—Mary concludes—"that ever I began the affair!" (15.15). By weaving the Fall and the Incarnation into a single, elliptical narrative, Frauenlob presents the tale from an oblique angle that defamiliarizes it. The shock of recognition lies not in *what* he tells but in *how* he tells it—and the cumulative effect of these shocks, distributed throughout the poem, is an aura of awe compounded by a faint whiff of scandal. Devotion is made sexy yet intellectually bracing. Mary herself, as the protean narrator of her own history, the herald of her own praises, seduces readers and hearers as she makes the call of Wisdom her own (Ecclus. 24:26): "Komt alle zu mir, die min gern. / ich wil, ich kan, ich muz gewern" ("Come unto me, all you who desire me: I will, I can, I must content you" 12.9–10). It was to awaken such desire that Frauenlob bent the resources of his extraordinary art.

There are many ways to use this book. Some readers will turn immediately to the translation, which is meant to stand on its own as an English poem even for those who have no German, while others may prefer to begin with the music, using the MHG text and the facing-page English version as an entrée to the performance. Chapters 1–5 introduce the poet-composer and his literary and intellectual world, enabling a more contextualized reading of the *leich*. The commentary is the most technical part of this volume. For students of Middle High German, it should ease the difficulties of Frauenlob's language as well as elucidating the content of his poem. While I hope that medieval Germanists will appreciate a more accessible text of the *Marienleich,* this volume is not meant exclusively for them; it is also meant for all who share an interest in the medieval lyric, the cult of the Virgin, or the heady fusion of sacred and secular love, sensuality, and learning that characterized thirteenth-century thought.

ABOUT THE TEXT, THE TRANSLATION,
AND THE RECORDING

The text of the *Marienleich,* established by Karl Stackmann and Karl Bertau, is reprinted from the Göttingen Ausgabe (GA): Frauenlob (Heinrich von Meissen), *Leichs, Sangsprüche, Lieder* (Göttingen: Vandenhoeck & Ruprecht, 1981), 1:236–81. I have not reproduced the editors' italics, brackets, manuscript indications, or other sigla, so readers wishing to make a more detailed study of the text should consult the GA directly. Karl Bertau's transcription of the music, not included here, can be found on the pages facing Karl Stackmann's text. A fragmentary Latin translation that is also a *contrafactum,* singable to the same tune as the original, appears in GA 1:284–90 and may have been composed by Frauenlob himself. For the editors' textual notes, on which I have relied extensively, see GA 2:613–64. I am grateful to Professors Stackmann and Bertau and their publisher, Vandenhoeck & Ruprecht, for permission to reprint their text.

In translating the *Marienleich* I have attempted the impossible—to produce a viable English poem that accurately (if not always literally) represents Frauenlob's meaning while approximating his virtuosic feats of rhyme and meter as closely as our contemporary tongue permits. My translation was nearing what must have been its nineteenth draft when I came across a wry comment by Ezra Pound, translator extraordinaire, on his youthful attempts at Englishing the work of another metrical acrobat, the troubadour Arnaut Daniel: "I have proved that the Provençal rhyme schemes are not *impossible* in English. They are probably *inadvisable.*"[1] Just how inadvisable the effort might be in Frauenlob's case is proven by the example of his previous translator, A. E. Kroeger, who dedicated his *Lay of Our Lady* to Henry Wadsworth Longfellow in 1877.[2] Kroeger, the author of a book on the minnesingers, actually replicated the ever-shifting

---

1. Anthony Bonner, ed. and trans., *Songs of the Troubadours* (New York: Schocken Books, 1972), 283.

2. Frauenlob (Heinrich von Meissen), A. E. Kroeger, trans., *Cantica Canticorum, or, The Lay of Our Lady* (St. Louis: Gray & Baker, 1877).

patterns of the *Marienleich,* line by line and rhyme for rhyme, though at considerable cost to readability and sense. Here is his version of strophe 8a on the coronation of the Virgin:

> Lo, what a rare life-full love-word!
> Maid, of all hoards the chiefest hoard!
> Thy figure and thy beauty
> O'er-beauty all throne's beauty.
> Loud cry men now: "Crown her, O King, in duty!"
> It fits so well
> Thy state to dwell
> At His right hand there seated.
> The apple, which thou bearst, grows mellow-meated;
> The flowers laugh both sides of thy valley wheated!
> Thy mouth with dewdrops gleams so pearly,
> They gleam as if they'd say: "Oh clearly,
> This maid of all the maidens born delights us dearly!"

It would be easy to ridicule the late Victorian excesses, the archaisms and convolutions of syntax on display here, but the passage has its virtues. It faithfully reproduces not only the demanding rhyme scheme but also the oscillation between short and long lines that is such a notable trait of Frauenlob's style yet so jarring to English ears. Although I too echoed such contrasts in several strophes, in this case I opted for a rough tetrameter broken by only two short lines:

> Ah, what a living word of love!
> Maiden, richest treasure trove!
> The beauty of your radiant face
> fills all heaven's thrones with grace.
> 5   "Crown her, king!" cries every voice.
> "It is truly just and right:
> Let the queen reign at your right.
> The apple that she bears grows ripe."
> On either side of the mountain,
> 10   dew-drunk, all the flowers wanton
> and laugh and sway
> as if to say,
> "The Maid of maids brings joy today."

This is far from perfect. While the *rime riche* of my lines 6 and 7 might have pleased Chaucer, it would have annoyed Frauenlob, and "wanton" in line 10 is an archaism more cavalier than the context demands. Still, I hope the passage illustrates what is to be gained by a more natural-sounding English. In general I have used fewer feminine rhymes (mountain/wanton) and many more slant rhymes (love/trove, grace/voice) than the original. While Frauenlob's prosody permits only pure rhymes, he uses them with a frequency that is not only difficult to sustain but also decidedly out of fashion, even in formal English verse. It goes without saying that my translation *is* formal verse. With a poet of Frauenlob's mannerist bent, it would be pointless to strive for a plain or colloquial style.

I have done my best to replicate many features of his prosody, especially the long lines broken by caesuras, the insistent use of internal rhyme, and above all, the principle of strophic responsion. Although I did not manage to employ exactly the same rhyme scheme in each half of a strophic pair, I preserved the same number of lines in each, and the same general pattern of long and short. In some cases Frauenlob uses rhyme not only within but across half-strophes, as in 12.3–8 and 12.22–27, an effect I tried to imitate. In strophe 13, similarly, the last lines of 13a and 13b must rhyme across a distance of twenty lines. Frauenlob of course composed his *leich* to be sung, so many such effects are amplified by his melodies, while my version aspires only to be read out loud.

Readers are entitled to expect accuracy as well as echoes of the original music, especially in a translation published by an academic press. For this reason, I have supplied literal translations of all German passages, whether of Frauenlob or other poets, cited in Chapters 1–5 and in the Commentary. But my poetic version of the *Marienleich* is as faithful as it dares to be, following the ancient principle of translating sense for sense rather than word for word. It is, I believe, considerably more accurate than Kroeger's version, and at least as faithful as the medieval Latin—and where the Latin translator and I diverge from the original, our deviations are at least instructive. In a few cases I have omitted an untranslatable idiom, such as *vor miner ougen anger* ("before the pasture of my eyes") in 1.4, which the Latin also omits, or a line of padding, such as 19.17, *zwar sie sint solcher slachte* ("that indeed is their nature"). But to his great credit and despite his exigent rhyme schemes, Frauenlob used very little padding. Conversely, I have in rare instances introduced my own fillers. Neither the line "I who am dark, but comely" (10b) nor "my Beloved is mine" (end of 11a) appears in the German text. On the other hand, both verses derive from the Song of Songs, Frauenlob's most important source, and both expand on hints that are indeed present in the original (*brunen*, 10.23; *da barg er sich mit fugen in*, 11.18).

I am under no illusion that I have done justice to my original. For English readers who desire a keener sense of Frauenlob's metrical virtuosity, his exotic coinages, his wild chiming music, and his fervent baroque piety, I can recommend two further options: learn Middle High German or read Gerard Manley Hopkins. Nevertheless, it has been a signal honor to spend the past three years singing duets with a 700-year-old poet. I am the richer for having done so, and I hope the reader will also be.

The CD included with this volume was first released in Germany in the year 2000 under the Deutsche Harmonia Mundi label and titled "The Celestial Woman: Frauenlobs Leich, oder der Guldin Fluegel, zu latin: Cantica Canticorum." I extend my cordial thanks to Benjamin Bagby, the director of Sequentia, and to their recording company, Sony/BMG, for permission to reissue the disc. The information that follows is adapted from the original liner notes.

LIST OF TRACKS AND PERFORMERS

1. Ei, ich sach in dem trone (Benjamin Bagby)	1:25
2. Nu merket, wie sie trüge (men)	2:35
Instrumental interlude	
3. Ein bernde meit und eren riche vrouwe (Benjamin Bagby, men)	1:55
4. Nu lougen nicht durch icht der schicht (men, Benjamin Bagby)	2:02
5. Sit irz die meit, die durch die wüstenunge zoget? (Benjamin Bagby, men)	1:23
6. Den siben kirchen schreib Johan (men)	1:30
7. Ob ich die warheit lerne (Benjamin Bagby, men)	1:13
8. Ei, welch ein lebendez minne wort (Benjamin Bagby, men, women)	3:29
9. Ich bin ez die groze von der kür (Barbara Thornton)	2:21
10. Ich bin erkennig, nennig, kurc (Lena Susanne Norin, Barbara Thornton)	2:38
11. Der smid von oberlande (women, Barbara Thornton)	5:25
12. Ich binz ein zuckersüzer brunne (Johanna Koslowsky, Barbara Thornton)	4:13
13. Sterke unde zierde hat mich ummehelset	3:57
(Lena Susanne Norin, Johanna Koslowsky, Barbara Thornton)	
14. Ein snider sneit mir min gewant (Karen Clark, Laurie Monahan, women)	6:47
Instrumental interlude	
15. Ich binz der sterne von Jacop (Suzie Le Blanc, women)	4:53
16. Ich binz der ersten sache kint (Johanna Koslowsky, women)	2:39
17. Ei, waz sich mischet und unmischet (Karen Clark, women)	3:42
18. Wie die döne löne schöne schenken uz der armonien (Laurie Monahan)	1:52
19. Nu lat iuch lüsten also hübsches meres (Lena Susanne Norin, women)	3:58
20. Gein berge climmen nach ir nar die geize (women)	5:26
Total playing time:	62:55

Conception, musical arrangements, and musical direction: Barbara Thornton and Benjamin Bagby
Female voices: Karen Clark, Johanna Koslowsky, Suzie Le Blanc, Laurie Monahan, Lena Susanne Norin, Barbara Thornton

Male voices: Benjamin Bagby, Stephen Grant, Eric Mentzel, Raimund Nolte, Matthias Senn
Harps: Benjamin Bagby, Cheryl Ann Fulton
Arrangements of harp music: Benjamin Bagby, Cheryl Ann Fulton
Instruments: Two Gothic harps and two *cithara anglica:* Rainer Thurau (Wiesbaden)
Language consultant and pronunciation coach: Andrea Fritz
Sources: The standard modern edition is Karl Stackmann and Karl Bertau, *Heinrich von Meissen: Leichs, Sangsprüche, Lieder,* which was used in the preparation of the recording and is reprinted in this volume. The *Marienleich* has survived in a number of incomplete musical sources that can be used to reconstruct the entire piece. In those places where there are gaps in the musical transmission, reconstructions were made by Benjamin Bagby based on existing melodies within the overall modal structure.
A & R direction: Daniela Haltmayer
Producer: Klaus L. Neumann (WDR Köln)
Recording engineer and original analog editing (1990): Siegfried Spittler (WDR Köln)
Digital restoration and remastering (1999): Dirk Franken and Barbara Valentin (WDR Köln)
Balance engineer: Werner Strässer
Recorded: 26–29 March 1990, in the church of St. Osdag, Mandelsloh
A recording of the Westdeutschen Rundfunks, Köln.

A NOTE ABOUT THE SEQUENTIA FRAUENLOB PROJECT
by Benjamin Bagby (1999)

In the history of Sequentia, important projects typically have demanded a long period of gestation and then have reemerged in various incarnations over the span of many years. Our initial contact with the *Marienleich* was during 1985, when we included sections of the piece in a program called "The Apocalyptic Imagination." Subsequent intensive study of the piece led to a theatrical production commissioned by the Alte Oper Frankfurt for the Frankfurt Feste in September 1987 and to concert performances in the Utrecht Festival Oude Muziek and other festivals. During 1989–90 the work was completely reenvisioned for this recording, and it continued to be performed in concert as late as 1994. In this version, for instance, a larger mixed instrumental ensemble was replaced by two gothic harps, instruments that are most suitable for accompanying a piece that unfolds through all eight modes. This production was the last analog recording made by Sequentia for the Westdeutscher Rundfunk. Because of technical problems with the editing process and the analog tapes, the recording's release was repeatedly delayed, until other projects (especially the Hildegard von Bingen complete works) began to take precedence. Finally, in 1995, after one final unsuccessful attempt to restore the tapes, Barbara Thornton and I decided to abandon the tapes and rerecord the work at a later date. In any case, we no longer agreed with some of the decisions we had made about the musical realization, and we believed we could do a better job if given another chance. What musician has not known this feeling? But following Barbara's tragic death in 1998, I asked Deutsche Harmonia Mundi and the Westdeutscher Rundfunk to allow one more attempt at remastering the tapes, especially in light of new technical possibilities for digital restoration that had not existed before.

I believe it is important that this performance now be heard, especially considering the enormous amount of energy put into the Frauenlob project by the ensemble, and in honor of Barbara Thornton's own deeply personal involvement with the piece over a period of ten years—it was very much her personal creation—and finally, as a record of her own vocal contributions, which would otherwise have remained unheard forever. The release of Frauenlob's *Leich*, exactly ten years after its recording, is not only a major testimony to the genius of one of Germany's most innovative and profound poet-composers. This CD is also a "historical recording," documentation of an important phase in the life of our ensemble, and a witness to the creative force of an artist whose voice was cruelly silenced in mid-career.

ABOUT THE ENSEMBLE SEQUENTIA

Founded in 1977 by Benjamin Bagby and the late Barbara Thornton, Sequentia is among the world's most respected and innovative ensembles for medieval music. Under the direction of Benjamin Bagby, Sequentia can look back on more than a quarter-century of international concert tours, a comprehensive discography spanning the entire Middle Ages (including the complete works of Hildegard von Bingen), film and television productions of medieval music drama, and a new generation of young performers trained in professional courses given by members of the ensemble. Sequentia has performed throughout Europe, the Americas, India, the Middle East, East Asia, Africa, and Australia and has received numerous prizes (including a Disque d'Or, several Diapasons d'Or, two Edison Prizes, the Deutsche Schallplattenpreis, and a Grammy nomination) for many of its more than two dozen recordings on the BMG/Deutsche Harmonia Mundi and Marc Aurel Edition labels. A recent release contains reconstructions of music from the ensemble's acclaimed 2001 program based on the Icelandic Edda, "The Rheingold Curse." The year 2004 witnessed the release of a new CD, on the Sony/BMG label, of the earliest known European songs: "Lost Songs of a Rhineland Harper." Sequentia's most recent recording is "Crown and Veil: Music from Medieval Female Monasteries," produced in conjunction with the exhibition of medieval monastic art at the Kunst- und Ausstellungshalle der Bundesrepublik Deutschland, Bonn, and the Ruhrlandmuseum Essen, March–July 2005.

Sequentia has created more than sixty innovative concert programs that encompass the entire spectrum of medieval music, in addition to their creation of such music-theater projects as Hildegard von Bingen's *Ordo Virtutum*, the Cividale *Planctus Marie*, the *Bordesholmer Marienklage*, Frauenlob's *Marienleich*, and the medieval Icelandic *Edda*. The work of the ensemble is divided between a small touring ensemble of vocal and instrumental soloists, and a larger ensemble of voices for the performance of chant and polyphony. After twenty-five years based in Cologne, Sequentia's home has been reestablished in Paris (www.sequentia.org).

This project was supported by a translation grant from the National Endowment for the Humanities and a residency at the Rockefeller Foundation's magnificent villa in Bellagio, Italy. I here express my deep gratitude for both. Frau Irmtraud Dewald and the Martinus-Bibliothek of Mainz helped me locate some out-of-the-way material pertaining to Frauenlob's monument and other memorials in that city. Audiences at the University of Minnesota and Brown University provided generous and helpful feedback. I would also like to thank the scholars who have offered their advice and support along the way, among them Paul Breslin, Richard Kieckhefer, Nigel Palmer, Miriam Wendling, and my two press readers, Francis Gentry and Anne Winston-Allen. I am especially grateful to my editor at Penn State, Peter Potter, for his steadfast encouragement and loyalty to such an unconventional project. Finally, I offer heartfelt thanks to Benjamin Bagby of Sequentia. This book is dedicated to the memory of the incomparable Barbara Thornton, without whom it would never have come to be.

FRAUENLOB'S SONG OF SONGS

MARIENLEICH

1. Ei, ich sach in dem trone
   ein vrouwen, die was swanger.
   die trug ein wunderkrone
   vor miner ougen anger.

5 Sie wolte wesen enbunden,
   sust gie die allerbeste,
   zwelf steine ich zu den stunden
   kos in der krone veste.

FRAUENLOB'S SONG OF SONGS

I. The Poet's Vision

1. Listen! I saw a vision:
   a Lady on a throne.
   Great with child, that woman
   wore a wondrous crown.

   How she ached for the hour
   of birth, the best of women!
   In her crown of power
   I saw twelve gemstones glisten.

2. Nu merket,
   wie sie trüge,
   die gefüge,
   der naturen zu genüge:
5 mit dem sie was gebürdet,
   den sach sie vor ir sitzen   mit witzen
   in siben liuchteren
   und sach in
   doch besundert
10 in eines lammes wise
   uf Sion, dem berge gehiuren.

   Sie tet rechte
   als sie solde,
   ja, die holde
15 trug den blumen sam ein tolde.
   vrouwe, ob ir muter würdet
   des lammes und der tuben,   iur truben
   ir liezet iuch sweren?
   da von mich
20 nicht enwundert,
   ob iuch die selbe spise
   kan wol zu der früchte gestiuren.

2. Now see
   how she
   so meekly
   bowed to Nature's ways.
   With visionary gaze
   she saw the child in her womb
   enthroned amid lampstands seven,
   and yet again she saw him
   in the form of a Lamb
   high on Mount Zion,
   the mount of heaven.

   She did
   as she should,
   noble and good,
   bore a flower like a scepter.
   Lady, if you would be
   mother of both Lamb and Dove,
   could you bear the weight
   of the vineyard's grape?
   I'll not be amazed
   if the fruit of that vine
   makes you fruitful from above.

3. Ein bernde meit und eren riche vrouwe,   din ouwe
   von dem grozen himeltouwe
   blumen birt in werder schouwe.
   man höret der turteltuben singen   erklingen,   volringen
5 nach süzes meien horden.
   hin ist des winters orden,
   die blünden winrebe diner frucht   sint vollen smachaft worden.

   Des soltu gan, din friedel rufet arten   dir zarten
   in dem heilwin tragenden garten:
10 'kom, lieb, kom', sust wirt sin warten
   dort uf dem lewenberge von mirren.   kein virren   sol irren
   dich, wan er wil erkosen
   sich mit dir in den rosen.
   des soltu, tochter, muter, meit,   mit liebem liebe im losen.

3. Fertile maid and   favored lady,
   your meadow wet with heaven's dew
   flowers in resplendent show.
   Hear the turtledoves singing   their song, loud-ringing,
   a song of longing
   for sweet May's treasure.
   Winter's ordeal is over:
   your vineyards blossom   with fruit so wholesome.

   Your beloved calls from the vineyard,   from the garden
   where hallowed grapes ripen:
   "Come, love, come!" He is waiting
   on the mountain of myrrh   where lions stalk.
   Your way cannot err
   should he wish to talk
   among roses. Listen with love
   most tender, daughter,   mother, maid, you must go!

4. Nu lougen nicht   durch icht   der schicht,   daz dich   sunderlich
der künig in sinen keler furte.
dich rurte
sin grüzen.

5 wie nu, ver meit, hat ir iuch wol versunnen?
wir gunnen
der wunnen
iu wol, daz ir den win habt getrunken
mit der milch   so süzen.

10 Ich wene wol,   iu sol   den zol   sin munt   machen kunt,
wa durch die murehüter quamen,
iu namen
den mandel.
waz sucht ir, meit, so spate in disen gazzen?
15 kein lazzen,
wir vazzen
die liebe. an iuwern wunden durchsunken
hat sin drilch   den wandel.

4. Tell no lie,   never try   to deny:
   you alone were meeting
   with the king
   in his cellar—
   you knew his greeting,
   you felt his touch.   How much,
   fair maid, did you dally?
   We do not envy the wine of bliss
   you drank there   with sweet, sweet milk.

   I know well   his own tongue should tell   you the toll—
   why the watchmen took
   your cloak,
   asking what do you seek,
   fair maid, so late
   in these alleys?   "Never cease,
   we must seize
   the beloved!" Deep in your wounds
   he's branded   his threefold mark.

5. Sit irz die meit,   die durch die wüstenunge zoget   mit richen
      smecken?
   iuch hat gemehelt der eren voget.   ir sit ein brut,
   daz prüfe ich an den worten,
   der künig durch iuwer pforten
5 quam uz und in   nach willen sin,
   die da beslozzen was und ist   an allen eren orten.

   David, der seit,   ir stündet zu der zeswen hant,   goltvar gekleidet
   iuch künig Salomon bevant.   gar überlut
   er gicht, daz iuwer löcke
10 gestalt sin sam rechböcke
   und iuwer huf,   da seit er uf,
   daz die viurguldin fürspan sin.   wol stan der kiuschen ir röcke.

5. Are you that maid   who came up through the wilderness   with rich
        perfumes?
   The honored prince   has made you his bride.
   This I prove as follows:
   the king comes and goes
   as he pleases through your portals,
   yet they were   and still are closed
   in every place to mortals.

   David says you stand   at his right hand   in cloth of gold.
   King Solomon found you,   I heard him declare
   the curls of your hair
   dance like gazelles,
   your thighs are jewels
   of golden fire.   The attire
   of a modest woman suits her well!

6. Den siben kirchen schreib Johan,
waz sie tun solden oder lan,
ob sie mit willen wolden stan
bi gote sunder valles wan.
5 do wart gebent der selden ban.
der engel siben vurten dan
die botschaft, als ich mich versan.
meit, sit din forme den bespan,
der alle forme tirmen kan,
10 diz wirken schuf ir kraft, der siben geiste.

Da von geliche ich dich zu stunt
den kirchen, ach du bernder grunt,
du minne, wisheit was dir kunt,
du senftekeit, du künste funt,
15 du rat, din sterke bleib gesunt,
din vorchte entsloz den grozen bunt:
meit, aller meide ein überwunt.
von disen geisten wart entzunt
din lip, din herze, des min munt
20 dich mizzet uf daz beste und uf daz meiste.

6. To the seven churches wrote St. John
   what they must do or leave undone
   if they wished to take their stand
   with God, and never fear to fall:
   thus he paved the path of blessings.
   Seven angels carried the tidings,
   if I understand the case at all.
   Maiden, since your form contained
   the One who fashions every form,
   by the craft of spirits seven,

   I compare you, giver of birth,
   to seven churches over all the earth.
   You are Love, and Wisdom is yours,
   you are Gentleness, Knowledge's source,
   you are Counsel and your Strength is whole,
   your Fear of God loosed the chains of hell.
   Maiden, fulfillment of every girl,
   these spirits kindled you, body and soul,
   and thus my craft with words well-formed
   must raise your praise to highest heaven.

7. Ob ich die warheit lerne,
   die siben liecht lucerne
   uz diner sele liuchten sam die sterne
   —von dir wart zitig sines geistes erne—,
5 da der jungalte zwischen saz
   gegerwet, als er sich vermaz
   in wizem kleide sunder haz.
   ei, tochter von Sion, vröu dich der mere.

   Die siben liecht erglesten
10 ob dines geistes vesten:
   din zucht, din kiusche liuchten mit den besten,
   din triuwe und ouch din stete vil wol westen,
   daz der geloube sie nicht floch,
   din güte schein da vollen hoch,
15 din diemut sich gein himel zoch,
   hie bi so bleip din wille an alle swere.

7. If all that I have learned is true,
   these seven lanterns shine from you,
   in your soul their starlight brightens,
   in you his spirit's harvest ripened—
   when the Ancient Youth sat in the clearing,
   robed in white, with gracious bearing—
   peaceful, like a king appearing—
   Daughter of Zion, celebrate!

   The seven lanterns brightly shimmer
   because your spirit does not waver.
   Your courtesy, chastity gleam with the best,
   your truth and constancy held ever fast
   to faith unforsaken
   with kindness unshaken:
   your humility soared to heaven
   and freed your will of every weight.

8. Ei, welch ein lebendez minne wort:
meit, alles hordes überhort!
wan din gestalt, din schöne
durchschönet alle tröne.
5 ir gelf, ir lut ist: 'cröna, künig, cröne.
ir richsen wol
zimt, als ez sol,
zu diner zeswen siten.
der aphel, den sie treit, beginnet ziten.'
10 die blumen lachen beidenthalb der liten,
ir münde hat der tou getwagen,
sie stan rechte als sie wellen sagen:
'die meit ob allen meiden muz uns wol behagen.'

Künic Salomon, der wisheit selch,
15 der gicht, din nabel ein guldin kelch
si voller edeler steine
fin, luter unde reine,
—die sint jacint genennet, als ich meine—
der kelch des suns,
20 dar in er uns
her sinen vater brachte.
wie wol die zarte tochter sich bedachte,
do uns der val des alten swindes schachte.
vil schöne ob allen vrouwen, sprich:
25 der schönen liebe ein muter ich,
der heilicheit ein hoffenunge nennet mich.

8. Ah, what a living word of love!
   Maiden, richest treasure trove!
   The beauty of your radiant face
   fills all heaven's thrones with grace.
   "Crown her, king!" cries every voice.
   "It is truly just and right:
   Let the queen reign at your right.
   The apple that she bears grows ripe."
   On either side of the mountain,
   dew-drunk, all the flowers wanton
   and laugh and sway
   as if to say,
   "The Maid of maids brings joy today."

   As Solomon the wise king told,
   your navel is a cup of gold
   studded with fair
   jewels so clear,
   called jacinths, as I hear.
   In this chalice
   without malice
   the Son brought his Father near us.
   The tender Daughter found a move to make
   when the Old One's fall put us in check.
   Loveliest of women, speak!
   "I am the Mother of love all glorious,
   Call me the hope of holiness."

9. Ich bin ez die groze von der kür,
   min wille ist kreftig und ouch mür.
   gein liebem liebe ich mich erbür.
   daz venster miner klosentür,
5 da gieng min lieb so triutlich vür.
   sin hant mich rurte, des ich spür,
   sie was von süzen touwe naz,
   ez duchte mich ein honigvaz.
   ich az den veim
10 und tranc den seim,
   do quam ich heim.
   des wart mir baz,
   waz wirret daz?

   Den slangen beiz min harm, ich wisel.
15 min süzer touwig morgenrisel
   durchbrach des herten fluches kisel.
   min wünschelrute sunder zwisel
   streich abe der swarzen helle misel.
   do wart gerötet sunder prisel
20 der palme, dem min grüzen quam.
   sprich, edeler, wiser friund Adam,
   wie min gesuch
   den dinen fluch
   brachte in unruch.
25 mir meide zam
   wol muter scham.

II. The Lady's Revelation

9. I am the great and chosen Lady,
   my will is ripe, my desire is mighty.
   For fervent love I must unbar
   the lattice of my cloister door—
   my love all passionate drew near.
   His hand caressed me, wet with dew—
   O taste of honey through and through!
   I ate the comb
   and drank the foam
   then came back home.
   My God, such bliss!
   What's the harm in this?

   I the weasel bore the ermine
   that bit the snake. With morning dew
   I split the hard rock of the curse.
   My divining rod, unforked,
   crushed the heads of hell's black vermin.
   When the palm tree of the Cross
   saw me, it reddened without dye.
   Speak, wise Adam, noble friend,
   and tell how I
   have come to end
   your ancient blight—
   I the Maid, by a mother's right.

10. Ich bin erkennig,   nennig,   kurc,
     des höchsten küneges sedelburg.
     min türne nieman kan gewinnen.
     min zinnen
  5 uz und innen
     sint mit liljen wiz gepinset.
     des trones wesen mir hilflich zinset.
     min gazzen sint geblümet.   swer mich nümet,
     ein balsem den durchgümet.
 10 der sunnen glesten ist min kleit,
     dar in so han ich mich gebriset und gereit.
     so hat der mane sich geleit
     zu minen füzen.
     ich kan büzen
 15 swere, des got geist mich rümet.

     Do er mich vester   swester   sagete,
     er jach, ich were so jung betaget:
     'wie well wir, daz sie sich gerüste
     bar brüste
 20 zu der lüste,
     durch die man sie sprechen solde?'
     nu merket, waz min friedel wolde!
     er warte siner lune,   daz mich brunen
     von senfte der alrunen
 25 wart slafern, durch so süzen smac
     in unser pforten leisten, durch so rich bejag.
     die wile und ich des slafes pflag,
     gein der naturen
     min behuren
 30 muste er vlechten unde ziunen.

10. I am famed,   acclaimed,   adored,
the palace of the highest Lord.
My towers none can storm.
Without, within,
white lilies trim
my ramparts strong.
The tribute of the Throne is mine.
My lanes are lined with flowers,
a taste of balsam overpowers
everyone who names me.
I am clothed in the shining sun,
laced within its rays.
At my feet the moon lies down.
I can lighten
every burden,
thus I earn the Spirit's praise.

Though I am young in days   he called me   strong sister:
"How can we expect her
who has no breasts
to be ripe for pleasure
on the day she is spoken for?"
Hear what my love had in mind!
He bided his time
till slumber claimed me,
lulled by the mandrakes' fumes—
I who am dark, but comely.
Allured by their sweet perfumes,
he passed through our doors
to claim his prize,
and while I lay amazed,
defying nature
he wove my pleasure.

11. Der smid von oberlande
    warf sinen hamer in mine schoz.
    ich worchte siben heiligheit.
    ich trug in, der den himel und die erden treit,
5   und bin doch meit.
    er lag in mir und liez mich sunder arebeit.
    mit sicherheit
    ich slief bi drin,
    des wart ich fruchtig, voller güte
10 süze in süze mir do sneit.
    min alter vriedel kuste mich,
    daz si geseit.
    ich sach in an, do wart er junc, des fröute sich
    die massenie da zu himel alle.
15 swie züchtig stolzer meide rum ich schalle,
    doch hoffe ich, daz ez ieman missevalle.
    er jach, min brüstel weren süzer dann der win,
    da barg er sich mit fugen in.

    Wie wol er mich erkande,
20 der sich so vaste in mich versloz!
    wer leit mich in der liljen tal,
    da min amis curtois sich tougen in verstal?
    ich binz der sal,
    dar inne man daz gespreche nam um Even val,
25 schone ich daz hal.
    secht, lieben, secht:
    min morgenröte hat erwecket
    hohen sang und richen schal,
    den niuwen tag der alten nacht.
30 ich binz der gral,
    da mit der eren künig den leiden übervacht.
    min spünne ernerte den von violvelde.
    mir wart ein hirzgewige an minem gelde,
    damit ich stiez den fluch uz dem gezelde.
35 ich worchte phriemen und enbant die alten recht,
    sus wart der stric des valles slecht.

11. The smith from the high country
    hurled his hammer in my womb
    and forged seven sacraments.
    I carried him who carries earth and sky
    and yet am still a maid.
    He lay in me and left me without labor.
    Most certainly
    I slept with Three—
    till I grew pregnant with God's goodness,
    pierced by sweetness upon sweetness.
    My ancient lover kissed me,
    let this be said:
    I gazed at him and made him young—
    then all the heavenly hosts were glad.
    (The proud Maid's praises must be sung—
    let none take it ill!)
    He said my breasts were sweeter than wine
    and drank his fill—
    my Beloved is mine.

    How intimate he was with me,
    locked in my little room!
    Who will lead me to the lily dell
    where my courtly lover hid so well?
    I am the high court's chamber
    where they heard the case of Eva's fall—
    I, the echo hall.
    Dear friends, remember:
    in the music of my dawn, I awake exalted song;
    from ancient night I bring the morn.
    I am the Grail
    that healed the noble King's great woe.
    With my milk I nursed the hero
    from the violet vale:
    he gave me the antlers of a deer
    to drive the curse out of the tent.
    I pierced the ancient punishment
    with awls, and broke the Fall's
    inveterate snare.

12. Ich binz ein zuckersüzer brunne
des lebens und der bernden wunne.
ich binz ein spiegel der vil klaren reinekeit,
da got von erst sich inne ersach.
5 ich was mit im, do er entwarf gar alle schepfenunge,
er sach mich stetes an in siner ewiclichen ger.
wie rechte wol ich tet im in den ougen,
ich zarter, wolgemuter rosengarte!
komt alle zu mir, die min gern.
10 ich wil, ich kan, ich muz gewern.
ich binz der lebende leitestern,
des nieman sol noch mag enbern.
min mut   gut   frut   tut.
ich binz die stimme, do der alte leo lut
15 die sinen kint uf von des alten todes flut.
ich binz die glut,
da der alte fenix inne sich erjungen wolte.
ich binz des edelen tiuren pelikanes blut
und han daz allez wol behut.

20 Ich binz ein wurzenricher anger,
min blumen, die sint alle swanger,
ir saffes brehender smac vil gelwer varwe treit.
ei, welch ein flüzzig, zinsig bach
die blumen min durchfiuchtet, daz sie stan nach wunsche
entsprungen.
25 ich binz ein acker, der den weize zitig brachte her,
da mit man spiset sich in gotes tougen.
ich drasch, ich mul, ich buch linde und nicht harte,
wan ich mit olei ez bestreich;
des bleib sin biz so süzlich weich.
30 ich binz der tron, dem nie entweich
die gotheit, sit got in mich sleich.
min schar   gar   clar   var:
ich got, sie got, er got, daz ich vor nieman spar.
ich vatermuter, er min mutervater zwar,
35 wan daz ist war.
ich wart, ich leit, ich brach den tot, ich warb, als ich do solde.
ich fur, ich quam, ich Adelheit, der tugende ein ar.
er leit do nicht, min Engelmar.

12. I am the well of life on earth,
    as sweet as sugar—and the joy of birth.
    I am the mirror of great purity
    in which God gazed before all time.
    I was with him when he formed creation,
    he gazed at me with desire unceasing.
    How my beauty gladdened his eyes—
    I, a garden of rose-red mirth.
    Come to me, all you who want me:
    I can, I will, I must content you.
    I am the living lodestar:
    without me none can travel far.
    My will stills all ills.
    I am the ancient lion's roar
    that roused its cub from death's first flood.
    I am the fire
    in which the phoenix renewed its youth.
    I am the precious pelican's blood,
    and well I know that this is truth.

    I am a richly planted field:
    my blossoms all bear fertile yield,
    with fragrant sap, in yellow symmetry.
    Ah, what a swiftly flowing stream
    drenches my blooms in exultation!
    I am the field that bore in season
    wheat for the sacred mysteries.
    I threshed, I milled, I baked the bread—
    soft, not hard, with smooth oil spread.
    I am the throne the Godhead
    never fled—since God slipped inside.
    Strong the throng where I belong!
    I God, they God, he God: this I will never hide.
    I am the Father's mother, my mother's father he—
    how can this be?
    I was born, I suffered; death I shattered;
    I did what I should; I went, I came,
    an eagle, Adelheid by name.
    My Engelmar—he knew no pain.

13. Sterke unde zierde hat mich ummehelset,
   ich schrecke als einer, der da bürge velset,
   wan ich bin uf geschozzen als ein lustig cederboum,
   den cipres ich verschönet han.
 5 ei, welch ein senftez, süzez riechen, swem ich kom in sinen goum.
   ich zoge über daz gebirge hin,
   zu sprechen minen vriedel han ich ganzen sin.
   den wagen ich spise, den der wise von holze werden liez zu
     prise,
   daz gütig nennet uns der grise.
10 min siulen silber meinen,
   min simz, anelein uz golde erscheinen,
   min ufganc purper, wol mich reinen!
   dar zwischen ist geströuwet inne
   die were, senfte, süze minne.
15 der aller bin ich ein beginne.
   genade hat sich in min lefsen uz der kefsen
   so volleclich gegozzen.
   die wisheit hat mir minen munt entslozzen,
   der ordenunge senftekeit min zunge hat genozzen.
20 des grüzet, lieben, grüzet mich.

   Die patriarchen sahen min figuren,
   sie sprechen von mir, daz in der naturen
   so schönez noch so reinez in al der werlte würde nie.
   wil ieman wizzen, waz ich kan?
25 ich salbe, ich heile, ich füre uz nöten, swaz man mir der wunden lie.
   ich binz ein liecht der starken tugend,
   der grundelosen güte ein endelose mugend.
   ich rufe, ich schrie, daz min krie in al der werlte trost gedie.
   hie mit ich mich vor ernste vrie,
30 nicht zornes hat min denken,
   ich kan uz siben hornen schenken,
   die man sach uf dem lamme lenken.
   swaz die propheten alle kunden
   —ir wort, ir rede sie uf mich bunden—
35 ich bir, niur himel minen friunden.
   gein mir so lan die ingesigel alle ir rigel,
   swie vaste er sie behalte,
   min schepfer und min vriedel der vil alte,
   der sich zu mir nach siner kust in drin personen valte.
40 des selben mutermeit bin ich.

13. Strength and beauty embrace me;
    I daunt the devil like a clifftop castle.
    I sprang up like a mighty cedar tree,
    I surpass the cypress in loveliness.
    What sweetness fills the mouth that names me!
    I went up over the mountains
    to speak to my love, my sole desire,
    in the litter of King Solomon,   carved from the wood   of Lebanon,
    as the ancient sage has told.
    My posts are made of silver,
    my seat of glimmering gold,
    my steps of purple splendor.
    Strewn everywhere within
    is sweet Love, true and tender:
    With me all loves begin.
    Abundant grace drips from my lips,
    wisdom has opened my mouth,
    my tongue has tasted the angels' truth.
    Greet me, friends, with greetings high!

    The patriarchs saw me in figures;
    they say that among all natures
    in all the world was none so fair.
    Do you wish to know what I can do?
    I salve, I soothe, I heal all wounds that men reveal.
    I am potent virtue's light,
    abyss of grace in boundless might.
    I shout, I call,   consoling all: thus I free myself from toil.
    My thoughts bear no one ill.
    I can pour from seven horns
    that curve upon the Lamb's white head.
    All that the prophets prophesied—
    of me alone their words were said.
    I bring but heaven to my friends.
    All locks fly open before me,
    however great their artistry.
    My Creator and my ancient Lover
    entered me in Persons three:
    maiden-mother of the same am I.

14. Ein snider sneit mir min gewant,
    sin sin den spehen list ervant:
    do mich gebriset het sin hant,
    er sach mich an und kos min cleider, als ein meister kiesen sol.
5   do stunden mir min cleider uz der mazen wol,
    daz sie gevielen in sinen mut.
    er tet ein spehe, die was nützlich unde gut.
    die wile und ich min cleider truc,   er was so cluc,
    daz er uz minen cleidern sneit im cleider an,
10 die waren baz dann mine cleider vil getan,
    und doch min cleider bliben ganz
    an allen bruch, an allen wanc, an allen schranz,
    vin unde luter, schöne ob aller schöne glanz.
    der meister heizet meister.

15 Als er daz wunderliche cleit
    het wunderlich an sich geleit,
    ez was so wit und was so breit,
    daz ez besloz den grozen, der da himel und erde in henden hat.
    doch ward an im verschroten sit die selbe wat.
20 er worchte ein spehez spiegelvaz.
    als erz volbrachte, san er mitten dinne saz
    und aventiurte meisterschaft   von vremder craft.
    daz spiegelvaz in doch besloz, swie groz er si.
    do blute er wider uz im, alsam ein blünder zwi
25 uz einem ganze boume tut
    und als der apfel uz der blünden blumen blut.
    daz spiegelvaz bleip ganz, an allen enden gut.
    sust ich verwant die geister.

14. A tailor cut for me a gown—
 his craft has won him great renown.
 With his hand he took my measure,
 then gazed at me and chose my clothes
 as a master ought to choose.
 So dazzling and well-dressed I was—
 my garments gave him pleasure.
 I wore them still   as, with his skill,
 out of my gown he cut his own,
 yet more finely wrought than mine,
 and all the while my robe remained
 inviolate and without stain,
 as fair and bright as beauty's sheen.
 The Master is indeed the Master!

 When he had wondrously put on
 this wondrous robe, this ample gown,
 its folds enclosed the One who holds
 earth and sky within his hands.
 And when that robe was torn to shreds
 he wrought by art a mirror-vial
 and sat down in its midst awhile
 to stake his skill   against ill will.
 The mirror-vial contained him
 in his greatness, framed him
 until he burst from it, unquenched,
 and blossomed like a flowering branch—
 whole the vial, intact, untouched.
 The demons I have mastered!

15. Ich binz der sterne von Jacop,
    an mir so lit der hochgeherten engel lop.
    ich binz die groze gotes stat,
    von der sant Augustin so vil gesprochen hat.
5 min pforten nie entslozzen wurden.
    doch quam min vriedel drin und nam min bürde,
    die ich da truc, und half mir tragen.
    daz sol iu allen lusticlichen wol behagen.
    er ward mit einer schönen meit
10 gein sinem vater überseit,
    des quam er sit in arebeit.
    daz ellende er gutlich leit.
    da mit er doch sin erbe erstreit,
    daz im sin vater het verjeit.
15 so wol und wol, daz ich der sachen ie begon.

    Vil lieben, tut mir ouch ein liep
    und merket, wie der götliche minnen diep
    sleich mitten in die sele min
    und trancte die mit suzekeit der süze sin.
20 sie wart verwunden mit der süze,
    daz sie vertruc des grozen gruzes grüzen
    und weste doch, waz ir geschach:
    nie leit, niur liep, nie we, niur wol, kein ungemach.
    die wechter miner bürge zwar
25 der tougen wurden nie gewar,
    wie got in mich sin kint gebar,
    daz ich gebar fürbaz al dar.
    die süze miner sele nar
    gebar den geist, ich menschen clar.
30 sust vater, sun, heiliger geist in mich sich span.

15. I am the star of Jacob,
    mine is the honored angels' praise.
    I am the city of God on high—
    St. Augustine spoke much of me.
    My gates were never open,
    yet my love came in and took my burden
    to help me bear the One I bore,
    a joy to you all forevermore.
    He and a lovely girl were hailed
    before his father's court—
    that was the cause of his travail.
    He bore his exile willingly,
    yet fought for the legacy
    from which his father cast him out.
    Blessed be the day I began it all!

    Dear ones, I would have you know
    how that heavenly thief of love
    slipped in and stole my heart and soul,
    drenched me in sweetness more and more,
    in wounding sweetness, that I might bear
    Love's greatest greeting wide awake.
    No pain but joy, no woe but bliss, no heartache.
    The watchmen of my turrets
    never knew my secrets—
    how God in me begot his child,
    the One I bore into the world.
    The sweetness that sustains my soul
    bore the Godhead; I, the manhood pure.
    Thus Father, Son, and Spirit clear
    in me were braided into one whole.

16. Ich binz der ersten sache kint,
   ich binz ein understant, in der gewelchet sint
   die dri und doch mazheftic kunden werden nie.
   er ist min wesen und ich daz sin, sun guter,
5 er kint und ich muter.
   er tet, ich leit,
   in wenne, uf wa, des habens ich gelegenheit.
   sin art, die mac man von mir sagen
   und min gestalt in sinen jagen.
10 welch underscheit mac daz geclagen?
   die menscheit unser eigen immer muz betagen,
   kein zuschicht noch kein abeschicht er mac getragen,
   ern si ein got den ich gebar.

   Daz wort mir von der höhe quam
15 und ward in mir ein so gebenediter nam:
   der name hie wart, daz wort was ane werden ie.
   von disen zwein ein rede wart gevlochten,
   der min witze tochten.
   ein meinen truc
20 die rede in ir, daz disputirete ich genuc,
   als mich der vrone bote sprach.
   mich wunderte e, wie daz geschach.
   daz wunder mir der engel brach.
   wan er bewisete ez in warer sprüche vach:
25 der nider ein grunt, der mitte ein zil, der höhe ein dach
   nam in mir bernder künste nar.

16. I am the child of the Primal One,
    I, the substance in which the Three
    beyond all measure took on form.
    He is my essence and I am his—good Son;
    he the child and I the mother,
    he acted, I suffered—
    I, the occasion
    of time and place and situation.
    From me his genus can be known;
    through his, my species may be learned.
    What difference can be discerned?
    Humanity remains our own:
    he cannot make it less or more—
    unless it's God that I bore.

    The Word came down from on high
    and became an ever-blessed Name.
    In me that Name became;
    the Word knew no becoming.
    From these two a speech was braided
    while I debated
    the meaning of God's coming.
    I wondered how this could be?
    The angel showed me the mystery
    in a web of sayings true:
    the ground of what lies below,
    the bound of what lies between,
    the roof of what lies above—
    all this I nursed with a scholar's love.

17. Ei, waz sich mischet und unmischet
und waz sich uz der mische drischet:
ob daz mischen nicht verlischet,
wie der ursprinc sich da vrischet,
5 und swaz ungemischet blibet,
wie daz mischen von im tribet!
werden und unwerden brechen
mit geburt, ob ich sol sprechen,
daz ich der bin ein beginne.
10 swie des geistes worchtlich minne
mit der liebe und mit der lüste
enget, witet ane unküste:
ich binz aller formen forme,
abgenomen nach des innern sinnes norme,
15 die durchblümet was und ist und immer muz ane ende sin.

Zwar ich binz aller tugent nature
und der materjen nachgebure.
swaz ich in dem sinne mure,
speher bilde ich vil behure.
20 ich binz aller himel mezzen
und swaz ir snelle hat besezzen;
wie gestecket in die firme
sint die sterne, daz ich tirme,
die sich werren mit der irre,
25 inguz, wandel, nehe, virre.
ich han geechset allen speren
beide ir hemmen und ir keren.
wite, lenge, tiufe, höhe
winkelmezic miner lust sich nicht entflöhe!
30 zal der dinge mit den sachen ligen in der gehügde min.

17. See what is mixed, what is unmixed,
    and what is threshed from the mixture.
    If the mixture keeps its force,
    how it rejuvenates the source!
    See how mixing is pushed away
    by that which remains unmixed.
    Becoming and unbecoming
    start with birth, so I may say:
    I am their pure beginning.
    The sea of the Spirit, quickening
    all that lives with love and rapture,
    ebbs and flows without a bourn.
    I am the Form beyond each form,
    drawn from the inmost meaning's norm,
    which was and is and ever shall be blooming.

    I am every virtue's nature
    and primal matter's neighbor.
    Whatever I design in will,
    I decorate with joyful skill.
    I take the starry heaven's measure
    and guide its motions;
    within the firmament I fix
    the stars in constellations.
    I weave their courses through the skies,
    through me the planets set and rise.
    I set all spheres on their axis
    to make them speed and slow and spin.
    I need no compass to delight
    in breadth and length and depth and height.
    In my mind all causes lie, and all things' reckoning.

18. Wie die döne löne schöne
schenken uz der armonien,
die sich modeln, dries drien,
wie die steige, velle schrien,
5 mac man hören
in niun kören
—den schal nieman mac zerstören—,
da min vriedel, der vil süze,
schaffet unser beider dinc.

10 Balde cröne, tröne, vröne
mir ein küssen, sun der gerten!
miner menscheit schiltgeverten
mich dem künige Jesse zerten.
sus in troume
15 wer min goume?
under einem apfelboume
wart erwecket ich so suzlich,
secht, daz tet ein jungelinc.

18. Voices nine   with joy divine
    intone the thrice-three modes
    in harmony abounding:
    they rise and fall, resounding
    in nine fair choirs
    as each ear hears—
    their melody unfurling
    since the day my love, my darling,
    composed our common theme.

    Quickly crown,   enthrone your queen!
    Kiss me, son of the Branch!
    My comrades in humanity
    plucked me from King Jesse's tree.
    Whom do I see
    watching over me?
    Under an apple tree
    one sweetly wakened me—
    the young man in my dream.

19. Nu lat iuch lüsten also hübsches meres:
   er was sun des alden gerteneres,
   der gebelzet het in sinem garten
   den boum, dar an er selber sit des todes wolde warten,
5 min muter an der menscheit da gewaldiclich zerbrochen und zerstöret
      wart,
   min kint des lebens tet nach sines vater art.
   nu secht, ich binz daz bette Salomones
   rich hochswebendes lones,
   daz die sechzic starken ummehalden:
10 vier und zweinzic ist der wisen alden,
   niur zwelfe sint der boten, die des cristentumes walden,
   der ordenunge niune sint, die nie min lop volzalten,
   dri patriarchen, vier ewangelisten wunder stalten,
   noch sint ir achte,
15 den ich sache,
   daz ir heilikeit min berndez lop bewache,
   zwar sie sint solcher slachte.

   Nu streuwet mir die blumen in min klosen,
   bestecket mich mit liljen und mit rosen!
20 er blume von mir blume wolde entspriezen,
   und daz was in der zit, daz sich die blumen schouwen liezen.
   die stat hiez Blume, da der blume uz mir blume warf sich in der blu-
      men zit,
   und mit dem blumen han ich mich geblümet wit.
   er schin, ich glast, wir liuchten und erglenzen,
25 merzen, meien, lenzen.
   swaz der sumer speher varbe erzücket,
   dar in so hat min vriedel sich gesmücket.
   er wil, daz ich sin herbest si, und hat in mich gedrücket
   die truben, da min vater sich hat selben in gebücket.
30 sust wart min kint min swager und min bruder ungestücket.
   des vluches winter
   wir verdrungen.
   ab dem blumen min ist trostes vil entsprungen.
   sünder, da birc dich hinder!

19. Now listen to a pretty song!
    'Twas the old gardener's son
    who grafted the tree—the very one
    on which he'd one day hang.
    My mother walked in that garden;   there she was brutally attacked.
    My child behaved with his Father's tact.
    Look! I am the bed of Solomon,
    rich in sublime rewards,
    flanked by sixty knights with swords.
    Twenty-four are the wise elders,
    twelve the apostles, Christendom's lords.
    Nine are the angel orders   that have never fathomed my praise.
    Patriarchs three, evangelists four,
    are wonder-workers evermore.
    Eight more stand
    at my command:
    their holiness guards my fruitful praise.

    Deck me with flowers round about,
    with lilies and roses strew my room!
    For a bud from my blossom wished to sprout
    in the month when fields begin to bloom,
    in the blossom-town in blossom-time.   Far and wide our fragrance
        flinging,
    see us marching, maying, springing,
    he a light and I aglow.
    My lover's robe's ablaze
    with summer's brilliant hues.
    He wants me to be his harvest-time:
    in me he pressed the vintage wine
    from grapes plucked by my Father,   and thus my Son became my
        brother
    and my Child, my husband's brother.
    We have reversed
    the winter's curse.
    Comfort bloomed when my blossom opened.
    Sinner, shelter in it!

20. Gein berge climmen nach ir nar   die geize,
   durch daz min har   ich dar   geleichen heize:
   der himel höhe han ich überclummen.
   mich hat die gotheit mit ir macht so meisterlich durchswummen.
5 ich kan über daz gebirge herten herzen komen
   und mit der sele schaffe ich mines vriedels vromen,
   des han ich ab den pinen mangen geist genomen,
   ich binz des wisen Noe trones arke,
   in die sich vor menschlicher sünden sintvlut barc der starke.
10 zwischen menscheit unde gote
   sten ich rechte mitten uf der marke:
   der vater ummehelset mich,
   der sun verslozzen lit in minem sarke.
   rubinröte gab er mir mit Simeonis swerte,
15 den smaragd ich in kiusche truc,
   der saphir zierte mich genuc.
   des herten vluches adamas zerbrochen wart
   mit sinem blute, sust er mich gewerte.

   Des siges jaspis, der daz blut   verstalte,
20 der kempfe gut,   die vlut   des jamers valte.
   erbrennet durch berillen warer minne
   daz trübe jachandine herze wart entzündic inne.
   sin topasieren mir in reiner lüste quam,
   do calcedonete ich, daz ez der züchte zam,
25 sust trug ich amatisten der vil bernden scham.
   der vröuden crisoliten mich durchslichen,
   do mir der angeborne nebel wart geistlich ab gestrichen.
   sust ein roup der mantel was,
   mir die röuber nimmerme entwichen.
30 alsust ich menschlich gotlich wart,
   ja gotlich menschlich, daz hat er getichen.
   vröut iuch alle, vröut iuch immer miner balsamiten!
   ich volles wunsches wurzesmac,
   min mitsam granatin bejac
35 den brasem des trostes heilsam an iuch strichen muz,
   sust werdet ir des himels margariten.

20. Goats scamper up the mountains seeking food;
I spring   like a stag   up the peaks of God.
I have mounted to heaven's loftiest height,
infused with the Godhead's masterful might.
The summit of a hardened heart I can scale
and shape the soul to my lover's will.
Thus have I snatched many lives from hell.
I am the ark, wise Noah's throne,
that sheltered the strong from the flood of sin.
Between God and humankind
I stand on the borderline:
the Father embraces me,
the Son is locked in my shrine.
With Simeon's sword he gave me the ruby red;
emerald I wore in chastity,
sapphire sanctified my beauty.
The adamant curse was cut by his blood,
in this way he preserved me.

The jasper of victory that stanches blood
fought well,   and stilled   the woeful flood.
Kindled by beryl, true love's stone,
the jacinth heart caught fire within.
He came topazing me with utmost courtesy,
I chalcedoned to him with maiden modesty.
My amethysts mark fruitful chastity.
I wore the chrysolites of joy
when the Spirit snatched the inborn cloud away.
Since the robbers stole my cape,
they can never again escape.
For, human, I became divine,
divine and human—such was his will.
Rejoice then always, one and all!
I am the fragrance of deep desire.
When the merits of my garnet pure
heal you with comfort of chrysoprase,
you shall be pearls of paradise.

1

THE PERFORMER, HIS PUBLIC, AND HIS PEERS

The poet-composer Frauenlob, a contemporary of Meister Eckhart and Dante, enjoyed a public career spanning four decades, with patrons in the great courts of central and northern Europe. When he died in 1318, his reputation was so great that he was buried in the cloister of Mainz Cathedral. According to the chronicler Albrecht von Strassburg, "on the vigil of Saint Andrew [November 29] in the year 1318, Heinrich, called Frauenlob, was buried in Mainz, in the cathedral cloister near the school, with exceptional honors. Women carried him from his lodgings to the sepulchre with loud lamentation and great mourning, on account of the infinite praises that he heaped on the whole feminine sex in his poems. Moreover, such copious libations of wine were poured on his tomb that it overflowed through the whole cloister of the church. He composed the *Cantica canticorum* in German, known in the vernacular as *Unser Frowen laich*, and many other good things."[1]

---

1. "Anno Domini M˙CCC˙XVII [*sic*] in vigilia sancti Andree sepultus est Heinricus dictus Frowenlob in Maguncia in ambitu maioris ecclesie iuxta scolas honorifice valde. Qui deportatus fuit a mulieribus ab hospicio usque in locum sepulture, et lamentaciones et querele maxime audite fuerunt ab eis propter laudes infinitas, quas inposuit omni generi femineo in dictaminibus suis. Tanta

After death, Frauenlob remained an influential figure, much admired and imitated up to the time of Hans Sachs two and a half centuries later. He is among the poets anthologized in the illuminated Manesse Codex, and one of only a handful of medieval German composers whose music comes down to us. Around 1364, the humanist John of Neumarkt sent the archbishop of Prague a Latin prose translation of one of Frauenlob's poems, praising him as *tantus et tam famosus dictans* and *vulgaris eloquencie princeps,* in much the same terms as he lauded Petrarch.[2] But in spite of his fame, these testimonies tell us most of what we know about Frauenlob apart from the manuscripts of his poems. His output was very large, yet the precise contours of his canon are unknown and probably always will be, since a great many texts composed by the "school of Frauenlob" were transmitted under the master's name. In fact, fully two-thirds of the strophes ascribed to him survive in a single manuscript each.[3] Aside from the well-known *Cantica canticorum* (or *Marienleich*) presented here, there is little overlap.

The meistersingers, who revered Frauenlob, maintained that he had founded the first "singing school" in Mainz, where he spent the last years of his life. Although this tradition cannot be verified for lack of evidence, it seems to have arisen early, for the illustration of the poet in the Manesse Codex (ca. 1340) shows him teaching at just such a school.[4] In this painting (fig. 1), Frauenlob presides from a lofty chair at an outdoor music lesson or performance. Over his striped tunic he wears a cloak of ermine and a coronet trimmed with the same fur, usually reserved for high nobility but here representing the gift of a particularly lavish patron. With his right hand raised in a stylized teaching gesture, the singer-poet holds in his left what looks—anachronistically—like a conductor's baton.[5] On a carpet below, stretched out by a piper on the right and a drummer on the left, a fiddler performs while other musicians listen, holding a variety of soft and loud instruments including flute, psaltery, and shawm. The *meister's* identity is confirmed by a symbolic coat of arms representing his Lady, the crowned Virgin, who extends her mantle over his shield in a gesture of protection and favor.[6] This painting immediately precedes the text of the *Marienleich* and reminds us that the German *leich* had always been an instrumental

eciam ibi fuit copia vini fusa in sepulcrum suum, quod circumfluebat per totum ambitum ecclesie. Cantica canticorum dictavit Teutonice, que vulgariter dicuntur 'Unser Frowen laich' et multa alia bona." Adolf Hofmeister, ed., *Die Chronik des Mathias von Neuenburg* [continuation by Albrecht von Strassburg], MGH.SS., n.s. 4, fasc. 1 (Berlin: Weidmann, 1924), 312. Frauenlob's original tombstone, extant until 1774, gave the year of his death as 1318; the present facsimile dates from 1783.

2. "Such a great and famous poet, . . . the prince of vernacular eloquence." Paul Piur, ed., *Briefe Johanns von Neumarkt,* no. 121 (Berlin: Weidmann, 1937), 178–80; Herbert Thoma, "John of Neumarkt and Heinrich Frauenlob," in *Mediaeval German Studies Presented to Frederick Norman* (London: University of London Institute of Germanic Studies, 1965), 247–54.

3. Olive Sayce, *The Medieval German Lyric, 1150–1300: The Development of Its Themes and Forms in Their European Context* (Oxford: Clarendon, 1982), 411.

4. Max Wehrli, *Geschichte der deutschen Literatur vom frühen Mittelalter bis zum Ende des 16. Jahrhunderts,* vol. 1 (Stuttgart: Philipp Reclam, 1980), 731. Our earliest documentary evidence of *Singschulen* is much later, from ca. 1450.

5. Frauenlob's title of *meister* is cognate with the Italian *maestro,* today used even in English for an orchestral conductor. This is short for *maestro di cappella* (German *kapellmeister*), an early eighteenth-century usage with remote antecedents in the late medieval *Singschule.*

6. For other interpretations of the painting (Heidelberg, Universitätsbibliothek, Cod. pal. germ. 848, fol. 399r), see Ewald

FIG. 1   Frauenlob directs his "singing school." Codex Manesse, CPG 848, fol. 399r

genre.[7] Frauenlob's great poem was undoubtedly meant for the kind of lavish musical perform-ance illustrated here, although—as is usual with medieval music—the manuscripts record only the vocal melody.[8] Instrumental parts would have been composed or improvised by the per-formers, as they are by Sequentia in the CD that accompanies this book.

A few folios earlier in the Manesse manuscript, Frauenlob appears in a very different role. This painting (fig. 2) introduces the poems of his archrival, Regenbogen, who was held to have been a smith and appears in his forge with hammer, anvil, and tongs. (The belief derives from a line in one of his poems; it may or may not have been literally true, since "forging" was also a favorite metaphor for crafting poetry.) Next to Regenbogen sits Frauenlob, sporting the same light beard and zigzag-striped tunic as in the *Singschule* illustration, but he no longer wears his honorific fur mantle. Instead, both poets, decked with identical garlands, raise their hands in aggressive, symmetrical ges-tures of debate. Regenbogen, prepared to wield his hammer at need and seconded by an apprentice with bellows, occupies the position of strength. In contrast to the musicians' scene, which flaunts the high honor Frauenlob enjoyed, this painting suggests the other side of his reputation as a contro-versial figure, one whose pride and ostentatious mannerism aroused resentment and criticism. The grounds of Frauenlob's feud with Regenbogen are now hard to ascertain, given the thorny prob-lems of authentication. But the two poets belonged to a literary culture in which fierce competition constituted a genre unto itself—the *Sängerkrieg*, or "singers' war"—so the legend of their rivalry lived on after their deaths in a fictional work, *Der Krieg von Würzburg* (The Battle of Würzburg).[9] In this text the two rivals come forth to fight as champions in a tournament, with Frauenlob defending the honor of women, and Regenbogen proclaiming the superiority of men. Although their debate ends in a draw, this fictional portrait shaped both singers' reputations for centuries to come.

PATRONS, PEERS, AND POLEMICS

Frauenlob is the most famous of a neglected group of poets who fill a key place in thirteenth- and fourteenth-century literature. Traditionally named *Spruchdichter*—an umbrella term for "lyric

---

Jammers, *Das Königliche Liederbuch des deutschen Minnesangs: Eine Einführung in die sogennante Manessische Handschrift* (Heidelberg: Lambert Schneider, 1965), 74–75; Hella Frühmorgen-Voss, "Bildtypen in der Manessischen Liederhandschrift," in *Werk—Typ—Situation: Studien zu poetologischen Bedingungen in der älteren deutschen Literatur, Hugo Kuhn zum 60. Geburtstag* (Stuttgart: Metz-ler, 1969), 184–216, at 194 and 204; Walter Koschorreck, ed., *Minnesinger in Bildern der Manessischen Liederhandschrift* (Frankfurt am Main: Insel, 1974), 111–12; *Codex Manesse: Katalog zur Ausstellung vom 12. Juni bis 2. Oktober 1988, Universitätsbibliothek Heidelberg* (Heidelberg: Edition Braus, 1988), 122. There is no consensus about the meaning of the image; some scholars interpret the fiddler as Frauenlob, and the enthroned figure as a patron. But

the crowned man's beard and costume, almost identical to those of Regenbogen's debating partner in the image discussed below, argue in favor of Wehrli's interpretation.

7. Sayce, *Medieval German Lyric*, 74, 368–70.

8. The music is transmitted in fragmentary form in six man-uscripts, of which the best is the fourteenth-century Vienna *leich* manuscript (W): Vienna, Österreichische Nationalbibliothek, Cod. Vind. 2701, fols. 2r–8r. See Fig. 4 for a specimen.

9. Karl Bartsch, ed., "Der kriec von Wirzburc," in *Meister-lieder der Kolmarer Handschrift* (Stuttgart: Litterarischer Verein, 1862), 351–62. See also Burghart Wachinger, *Sängerkrieg: Unter-suchungen zur Spruchdichtung des 13. Jahrhunderts* (Munich: Beck, 1973), 287–88.

FIG. 2   Frauenlob debates with Regenbogen. Codex Manesse, CPG 848, fol. 381r

poets who were not minnesingers"—these itinerant artists have more recently been characterized as "poet-minstrels."[10] Their repertoire, called *Sangspruchdichtung,* comprised sung poetry on a variety of subjects, religious, political, and moral; but this is more properly a sociological term than a generic one. Unlike minnesingers, who were for the most part noble amateurs, the *Spruchdichter* were professional traveling minstrels, usually of bourgeois origin, who embraced the arts of poetry and song as a vocation rather than as a polite accomplishment. Since they made their living by their art, contemporaries called them singers who "took *guot* for *êre,*" that is, received payment in money and kind for the praise of their patrons. The term was not always a pejorative one, although in the sermons of friars it took on a disapproving tone.[11] Normally, the willingness of nobles to support such traveling artists (if all too scantily in material terms) shows how highly they valued them for both the prestige and the entertainment they could offer. In contrast to France, where a class distinction separated the noble poet-composers (*troubadours* or *trouvères*) from the more plebeian musicians (*joglars* or *jongleurs*) who traveled from court to court performing their songs, the *Spruchdichter* filled both roles—nor was the art of performance seen as demeaning, except by clerical moralists. A rare biographical notice on Frauenlob mentions that one of his patrons, Duke Heinrich von Kärnten, in 1299 gave him the lordly sum of fifteen marks to buy a horse. The Latin manuscript describes the poet as an *ystrioni dicto Vrowenlop*—"an entertainer called Frauenlob."[12]

A horse was a necessity in his line of work, since the instability of the political situation—and the performer's need for ever-new audiences—required constant travel. Unlike such fourteenth-century court poets as Geoffrey Chaucer, Frauenlob and his German contemporaries could not expect stable long-term patronage, but moved frequently, settling for a time at any court where they found a warm welcome and a solvent prince. This itinerant lifestyle was a mixed blessing. On the one hand, it rendered poet-singers marginal and highly suspect to the arbiters of morality. Like goliards, or wandering students, they traveled too much to be trusted, for they seldom stayed in one place long enough to become permanent members of parishes, households, or other stabilizing institutions. If accused of any crime, they lacked local family connections and long-term acquaintances to vouch for them. On the other hand, the minstrel's wandering ways enhanced his value to his patrons. Court records and account books show that, when they were not performing, poet-minstrels filled a variety of useful and remunerative roles as messengers, heralds, watchmen, interpreters, and spies.[13] Well-traveled, versed in a range of

10. Maria Dobozy, *Re-Membering the Present: The Medieval German Poet-Minstrel in Cultural Context* (Turnhout: Brepols, 2005). On the term *Spruchdichter* and its inadequacies, see Eva Kiepe-Willms, "*Sus lêret Herman Dâmen*: Untersuchungen zu einem Sangspruchdichter des späten 13. Jahrhunderts," *Zeitschrift für deutsches Altertum und deutsche Literatur* 107 (1978): 33–49. Many professional poets, including Frauenlob, also composed minnesang, but amateur minnesingers rarely worked in other genres.

11. Joachim Bumke, *Courtly Culture: Literature and Society in the High Middle Ages,* trans. Thomas Dunlap (Berkeley and Los Angeles: University of California Press, 1991); Dobozy, *Re-Membering the Present,* 227–38.

12. Karl Stackmann, "Frauenlob," in *Die deutsche Literatur des Mittelalters: Verfasserlexikon,* 2nd ed. (Berlin: Walter de Gruyter, 1980), 2:865–77, at 866. This article is the best source for the little we know of the poet's biography.

13. Dobozy, *Re-Membering the Present,* chap. 4.

dialects, and welcomed by all social strata, such performers could be skilled information-gatherers. A poet as learned as Frauenlob might even have placed his clerical skills at his patrons' service—for example, in reading and transcribing letters—but this must remain con-jectural, given the frustrating lack of documents on the lives of individual *Spruchdichter*. Finally, at important festivals, such as knightings, weddings, and coronations, a seasoned enter-tainer would be given the role of "minstrel king," responsible for devising ensemble perform-ances and serving as master of ceremonies. This is another possible interpretation of Frauenlob's role in the Manesse illustration.

We know the identity of his lords almost exclusively from the poems he wrote in their honor. In addition to Heinrich von Kärnten, Frauenlob's patrons included Duke Heinrich IV of Breslau in Silesia (d. 1290); Count Otto II von Oldenburg (d. 1304); Archbishop Gieselbrecht of Bremen (d. 1306); Count Otto III von Ravensberg in Westphalia (d. 1306); Count Gerhard von Hoya in Lower Saxony (d. 1311); Duke Heinrich (I or II) von Mecklenburg; Margrave Waldemar von Brandenburg (d. 1319); Prince Wizlav von Rügen (d. 1325); a Danish king, probably Erik VIII (d. 1319); and finally, Peter von Aspelt, archbishop of Mainz (d. 1320).[14] Unfortunately, we cannot trace the chronology of the singer's wanderings before his final decade, much less establish a biography, for his poems mention few datable events. But among those few are a feast of Rudolf of Habsburg, held in 1278 to celebrate his victory over the Bohemian king Přemysl Ottokar II, and the knighting in 1292 of Ottokar's successor, Wences-las II. Frauenlob also composed lamentations on the death of Rudolf in 1291 and Wenceslas in 1305.[15] Given these Bohemian connections, most scholars believe he spent some time at the court of Prague, probably at the beginning of his career. His birthplace of Meissen in Saxony was not far from Bohemia, and the allure of that glittering court would have made it a natural magnet for an ambitious young singer.[16]

That Frauenlob *was* an ambitious young singer is clear from an interesting polemic against him, couched in the form of ironic praise. Echoing twelfth-century Latin satire against "beard-less masters,"[17] an anonymous critic writes:

---

14. For a collection of Frauenlob's poems in honor of these lords, see Joachim Bumke, *Mäzene im Mittelalter: Die Gönner und Auftraggeber der höfischen Literatur in Deutschland, 1150–1300* (Munich: Beck, 1979), 636–45.

15. The lament on King Rudolf's death is GA V.81. The lamentation for Wenceslas is no longer extant, but it is mentioned by Ottokar von Steiermark in his *Österreichische Reim-chronik*, lines 86, 552–58, ed. Joseph Seemüller, MGH.SS., vernac. 5 (Hannover: Hahn, 1890–93), 2:1129: "Die sungen manic klageliet / mit grôzer zeher gusse / sînem lop ze gehugnusse / klagebaer und lobelich, / Frouwenlop meister Heinrich, / der ûf die kunst ist kluoc, / und ander singaer gen-uoc" (At the king's funeral "many sang lamentations in a great

outpouring, to call his praise to mind in the manner of eulogy and lament—Master Heinrich Frauenlob, who is skilled in art, and many other singers").

16. Hans-Joachim Behr tries, with mixed success, to refute the evidence for Frauenlob's sojourn in Bohemia: *Literatur als Machtle-gitimation: Studien zur Funktion der deutschsprachigen Dichtung am böhmischen Königshof im 13. Jahrhundert* (Munich: Wilhelm Fink, 1989), 234–39.

17. See for example John of Hauville, *Architrenius* 5.72–77, ed. and trans. Winthrop Wetherbee (Cambridge: Cambridge University Press, 1994), 120–21: "Here too anyone may clamber into the teacher's chair (*cathedras*), usurping the divine title of 'master' (*rapta deitate magistri*), and become pregnant of bombast

Wa bistu gewest zu schule,	Where did you go to school,
daz du so hohe bist gelart?	that you acquired such great learning?
man sprichet dich also kindes,	They say you are such a child
daz in der niuwe si din bart.	that your beard is still new.
drizehen jar der hastu noch nicht,	You are not yet thirteen years old—
nu la dich got vierzehen mit eren leben.	now may God grant you to live fourteen years with honor!
Du macht uf meisters stule	You may well sit in the master's chair,
gesitzen wol, des höre ich jehen,	so I hear people say;
unt daz von dinen jaren	and [they say] that no one your age
nie din geliche wurde gesehen.	was ever seen to be your equal.
wol dir der seldehaften schicht,	Lucky you that, on account of this fortunate tale,
daz nu din pris so ho beginnet sweben.	your praise now begins to soar so high!
Man gicht, in diutischem riche	They say that in the German realm
si niender phaffe din genoz	no priest is your equal,
noch singer din geliche.	nor is there any singer like you.
und macht du daz bewisen,	If you can prove this—
daz dir da her von himele vloz	namely, that wisdom flowed down from heaven
unde in din herze sich besloz	and enclosed itself wholly in your heart—
die wisheit gar, vür war,	this indeed is deserving of praise!
daz muz man prisen.[18]	

(GA VII.42G)

The skeptical or jealous or—just possibly?—admiring author of this strophe compares the precocious Frauenlob to Jesus at the age of twelve, who amazed the rabbis of Jerusalem with his wisdom (Luke 2:42–48). According to appreciative rumors, says the satirist, there was not only no singer but also "no priest" to equal the young poet's wisdom "in the German (*diutischem*) realm," a phrase that sounds teasingly like "the Jewish (*jüdischem*) realm." So this poem, which must have been written early in Frauenlob's career, indicates that he chose the life of traveling

---

by this empty dignity. Though both chin and mind are beardless, though he is still a mere green sapling taking precedence over strong and mature timber, he does not hesitate, decked in his hastily bestowed laurels, to lay claim to rewards held in store for age."

18. All poems by Frauenlob, along with a few polemical poems addressed to him, are cited from Frauenlob (Heinrich von Meissen), *Leichs, Sangsprüche, Lieder*, ed. Karl Stackmann and Karl Bertau, 2 vols. (Göttingen: Vandenhoeck & Ruprecht, 1981). Poems are identified by section, strophe, and line numbers.

poet while still quite young (eighteen perhaps, if not twelve) and quickly gained a reputation for theological learning.

We cannot definitively answer the satirist's question "Where did you go to school?" But the likeliest guess is the cathedral school at Meissen, where the novice poet would have obtained a thorough grounding in the liberal arts and in theology. His title of *meister* does not mean that he earned the degree of *magister artium,* for the oldest university in the empire (Prague) was founded only in 1348. Vienna, Heidelberg, and Cologne followed later in the fourteenth century. Nevertheless, *meisterschaft* in the double sense of learning and artistic skill was crucial to the self-image of Frauenlob and his peers, who sometimes used the term as a near-equivalent for *magisterium,* the teaching authority of the church.[19] The *Spruchdichter* were the German vernacular theologians of their age, dwelling by choice on the Trinity, the Incarnation, the glories of the Virgin, the marvels of nature, and other philosophical and religious themes.[20] Frauenlob himself was instrumental in creating a vernacular lexicon for the terms of Platonic metaphysics and Aristotelian logic, playing a key role as well in the German reception of such twelfth-century masters as Alan of Lille.[21] A *meister* denoted both a master craftsman and a wise teacher: to sing *meisterlich* and with *wîsen sinn* (wise sense) was the thirteenth-century artistic ideal from which the later meistersingers derived their self-concept. When they celebrated great poets of the past, they tended to list precisely twelve "old masters" by analogy with the apostles—although two of Frauenlob's contemporaries composed sly lists of eleven, leaving their listeners to identify the present singer as the twelfth.[22]

Meisterschaft in Frauenlob's own poetry describes such phenomena as the skill of the artist; the ennobling power of woman's love (VII.35.18); the creative bounty of the First Cause (VII.9.4); and above all, the mastery of God. In the Incarnation, he sings, Christ *aventiurte meisterschaft von vremder craft* (I.14.22): "he embarked on an adventure that risked (or revealed) his mastery against (or over) an alien power." By his victory he proved himself the ultimate craftsman: *der meister heizet meister,* "let the Master be called a master indeed!" (I.14.14).[23] The poet's personal mastery likewise stems from God, for artistic inspiration is a divine gift. In response to contemporaries who lamented that the golden age of art was over, Frauenlob proclaimed defiantly

---

19. On the various meanings of *magister* and *magisterium,* I am indebted to Jan Ziolkowski, "Mastering Authority and Authorizing Masters in the Long Twelfth Century," paper delivered at the 40th International Congress on Medieval Studies, Kalamazoo, Michigan, May 2005.

20. Peter Kern, *Trinität, Maria, Inkarnation: Studien zur Thematik der deutschen Dichtung des späteren Mittelalters* (Berlin: Erich Schmidt, 1971).

21. Christoph Huber, *Die Aufnahme und Verarbeitung des Alanus ab Insulis in mittelhochdeutschen Dichtungen* (Munich: Artemis, 1988), 136–99.

22. Nikolaus Henkel, "Die zwölf alten Meister: Beobachtungen zur Entstehung des Katalogs," *Beiträge zur Geschichte der deutschen Sprache und Literatur* 109 (1987): 375–89. The best-known canon of twelve includes Walther von der Vogelweide, Reinmar von Zweter, Der Marner, Regenbogen, Boppe, Stolle, Konrad von Würzburg, Der Kanzler, Wolfram von Eschenbach, Klingsor, Heinrich von Ofterdingen, and Frauenlob. Of these, Klingsor and Heinrich von Ofterdingen are fictional characters; the rest, except for Walther and Wolfram, are *Spruchdichter.* Joachim Bumke, *Geschichte der deutschen Literatur im hohen Mittelalter* (Munich: Deutscher Taschenbuch, 1990), 318.

23. See also Commentary, below, under strophe 14.

that singers of his own day are in no way inferior to those of the storied past, for creativity is inexhaustible as the force of nature:

Prüft regen mit den winden:	Consider the rain and the winds!
die han hiute also groze kraft	They have as much power today
von gotes haft	by God's covenant
als über zwei tusent jare. meisterschaft	as two thousand years ago. So too
si dar gebogen.	with mastery in art.

(VI.1 2.6–1 0)

Frauenlob knew the songs of some of the great minnesingers, especially Walther von der Vogelweide, but he was more deeply influenced by the generation of *Spruchdichter* preceding him, in particular Hermann Damen, Reinmar von Zweter, and Konrad von Würzburg. Damen (d. ca. 1300) was not himself a major talent, but he was once thought to have been Frauenlob's teacher on the basis of four illuminating strophes he directed to the younger poet.[24] One of these addresses Frauenlob by name, while the others appeal to an unnamed "child." Like the satirist cited above, Damen chastises the youthful poet for his arrogance. Although still "a child in childish years" (*ein kint in kindes jaren*), he already presumes to write about all the wonders of creation—*Waz dem himel obe unde unde / si und in abysses grunde* ("Whatever may be above and beneath the heaven, and in the depths of the abyss"). Moreover, he boasts shamelessly, professing to surpass "the art of all singers" living and dead—a charge based on a notorious song of self-praise that, as we shall see, was probably the work of a malicious parodist. But if it was, Frauenlob must already have earned a reputation for overweening pride, or else such a parody could never have fooled colleagues who knew him. Hence Damen counsels the young singer to learn some humility by apprenticing himself to a more seasoned poet:

Durch vriuntschaft unt durch guot,	Out of friendship and kindness,
wend ich dir guotes vil wol gan.	I hope much good will come your way.
vür war, sus stet min muot:	Truly, this is my offer:
waz ich dir guotes lernen kan,	whatever good I can teach you,
des wil ich weinic sparen.	I will withhold none of it.
Dunkstu aber dich so here,	But if you think so highly of yourself
daz dir tüge niemans lere,	that no one's teaching is of use to you—
daz wirt dines herzen swere,	that will be a burden on your heart
wiltus nicht bewaren.[25]	if you do not wish to guard it.

24. For an edition of these strophes, see Wachinger, *Sängerkrieg,* 182–84, as well as Kiepe-Willms, "*Sus lêret Herman Dâmen.*" This poet is sometimes referred to as "der Damen" or "von Damen."

25. Hermann Damen, strophe 5.7.9–17, ed. Wachinger, *Sängerkrieg,* 183–84.

Frauenlob left us a single appreciative line about Damen, so he seems not to have resented this fatherly offer.[26] But it is most unlikely that he accepted it, since he was to choose an artistic path quite different from the older poet's didactic plain style.

Damen's strophe addressing Frauenlob by name is of special interest because it sheds some light on the poet's sobriquet. Like performing artists today, many traveling minstrels adopted stage names. The roll call of these poets includes such flamboyant characters as Der Helleviur (Hellfire), Der Marner (the Steersman), Der Unverzagte (the Undaunted), Regenbogen (Rainbow), Singuf (Sing Out), Rumelant (Land of Praise), Der tugendhafte Schreiber (the Virtuous Scribe), Suchensinn (Seek the Sense), and Muskatblut (Nutmeg). Since Frauenlob was still a "child" at the time Damen addressed him, he must have chosen his own sobriquet at the outset of his career, leading rivals to speculate on the reason for it:

Vrouwenlob, des hastu scande.	Frauenlob, this [boasting] is shameful!
vrouwen lob in scanden bande	The praise of ladies in a fetter of shame
stuont nie halben tac zuo phande.	will never stand as pledge for half a day.
merken diz beginne,	Consider this for a beginning:
Wie vil eren habe der name!	how much honor there is in the name!
vrouwen lob in eren krame	The honorable praise of ladies
spilt vil schone sunder schame	plays beautifully without disgrace
nach heiles gewinne.	and profits toward salvation.
Uns tuot her Reimar kunt,	Herr Reinmar tells us
der vrouwen lob si reinez leben.[27]	that praise of ladies is a pure life.
du triffs der selden vunt,	You have hit upon the fount of blessings
ist dir der name durch daz gegeben;	if this is the reason for your name;
so soltu vrouwen minne	so you should extol the love of ladies
Prisen und ir wibheit eren	and honor their womanhood
und ir lob mit sange meren.	and enhance their praise with song.
wil dir ieman daz vurkeren,	If anyone dissuades you from this,
daz kumpt von unsinne.[28]	it comes of foolishness.

Not unreasonably, Damen assumed that "Frauenlob" meant *vrouwen lob,* the courtly praise of ladies, so he advised the young poet to adopt the idiom of traditional minnesang instead of busying himself

26. "Kunde ich baz dan Herman der Damen / ein lobes vaz mit sange amen" ("If I could fill a barrel of praise with song better than Hermann Damen"): GA V.8.17–18.

27. "Vrouwen lop ist reinez leben": Reinmar von Zweter, strophe 36.1. *Die Gedichte Reinmars von Zweter,* ed. Gustav Roethe (Leipzig: Hirzel, 1887), 429. Hermann Damen has already taken

Reinmar's line out of context. In the original poem, Reinmar states that a "pure life" of chastity, modesty, kindness, and gentleness is the source of a woman's praise, whereas Damen tells Frauenlob that the *poet* who wishes to praise ladies should possess these virtues.

28. Damen 5.5.1–17, ed. Wachinger, *Sängerkrieg,* 182–83.

with the mysteries of divinity and natural science. But this, it turns out, is precisely what Frauen-lob did *not* wish to do—for it was the *Ewig-Weibliche*, the Feminine as a cosmic principle, that he truly loved. To honor Woman in the style he intended, he needed not to abandon but to immerse himself ever more deeply in the mysteries that Hermann Damen would have had him forswear.

Reinmar von Zweter (d. ca. 1260), cited in Damen's cautionary poem, is the second singer who demonstrably influenced Frauenlob. This prolific blind poet,[29] a native of the Rhineland, grew up in Austria and served a number of patrons, including Duke Leopold VI of Austria and King Wenceslas I of Bohemia (reg. 1230–53) in the early years of his reign. It may well have been in Prague, a generation later, that Frauenlob encountered his songs. Reinmar composed some 229 strophes of *Spruchdichtung*, but it is his religious *leich* that Frauenlob most clearly echoes, though the debt has been little noticed.[30] Reinmar's innovative *leich* praises the Trinity, the Incarnation, and the Virgin as linked manifestations of Minne (personified Love), using the "crossover" mode that enjoyed immense pan-European popularity in the mid-thirteenth cen-tury. The imperious feminine figure of Minne fuses with her Latin counterpart, Caritas, linking the tropes of courtly love with a tradition of Song of Songs exegesis and religious allegory nur-tured by such twelfth-century greats as Hugh of St.-Victor and Bernard of Clairvaux. A similar convergence between God and Frau Minne can be seen in many of Reinmar's contemporaries, including the Netherlandish mystical minnesinger Hadewijch, as well as the beguine Mechthild von Magdeburg and the Franciscan poet Lamprecht von Regensburg, a director of nuns.[31] It is in this tradition that Reinmar sings:

Des vater Minne unt ouch des suns
der gotheit in ir herze dranc
unt clagte in beiden, wie daz uns
der êrste val ze valle twanc:
dar an uns allen misselanc.

   Got hêrre unüberwundenlich,
wie überwant diu Minne dich!
getorste ich sprechen, sô spraech ich:
"si wart an dir sô sigerîch,
daz si den val nam über sich."[32]

The Love of the Father and the Son
urged the heart of the Godhead
and lamented to both of them
how the first Fall compelled us to fall
and brought us all to grief.

   O God, invincible Lord,
how Minne has vanquished you!
If I dared speak, I would say,
"she won such a victory over you
that she took the Fall upon herself."

29. Frühmorgen-Voss, "Bildtypen," 188. In the Manesse image of Reinmar (fol. 323r), the poet's eyes are closed and he is dictating to a page, who transcribes his poems on wax tablets, and to a lady, who makes a fair copy on parchment.

30. On the religious *leich* in general, see Karl Bertau, "Über Themenanordnung und Bildung inhaltlicher Zusammenhänge in den religiösen Leichdichtungen des XIII Jahrhunderts," *Zeitschrift für deutsche Philologie* 76 (1957): 129–49.

31. See my *God and the Goddesses: Vision, Poetry, and Belief in the Middle Ages* (Philadelphia: University of Pennsylvania Press, 2002), chap. 4.

32. *Leich*, 11–20, in *Die Gedichte Reinmars*, 401. These lines closely echo Hugh of St.-Victor's encomium, *De laude charitatis* (PL 176:969–76).

Minne, the love that galvanizes Father and Son into action, turns out to be another name for the Holy Spirit: "Der minne schenke ist aller meist / der übersüeze Gotes Geist: / dem er die wil schenken" ("The gift of Love is above all the Spirit of God, surpassingly sweet to whomever he will give her"). It is through Minne that God becomes incarnate:

<table>
<tr><td>Durch minne wart der alde junc,</td><td>Through Love the Old One became young,</td></tr>
<tr><td>der ie was alt ân ende:</td><td>he who was forever ancient without end:</td></tr>
<tr><td>von himel tet er einen sprunc</td><td>from heaven he leapt down</td></tr>
<tr><td>her ab in diz ellende,</td><td>below, into this exile.</td></tr>
<tr><td>ein Got unt drî genende</td><td>One God and three persons</td></tr>
<tr><td>Enphienc von einer meide jugent,</td><td>received youth from a maiden!</td></tr>
<tr><td>daz geschach durch minne:</td><td>It was through Love that this happened.</td></tr>
<tr><td>ir gap des heilegen Geistes tugent</td><td>The virtue of the Holy Spirit gave her</td></tr>
<tr><td>minnebernde sinne:</td><td>senses made fruitful by Love:</td></tr>
<tr><td>des wol dir, küniginne![33]</td><td>therefore, Queen, you are blessed!</td></tr>
</table>

Frauenlob similarly links the Virgin, the Holy Spirit, and an all-powerful Minne who transforms the ageless God into a youthful lover or a newborn babe. Reinmar was by no means his only source for these motifs, but Frauenlob's many verbal echoes of his *Leich* reveal a deep respect for him.

Konrad von Würzburg, the most influential of Frauenlob's precursor poets, has lately been recognized as "the single most versatile and prolific [German] author of the thirteenth century."[34] He traveled widely, visiting France, Switzerland, and the Netherlands as well as German courts, and eventually settled in Basel where he is buried. Unlike most of his peers, Konrad composed in multiple genres including minnesang, brief tales (*märe*), hagiography, epic, and courtly romance, in addition to the religious and political lyrics that were the staple of wandering poets. Like Reinmar, he also composed a religious *leich*, which Frauenlob undoubtedly knew, but his most famous work was *Die goldene Schmiede* (The Golden Forge), an elaborate Marian praise-poem of two thousand lines, extant in more than thirty manuscripts. A pioneer of the *geblümter Stil*, or "flowery style," which Frauenlob would carry to hitherto unimagined heights, Konrad introduced the floral lexicon of this new aesthetic into the modesty preface of *Die goldene Schmiede*, where he laments his inability to weave Mary the garland she deserves:[35]

33. *Leich*, 51–60, p. 403.

34. Maria Dobozy, "Konrad von Würzburg," in *The Literary Encyclopedia* (2003), online at www.litencyc.com/php.

35. On this celebrated prologue, see Mireille Schnyder, "Eine Poetik des Marienlobs: Der Prolog zur *Goldenen Schmiede* Konrads von Würzburg," *Euphorion* 90 (1996): 41–61, and Peter Ganz, "'Nur eine schöne Kunstfigur': Zur 'Goldenen Schmiede' Konrads von Würzburg," *Germanisch-Romanische Monatsschrift* 29 (1979): 27–45.

er muoz der künste meienris
tragen in der brüste sin,
swer diner wirde schäpelin
sol blüemen unde flehten,
daz er mit roeselehten
sprüchen ez floriere,
und allenthalben ziere
mit violinen worten,
so daz er an den orten
vor allem valsche ez liuter,
und wilder rime kriuter
darunder und da'nzwischen
vil schone künne mischen
in der süezen rede bluot.[36]

He who would braid and decorate
your noble chaplet with flowers
must bear within his breast
the blooming May-branch of the arts
in order to adorn it
with rose-red phrases
and decorate it all around
with words like violets,
to purify it utterly
of everything false,
and most beautifully interweave
the herbs of exotic rhymes
beneath, around, between
the blossoms of sweet speech.

In a lament he composed on Konrad's death in 1287—his only eulogy for another poet—Frauenlob paid the supreme tribute of complimenting the master in his own terms, fusing the aesthetic tropes of "blossoming speech" and the "golden smithy" in which the artist labors to forge poetic praise. But where Konrad is ornate yet clear, Frauenlob is deliberately hermetic and obscure, recalling the *trobar clus*, or "closed style," of some of the Provençal troubadours. His lament for Konrad is in fact a demanding expression of his own aesthetic program:

Gefiolierte blüte kunst,
dins brunnen dunst
und din geröset flammenriche brunst,
die hete wurzelhaftez obez
gewidemet: in dem boume künste riches lobes
hielt wipfels gunst
sin list, durchliljet kurc.

Durchsternet was sins sinnes himel,
glanz, als ein vimel
durchkernet. luter golt nach wunsches stimel
was al sin blut, geveimt uf lob,
gevult mit margariten nicht zu kleine und grob;

36. Konrad von Würzburg, *Die goldene Schmiede*, 60–73, ed. Edward Schröder (Göttingen: Vandenhoeck & Ruprecht, 1926). The edition is not paginated.

sins silbers schimel
gap gimmen velsen schurc.

Ach, kunst ist tot! nu klage, armonie,
planeten tirmen klage, nicht verzie
polus jamers drie.
genade im, süze trinitat,
maget reine, entfat:
ich meine Conrat,
den helt von Wirzeburc.

(VIII. 26)

[Exquisite art, decked with blossoming violets! The vapor rising from your fountain and your rose-red, flaming fire have brought forth deeply rooted fruit. In the tree of artistic praise-poetry, his mastery, adorned with twining lilies, enjoys the summit of favor. The heaven of his skill glittered with stars, radiant, firm as a miner's axe. All his blossoms were pure gold, purged of dross, refined to win praise, according to the goad of his intention—filled with pearls, neither too small nor too coarse. The shimmering of his silver (axe) thrust against rocks to yield jewels. Alas, art is dead! Lament now, music of the spheres! Planetary plowers, lament! Let the heavens triple their outcry! Have mercy on him, sweet Trinity; pure Virgin, receive him. I mean Konrad, the hero of Würzburg.][37]

FRAUENLOB'S SELF-PRAISE: LITERARY BOAST OR MALICIOUS PARODY?

This mannered style won both admirers and detractors. In his relatively mild censure of Frauenlob's pride, Hermann Damen had accused him of claiming to surpass not only present rivals, but also the greatest singers of the past, with his superlative artistry. Throughout his life and long afterward, Frauenlob's reputation labored under the charge of monumental arrogance, resting on a literary boast that rivals those of Homeric heroes. The fabled boasting poem has provoked attacks far more savage than Damen's, extending well into the twentieth century; but its authenticity has recently and, in my view, convincingly been challenged by Johannes Rettelbach.[38] Yet the poem and the counterattacks it inspired still have a great deal to tell us about

37. My translation is indebted to Karl Stackmann, "Bild und Bedeutung bei Frauenlob," *Frühmittelalterliche Studien* 6 (1972): 441–60; Sayce, *Medieval German Lyric*, 427; and Gert Hübner, *Lobblumen: Studien zur Genese und Funktion der "Geblümten Rede"* (Tübingen: A. Francke, 2000), 71.

38. Johannes Rettelbach, "Abgefeimte Kunst: Frauenlobs 'Selbstrühmung,'" in Cyril Edwards, Ernst Hellgardt, and Norbert Ott, eds., *Lied im deutschen Mittelalter: Überlieferung, Typen, Gebrauch, Chiemsee-Colloquium 1991* (Tübingen: Niemeyer, 1996), 177–93.

Frauenlob's ambitions, his enemies, and his literary culture—all the more so if the original boast is a forgery. Here is what Hermann Damen and others thought the poet had sung of himself:

Swaz ie gesang Reimar und der von Eschenbach,
swaz ie gesprach
der von der Vogelweide,
mit vergoltem kleide
ich, Vrouwenlob, vergulde ir sang,   als ich iuch bescheide.
sie han gesungen von dem feim,   den grunt han sie verlazen.

Uz kezzels grunde gat min kunst, so gicht min munt.
ich tun iu kunt
mit worten unt mit dönen
ane sunderhönen:
noch solte man mins sanges schrin   gar rilichen krönen.
sie han gevarn den smalen stig   bi künstenrichen strazen.

Swer ie gesang und singet noch
—bi grünem holze ein fulez bloch—,
so bin ichz doch
ir meister noch.
der sinne trage ich ouch ein joch,
dar zu bin ich der künste ein koch.
min wort, min döne traten nie   uz rechter sinne sazen.

(V.115)

[Whatever Reinmar (von Zweter) and (Wolfram) von Eschenbach ever sang, whatever (Walther) von der Vogelweide ever said—with gilded garments I, Frauenlob, gild their song, as I inform you. They have sung of the froth and left the depths untouched. My art comes from the bottom of the cauldron—so I proclaim. I make it known in words and melodies, without a trace of ridicule: the shrine of my singing ought to be nobly crowned. Singers until now have traveled the narrow path that runs alongside the highway of rich art. Above all who have ever sung and are singing still, I am their master! They are like a rotten stump compared to a living tree. I bear the yoke of artistic skill; I am a master chef of the arts. My words and melodies have never overstepped the bounds of proper meaning.]

As Burghart Wachinger has noted, this poem is unparalleled in all medieval German literature for its unabashed, extravagant self-praise.[39] Its assertive gesture of self-naming ("ich, Vrouwenlob") is found nowhere else except in fictional "singers' wars" like *Der Krieg von Würzburg* (composed after Frauenlob's time) and the earlier *Wartburgkrieg*, which he knew. In that work of dramatic fiction, which presents rival singers competing to produce the best praise-poem, Walther von der Vogelweide and Wolfram von Eschenbach are prominent characters, and it is probably for that reason that the boast cites them. (Otherwise it would have made little sense for Frauenlob to compare himself with Wolfram, a much earlier epic poet, rather than a fellow *Spruchdichter*.)[40] The "Reimar" of the boast is surely Reinmar von Zweter, although some critics have mistakenly identified him as Reinmar der Alte, a minnesinger who lived a century before Frauenlob but is now more famous than von Zweter. In vaunting his superiority to these precursors, Frauenlob—or the singer impersonating him—boasts of two qualities in particular: that his poetry is more highly crafted ("with gilded garments I gild their song") and that it has greater philosophical depth (he sings "from the bottom of the cauldron," as opposed to the superficial froth of others). Both the depth and the verbal ornament are illustrated by a series of self-conscious metaphors—the cauldron of art with its "master chef," the laureate's crown, the high road of true song alongside the narrow paths of impostors, the flourishing green tree beside the dead wood of the past. Much of the poem, like the elegy for Konrad von Würzburg, is deliberately riddling and obscure.

The Manesse Codex transmits two counterstrophes attacking this poem, both ascribed to Regenbogen. The first begins with open abuse and proceeds to a passionate defense of the old masters:

> Braggart, nitwit, fool, idiot—shut up about the art of the dead! My mouth contradicts you; you get no sympathy from me. You claim that you gild the song of the masters with a gilded garment—they who plucked so many roses of skillful invention from the field of art, and still do? I will be the champion of them all! Your art will stumble: I will engrave the cauldron of your notions for you. Your art seems to me more like a nettle than the violets of mastery. How dare you mount the throne of art on which they sat! I come forth as the defender of them all. Whether you believe it or not, I'll be a shield for them all. My song will strike you right on target, for your boasting annoys me no end. My art will pound you through the cauldron! If the dead and the living leave you free, then try just once to slip out of my fetters![41] (V.116G)

39. Wachinger, *Sängerkrieg,* 252.

40. Karl Stackmann, "Frauenlob und Wolfram von Eschenbach," in Kurt Gärtner and Joachim Heinzle, eds., *Studien zu Wolfram von Eschenbach: Festschrift für Werner Schröder zum 75. Geburtstag* (Tübingen: Niemeyer, 1989), 75–84.

41. "Gum, giemolf, narre, tore, geswig der toten kunst! / min munt, min gunst, / die widersagen dir beide. / gichst, mit vergultem kleide / vergultest du der meister sang, die uf der künste heide / gebrochen han und brechen noch vil rosen speher fünde? // Der kempfe wil ich aller sin: din kunst muz snaben, /

In a second counterstrophe, Regenbogen ridicules Frauenlob's esoteric poetry as an "art of the balance and the pumice stone" and mockingly calls for an interpreter to translate it—a plea with which even more appreciative readers can still sympathize. Contrasting Frauenlob unfavorably with Wolfram, Walther, and "the two Reinmars"—in a pointed claim to possess wider poetic knowledge than the author of the boast—his rival declares Frauenlob's song to be no "gilded garment" but threadbare and "formless as clothes without a waistline." Yet another counterstrophe, transmitted anonymously in the Jena manuscript, claims that Walther and Reinmar both excelled in the praise of ladies (*vrouwen lob*), whereas Frauenlob's dull singing "pours out nothing but fool's wine."[42]

Although at least three contemporaries, including Hermann Damen and Regenbogen, responded to the boast as an actual song by Frauenlob, its authenticity has been questioned more than once. Karl Stackmann noted the problem of reconciling its claim to unrivaled mastery with Frauenlob's exaltation of Konrad, in whom "art itself died."[43] Beate Kellner points out that in medieval literary culture such boasts are less a function of individual personality than of genre: self-praise is suited to a poetic competition, praise of a colleague to eulogy, and contemporaries would not necessarily have been troubled by a contradiction between them.[44] Rettelbach, however, presents compelling evidence that Frauenlob could not have written the boast, for it contains an elementary technical error. In the *Abgesang*, or final third of the strophe, the word *noch* is made to rhyme with itself. Although English and French poets used *rime riche* as an ornament, German poets considered identical rhyme a serious flaw and scrupulously avoided it. It is unthinkable that a virtuoso like Frauenlob would have committed such a fault—and moreover, both counterstrophes ascribed to Regenbogen display the same flaw, as if pointedly mocking it.[45] If read closely, the boast reveals other signs of parody as well. The "cauldron of art" sounds like a travesty of Frauenlob's crucible image in the lament for Konrad, and the metaphor of the broad highway in fact reverses a familiar trope in which the most artful poets take the narrow paths, while it is hacks who follow the broad road. Similarly, "gilded" (*vergoltem*) is an equivocal term that can also mean "counterfeit."

It appears, then, that the notorious boast was not Frauenlob's own but the work of a wickedly skillful parodist who wrote it—and perhaps also the counterstrophes—in order to do lasting harm to his rival's reputation. This could well have been Regenbogen, whom the Manesse Codex presents both verbally and pictorially as Frauenlob's archrival. Yet Rettelbach

---

ich wil durchgraben / dir dines sinnes keʒʒel. / din kunst ist mir ein neʒʒel / gein violricher meisterschaft. sitze ab der künste seʒʒel, / dar uf sie saʒen! des wil ich wol sin ir aller urkünde, // Ob du des nicht gelouben wilt: / wol her, ich für ir aller schilt. / min sang dir gilt / gar unverʒilt. / dins giudens mich gar sere bevilt, / min kunst dir durch den keʒʒel spilt. / lan tote und lebende dich vri, sluʒ uf min eins gebünde." My translation is indebted to Rettelbach, "Abgefeimte Kunst," 183–84 n. 26.

42. These two strophes are GA V.117G and V.119G.

43. Stackmann, "Frauenlob und Wolfram," 80.

44. Beate Kellner, "*Vindelse*: Konturen von Autorschaft in Frauenlobs 'Selbstrühmung' und in '*wip-vrowe*-Streit,'" in Elizabeth Andersen, Jens Haustein, Anne Simon, and Peter Strohschneider, eds., *Autor und Autorschaft im Mittelalter: Kolloquium Meissen 1995* (Tübingen: Niemeyer, 1998), 255–76, at 260.

45. Rettelbach, "Abgefeimte Kunst," 180–81.

nominates Rumelant, another foe, as the parodist because he was the better poet. Circumstantial evidence also suggests that Frauenlob may have ousted Rumelant from his position as court poet to King Erik VIII of Denmark, providing a likely motive for revenge.[46] The conjecture cannot be proven, but the whole incident nicely illustrates the intense rivalry of the *Spruchdichter* and the competitive atmosphere surrounding court patronage, as well as Frauenlob's widely recognized ambitions and the distinctiveness of his style. It is a striking fact that, for all the frequency of polemic and ritual aggression among these traveling poets, Frauenlob alone inspired stylistic parodies.[47]

Enemies notwithstanding, the singer's list of illustrious patrons (including Erik VIII) testifies to the wide esteem he enjoyed. At least two of these patrons were themselves poets—King Wenceslas II of Bohemia and Prince Wizlav of Rügen, who both composed love songs in accord with the time-honored tradition of the noble amateur.[48] It is interesting that language differences do not seem to have hindered Frauenlob's reception. His native dialect was a form of Middle German, but he spent much of his career in the Low German–speaking regions of the north: Lower Saxony, Brandenburg, Mecklenburg, even Denmark and the Baltic island of Rügen. The last datable event that he mentions is a chivalric feast in the Hanseatic port city of Rostock in 1311. Shortly afterward, however, he settled permanently in Mainz, a High German–speaking city in the Rhineland. His patron there was the powerful archbishop Peter von Aspelt, who may have met the poet in the Bohemian court as early as the 1280s. A high-ranking political figure, Peter had been physician and chaplain to Rudolf of Habsburg (1286), then protonotary to King Wenceslas II (1289), chancellor of Bohemia and bishop of Basel (1296), and finally archbishop of Mainz (1306). It may have been Peter's patronage that gave Frauenlob the stability to establish a "school," or at any rate to do some sort of teaching under the auspices of the cathedral, ultimately inspiring the Manesse illustration and the meistersinger tradition.[49] The large corpus of inauthentic poems ascribed to him in the manuscripts might best be explained as the work of his many disciples. At any rate, Frauenlob surely owes his illustrious burial place to Peter's friendship. Two manuscripts transmit a poignant notice claiming that the poet wrote the first strophe in his Langer Ton (Long Tune) "an sinem leczsten end in der stunde, als im der erczbischoff ze Mencz gotz lichnam mit sinen henden gab" ("at the end of his life, in the hour when the archbishop of Mainz gave him God's body with his own hands").[50]

---

46. Rettelbach, "Abgefeimte Kunst," 193 n. 56. In GA XI.1.17 Frauenlob identifies himself in a praise-poem for Erik as *priser des küniges* ("praiser of the king"), as if denoting a quasi-official post. Rumelant had written a praise-poem for the same king earlier in his reign.

47. Wachinger, *Sängerkrieg,* 314–15.

48. For Frauenlob's influence on the king's poetry, see Burghart Wachinger, "Hohe Minne um 1300: Zu den Liedern Frauenlobs und König Wenzels von Böhmen," in Werner Schröder,

ed., *Wolfram-Studien* 10: *Cambridger "Frauenlob"-Kolloquium 1986* (Berlin: Erich Schmidt, 1988), 135–50.

49. Uwe Ruberg speculates that Frauenlob may have held some secular office at the cathedral during Peter's tenure: "Frauenlob-Gedenken: Das Begräbnis des Dichters im Mainzer Domkreuzgang," *Domblätter: Forum des Dombauvereins Mainz e.V.* 3 (2001): 77–83, at 79.

50. Stackmann, "Frauenlob," *Verfasserlexikon,* 867.

The attentive reader will have noticed that, in the fairly long list of Frauenlob's patrons, no female names occur, nor do we find any among his fellow poets. This is not Frauenlob's fault; he did not create the culture in which he sang. But in view of his exalted praise of Woman, a defining mark of his oeuvre, we should not forget that the world of secular German poetry was overwhelmingly male.[51] In striking contrast to medieval France, it offers no counterpart to Eleanor of Aquitaine or Marie de Champagne, no Marie de France or Comtessa de Dia, much less any Christine de Pizan. We do find female-voiced lyrics by male poets,[52] as well as out-standing female religious writers. In fact, *all* the substantial Latin texts composed by women after 1150 stem from German-speaking lands—a remarkable fact that testifies to the high educational level of nuns and canonesses in the empire, far surpassing the norm for other parts of Europe.[53] Among vernacular sacred writers, Mechthild of Magdeburg (d. 1282) offers some points of comparison with Frauenlob, so we shall return to her. But the poet is not likely to have known her book—or indeed, the work of any female author—unless he encountered some lyrics or other texts by Hildegard of Bingen during his late years at Mainz, where she enjoyed a significant cult. Otherwise, women figure not at all among Frauenlob's patrons, his fellow *Spruchdichter,* or his literary influences. More surprising, perhaps, is that this great apostle of Woman's praise shows no sign of reverence for any private muse: his few *Minnelieder* reveal no engagement with any flesh-and-blood woman, let alone a Beatrice. The poetic speaker in his debate poem, *Minne und Welt,* does give thanks for his beautiful wife, but he does so to set an argument in motion; there is no reason to take his statement as autobiographical. Though Frauenlob may well have been married, we know nothing whatsoever of his wife or possible children.

Pace Hermann Damen, then, the "praise of ladies" by which Frauenlob chose to define his poetic self had very little to do with courtly love, and even less with female conversation part-ners in the world. Rather, all his women are goddesses: Natura, Minne, Sapientia, and above all, the double-natured Lady of the *Marienleich,* the divine-human Mary, partner of the Trinity, who incarnates both God and the Eternal Feminine.[54] It is such figures as these that we will encounter as we explore the poet's oeuvre.

---

51. For the scanty evidence of female musicians (not com-posers), see Dobozy, *Re-Membering the Present,* 177–81.

52. See William E. Jackson, *Reinmar's Women: A Study of the Woman's Song ("Frauenlied" and "Frauenstrophe") of Reinmar der Alte* (Amsterdam: Benjamins, 1981); Ingrid Kasten, ed., *Frauen-lieder des Mittelalters* (Stuttgart: Philipp Reclam, 1990); Albrecht Classen, ed., *Women as Protagonists and Poets in the German Middle Ages: An Anthology of Feminist Approaches to Middle High German Literature* (Göppingen: Kümmerle, 1991).

53. These include the Latin works of Hildegard of Bingen, Elisabeth of Schönau, Herrad of Hohenbourg, Gertrude of Helfta,

and Mechthild of Hackeborn, as well as the *Vitae sororum* of Unter-linden and the letters and sermons of the nuns of Admont—an impressive corpus indeed. On their world, see the essays in *Krone und Schleier: Kunst aus mittelalterlichen Frauenklöstern,* ed. Kunst-und Ausstellungshalle der Bundesrepublik Deutschland, Bonn, and Ruhrlandmuseum, Essen (Bonn and Essen, 2005). I exclude the extant Latin texts by Angela of Foligno and Birgitta of Swe-den, which were translated by their confessor/scribes from the women's Italian and Swedish vernaculars.

54. For a full account of these figures, see my *God and the God-desses,* which could well be read as a "preface to Frauenlob."

2

FRAUENLOB'S CANON

A convenient point of entry into Frauenlob's oeuvre is afforded by a series of short poems known as the *wip-vrouwe* debate—a literary argument between Frauenlob and some rivals about the noblest way to praise women.[1] Since this debate is closely linked with the poet's stage name and the critiques of his precocity, it probably took place at an early point in his career. In these strophes we see the young singer developing and defending his poetic program in polemical conversation with both *antiqui* and *moderni*. Just as he elaborated a stylistic credo in his eulogy for Konrad von Würzburg, in the *wip-vrouwe* debate he developed a philosophical rationale for his "praise of ladies" in dialogue with Walther von der Vogelweide.

1. The most thorough study of these poems is now Margreth Egidi, *Höfische Liebe: Entwürfe der Sangspruchdichtung, Literarische Verfahrensweisen von Reinmar von Zweter bis Frauenlob* (Heidelberg: Carl Winter, 2002), 245–337. See also Wachinger, *Sängerkrieg*, 188–246, and Kellner, "*Vindelse*: Konturen von Autorschaft."

By the time Frauenlob took up the theme, the relative value of the terms *wip* ("woman") and *vrouwe* ("lady") was already a hoary topos in German poetry. In a well-known song, Walther had opined:

> Wip muoz iemer sîn der wîbe hôhste name,
> und tiuret baz denne vrowe, als ich ez erkenne.[2]

> [*Wip* must always be the highest name of woman
> and honors her more than *vrouwe*, as I understand it.]

Walther reasons that *wip* is the more inclusive category because all ladies are women, but not all women are ladies (that is, of high social rank). Further, the category of *vrouwen* includes *unwip* or ladies who behave shamefully. Opposing this stance, Frauenlob throws down the gauntlet on behalf of *vrouwenlop*, his own agenda. His opening salvo divides womankind into three classes, in an ascending hierarchy of value based on biological status: *maget* (*virgo*, or maiden), *wip* (*deflorata*, or sexually experienced woman), and *vrouwe*. Against all precedent, Frauenlob defines the *vrouwe* not as a lady of rank but as a *mother*, further proclaiming that, while all women are worthy of praise, the highest laurels belong to the *vrouwe* (V.102).

These distinctions run counter to tropes long familiar in Latin as well as German linguistic spheres, both of which tended to polarize women. It was a commonplace that only after sexual initiation did a maiden *become* a woman (*wip* or *femina*). Marian hymns set up an opposition between virgins and mothers to proclaim that Mary alone was both, while minnesingers often distinguished between good women and bad, amorous and chaste, or low-born and high-born (*vrouwen*). The only tripartite distinction in common use derived from ecclesiastical writing. In commentaries on the parable of the sower (Matt. 13:1–23), exegetes liked to identify the rich harvest of the divine seed with three classes of women: the married bear a thirtyfold yield, widows sixtyfold, and virgins a hundredfold.[3] In other words, a woman's spiritual value instantly doubles when she ceases to be sexually active, whereas a virgin's merits are worth more than three times those of a wife. Although the parable is explicitly about fertility ("bearing fruit"), motherhood does not figure in this exegetical schema. Frauenlob not only inserts it, replacing widows with mothers under the unexpected name of *vrouwen*, but also, more boldly, inverts the

2. Walther von der Vogelweide, *Leich, Lieder, Sangsprüche,* 25.4.1–2, ed. Christoph Cormeau, 14th ed. (Berlin: Walter de Gruyter, 1996), 101.

3. This topos originates with Jerome; see his *Adversus Jovinianum* 1.3 (PL 23:213); *Commentariorum in Matheum Libri* 2, ed. D. Hurst and M. Adriaen, CCSL 77 (Turnhout: Brepols, 1969),

106; and *Epistulae* 49.2–3 and 123.8, ed. Isidore Hilberg, CSEL 54:353–54 and 56:82 (Vienna: Tempsky, 1910–18). A well-known source from medieval Germany is the *Speculum virginum*, part 7, ed. Jutta Seyfarth, CCCM 5 (Turnhout: Brepols, 1990), 217. The work was written by Conrad of Hirsau around 1140.

values of the clerical hierarchy. Thus the *maget*, or lovely spring blossom, is good, but the *wip*, or fallen blossom of summer, is even better, and the *vruht*, or autumn harvest, is best of all. To stress that sexual initiation does not reduce a woman's worth, he derives *wip* etymologically as the acronym of *Wunne Irdisch Paradis*: joy, earthly paradise (V.102.11). Despite their orientation toward male pleasure, these terms refreshingly break with the clichés of minnesang and clerical misogyny alike. Frauenlob's valuation of fertility, unprecedented in the poetry of *hohe Minne*, remained constant throughout his oeuvre, anticipating the naturalism we find in his *Minneleich*, *Minne und Welt*, and *Marienleich*.

In a subsequent strophe, the poet derives the name *vrouwe* (also spelled *vrowe*) from *vro* plus *we*, or joy and woe. A *vrowe*, or mother, is "vro von der lust, we durch die burt": "glad from sexual pleasure, [but she experiences] woe through the pangs of birth" (V.112.12). This etymology, repeated with variants elsewhere, is surprisingly gynocentric and sharply opposes the misogyny of the Latin tradition, which derived *mulier* from *mollities* (weakness) and *femina* from *fide minus* (of lesser faith)[4]—not to mention the Middle English folk etymology, *woman* is the *wo* of *man*. A set of counterstrophes, some ascribed to Regenbogen or Rumelant, take issue with Frauenlob's revisionist position. They argue variously that *wip* and *vrouwe* are mere synonyms, though Walther was correct to prefer *wip* (V.107G), and that the old masters far excelled Frauenlob in the praise of ladies, which he should not pretend (implicitly through his stage name) to have invented (V.119G). The most interesting of these counterstrophes (V.108G) makes an exegetical argument, pointing out that in John's Gospel Jesus twice addressed Mary as *mulier*—that is, *wip* (John 2:4 and 19:26)—a devastating critique, since Christ would surely have used the most honorable name for his own mother.

Frauenlob's response evinces his keen awareness of language as well as his immersion in Latin learning. To the biblical argument he offers a two-pronged reply (V.111–12). First, *mulier* is more suitably translated as *vrouwe* because *wip* implies sexual experience and Jesus would hardly have used a term that might have led the Jews to impugn his mother's virginity. Hence "Die glose ist valsch, got sprach nicht 'wib,' sin wort sich 'vrouwe' erzeiget" ("The gloss is false: God did not say *wip*, his word means *vrouwe*," V.112.19). In any case, Jesus was not speaking Latin but Hebrew or Aramaic (*jüdisch*), so the German term is only a translation of a translation (V.112.7). This remarkable point about Christ's vanished *Urwort* may recall Dante's near-contemporary musings on the lost language of Adam.[5] Frauenlob too brings Adam into the discussion in another of his strophes (V.103), where he rhetorically asks the first man how he named his "rib." In a poem that closely follows the Vulgate, Adam replies that he gave his wife

---

4. Isidore of Seville, *Etymologiae* 11.2.18 (*mollities*), PL 82:417; Heinrich Kramer and James Sprenger, *Malleus maleficarum* 1.6 (*f[id]e minus*), trans. Montague Summers (New York: Dover, 1971), 44.

5. In *Paradiso* 26.124–38, Adam tells a curious Dante that the archetypal language was extinct even before his descendants

built the tower of Babel, for no work of the human mind is eternal: "The usage of mortals is like a leaf on a branch, which goes and another comes" ("l'uso de' mortali è come fronda / in ramo, che sen va e altra vene," 137–38). Dante Alighieri, *Paradiso*, ed. and trans. John Sinclair (New York: Oxford University Press, 1961), 378.

three names: first *mennin* (*virago*, Gen. 2:23), then *weichelmut* ("inconstancy," cf. Gen. 3:12), and finally *gebererin* (*mater cunctorum viventium*, Gen. 3:20). These names, conveying Eve's triple status as created, fallen, and fertile, loosely parallel Frauenlob's original triad of *maget, wip,* and *vrouwe.* At the price of tainting *wip* with the misogynist connotations he had earlier resisted, they validate *vrouwe* in the sense of "mother" as the ultimate name of woman. But the poem does not end there, for Frauenlob goes on to create a secular mythology of naming parallel to the sacred:

Mennor der erste was genant,	Mennor was the name of the first man
dem diutisch rede got tete bekant.	to whom God revealed the German tongue.
er sprach zuhant:	He said at once:
"vro-we, din bant	"woman (joy/woe), your union with man
manlichez, wirde ein vollez lant,	gave us honor and a populous land,
din we uns hie heil, selde vant."	your pangs brought us salvation and bliss."[6]

(V.103.13–18)

In this bravura performance, Frauenlob invents an archetypal German poet, an *Ursprecher* whose first speech-act is to name and praise *vrouwe,* not only vindicating this particular term but affording a paradigm for *vrouwenlop* as the essence of virtuous speech. What is more, "Mennor" is represented as a prophet on the model of Adam. Just as the first man, in acknowledging Eve as "bone of my bones and flesh of my flesh" (Gen. 2:23–24), is supposed to have prophesied the marriage of Christ and the Church (Eph. 5:31–32), so Mennor proclaims that the union of woman with man has brought not only honor (*wirde*) and prosperity (*ein vollez lant*) but also "salvation and bliss"—a hint that Eve's "woe" will be reversed by Mary's joyful fertility. To conclude this elevation of *vrouwe* over *wip,* the poet in a companion strophe (V.104) derives the name *wip* from a second invented figure, the French king "Wippeon." But this king, unlike Mennor, did not respect women; he raped virgins, and as soon as a girl in his harem became pregnant, she was banished from his realm. Because Wippeon dishonored maidens and rejected mothers, taking all his pleasure in the "middle sort," the word *wip* was derived from him. Ironically designating it *kurtois,* a "courtly" name because of its royal pedigree, the poet asks, "O vrouwe, sich, ist diz wort din stam?" ("Look, Woman—is this word your source?" V.104.17). In view of such origins, to prefer the *vrouwe* to the *wip,* Frauenlob implies, is to be at once more ethical, more biblical—and more German.

6. My translation of the last three lines is conjectural because of the convoluted syntax. I take *din bant manlichez* to mean "your sexual union with man" and *din we,* "your pain in childbirth," as in V.112.12. The two together represent woman in her capacity as *vrouwe,* and both are subjects of the verb *vant* (found or brought) with reference to the indirect object *uns hie,* "us (men or humans) here on earth." The joyful union of man and woman brings honor (*wirde*) and a thriving population (*ein vollez lant*), while a mother's fertile labor brings *heil* (health/salvation) and *selde* (blessing)—terms that can be interpreted in either a worldly or a religious sense.

If, from a distance of seven centuries, these strophes sound like a quibble over semantics, it is in part because of their ludic element. Like much of Frauenlob's work, they revel in virtuosity for its own sweet sake.[7] Yet much is also at stake in them. The *wip-vrouwe* debate reveals a young singer determined not only to praise ladies, as German poets had been doing for the past century, but to do so in his own idiosyncratic way: with a proud sense of distinction from precursors and peers alike; with deep learning, worn exuberantly if seldom lightly; with wild inventiveness; with equal immersion in his Latin and vernacular sources; and with a penchant for erotic reciprocity, sexuality, and fertility that sets him apart from the more idealizing strain in minnesang but aligns him with the naturalism of such twelfth-century authors as William of Conches, Bernard Silvestris, Alan of Lille, and Hildegard of Bingen. Finally, having taken his very name from what he praised, Frauenlob set himself on a paradoxical path. On the one hand, his exaltation of Woman as *vrouwe* shades too easily and overtly into self-exaltation, hence the bitterness and irritation of the counterstrophes. On the other hand, this total identification of his poetic persona with the sublime Feminine enabled him ultimately to achieve, on a grand scale, something that no poet before or after him even attempted: to submerge his voice completely in the Virgin's and so to *become* Mary, to utter her divine self-praise in her own first-person voice.

MINNELEICH

Like most of his *Spruchdichtung*, Frauenlob's three *leichs* are impossible to date. Karl Bertau hypothesized fifty years ago that the *Marienleich* belongs to the poet's early Bohemian period, since it could have been composed for performance before Wenceslas II, whose Marian piety is well attested (if scarcely unusual).[8] But no evidence bears one way or another on this thesis, and one might just as easily argue that the *Marienleich,* its author's supreme accomplishment, must be a late work.[9] It is the *Minneleich* that has a better claim to early composition, given its close links with the *wip-vrouwe* strophes. It too, for example, presents the three classes of women and the *Wunne Irdisches Paradis* etymology for *wip*, though without the polemical thrust of the debate poems.

As a minor genre of love poetry, the *minneleich* normally explored the familiar themes of the lyric—praise of ladies, love laments, pleas for mercy—in the longer, more rhetorically and metrically ambitious form of the *leich*. The surviving canon is small, including specimens by

---

7. In fact, the recently discovered Marburg fragment (Z) contains a Frauenlob strophe that flatly contradicts the poems just discussed, declaring: "Got hohern namen nie gegab / uf erden hie wan wibes nam" ("God never gave a higher name here on earth than the name of *wip*," VIII.19.10–11): Stackmann, "Frauenlob und Wolfram," 80–82. Like the fourteenth-century French poet Jehan Le Fèvre, who wrote both misogynist and proto-feminist texts, Frauenlob in his *wip-vrouwe* poems may have been more eager to demonstrate rhetorical versatility than firm conviction.

8. Christoph März, *Frauenlobs Marienleich: Untersuchungen zur spätmittelalterlichen Monodie* (Erlangen: Palm & Enke, 1987), 53–60. See also Karl Bertau, "Untersuchungen zur geistlichen Dichtung Frauenlobs" (dissertation, Göttingen 1954).

9. On the difficulties of establishing a chronology, see Christoph Huber, "*Gepartiret und geschrenket*: Überlegungen zu Frauenlobs Bildsprache anhand des Minneleichs," in Jens Haustein and Ralf-Henning Steinmetz, eds., *Studien zu Frauenlob und Heinrich von Mügeln: Festschrift für Karl Stackmann zum 80. Geburtstag* (Fribourg, Switzerland: Universitätsverlag, 2002), 31–50, at 35.

Konrad von Würzburg and an experimental poet who called himself Wild Alexander.[10] But Frauenlob's contribution, as usual, breaks the rules through its intellectual ambition and novelty. The poem—transmitted in two manuscripts, one with the melody—consists of thirty-three strophic pairs, varying in length from four to twelve lines apiece.[11] These strophes are clustered in thematic groups of three, four, five, and seven, forming a complex numerological structure, such as we shall find again in the *Marienleich*.[12] In the first seven strophes, the poet-speaker holds a dialogue with Herr Sinn, his personified inspiration, about the praise of ladies. He begins by asserting that Woman (*wip*, now shorn of pejorative connotations) should be highly honored on account of three blessings: *gesellschaft*, or companionship; *der formen cleit*, the garment of form or beauty; and *der hochsten vrouwen minne*, "the love of the highest Lady" (Mary).[13] He then asks Herr Sinn for a model of ideal womanhood:

"Her Sin, nu bildet mir ein wip,

sit ich ouch trage eines mannes lip."
"ob ich erkenne ir bernden lobes künne,
Ich tunz mit willeclicher hege."

"Sir Thought, portray a woman for me now
since I myself bear a man's body.
If I learn the nature of her fruitful praise,
I will perform it most willingly."

(III.2.1–4)

Herr Sinn responds with three paradigms. The first, Queen Esther, wins only brief praise as a paragon of virtue. The other two are goddesses—first, Natura as she appears in Alan of Lille's *De planctu Naturae*, then Minne in the esoteric form of a hermaphrodite. Frauenlob was the first German author to cite Alan, whose Natura figures so prominently in the *Roman de la Rose* by his French contemporary Jean de Meun. In the *Minneleich*, Herr Sinn asks the poet if he recalls "waz feien sach Alanus uf der glanzen gru" ("what 'fairy' Alan saw on the shining meadow") at the beginning of his dream-vision (III.4.2). Alan had called his Natura by a variety of names: *mulier, puella, virgo, nutrix, dei vicaria, dei proles*; above all, she is the daughter and deputy of God.[14]

10. Ingeborg Glier, "Der Minneleich im späten 13. Jahrhundert," in *Werk—Typ—Situation: Studien zu poetologischen Bedingungen in der älteren deutschen Literatur. Hugo Kuhn zum 60. Geburtstag* (Stuttgart: Metzler, 1969), 161–83.

11. The manuscripts are the Wiener Leichhandschrift W (Vienna, Österreichische Nationalbibliothek, Cod. Vind. 2701) from the fourteenth century, with music, and the mid-fifteenth-century Weimar Frauenlob manuscript F (Weimar, Zentralbibliothek der deutschen Klassik, Q 564). The same two manuscripts transmit the *Kreuzleich*. In W both *leichs* lack attribution, but in F they appear within a lengthy section of Frauenlob's authentic works, and there is no other contemporary poet of comparable style, intellectual interests, and artistic merit to whom they could plausibly be ascribed. Stackmann's textual work and a series of important critical studies have put to rest the doubts of earlier

critics, such as Olive Sayce, who believed the *Minneleich* to be "certainly spurious" (*Medieval German Lyric*, 411).

12. Karl Stackmann, "Frauenlob, Verführer zu 'einer gränzenlosen Auslegung,'" in Werner Schröder, ed., *Wolfram-Studien 10: Cambridger "Frauenlob"-Kolloquium 1986* (Berlin: Erich Schmidt, 1988), 9–25, at 13–14.

13. The phrase "der formen cleit" could mean either Woman's beauty or, more likely, her power to bestow form by giving birth to new life. The whole passage is indebted to Reinmar von Zweter's *Leich*, 184–86: "Sich din starke goteheit / durch minne lie besliezen / in unser armen forme cleit!" ("Your mighty Godhead let itself be enclosed for love in the garment of our poor form"), *Die Gedichte Reinmars*, 408.

14. Alan of Lille, *Liber de planctu Naturae*, ed. Nikolaus Häring, *Studi Medievali*, terza serie, 19.2 (1978): 797–879.

Frauenlob terms her a *feie*, a numinous female being of exceptional beauty, asking Herr Sinn how he should compare Woman-as-such to the creativity of Nature:

"Die feie, die Alanus sach,	"The numinous being that Alan saw
truc aller creatiuren dach	upheld the summit of all creation
und ouch der elementen vach,	and also the web of the elements,
planeten mit der firme.	the planets with the heaven of fixed stars.
Den allen si besloz ir art,	All this she enclosed in her fashion,
complexen und ir mische vart."	the complexions and the manner of their mixing.
"wie sol ich wip, der triuwen zart,	How should I compare Woman,
gelichen zu der tirme?"	true love's darling, to her figure?"

(III.5.1–8)

Herr Sinn replies that, just as Natura "enclosed within herself the power of all creatures," so a woman's body "contains the impulse of all the joys that the thought of a human heart has ever woven."[15]

Further, just as Nature braids the elements of life in a cord of many strands, "sust vrouwen bilde und vrouwen nam / menschlicher vrucht zu vröuden quam" ("so by the image and name of Woman, the fruit of humanity ripens to joy," III.7.4–5). In other words, woman is the source of man's bliss (as *wip* or sexual partner) and the giver of life (as *vrouwe* or mother). In both capacities she mirrors the bounty of Natura, Alan's luminous *feie*. The comparison can be read in two directions: Natura is a fictive image of the Eternal Feminine, a cosmic creative principle, or Woman is the earthly embodiment of Nature, the concrete source of life, fertility, and the joys of love.

From this vision the *leich* proceeds immediately to another, ascribed to a seer named "Selvon"—apparently an imaginary character like Mennor and Wippeon.

> Selvon, der sach ein dunstlich bilde,
> halp maget, halp man, geteilet nach der lenge,
> Daz truc die vier complexen wilde
> in siner hant, ez vloz in twalmes henge.
>
> Kalt unde trucken truc ez in der vrouwen hant,
> warm unde viuchte truc sin manlich ellen.
> Ein sinnic man, der sinnet, waz ez tut bekant.
> spreche ich da von icht mere, ez were gevelle.

15. "Sust vrouwen lip / und wiplich wip / besliuzet aller
vröuden trip, / die menschlich herzen sin ie vlacht." III.6.5–8.

Die forme, halp gecrönet
nach küniges recht
und halp ein meitlich borte,
Sie was so clar geschönet.
Selvon, der knecht,
ein got wart in ir worte.

$\qquad$ (III.9–11)

[Selvon saw a misty image—half maiden, half man, divided lengthwise down the middle. It carried the four untamed complexions in its hands; they flowed forth in the form of vapor (*pneuma, spiritus vitalis*). Cold and dry it bore in its feminine hand, warm and moist in the masculine. Let a wise man understand what this signifies! If I were to speak any more of it, it would be dangerous. The form—half crowned as befits a king, half with a virginal braid—was so radiantly beautiful that Selvon, the servant, became a god in her words.]

The text then describes the actions of this hermaphrodite, still unnamed. Whenever she finds "lascivious senses" (*bröde sinne*), she flings out her mysterious *twalm* or vapor, setting in motion "the whole exaltation of love" (*ganzer liebe vrevel*, III.13.1). Amorous gazes pass to and fro until the "four complexions" intertwine—a figure for sexual intercourse but also for the creation of new life through the intermingling of humors in the womb.[16] Finally, the figure's identity is revealed—with the rider that, despite its dual gender, it is ultimately a "she" and therefore pertains to the praise of Woman.

Die forme hiez der minnen kraft,
an tougen buchen daz erschein.

Sie wart geheizen sie durch ganze süze.
sich, wip, durch dine süze saffen blumen,
Sit dir die geiste jen alsüzer grüze.

$\qquad$ (III.13.5–6; 14.1–3)

[The figure was called the power of Love;
this appears in books of secrets.

16. For Frauenlob's "scientific" understanding of erotic psychology and physiology, see Christoph Huber, "Frauenlob zum Minneprozess," in Schröder, ed., *Wolfram-Studien* 10:151–58, and idem, *Aufnahme und Verarbeitung*, 166–71. The fullest study of the *Minneleich* is Thomas Bein, "*Sus hup sich ganzer liebe vrevel*": *Studien zu Frauenlobs Minneleich* (Frankfurt am Main: Peter Lang, 1988).

She was called "she" because of her utter sweetness.
See, Woman, because of your sweet, ripening flowers,
to you the spirits grant the all-sweet greeting.][17]

Not least of the mysteries in this much-discussed passage is the replacement of Frau Minne, a feminine figure elsewhere in medieval German poetry (including Frauenlob's),[18] with a hermaphrodite—and this in a context delineating models of the ideal woman! Because Selvon's vision is so precisely described, scholars have naturally looked for iconographic models. Twelfth-century "microcosmos" diagrams often represented the four elements (earth, water, fire, and air), their qualities (warm, cold, moist, and dry), and their mixtures or "complexions" (sanguine, choleric, phlegmatic, and melancholic), which belong to mainstream humoral medicine. Such diagrams feature a *homo quadratus* with arms outstretched in the midst of a square or circle, as in the famous examples from Hildegard's *Liber divinorum operum* and Herrad of Hohenbourg's *Hortus deliciarum*. In Frauenlob's lifetime, such a figure (possibly meant as a representation of Adam) appeared on the rood screen of Mainz Cathedral.[19] But these figures are always male, in contrast to the hermaphrodite of Selvon's vision. To find images such as Selvon sees, we must turn to alchemical books, a possible referent for Frauenlob's "books of secrets" (*tougen buchen*). Hermaphrodites like the one he describes do appear in these texts, but the earliest extant illustrations date to a century after his death. The *Buch der heiligen Dreifaltigkeit* (Book of the Holy Trinity), written by a peripatetic Franciscan during the Council of Constance (1414–18), includes some particularly celebrated examples.[20] Frauenlob may have known earlier specimens that are no longer extant, but it is just as likely that he himself exercised a significant influence. For the *Buch der heiligen Dreifaltigkeit* is at least as interested in Mariology as it is in alchemy, arguing a radical thesis very much along the lines of the *Marienleich*: the androgyny of God is revealed to mortals through the double-natured "divine humanity" shared by Jesus and his mother, who is elevated into the Trinity in place of (or as equivalent to) the Holy Spirit.[21] Among the *Buch* author's patrons were the Holy Roman Emperor Sigismund, king of Bohemia and Hungary (1368–1437), and Friedrich, margrave of Brandenburg. Both these courts had hosted Frauenlob a century earlier and might have preserved manuscripts of his works.

17. Line III.14.3 is ambiguous. *Die geiste* could mean simply the spirits of men attracted to female beauty, or numinous spirit-beings like Natura and Minne (as Stackmann suggests; *Wörterbuch*, 107), or the *spiritus* (*pneumata*) of medieval physiology—very fine material substances through which the soul acts on the body, equivalent to Frauenlob's *twalm*. But *geiste* and *grüze* in such close proximity also hint at the Annunciation, giving a Marian tinge even to this passage on the mechanics of sexual attraction.

18. "Vrou Minnen warte"—"the expectation of Lady Love"—is in fact mentioned in III.8.2, just before the Selvon vision. The feminine Minne also figures in *Minne und Welt*, the *Marienleich*, and many of Frauenlob's *Sprüche* and *Minnelieder*.

19. Ruth Finckh, *Minor Mundus Homo: Studien zur Mikrokosmos-Idee in der mittelalterlichen Literatur* (Göttingen: Vandenhoeck & Ruprecht, 1999), 391–93, 420.

20. Alexander Roob, *The Hermetic Museum: Alchemy and Mysticism*, trans. Shaun Whiteside (Cologne: Taschen, 1997), 462–63.

21. Uwe Junker, ed., *Das Buch der heiligen Dreifaltigkeit in seiner zweiten, alchemistischen Fassung (Kadolzburg, 1433)* (Cologne: F. Hansen, 1986); see also Newman, *God and the Goddesses*, 240–43.

Yet in the *Minneleich* itself, the context of Selvon's hermaphrodite is not alchemy but sexual physiology and psychology. The *leich* evokes a tradition of esoteric science bordering on natural magic, with power to deify the visionary "Selvon, der knecht"—perhaps conflating magical practice and a belief that union with the cosmic Feminine could render man godlike.[22] On the other hand, the term "books of secrets" was applied not only to alchemical and magical texts but also to manuals of gynecology, which often made prurient appeals to secrecy in order to titillate male readers.[23] One of the most popular such books was falsely ascribed to Albertus Magnus (d. 1280), a highly influential scientist, philosopher, and theologian as well as a reputed magician, whose authentic works Frauenlob could have known.[24] Whatever the tangled sources of the Selvon vision, its meaning in context is fairly clear. Minne appears as a hermaphrodite because the purpose of erotic love is to transcend the polarity of the sexes, yet—assuming an androcentric perspective—"she [is] called 'she' because of her utter sweetness" to her lover. Together, then, the figures of Natura and Minne supply a philosophical basis for *vrouwenlop*, to which the rest of the *leich* is devoted.[25]

In the remaining strophes, the singer praises *meit* (*maget*), *wip*, and *vrouwe* as the *dri genende*, the "three names" or persons of womanhood (III.21.5–6)—echoing a phrase more often used of the Trinity.[26] Woman is the "temple of all joys" whom the poem extols in a series of three anaphora sequences—cascades of similes and rhetorical questions beginning with the words *noch süzer dan* ("still sweeter than"), *wer kan* ("who can?"), and *wa lit* ("where lies?"). In the first sequence, Woman is the source of bliss; in the second, the allayer of sorrows; in the third, the shrine of virtues. A portion of the *noch süzer* sequence bears citing as a specimen of the *geblümter Stil* in full blossom.

> Sweeter than a cool wind to the hot traveler,
> sweeter than a cold spring to the thirsty plowman,
> sweeter than shade in the blazing sun of August,
> sweeter than the chime of sweet harmonies to the newborn babe,
>
> Sweeter than its father's quickening roar to the lion cub,
> sweeter than a splendid virgin to the unicorn in flight,

22. For an alternative view of Selvon's apotheosis, see Finckh, who believes it may be based on a microcosmos-figure with a text or speech-scroll referring to man as the image and likeness of God: *Minor Mundus Homo*, 393. Ralf-Henning Steinmetz links the enigmatic words with a passage in Boethius's *Consolation of Philosophy* (bk. 3, prose 10) that promises deification to anyone who participates in the Divine through virtue: "Omnis igitur beatus deus. Et natura quidem unus [deus]; participatione vero nihil prohibet esse quam plurimos." Steinmetz, *Liebe als universales Prinzip bei Frauenlob: Ein volkssprachlicher Weltentwurf in der europäischen Dichtung um 1300* (Tübingen: Niemeyer, 1994), 145–46.

23. Karma Lochrie, *Covert Operations: The Medieval Uses of Secrecy* (Philadelphia: University of Pennsylvania Press, 1999), 118–31.

24. Steinmetz, *Liebe*, 50–57, 103–9, 146–48.

25. Bernward Plate notes that Frauenlob is the first German writer to represent Natura as a cosmic force in which Minne is philosophically grounded. "Natura Parens Amoris: Beobachtungen zur Begründung der *minne* in mittelhochdeutschen und frühneuhochdeutschen Texten," *Euphorion* 67 (1973): 1–23.

26. Cf. "ein got und dri genende" ("one God and three persons," V.4.19); the same phrase appears in Reinmar's *Leich*, line 55 (cited above, p. 55).

sweeter than a shining fountain to the eagle in its molting,
sweeter than its transformation to the phoenix after burning,

Sweeter than the taste of honeyed flowers to the bee,
sweeter than flickering fire to the salamander,
sweeter than the air to the chameleon, . . .

Still sweeter is the day of form-bestowing joys
that dazzles you like lightning from a woman's form,
flashing through your eyes into your very heart.[27]

After much more in this vein, the poem ends as it began with a gesture toward Mary—the woman "durch die man alle vrouwen eret" ("through whom all women are honored," III.33.8).

MINNE UND WELT

Minne and Natura both return in the fascinating debate poem that its editors have titled *Minne und Welt* (Love and the World), but the second goddess is there conflated with *Frau Werlt*, an allegorical stalwart first personified by Walther von der Vogelweide.[28] *Minne und Welt* occupies a problematic place in Frauenlob's canon because it survives in only one mid-fifteenth-century manuscript, where it has no attribution and a badly corrupt text.[29] Nevertheless, both the manuscript context and the poem's stylistic and thematic affinities with other works of Frauenlob speak for his authorship. A series of important studies by Christoph Huber, Ralf-Henning Steinmetz, and Ruth Finckh have done a great deal to contextualize this philosophical poem and illumine its thought.[30] Finckh in particular has clarified Frauenlob's intellectual lineage, placing him in a tradition of Neoplatonic, hermetic, and patristic ideas, mediated in part by John Scotus Eriugena, which he shares with such twelfth-century figures as Honorius Augustodunensis, Hildegard of Bingen, Bernard Silvestris, and Alan of Lille. Among the most important of these themes are a cosmology and physiology based on the four elements and their mixtures, as we

27. "Noch süzer dan ein küler wint dem heizen pilgerine, / noch süzer dan dem durstendigen ackerman ein kalt ursprinc, / Noch süzer dan ins lewen hitzic sunne ein schate schine, / noch süzer dan dem niuwen leben der süzen armonien clinc, // Noch süzer dan des lewen welf ir vater quickendiger gelf, / noch süzer dan ein stolze meit in vlucht dem eingehürne, / Noch süzer dan dem adelar in siner muze ein brunne clar, / noch süzer dan dem fenice sin wandel nach der bürne, // Noch süzer dan der honiktrage / der blüte honicsaffec nage, / noch süzer dan dem salamander viures wage, / noch süzer dan der luft dem gamalione, / . . . // Noch süzer ist der formelicher vröuden tag, / der dir uz wibes bilde bliczet durch din ougen in dins herzen eigen." *Minneleich* 16–17; 18.1–4; 19.1–2. Two of the bestiary examples, the lion cub and the phoenix, appear again in *Marienleich* 12.14–17; the Virgin with the unicorn was also a common figure for Mary.

28. Huber, *Aufnahme und Verarbeitung*, 154. The personification was also used by Reinmar von Zweter and Konrad von Würzburg.

29. This is the Weimar MS F; see note 11, above.

30. Huber, *Aufnahme und Verarbeitung*, 152–83; Steinmetz, *Liebe*, 9–57; Finckh, *Minor Mundus Homo*, 394–407.

saw in the Selvon vision; a conviction that human creativity and sexuality both derive from—
and mirror—the creativity of God; a doctrine of man as at once *imago Dei* and microcosm of the
universe, whose parts correspond with parts of the human body; and a psychological corollary
that finds cosmic resonance in the organization of soul as well as body. Frauenlob, however,
goes further than any of these Latin authors toward rejecting the soul-body dualism that is such
a persistent element in both Platonic and Pauline traditions. Honorius, while popularizing Eri-
ugena's Neoplatonist cosmology, teaches a rigorous ethical and eschatological dualism; Hilde-
gard's writing about sexuality and the body is uneasily torn between Augustinian pessimism
and a more "naturalistic" optimism; Bernard Silvestris, while glorifying sex, also depicts the
human microcosm as inferior to the macrocosm and portrays preexistent souls weeping at the
prospect of their embodiment; and Alan of Lille ultimately propounds a supernaturalism that
draws a firm line between Natura's sublunary world and the Incarnation, which she cannot
comprehend.[31] By contrast, if Frauenlob at one point in the *Marienleich* asserts that the Virgin
conceives "against nature," he tries more consistently and emphatically to show that she *is*
Nature—as well as the other pertinent goddesses, Minne and Sapientia.

   Minne und Welt is a pivotal poem in which Frauenlob explores not only his explicit theme—
the rivalry between "love and the world"—but also the nature of both entities, weighing
whether the terms are to be predicated univocally or equivocally of the phenomena they
denote.[32] Each goddess is dual or, at any rate, has dual aspects that may prove to be either com-
plementary or opposed. "Die Werlt" is Natura, the physical matrix of the world, and especially
its powers of procreation and reproduction. But she is also "Frau Werlt," a negative personifica-
tion of worldly transience, figured iconographically as a woman whose face is lovely while her
back is devoured by maggots. Minne of course is Love, an everyday term freighted with the
most complex and competing senses. Theologically she is *caritas,* a biblical name for God (1 John
4:8) and, in Augustinian doctrine, the Holy Spirit as the special bond of love uniting Father
and Son. Poetically, however, she is *hohe Minne,* or "courtly love," with all the ennobling traits
lauded in minnesang and romance yet centering firmly on sexual attraction. Die Werlt's strat-
egy throughout the debate is to drive a wedge between these two aspects of Minne, insisting
that divine and erotic love have only the name in common, and identifying her rival with the
latter, which she denounces. Minne's opposing tactic is to defend the univocity of her own
nature while insisting on her superiority to die Werlt as *creatrix* to *creatura.*

   The debate begins with a statement by the poet, who asserts the priority of Minne:

31. I here summarize the arguments I developed at length in
God and the Goddesses, chap. 2, and in *Sister of Wisdom: St. Hilde-
gard's Theology of the Feminine* (Berkeley and Los Angeles: Univer-
sity of California Press, 1987), chap. 4.

32. Steinmetz highlights the debate over different forms of
predication in *Liebe,* 157–58. He observes that for Thomas

Aquinas the different meanings of *amor* (corresponding to Frauen-
lob's Minne) are predicated analogously, while for die Werlt in
the debate, they are equivocal. But for Minne and evidently for
the poet himself, they are univocal.

Ich han der Minne und ouch der Werlte
    craft gewegen,
nu dünket mich, daz ich enmag
ir beider keine wis entbern.
ich weiz doch wol, welche unter in
    zwein me wirden hat.
	I have weighed the power of Minne and
	    also of the World.
	Now it seems to me that I cannot
	by any means do without both of them.
	Yet I know well which of the two has
	    greater worth.

Lieb unde lust der Minnen amtes müzen
    pflegen,
die wirken allez, daz der tag
erliuchtet.   alle ding begern
geminnert und gemeret sin nach Minne
    rat,
	Desire and pleasure are bound to fulfill
	    the office of Love:
	they accomplish all that the day
	illumines. All things long
	to be diminished and increased according
	    to Love's counsel.

Wurm, vogel, visch, tier,
wurz unde crut, stein unde holz, die han
    ir gir.
sus Minne ez allez wirken kan:
sich, Werlt, des wis ir untertan.
	Worm, bird, fish, beast,
	herb and plant, stone and wood, have a
	    desire for her.
	Thus Love can do everything;
	for this reason, World, I know you are
	    subject to her.

(IV.1.1–12)

Yet the poet-speaker at once qualifies this statement by thanking die Werlt for his own powers—heart and mind, body and senses—as well as for his pretty wife. For these blessings he praises her as *du bernder grunt* ("you fertile ground," IV.2.10)—a term he will apply to the Virgin in the *Marienleich* (I.6.12). But Minne responds indignantly that it was she, not die Werlt, who joined the poet with his wife; and so their debate begins.

    The argument falls into two parts, the first cosmological (strophes 3–10), and the second ethical (strophes 11–21). In the first section, die Werlt (as Natura) argues her priority over Minne on the grounds that she is both an eternal and a material being, whereas Love is merely an incidental "worker on her foundation," having no proper substance of her own. Minne retorts that, on the contrary, she is "a creator and a messenger of the first cause," and that in fact she herself is God: "er ist ouch ich und ich bin er" ("He indeed is I, and I am he," IV.5.11).[33] Die Werlt,

---

33. Cf. Lamprecht von Regensburg, *Tochter Syon*, 3192–93, "Diu minne ist got, got ist diu minne, / einz ist in dem andern inne" ("Minne is God, God is Minne; the one dwells in the other"), in Karl Weinhold, ed., *Sanct Francisken Leben und Tochter Syon* (Paderborn: F. Schöningh, 1880), 445. Such identifications were not uncommon in the thirteenth century. On the other hand, Frauenlob makes a similar pronouncement about honor: "Nu minnet ere! got ist ere, und ere ist got" ("Now love honor! God is Honor and Honor is God," GA V.61.7). All personified virtues could be identified with God via the Platonic (and Boethian) doctrine of participation; see note 22, above.

refusing to take such exalted claims seriously, compares Minne to a mirror image or a rainbow—a mere appearance, therefore easily deceived by appearances. Mocking her rival's foolishness, Minne identifies herself as the world soul, the *anima mundi*: just as the human soul is one yet has many functions, causing the feet to walk, the hands to grip, and the eyes to see, so she acts within the cosmos: "ich einig bin und han manig amt dort und in dir" ("I am one and have many offices there" (in heaven) "and in you" (on earth), IV.7.10). Minne is echoing the praise of divine Wisdom, "et cum sit una omnia potest" (Wisd. of Sol. 7:27), an index of the divinity Frauenlob ascribes to her. Yet the World still insists that Minne's function is merely to serve her, asserting in effect that, *qua* sexual love, her sole purpose is to maintain the world through procreation. Minne admits that she serves, but this only enhances her claim to divinity because God too serves his own creatures:

Got dienet allez daz, daz er gewirdet hat.	God serves all that he has caused to be.
sich, Werlt, also diene ich ouch dir:	See, World—thus I also serve you:
ich bin din ursprung und din zil.	I am your origin and your end.
ob ich drivaltig si, daz nim in dinen mut:	Bear in mind, am I not threefold?
Zu himel zwischen Crist und sines vater rat,	In heaven, between Christ and his father;
hie zwischen man und wibes gir,	here, between the desires of man and woman;
daz dritte ich dir nicht sliezen wil,	the third I will not conceal from you,
daz ist an aller frucht. der drilch mir wirde tut.	that is in all fruitfulness. My threefold nature does me honor.

(IV.9.1–8)

In this speech Minne emphatically asserts the unity of her nature; there is distinction, but no contradiction, among the three spheres of her activity as Holy Spirit ("between Christ and his father in heaven"), *anima mundi* or *genetrix rerum* (maintaining fruitfulness on earth), and *hohe Minne* (uniting the sexes in erotic love). At the same time, the very fact that she is triple identifies her with the Trinity, which is similarly characterized as a *drilch,* or threeness, in the *Marienleich* (I.4.18). Die Werlt responds gleefully that she is even "more perfect" (*volkomener*) because her own activity is fourfold: she works not only in humankind, on earth, and in heaven but also in hell, where Minne has no place! But this retort is comic, for activity in hell is hardly a perfection, and in numerology four—the cosmic number of the elements and compass points—cannot trump the divine Three.[34]

34. Helmut de Boor, "Frauenlobs Streitgespräch zwischen Minne und Welt," *Beiträge zur Geschichte der deutschen Sprache und Literatur* 85 (1963): 383–409, at 400.

Minne thus handily wins the first part of the debate. In its second and longer portion, the odds are more even.[35] Minne opens by boasting of her virtues, specifically *maze* (measure) and *bescheidenheit* (prudence or modesty). Die Werlt counters by citing such famous literary lovers as Gachmoret (the father of Parzival) and Paris (the lover of Helen), who conspicuously lacked these virtues. This charge compels Minne to acknowledge that she is eternal only in eternal beings. Love in mortals is ephemeral, but that is precisely the World's fault, for she is the cause of their transience. The rivals next attack each other on the grounds of iconography, die Werlt charging that Minne's true nature is exposed in the image of a blind, "blood-naked" (*blutnacket*) child with dangerous weapons, while Minne cites the worm-eaten backside of Frau Werlt as proof of her treachery. The two finally concur that neither is to blame for human sinfulness, since God has given mortals free will and they must take responsibility for their own misdeeds. Nevertheless, Minne notes that the World rewards even her best servants with a linen shroud and seven feet of earth, whereas she, Love, bestows eternal blessings. Predictably, she gets the last word:

Din rede nicht scheit	Your speech cannot separate
got unde mich: wir bliben ein, die schrift	God and me: we remain one, just as
daz seit.	Scripture says.
din falscheit gar dar nider lit,	Your falsehood is laid utterly low;
sust hast du, Werlt, verlorn din strit.	thus you, World, have lost your fight.

(IV.21.9–12)

Despite this forceful declaration of victory, Frauenlob's poem—like others of its genre—does not really seek to determine "which is better" so much as to explore a polarity, a relationship of mutual dependence. Within the constantly shifting perspectives of the debate, Love and the World can be compared as Creator to Creation, *anima mundi* to *mundus*, *Spiritus sanctus* to *Natura elementans*,[36] eternity to temporality, pure form to the compound of form and matter. Minne's self-perception is Platonic; she is in debt to the bold early twelfth-century thinkers—Thierry of Chartres, William of Conches, and Peter Abelard—who had tried to reconcile Plato's *Timaeus* with Genesis by identifying the Holy Spirit with the world soul. Abelard noted with characteristic subtlety that the Spirit, *qua* divine love in the Trinity, is eternal, but *qua* world soul it is not, since the world which it animates had a beginning in time.[37] Die Werlt may be evoking

35. Steinmetz, *Liebe*, 24–26.

36. This term is used in Bernard Silvestris, *Cosmographia*, to denote Natura as the creative force who actively mixes the four elements to produce living creatures. "Nature" in the passive sense is *Natura elementata*. See Huber, *Aufnahme und Verarbeitung*, 146–48; Winthrop Wetherbee, trans., *The "Cosmographia" of Bernardus Silvestris* (New York: Columbia University Press, 1973), 88.

37. "[Plato] called the Holy Spirit 'soul' (*anima*) rather than 'spirit' from its activity of 'animating,' that is, giving us life by

the gifts of grace through the increase of virtues. The Spirit was not always a soul, that is, a life-giver, since before there were any creatures to which it might distribute its gifts, it did not distribute them. Therefore we say the Holy Spirit, which in itself is altogether simple, is nonetheless multiple and even 'seven spirits' according to the diversity of gifts. . . . *Spiritus* is the name suited to its nature and *anima* to its function, that is, giving life." Peter Abelard, *Theologia "summi boni"* 3.94, ed. Eligius Buytaert and Constant Mews, CCCM 13 (Turnhout: Brepols, 1987),198.

some such reservation when she denigrates Minne as a mere "worker on [her] foundation," not a self-sufficient power. Unlike her rival, die Werlt is a firm Aristotelian: it seems self-evident to her that, as a being compounded of form and matter, she is superior to—because "more real than"—Minne, a mere insubstantial form.[38] Yet the two are not only interdependent, but both must collaborate in the poem's central concern, reproduction: Minne causes sexual attraction whereas die Werlt provides the matter for procreation. As she says of herself, "Swaz die vier element gebern, / daz bir ich ouch" ("Whatever the four elements bring forth, I bring forth also," IV.4.3—4).

It is in this very sphere, however, that both goddesses stand revealed—at least in their rivals' eyes—as "fallen." If die Werlt is Natura in the positive sense, the creative goddess whom Alan of Lille celebrated as "dei proles genitrixque rerum, / Vinculum mundi stabilisque nexus,"[39] she must also be Natura in the negative sense, the realm of biological change that Aristotle called "generation and corruption." Likewise, if Minne is divine *caritas* binding the Trinity and humankind in holy love, she is also *concupiscentia* or destructive passion, bringing ruin on reckless lovers like Paris and Gachmoret. While allowing the two goddesses to voice these accusations with full force, the debate also works to exonerate both as far as possible by locating moral responsibility with humans. Nevertheless, Minne is the more fully vindicated of the two, for cosmic Love is not finally to blame for the vices that infect human love, whereas Natura or die Werlt *is* to blame for the fact of mortality. Her duplicity is expressed in a more explicitly Christian strophe that represents Nature as a self-contradictory goddess, both creative and destructive, much as in Alan's *De planctu*:

Naturen lust gab apfels bruch,	Nature's desire caused the transgression of the apple,
nature brach naturen spruch.	Nature broke Nature's own edict.
sol ich nature melden?	Should I account for Nature?
nature der naturen selbe stal ir fluz.	Nature stole from Nature's self her own life-giving flow.

(X.2.9—12)

Frauenlob's final resolution of this debate lies not in *Minne und Welt* but in the *Marienleich*, where he adopts the extraordinary solution of melding both goddesses with the person of Mary. His Virgin embodies a chaste but passionate Minne as well as a redeemed, immortal Natura,

---

38. My distinction between Minne's Platonism and die Werlt's Aristotelianism is indebted to Brunhilde Peter, *Die theologisch-philosophische Gedankenwelt des Heinrich Frauenlob* (Speyer: Jägersche Buchdruckerei, 1957), 30. Steinmetz argues that Frauenlob understood his Minne less as a Platonic idea than as an Aristotelian *substantia separata*. Several propositions concerning the eternity and causality of "separated substances" were among those condemned at Paris in 1277. Steinmetz, *Liebe*, 50—57.

39. "O child of God and mother of the universe, chain of the world and stable bond." Alan of Lille, *De planctu Naturae*, metrum 4.1—2.

subsuming the functions of the world soul while remaining what the Mary of Christian devotion had always been: human mother of Jesus, bride of God, and mediatrix between sinners and the righteous Judge. As Christoph Huber notes, Frauenlob's poetry tends toward synthesis rather than differentiation of its diverse sources: Mary is the figure par excellence in whom "Christian, classical-philosophical, and secular-courtly elements converge."[40] According to Ralf-Henning Steinmetz, the *Marienleich* reunites the principles that *Minne und Welt* analytically separated: "Like the Abelardian Holy Spirit, like the Platonic Anima mundi, like the Chartrain Natura, Frauenlob's Mary imparts God—imparts the Trinity, raised by her to a quaternity—to the creation and to God's creatures here below."[41] For Ruth Finckh, Mary as incarnate Minne "unites not only humankind and God, but also microcosm and macrocosm, for she informs and leaves her mark on both alike." The Lady of the *Marienleich* "stands for the union of matter and spirit: she takes on the role of a numinous, creative power and presents herself as an aspect of God, but at the same time she emerges in her historical role as the bearer of God's Son and reflects a part of her glory on earthly mothers."[42] Since these poems mutually illumine each other, the *Marienleich* is most fruit-fully read in the context of other texts, especially the *Minneleich* and *Minne und Welt*, that represent the same personified forces. But the two Minne poems do not treat an additional theme that looms large in the *Marienleich*—the relationship between the eternal Trinity and the incarnate Christ. For this we must turn to Frauenlob's *Kreuzleich*, the least-studied of his three *leichs*.[43]

KREUZLEICH

The religious and secular *leich*, though formally similar, were in practice such separate genres that, apart from Frauenlob, only Konrad von Würzburg wrote one of each.[44] Konrad's religious *leich*, like those by Walther von der Vogelweide, Reinmar von Zweter, and Hermann Damen, covers all the major themes of Christian theology, with sections devoted to the Trinity, the Virgin, the Incarnation, and the Redemption.[45] Reinmar, as we have seen, also gave extensive treatment to Minne qua Holy Spirit. But Frauenlob alone composed two distinct *leichs*, one hon-oring Mary, the other the Cross. Both return to the problem he considered in *Minne und Welt*, the relationship between eternal Love and the temporal world, with the Trinity now filling the transcendent role of Minne in the debate poem. Despite its central focus on redemption, the

---

40. Huber, *Aufnahme und Verarbeitung,* 187.

41. Steinmetz, *Liebe,* 59.

42. Finckh, *Minor Mundus Homo,* 416.

43. There is a (conjectural) modern German translation by Eva and Hansjürgen Kiepe in their edited volume, *Gedichte 1300–1500, nach Handschriften und Frühdrucken in zeitlicher Folge,* vol. 2 of Walther Killy, ed., *Epochen der deutschen Lyrik* (Munich: Deutscher Taschenbuch, 1972), 19–29. See also Stackmann,

"Frauenlob, Verführer," 17–20, and Peter Kern, "*Heilvlies und selden holz*: Überlegungen zu Frauenlobs Kreuzleich," in Johannes Janota, ed., *Festschrift Walter Haug und Burghart Wachinger* (Tübingen: Niemeyer, 1992), 2:743–57.

44. Sayce, *Medieval German Lyric,* 372.

45. Bertau, "Über Themenanordnung und Bildung"; Sayce, *Medieval German Lyric,* 389–92.

Kreuzleich also deals with the Trinity and the Virgin, devoting more than half of its twenty-two strophes to them:

Strophes 1–6: The Trinity and the eternal generation of the Word
Strophes 7–9: Old Testament theophanies
Strophes 10–12: The Incarnation and the Virgin Birth
Strophe 13: The seven "leaps" of God
Strophes 14–21: The Cross and the Redemption
Strophe 22: Closing prayer

The number of strophes is not incidental, for the Hebrew alphabet has twenty-two letters and, in consequence, Psalm 119 is divided into twenty-two sections, the Apocalypse into twenty-two chapters, and Augustine's *City of God* into twenty-two books. So in medieval numerology this number symbolized completeness. As in the *Marienleich*, however, the strophes are not of equal length, but the sections dealing with the Cross are much longer than those in the first part, giving the poem a rough balance. Strophe 5 provides another index of Frauenlob's attention to numerology. Elsewhere in the *Kreuzleich*, as in the *Minneleich* and *Marienleich*, a strophe consists of two metrically identical halves, the second echoing the first. But *Kreuzleich* 5, dealing with the three Persons of the Trinity, contains three identical sections of three lines apiece, each devoted to one divine Person.[46] Thus this *leich* has an odd number of lines—a total of 249, making it slightly less than half the length of the *Marienleich* at 508.

The opening section reveals Frauenlob's bent for speculative theology, which made such a potent impression on his contemporaries and followers. Using an analogy from Augustine's *De Trinitate*,[47] he describes the eternal generation of the Word from the Father's heart, crafting a highly ornamental verse rendered difficult by the intensive use of internal rhyme and the rare technique of enjambment from one strophe to the next:

Sam von der sunnen tut der schin,	As a ray of light streams from the sun
ouch sam von den brunnen schiuzet,	and as a river rushes, gushes, pours
diuzet, vliuzet	itself from a spring
ein rivier, daz die wurze ergiuzet,	to water the plants,
runsic, seffec unde fin,	liquid, luscious and pure;
Wie biltsam uz des herzen schrin	As, by analogy, an intended word
sich daz wort in willen dringet,	slings, flings, hurls itself
swinget, slinget,	from the heart's shrine

---

46. Strophe 18 of the *Minneleich* is also tripartite, for no obvious reason.

47. Augustine, *The Trinity* 15.11, trans. Stephen McKenna (Washington, D.C.: Catholic University of America Press, 1963), 476–78.

swenn ez die zunge luftic twinget,
    sust gebar der vater sin
	when the tongue compels it with breath,
	    even so the Father's mind

Den sun.	Begot the Son.

(II.3.1—6; 4.1)

Frauenlob continues with the procession of the Holy Spirit from both, likening the three Persons of the Trinity to those of grammar:

Sprich, vaterlich persone:
"mich, min, mir;   sun: dich, din, dir;   geist: er, sin, im.
nu merket, daz ich allez bin."

Der sun uz kindes vrone:
"vater min,   in dir ich din,   in mir du nim
den erben, ja ich, du vatersin."

Der geist uz beider done:
"er, du; ich   —uz dir in dich—   iu beiden zim:
drivaldic got, doch ein begin."

(II.5.1—9)

[Speak, person of the Father: "Me, mine, to me. The Son: You, yours, to you. The Spirit: He, his, to him. Now observe that I am all." The Son (speaks) out of his majesty as Child: "My Father, in you I am yours, in me you have an heir—even I, O paternal Mind." The Spirit intones from both: "He, you, I—(proceeding) out of you (the Father) into you (the Son)—I belong to you both: threefold God, yet one beginning."]

This odd passage points clearly to its source: none other than Abelard, who introduced the nonstandard grammatical analogy in his *Theologia* "*summi boni.*" Using *Sprachlogik* as a novel approach to dogma, the philosopher explained that the rules of grammar refer to one and the same man as three "persons" positioned differently with regard to speech: the first person speaks, the second is spoken to, and the third is spoken about. Just as these grammatical persons represent three properties but only one substance, so also with God, who begets as Father, is begotten as Son, and proceeds as Holy Spirit.[48] Abelard's theological summa also includes his teaching on the world soul and a representation of the Holy Spirit as God's love for creation (not merely his intra-Trinitarian love, as Augustine had taught). Given these multiple echoes, it

---

48. Abelard, *Theologia "Summi boni"* 2.108—9 and *Theologia* "*scholarium*" 2.108, CCCM 13:153, 460.

seems likely that Frauenlob either knew a version of Abelard's *Theologia* directly or had studied with someone who did.

These abstract strophes on the triple Godhead yield to an easier set of analogies in which the poet claims to "learn of the Three from threes" (*sust drie von drien ich lerne*, II.6.5). Ice, water, and snow are three forms of one substance; the apple's skin, pulp, and core comprise a single fruit; a candle's wick, wax, and fire yield but one light; the musician's mind, strings, and hand produce a single tune. All these images stem from popular preaching, and all would be recycled by the meistersingers.[49] To confirm that the whole Trinity revealed itself to the patriarchs and prophets, Frauenlob continues with a torrent of rhetorical questions reminiscent of the *Minneleich*:

> Who fed you, Jonah, in the fish's belly?
> Who helped Daniel out of the hungry lions' den?
> Who twice sent Elijah food by means of the raven?
>
> Who slew the Egyptians with afflicting flame?
> Who saved your troubled soul, Joseph, sold into bondage?
> Isaac, speak! "Father, who restrained your deadly sword?"[50]

Like the Trinity passage, these questions display the poet's fascination with dialogue and direct speech. In fact, Frauenlob may have intentionally used all three grammatical persons to cement the analogy of strophe 5—composing one line in the first person, two in the second, and three in the third. Having already commanded God the Father to speak, he does not hesitate to give orders to a biblical patriarch. This unusual device culminates in the *Marienleich* where the poet's command "Vil schöne ob allen vrouwen, sprich" ("Loveliest of women, speak!" I.8.24) introduces twelve strophes of first-person discourse.

Strophes 10–12 introduce the Virgin to the *Kreuzleich* via biblical and extrabiblical types: the mystical unicorn hunt, Aaron's blossoming rod, Gideon's dewy fleece, the ray of sunlight that passes through glass without breaking it. None of these recur in the *Marienleich*, suggesting that Frauenlob deliberately avoided repeating himself. His language in strophe 11 is especially striking:

> Alrerst viel der reine, wise, starke, gute
> uz hohen himelvelsen her.

49. Kern, *Trinität, Maria, Inkarnation*, 144, 152–63, 171–74. For the analogy of the harpist with *ars, manus,* and *chorda,* see the pseudo-Augustinian sermon 245, "De mysterio Trinitatis et incarnationis" (PL 39: 21 97a).

50. "Wer nerte, Jona, dich in visches wamme? / wer half uz hungerlewen velsen Daniel? / wer sante bi dem raben spise Elie zwir? / Wer slug Egipten kummer tragender vlamme? / wer gap, verkoufter Joseph, heil der trüben sel? / Isac, sprich: vater, wer gap wider din mortswert dir?" *Kreuzleich* II.7.1–6.

swaz er   mit ger   in der   propheten kramen
het behalden, secht, daz wolde er melden mit dem gotelichen samen.

$$(\text{II.11.1--4})$$

[First of all the pure, wise, strong, and good One
fell from the high cliffs of heaven here below.[51]
What he desired to withhold from the prophets' wares,
see! through the divine seed he willed to make known.]

Christ's "fall" from the cliffs of heaven introduces a set piece, the seven leaps of God (II.13), whereby the Son "springs" out of his Father in eternity; into the Word; into the Virgin's womb; onto the Cross; into the realm of endless darkness (the Harrowing of Hell); up to the throne of Solomon (the Ascension); and finally "into pure hearts," who are willing to receive him—probably referring to the Eucharist.[52] This trope, inspired by Canticle 2:8 ("ecce iste venit, saliens in montibus, transiliens colles"), derives from a famous Ascension sequence by Notker of St. Gall.[53] The number and nature of Christ's leaps were variable. Notker himself mentions four (the Incarnation, the Nativity, the Harrowing of Hell, and the Ascension), while the St. Trudperter Hohelied lists eight: from heaven into the Virgin's womb and thence to the crib, to the waters of baptism, to the Cross, to the grave, to the Harrowing of Hell, to the Resurrection, and to the Ascension.[54] Frauenlob's inclusion of not one but two preincarnational leaps typifies his perspective in all three leichs, where the temporal is always framed by the eternal. In the Kreuzleich a third term, the liturgical, mediates between the two. Thus strophe 13 on the leaps of Christ is paralleled by strophe 16, which interprets the sign of the cross as a devotional gesture. The first touch on the forehead signifies God's eternal begetting of the Son; the second, on the breast, his descent into the Virgin; the third, on the left, his descent into hell (the "sinister" side); and the fourth, on the right, his return to the Father's right hand.[55] A final

51. The language is unusual; Christ is not usually represented as "falling." But see Julian of Norwich's *Revelation of Love*, chap. 51, about a century after Frauenlob: "When Adam felle, Godes sonne fell . . . into the slade [hollow] of the maidens wombe, which was the fairest doughter of Adam." *The Writings of Julian of Norwich*, ed. Nicholas Watson and Jacqueline Jenkins (University Park: The Pennsylvania State University Press, 2006), 283.

52. This is the view of Kern, "Heilvlies und selden holz," 744, and Kiepe, *Gedichte 1300–1500*, 23. Ludwig Pfannmüller on the other hand saw here an allusion to Meister Eckhart's teaching about the eternal birth of the Word in the soul: Frauenlob (Heinrich von Meissen). *Frauenlobs Marienleich* (Strassburg: Karl Trübner, 1913), 115–16, 130.

53. "Nam transilivit / omnes strenue montes / colliculosque Bethel. // Saltum de caelo dedit . . . / in virginalem ventrem, /

inde in pelagus saeculi. // Postquam illud suo / mitigavit potentatu, / tetras Flegetontis / assiliit tenebras. // . . . / Denique saltum dederat / hodie maximum . . . / nubes polosque . . . / cursu praepeti transvolans." Wolfram von den Steinen, ed., *Notker der Dichter und seine geistige Welt*, 2 vols. (Bern: A. Francke, 1948), 2:50.

54. Friedrich Ohly, ed., *Das St. Trudperter Hohelied: Eine Lehre der liebenden Gotteserkenntnis* (Frankfurt am Main: Deutscher Klassiker Verlag, 1998), 84.

55. Kern, "Heilvlies," 744–47. For the meaning of the sign, see Jean Beleth, *Summa de ecclesiasticis officiis*, chap. 39, CCCM 41a, ed. Herbert Douteil (Turnhout: Brepols, 1976), 72; William Durandus, *Rationale divinorum officiorum* 5.2.13, CCCM 140a, ed. A. Davril and T. M. Thibodeau (Turnhout: Brepols, 1998), 20–21.

gesture parallels Christ's final leap into pure hearts: this is the consecration of the Host at mass, when "God stoops low in the hand of the priest" (II.16.18).

The *leich*'s praise of the Cross centers on the essential unity of Fall and Redemption. Frauenlob recounts the apocryphal legend of Adam, who on his deathbed sent his son Seth to fetch a branch from the tree of Paradise as a remedy. Returning too late, Seth planted the sprout on his father's grave, where it grew into the mighty tree that became first a doorpost in Solomon's temple and, later, the True Cross.[56] Thus the tree of death and the tree of life are physically as well as symbolically one. In a particularly baroque passage, Frauenlob even compares Christ's body, twisted in death, to the serpent wound around the tree in Eden (II.14.1−2). Further, the Cross is a noble winepress, a rich table laden with food, a holy altar anointed with oil and chrism, indeed, "God's butcher block" on which the Lamb was slaughtered and "Death broke his bread" ("der tot / brach sin brot," II.18.3−4). Most surprising is that the Cross is also a mother:

Des cristentumes ouwe, daz	The pasture of Christendom,
criuce ich heize ein vrouwe.	I call the Cross a woman.
sie gebar daz lebende leben,	She gave birth to the living Life,
sie truc ein kint al unbewollen, rede ich eben,	she bore a child all undefiled, so I say truly,
ein liecht der sacramente wert.	a light of the precious sacraments.
ir griezstange und ir sigeswert,	As her battle-staff and sword of victory,
himelzeichen, gotes marc, wir cristen han daz criuze.	sign of heaven, mark of God—we Christians have the Cross.

(II.19.8−14)

What this means in a quasi-literal sense is that the Cross "bore" Christ by supporting his body and "gave birth to life" in that the sacraments of baptism and the Eucharist arose when his side was pierced by the spear, yielding blood and water. But these meanings are overshadowed by the explicitly Marian language applied to the rood. Poetic personification of the Cross was not unheard of, although it was rare. In the Old English *Dream of the Rood*—a poem Frauenlob would have loved if he had known it—the Cross is not only personified as a loyal thane of Christ, the divine warrior, but also narrates much of the poem. At one point he/it remarks that the Lord of glory has exalted the Cross above all trees of the wood, just as he has glorified his mother Mary above all women.[57] As twin foci of devotion, the Cross and the Virgin were paired in other contexts as well. For example, in the dramatic and devotional lyrics known as *planctus*

56. See also Commentary on the *Marienleich,* strophe 19.

57. "Hwaet, me þa geweorðode wuldres Ealdor / ofer holt-wudu, heofon-rices Weard, / swelce swa he his modor eac, Marian selfe, / aelmihtig God, for ealle menn / geweorðode ofer eall wifa cynn" ("Look! The Lord of glory, the Warden of heaven, almighty God, has exalted me over the trees of the wood for all men's sake, just as he also exalted his mother, Mary, over all womankind"). *Dream of the Rood,* lines 90−94, ed. John C. Pope, *Seven Old English Poems* (Indianapolis: Bobbs-Merrill, 1966), 12−13.

Mariae, the Virgin laments at the foot of the Cross, reproaches it, or engages in dialogue with it.[58] But it was reserved for Frauenlob to assert, in effect, that the Cross *is* Mary, because even in this context he could not envisage salvation without the presence of a *vrouwe.*

SANGSPRÜCHE AND THE NINE TONES

In addition to his three *leichs* and *Minne und Welt,* Frauenlob composed perhaps 450 *Sangsprüche,* or strophic songs—a canon that must remain ill-defined because of the difficulty of distinguishing Frauenlob's songs from those of his imitators.[59] The *Sprüche* deal with a great variety of themes, including the Trinity, the Incarnation and death of Christ, the Virgin Mary, Nature and her powers, macrocosm and microcosm, the paradox of time, the four elements and their qualities, chivalric virtues, courtly love, praise of patrons and ladies, advice to princes, duties and vices of the clergy, Arthurian heroes, social classes, youth and age, to mention only a sampling. Given the size and diversity of this canon, there can be no question of even a general survey.[60] But the *Sprüche* afford a perfect opportunity to examine the interaction of text and music in Frauenlob and his peers—a complex relationship that differs significantly from other vernacular traditions.

The *Spruchdichter* composed their songs within formal templates known as *Töne,* which are simultaneously melodic structures ("tunes") and metrical patterns incorporating rhyme schemes, number of feet per line, and number of lines per unit. Singers were judged not only on the quality of their lyrics but also on the melodic beauty and rhythmic ingenuity of their *Töne,* which could be preserved and imitated as poetic-musical patterns independently of any particular lyric. Their use therefore enabled a widespread, organized practice of *contrafactura,* the performance of multiple lyrics with the same metrical pattern to the same tune. (In a *Sängerkrieg* such as the *wip-vrouwe* debate, rivals composed their rebuttals in the same *Ton* as the piece that initiated the exchange.) Each *Ton* was given its own distinctive name, if not by its composer then by his contemporaries and scribes, to facilitate the classification of songs. Although a great variety of *Töne* are ascribed to Frauenlob in the manuscripts, his editors have accepted only nine as authentic: the Langer Ton (Long Tune), the Flugton (Flight Tune), the Grüner Ton (Green Tune), the Zarter Ton (Delicate Tune), the Würgendrüssel ("Choking Snout," so-called because it contains a melodic passage high enough to strain most singers' voices),[61] the Vergessener Ton

---

58. Sandro Sticca, *The "Planctus Mariae" in the Dramatic Tradition of the Middle Ages,* trans. Joseph Berrigan (Athens: University of Georgia Press, 1988), 34–37, 72–77.

59. The GA contains a total of 451 strophes but excludes at least forty from Ettmüller's 1843 edition on grounds of inauthenticity. For these excluded strophes and many more ascribed to Frauenlob in the manuscripts, see Jens Haustein and Karl Stackmann, eds., *Sangsprüche in Tönen Frauenlobs: Supplement zur Göttinger Frauenlob-Ausgabe,* 2 vols. (Göttingen: Vandenhoeck & Ruprecht, 2000).

60. In *Höfische Liebe,* Margreth Egidi offers detailed analyses of Frauenlob's strophes on love and the praise of ladies in their vernacular context.

61. Horst Brunner, "Die Spruchtöne Frauenlobs: Bemerkungen zur Form und zur formgeschichtlichen Stellung," in Jens Haustein and Ralf-Henning Steinmetz, eds., *Studien zu Frauenlob und Heinrich von Mügeln: Festschrift für Karl Stackmann zum 80. Geburtstag* (Fribourg: Universitätsverlag, 2002), 61–79 at 75.

(Forgotten Tune), the Neuer Ton (New Tune), the Goldener Ton (Golden Tune), and the Kurzer Ton (Short Tune). All these melodies, except for the Kurzer Ton, have survived. The number nine is itself significant: in *Marienleich* 18, Frauenlob praises the "thrice three" tones of the nine choirs of angels, so he might have limited his own composition of *Töne* to this number to imitate the celestial choirs. Later tradition, however, attributes to him many other spurious ones. Aside from the standard medieval practice of ascribing recent compositions to famous names from the past, these attributions may have had a further motive, for after the meistersingers established their singing schools in the fifteenth century, they "closed the canon" for a time by limiting all new compositions to the *Töne* of the old masters, including Frauenlob.[62]

To see how a *Spruchton* works metrically, we can analyze Frauenlob's eulogy for Konrad von Würzburg, a composition in his Zarter Ton (see text on pp. 56–57, above). The standard thirteenth-century *Ton* was a tripartite form. Its first two units, called *Stollen*, are identical and together comprise the *Aufgesang*, or "rising song," while its third unit, the *Abgesang* ("falling song"), differs in its metrical and melodic structure and rhyme scheme. We can diagram the three units of the Zarter Ton as follows, with the numbers representing feet per line and the letters, the rhyme scheme.[63]

$$4\ 2\ 5\ 4\ 6\ 2\ 3 \qquad 4\ 2\ 5\ 4\ 6\ 2\ 3 \qquad 5\ 5\ 3\ 4\ 2\ 2\ 3$$
$$a\ a\ a\ b\ b\ a\ c \qquad d\ d\ d\ e\ e\ d\ c \qquad f\ f\ f\ g\ g\ g\ c$$

The extreme variation in line lengths is typical of the *Spruchdichter,* in contrast to Latin hymns and early troubadour lyrics where "isometric" stanzas (with lines of equal length) predominate.[64] Also typical is the fact that in this song of twenty-one lines Frauenlob uses only seven rhyme sounds, with the final c-rhyme linking the two *Stollen* and the *Abgesang* to unify the piece. Rhyming lines and rhythmic structures do not necessarily coincide (for example, the a-rhyme occurs in lines of four feet, two feet, and five feet), while melodic repetitions form a third pattern that may coincide with neither, giving each *Ton* a pleasing intricacy. For the melody of Frauenlob's Zarter Ton, listeners can consult a recent disc by Sequentia. It is interesting that the lyrics of the recorded piece (by an unknown meistersinger) praise the superiority of song over instrumental music, as if in disapproving comment on the Manesse portrait of Frauenlob.[65]

---

62. Henkel, "Die zwölf alten Meister"; Wehrli, *Geschichte der deutschen Literatur,* 1:730–31.

63. Brunner, "Die Spruchtöne Frauenlobs," 63. A foot includes a single stressed syllable; this poetry allows some latitude as to the number and placement of weak syllables.

64. Sayce, *Medieval German Lyric,* 47, 112.

65. "Crown and Veil: Music from Medieval Female Monasteries," directed by Benjamin Bagby (2005), produced by the Kunst- und Ausstellungshalle der Bundesrepublik Deutschland, Bonn, and the Ruhrlandmuseum Essen. The Frauenlob piece is track 13, "Ich wil verbannen und verban"; for an edition of the text, see Haustein and Stackmann, *Sangsprüche in Tönen Frauenlobs,* 1:226–29. The poem asserts that strings, pipes, and organs can offer a pleasing but meaningless sound, whereas "sang ist ein hort, / des got selber begert" ("singing is a treasure that God himself desires").

Finally, we turn to the least-known works in Frauenlob's canon: his seven *minnelieder,* or love songs. Long thought to be his most conventional pieces, a last gasp of the moribund minnesang, these songs now appear in a more innovative light, drawing new attention for their resemblance to the oeuvre of the *stilnovisti.* Like some of his Italian contemporaries, especially Guido Cavalcanti, Frauenlob in these songs focuses intensely on the inner psychic experience of the lover, the "lyric I," to the near exclusion of an objectively real beloved.[66] This "I" is typically fragmented, introspective, unrewarded, and impotent against the power of Minne, to whom he desperately appeals for help. For instance, in the poet's seventh song Minne explains to a despairing lover that he has lost all power over himself because he is now a divided being; his *herze* and *mut* (heart and mind) have taken his lady's side and abdicated all power into her hands. The "I" then asks Minne to help him enter his lady's heart as she has entered his, but Minne warns that this would be dangerous because she might resist his love and attack him. In the last strophe, the lover asks how he should behave if he does breach the defenses of his lady's heart, and Minne replies, "Like a raging madman" ("toben soltu . . . alsam du sist von sinnen komen," XIV.35.2–3). Realizing that such behavior would cause the beloved to suffer the same pain that he himself endures, the lover draws back in dismay. In their subjective and inward-looking character, these *minnelieder* differ from Frauenlob's *leichs* and even his *wip-vrouwe* poems, which strongly insist on the woman's physical presence (though scarcely on what we would call her individual self). Even in the *lieder,* however, the poet praises sexual consummation, having no use for the "pure" love upheld by minnesingers like Reinmar der Alte and his early patron, King Wenceslas of Bohemia.[67]

In an excellent new study of the *lieder,* Susanne Köbele sketches a comparison between Frauenlob and Dante that may be even more pertinent for the *Marienleich* than for the songs she analyzes.[68] Both poets, she argues, conceived of the "I" as essentially loving, imaginative, and visionary—an "absolute" self rather than a modern "individual." Both were steeped in Latin learning yet committed to the vernacular, which they held fully capable of expressing philosophical and theological ideas hitherto discussed only in Latin. Finally, and most crucial, both believed in a cosmic, absolute, unlimited Love at the heart of the universe and set it at the center of their literary projects. Thus Frauenlob's poetry (especially the *Marienleich* and *Minne und Welt*) shares with Dante's *Vita Nuova* and *Commedia* a convergence between "secular" and "spiritual" perspectives on love. A single, overarching Minne or Amore embraces both God and

66. Harald Bühler, "Zur Gestaltung des lyrischen Ichs bei Cavalcanti und Frauenlob," in Schröder, ed., *Wolfram-Studien* 10:179–89.

67. Wachinger, "Hohe Minne um 1300," 144.

68. Susanne Köbele, *Frauenlobs Lieder: Parameter einer literarhistorischen Standortbestimmung* (Tübingen: A. Francke, 2003), 209–15.

eros, uniting the phenomena that moral theology had set in opposition under the names of *caritas* and *concupiscentia*. Although the *language* of what I have called "crossover"—the use of secular erotic imagery for divine love or vice versa—is ubiquitous in the thirteenth century, the serious, theological articulation of their convergence remains rare.[69] In Dante's reception, we can see the resistance to this convergence theology in the endless critical argument over whether Beatrice is "really" an allegory of grace or a concrete, historical woman whom Dante loved, when in truth she is really simultaneously both. In the case of Frauenlob, as Köbele observes, resistance appears even in the scribal tradition. Compilers of manuscripts hierarchically separated "religious poems" (*tichten von gote*) from "poems about love" (*tihten von der mynne*), thus necessarily making interpretive choices about songs sometimes so ambiguous that one can hardly tell whether the Lady being praised is the Virgin Mary or *Vrouwe* in general.[70] Even Frauenlob's greatest admirers in the next generation, such as Heinrich von Mügeln, tended to rehierarchize earthly and heavenly love, presenting them as analogous rather than consubstantial. Köbele thus contrasts von Mügeln's more conventional technique of *Nebeneinander* or juxtaposition with Frauenlob's *Ineinander* or coinherence.[71] Whether in the *minnelieder* or the *Marienleich*, Frauenlob was not charting a passage "from" the sensual "to" the spiritual, but representing a love that is, like Dante's for Beatrice, simultaneously both.

This exalted yet introspective notion of love leads us to expect passages bordering on the mystical in Frauenlob's work, and indeed we find them. His sixth *lied* raises the very Dantesque question whether lamenting his own amorous pain serves his ultimate goal, which is his lady's praise. One passage describes an ecstatic self-annihilation that might have come from the pages of Mechthild of Magdeburg or Meister Eckhart:

Ich suchte mich,	I sought myself,
da vant ich min da heime nicht.	yet I found nothing of myself at home.
ich wante, ein ding daz wolte	I believed there was something
mich töten gar mit lüste.	that wished to kill me wholly with desires.
lip, wa was ich do?	Body, where was I then?

(XIV.28.1–5)

Köbele compares this passage with the last strophe of the *Granum sinapis* (Mustard Seed), a mystical sequence in the Eckhartian mode from the early fourteenth century:[72]

69. On the crossover phenomenon, see Barbara Newman, "Love's Arrows: Christ as Cupid in Late Medieval Art and Devotion," in Anne-Marie Bouché and Jeffrey Hamburger, eds., *The Mind's Eye: Art and Theological Argument in the Medieval West* (Princeton: Princeton University Press, 2005), 263–86; and Hildegard Keller, *My Secret Is Mine: Studies on Religion and Eros in the German Middle Ages* (Leuven: Peeters, 2000).

70. Köbele, *Frauenlobs Lieder*, 226.

71. See also Susanne Köbele, "Umbesetzungen: Zur Liebessprache in Liedern Frauenlobs," in Christoph Huber, Burghart Wachinger, and Hans-Joachim Ziegeler, eds., *Geistliches in weltlicher und Weltliches in geistlicher Literatur des Mittelalters* (Tübingen: Niemeyer, 2000), 213–35.

ô sêle mîn	O my soul,
genk ûz, got în!	go out [of yourself, let] God in!
sink al mîn icht	May I sink all my "something"
in gotis nicht,	into the nothingness of God,
sink in dî grundelôʒe vlût!	sink into the bottomless flood!
vlî ich von dir,	If I flee from you,
du kumst ʒu mir.	you come to me.
vorlîs ich mich,	If I lose myself utterly,
sô vind ich dich,	in this way I find you,
ô überweselîches gût!	O supersubstantial Good!

Though such passages are rare, they point to *Minnemystik* as yet another spring from which Frauenlob's versatile muse drew nurture. In the *Marienleich,* all the streams—formal theology, biblical exegesis, mystical love, cosmology, *hohe Minne,* devotional lyric—converge to produce a work of unparalleled grandeur.

72. Kobele, *Frauenlobs Lieder,* 238; see also Wachinger, "Hohe Minne," 149. For the *Granum sinapis,* see Kurt Ruh, "Textkritik ʒum Mystikerlied 'Granum Sinapis,'" in *Kleine Schriften,* ed. Volker Mertens (Berlin: Walter de Gruyter, 1984), 2:77–93; and the website http://www.eckhart.de/index.htm?granum.htm.

3

THE *MARIENLEICH* IN CONTEXT

Setting the *Marienleich* in context is both easy and hard. It is easy because, by the time of Frauenlob's birth in the mid-thirteenth century, Mary's visual, textual, and devotional presence in European culture was already ubiquitous. So nothing can be less surprising than the choice of her praise as the topic for an ambitious vernacular poem. In Patrick Diehl's words, the *Marienleich* "was the equivalent of Milton's 'Lycidas' or Hopkins's 'Wreck of the Deutschland' or Crane's 'The Bridge': a conscious try for a masterpiece, in the highest style and form available, that stretched the poet's powers to the utmost and consummated a subject and tradition central to the poet's age."[1] But contextualizing the *leich* is hard for exactly the same reason. In the Virgin's kingdom were many mansions, and not all Marian traditions are pertinent.[2] The goal of this chapter, then, is to introduce a reading of the

1. Patrick Diehl, *The Medieval European Religious Lyric: An Ars Poetica* (Berkeley and Los Angeles: University of California Press, 1985), 97.

2. I mention only a handful of general works: Hilda Graef, *Mary: A History of Doctrine and Devotion*, 2 vols. (New York: Sheed & Ward, 1963, 1965); Walter Delius, *Geschichte der Marienverehrung*

leich by highlighting the most important contexts that the poet and his ideal audience would have brought to the work. These include biblical sources mediated through Marian liturgy and exegesis; the twelfth-century learned traditions surrounding Plato's *Timaeus* (once identified with the "school of Chartres"); the curricular structure of the seven liberal arts, including Aristotelian logic; vernacular *Marienlob*, especially the poetry of Konrad von Würzburg; and the German mystical tradition. My aim is not to provide a textbook account of any of these but to show how they bear on Frauenlob's text.

Marienleich is merely an editorial title. Some manuscripts leave the work untitled, while one calls it simply "Heinrich frawenlobs laich." Two others, with the chronicle of Albrecht von Strassburg, suggestively entitle the poem *Cantica canticorum*. The fullest inscription appears in a fifteenth-century Colmar song manuscript: "Unser frauwen leich oder der guldin flügel zu latin Cantica canticorum" ("Our Lady's *leich,* or the golden wing on the Latin Song of Songs").[3] According to Kurt Gärtner's count, there are no fewer than sixty Song citations in this poem of only 508 lines—more than all other biblical allusions combined. Every chapter of the Song is cited, and thirteen of the *leich*'s twenty strophes adapt lines from it.[4] Moreover, because the poem bears few traces of explicit allegory, it preserves more of the biblical text's erotic intensity and drama than many other, equally Song-laden medieval writings. The Colmar title provocatively suggests that Frauenlob has grafted a "golden wing"—a flight of aureate eloquence—onto the biblical love song.

MARY AND THE SONG OF SONGS TRADITION

If the twelfth century was the age of the great Latin Song commentaries, it was the thirteenth that saw a massive infusion of pomegranates and turtledoves into the vernacular. Yet Mary was a relative newcomer to this erotic landscape. Before 1100, the normative Bride in Song of Songs exegesis had been Ecclesia, the personified Church—a reading authorized by Ephesians 5, Apocalypse 21, and a long rabbinic tradition interpreting the impassioned lovers as God and Israel. *Anima*, the loving and believing soul, held an honorable second place.[5] In the wildly successful

(Munich: Ernst Reinhardt, 1963); Marina Warner, *Alone of All Her Sex: The Myth and the Cult of the Virgin Mary* (New York: Knopf, 1976); Klaus Schreiner, *Maria: Jungfrau, Mutter, Herrscherin* (Munich: Carl Hanser, 1994); Jaroslav Pelikan, *Mary Through the Centuries: Her Place in the History of Culture* (New Haven: Yale University Press, 1996). A useful study of Latin hymnody is Joseph Szövérffy, *Marianische Motivik der Hymnen: Ein Beitrag zur Geschichte der marianischen Lyrik im Mittelalter* (Leyden: Classical Folia Editions, 1985).

3. Stackmann, notes to *Marienleich,* GA 2:613, 656.

4. Kurt Gärtner, "Das Hohelied in Frauenlobs Marienleich," in Werner Schröder, ed., *Wolfram-Studien 10: Cambridger "Frauenlob"-Kolloquium 1986* (Berlin: Erich Schmidt, 1988), 105–16; register of quotations, 113–16.

5. On the history of exegesis, see Friedrich Ohly, *Hohelied-Studien: Grundzüge einer Geschichte der Hohelied-Auslegung des Abendlandes bis um ca. 1200* (Wiesbaden: F. Steiner, 1958); E. Ann Matter, *The Voice of My Beloved: The Songs of Songs in Western Medieval Christianity* (Philadelphia: University of Pennsylvania Press, 1990); Ann Astell, *The Song of Songs in the Middle Ages* (Ithaca: Cornell University Press, 1990); Denys Turner, *Eros and Allegory: Medieval Exegesis of the Song of Songs* (Kalamazoo, Mich.: Cistercian Publications, 1995); Rachel Fulton, *From Judgment to Passion: Devotion to Christ and the Virgin Mary, 800–1200* (New York: Columbia University Press, 2002), part 2.

Sermons on the Song of Songs preached by Bernard of Clairvaux, for all his fame as *doctor marianus,* the Virgin still plays a minor role. But as the century proceeded and the volume of commentaries swelled from a trickle to a flood, her position grew stronger. The first thoroughgoing Marian exegeses prove to have been Honorius of Regensburg's *Sigillum sanctae Mariae* (Seal of St. Mary), composed in England, and a much longer, highly influential commentary by Rupert of Deutz. These were followed by others: Alan of Lille, Philip of Harvengt, William of Newburgh, Alexander Nequam. Although none of these commentaries attained the same currency as Saint Bernard and his Cistercian continuators, they testify to a growing sense of the Virgin's centrality in the scheme of things. Characterized by their variety and originality, the Marian commentaries incorporate both strands of "classic" interpretation, for the Virgin is at once a type of the Church and a model for the loving soul; she is simultaneously daughter, mother, and bride; she can be found on all four levels of exegesis.[6] In a fine study of these commentaries, Rachel Fulton has shown that if they are deeply felt, they are also ingeniously wrought, integrating thought with feeling to probe "the mystery of a love so absolutely complete that there was nothing beyond it, nothing of body or spirit, humanity or divinity, creation or generation, in which it did not participate. It was a love that was itself the very perfection of empathy, beyond the experience of the meditant who might know Christ only through contemplation, beyond the experience of the communicant who might know Christ in body only through bread, beyond the experience of the flagellant who might know Christ only in pain. For . . . Mary had known—and still knew—Christ in all of these ways, with this difference: she alone knew what it had been to carry God in her womb."[7]

These comments apply also to Frauenlob: in his *leich,* Mary is the ultimate *vrouwe,* and her all-encompassing love affair with her Son is the ultimate *minne.* But how would he, as a layman, have been familiar with Song commentaries at all? Most studies assume a monastic readership for these texts, and we do not normally imagine traveling poets poring over volumes of Latin exegesis. Yet Frauenlob was no ordinary minstrel. As we have seen, he won an early and persistent reputation for learning; a late meistersinger tradition even took him for a doctor of theology.[8] A modern critic, Gerhard Schäfer, has gone so far as to represent Alan of Lille's *Elucidatio in Cantica canticorum* as an indispensable key for interpreting the *Marienleich.*[9] Though Schäfer overstates his case, the *Marienleich* shows at least one undeniable debt to this commentary, which was available in such German monasteries as Klosterneuburg and St. Marien, Trier.[10] Moreover, Frauenlob took an exceptional interest in Alan's writings. Alone among German

---

6. Matter, *Voice of My Beloved,* 168.

7. Fulton, *From Judgment to Passion,* 464.

8. Adam Puschmann, "Herr Frawenlob war ein Doctor . . . / Herr Mügeling geehret, / War ein Doctor gelehret, / Beide warens Theologi," in Bert Nagel, ed., *Meistersang: Meisterlieder und Singschulzeugnisse* (Stuttgart: Philipp Reclam, 1965), 129. See Stackmann, "Frauenlob," *Verfasserlexikon,* 875.

9. Gerhard Schäfer, *Untersuchungen zur deutschsprachigen Marienlyrik des 12. und 13. Jahrhunderts* (Göppingen: Alfred Kümmerle, 1971), 81–142. For Alan's commentary, see PL 210:51–110; partial translation in Turner, *Eros and Allegory,* 291–307.

10. Matter, *Voice of My Beloved,* 165; and see Commentary, below, strophe 4.

authors of his time, he knew both the *Anticlaudianus* and the *De planctu Naturae,* and probably also the "Rhythmus de incarnatione," so he might well have sought out the *Elucidatio.* But Rupert's earlier Marian commentary, *De incarnatione Domini* (ca. 1125), was even more accessible because his patron, Bishop Cuno of Regensburg, had circulated it throughout the monasteries of Germany and Austria, so that more than forty manuscripts survive.[11] Rupert's intensely personal voice, which appropriates Mary's union with her Beloved to discuss his own mystical experiences, makes an instructive contrast with Alan's cool didactic mode, and it is Rupert who comes closer to the fervent eroticism of the *Marienleich.* A look at these two commentaries, then, can suggest what Frauenlob might have gleaned from twelfth-century exegesis of the Song.

Rupert of Deutz reads its "historical" sense as an account of events in the lives of Jesus and Mary—that is, he takes the Song as a narrative of literal events constructed through allegorical readings. The first such event, the Incarnation, is poetically the "kiss of the mouth," for which the Bride yearns: "What is this exclamation so great, so unlooked for? O blessed Mary, the inundation of joy, the force of love, the torrent of delight, covered you entirely, possessed you totally, intoxicated you inwardly, and you sensed what eye has not seen and ear has not heard and what has not entered into the heart of man, and you said: 'Let him kiss me with the kiss of his mouth!'"[12] As the commentary proceeds, Rupert transparently identifies with Mary. Arriving at the most sexually explicit verse of the Song (5:4), he wonders how her beloved "put his hand through the hole" so that her "womb trembled at his touch," then answers his own question by recounting the contemporary erotic vision of "a certain girl" (*adulescentula*) who is a stand-in for the exegete himself, as medieval marginalia at this passage recognize.[13] Further, Rupert not only expects but encourages the reader to engage in a similar holy voyeurism. Citing a pornographic passage from Ezekiel 23:11–21, he recalls how the harlot Ooliba (an allegory of whorish Jerusalem) fell in love with the handsome Chaldean warriors after seeing them painted in a mural and decided to take them for her paramours. The reader of the Song should do likewise, admiring the Bridegroom's beauty portrayed in its sacred words until she too, like Mary, burns to "taste and see how sweet the Lord is" (Ps. 33:9).[14]

Unlike Rupert, Frauenlob never inserts his own voice in such an overtly personal way. The speaker of his first eight strophes is a more generic figure, a visionary modeled on Saint John the Divine, not the poet as an individual. In another sense, however, he identifies with Mary still more deeply than Rupert in that he speaks for her, placing a torrent of first-person discourse in her mouth—374 lines, to be exact, or nearly three-fourths of the poem. Even the authors of mystery plays rarely gave her that many lines, and lyric poets never did. For the Virgin of the Gospels is famously reticent; medieval writers were reluctant to break her silence with too many imputed words. But Rupert and the commentators in his lineage discovered that the best

11. Fulton, *From Judgment to Passion,* 314, 345.

12. Rupert of Deutz, *Commentaria in Canticum canticorum* 1:1, ed. Hraban Haacke, CCCM 26 (Turnhout: Brepols, 1974), 10; trans. Fulton, *From Judgment to Passion,* 324.

13. Rupert, *Commentaria* 5:2–8, pp. 110–11; Fulton, *From Judgment to Passion,* 334–37.

14. Rupert, *Commentaria* 5:10–16, p. 130.

way to hear Mary speak—"sonet vox tua in auribus meis, vox enim tua dulcis" (Cant. 2:14)—was to let her speak the words of the Canticle. Frauenlob's "golden wing" extends her speech not only into the vernacular but also far beyond any translation or paraphrase. Yet, especially in strophes 9–11 and 15, what Mary narrates is still her erotic experience, the Incarnation as a "kiss of the mouth":

mit sicherheit	Most certainly
ich slief bi drin,	I slept with Three—
des wart ich fruchtig, voller güte	till I grew pregnant with God's goodness,
süze in süze mir do sneit.	pierced by sweetness upon sweetness.
min alter vriedel kuste mich,	My ancient lover kissed me,
daz si geseit.	let this be said:
ich sach in an, do wart er junc.	I gazed at him and made him young.

(I.11.7–13)

Like Rupert too, the Mary of Frauenlob's *leich* invites her audience to identify with her experience, appealing at several points to the empathy of her "friends":

Vil lieben, tut mir ouch ein liep	Dear ones, do me too a kindness
und merket, wie der götliche minnen diep	and mark how the divine thief of love
sleich mitten in die sele min	stole into the midst of my soul
und trancte die mit suzekeit der süze sin.	and drenched it with sweetness from his own sweet.

(I.15.16–19)

Another element Frauenlob might have borrowed from Rupert, or the tradition he launched, was his portrayal of Mary as a visionary prophet. It was a commonplace that she had prophesied when she proclaimed her Magnificat, but Rupert goes further. The Virgin's conception not only fulfills Old Testament prophecies but also makes her into a prophetess—indeed, the greatest prophet of all. Filled with the Holy Spirit, she knows from the first moment of her pregnancy what is to come; as she nurses the infant Jesus she foresees the horror of his Passion, her mind's eye already fixed on the Cross.[15] Frauenlob does not concern himself with the Passion, having treated it separately in the *Kreuzleich*, but gives his pregnant Mary an apocalyptic vision instead:

mit dem sie was gebürdet,		The one whom she carried,
den sach sie vor ir sitzen	mit witzen	she saw sitting before her with her mind's eye

15. Rupert, *Commentaria* 1:11–13, pp. 31–32; Fulton, *From Judgment to Passion*, 328.

in siben liuchteren	amid seven lampstands—
und sach in	and yet again she saw him
doch besundert	in a separate form,
in eines lammes wise	in the guise of a Lamb
uf Sion, dem berge gehiuren.	on Zion, the lovely mountain.

(I.2.5–11)

This representation of Mary as seer immediately follows the speaker's vision of her on the celestial throne. The structure thus creates a parallel between the Lady and the author as fellow visionaries, not unlike the situation in Rupert's commentary. While this scarcely constitutes proof that Frauenlob had read Rupert's text, it places him within the same tradition of reading Mary's whole experience empathetically, *sub specie aeternitatis*. Hers is not a linear history but a "pattern of timeless moments" in which each event—angelic proclamation, pregnancy, nativity, and so forth—opens onto future and eternal glory and remains accessible to the believer's participation.[16]

This principle of fluid or circular chronology is explained by Alan of Lille in his late twelfth-century commentary: "it is the custom of prophets that just when they are speaking about present and future things, they suddenly revert to past things, even as the Holy Spirit was touching their hearts."[17] Since Mary as a prophetess uttered her Song in this fashion, the exegete has license to leap back and forth in time from the Assumption to the Annunciation to the Passion, as he weaves a coherent narrative from the elliptical scenes of the biblical text. Frauenlob does not follow the Song from beginning to end, but he does imitate its disjunctive temporality, hovering insistently around the decisive moment of the Incarnation, yet circling back to Mary's presence at the creation (as Eternal Wisdom) and forward to her crowning as Queen of Heaven. This initially disconcerting aspect of the *leich* is best explained as a deliberate imitation of the Song, as it was understood by its twelfth-century interpreters. Frauenlob's public called his poem *Cantica canticorum* for more reasons than one.

In contrast with Rupert, Alan interprets Mary's "kiss of the mouth" as less a personal rapture than a multifaceted symbol. The Bride longs for three kisses from the mouth of God: the Incarnation, which unites the human nature with the divine; the Holy Spirit, who is the mutual "kiss" of Father and Son; and the teaching of Christ, which proceeds like a kiss from his holy lips. In return, Christ longs for his mother's breasts, calling them "sweeter than wine"—literally, for they nurse him with the pure milk of virginity, and spiritually, for they signify her virtues of chastity and humility.[18] It would be possible to read some such meaning into *Marienleich* I.11.17–18:

16. Compare Diehl, *Medieval European Religious Lyric*, 180: "It is the seeing not the seen that belongs to time; Mary's multiple roles are a single eternal fact, always ready for the human eyes that will open to behold her."

17. Alan of Lille, *Elucidatio in Cantica canticorum*, chap. 5, PL 210:85a; trans. Astell, *Song of Songs*, 65.

18. Alan, *Elucidatio*, chap. 1, PL 210:53–54; trans. Turner, *Eros and Allegory*, 295–97.

er jach, min brüstel weren süzer dann der win,
da barg er sich mit fugen in.

[He said my breasts were sweeter than wine—
then meetly sheltered himself within.]

But the availability of such a reading does not prove its necessity. This is where program-
matic interpretations like Schäfer's go astray. The commentary tradition, after all, aimed to
exploit the sensuous language of the Song while neutralizing and "spiritualizing" it more or
less thoroughly (more in Alan's case, less in Rupert's). Yet Frauenlob was composing a song, not
a commentary, and had no wish to neutralize anything. On the one hand, his *Marienleich* would
have been unthinkable *without* the commentary tradition. Its grounding in this realm is indi-
cated on the semantic level by such tags as *nu merket* (nota bene, I.2.1) and *daz prüfe ich an den
worten* ("I prove it by these words," I.5.3). More important, readers and listeners must know on
a deep level that the Beloved's kiss "is" the Word made flesh. By the same token, they must be
aware that the passionate Bride is a perpetual virgin; that her breasts *may* symbolize chastity,
humility, wisdom, or compassion; and much more that could be learned from the exegetes. On
the other hand, these meanings constitute the soil in which the poem is rooted, not the poem
itself. If its roots are exegetical, its blossoms are lyrical—all its gorgeous, many-petaled *blumen*
with their intoxicating perfumes—and a fine perfume is never explicit. In short, to ignore the
exegetical tradition would risk seriously misunderstanding the poem, but to reduce the poetry
to exegesis would kill it outright.[19]

LITURGY AND LITURGICAL CHANT

Most of Frauenlob's hearers had never read a biblical commentary, but everyone would have
attended the liturgy, which provides the framework for his allusions. Gärtner's register of cita-
tions confirms what should be intuitively obvious: the Song of Songs is used in its entirety, but
other allusions cluster around those texts that had already been taken up in the Divine Office for
the Virgin's feasts. Among these are Genesis 2 (the creation of Eve); Psalm 44 (the royal epithal-
amium); Proverbs 8, Ecclesiasticus 24, and Wisdom of Solomon 7–8 (praises of divine Wis-
dom); Isaiah 11 (gifts of the Holy Spirit); Luke 1 (the Annunciation); and Apocalypse 12 and 21
(the woman clothed with the sun and the New Jerusalem).[20] But Frauenlob's immersion in the
Marian liturgy raises further questions, since the most extensive performance of these texts,

19. Cf. Timothy R. Jackson, "Erotische Metaphorik und
geistliche Dichtung: Bemerkungen zu Frauenlobs 'Marienleich,'"
in Schröder, ed., *Wolfram-Studien* 10:80–86; idem, "Erotic
Imagery in Medieval Spiritual Poetry and the Hermeneutics of

Metaphor," in Bernhard Debatin, Timothy R. Jackson, and Daniel
Steuer, eds., *Metaphor and Rational Discourse* (Tübingen: Niemeyer,
1997), 113–24; Kobele, *Frauenlobs Lieder*, 229–40.
20. Gärtner, "Das Hohelied," 114–16.

along with the antiphons and responsories based on them, took place in the Divine Office per-formed by priests and monastics, rather than in the masses heard by laypeople. So far as we know, Frauenlob never belonged to any religious community. But he did spend portions of his life in the ambit of great cathedrals, during his education at the school of Meissen and again dur-ing his late years in Mainz, under the archbishop's patronage. Gieselbrecht, archbishop of Bre-men (reg. 1274–1306), was another of his patrons, though we do not know exactly when or for how long.

More to the point, perhaps, Frauenlob's early years in Prague would have exposed him to a court life saturated with Marian piety. The chronicle of Peter von Zittau, a contemporary of the poet, provides some fascinating details on the reign of Wenceslas II. Ambitious to enhance the scope of learning and culture in Bohemia, Wenceslas spent two hundred marks in silver to pur-chase books from Paris in 1293, and two years later he made an abortive attempt to found a uni-versity and *studium generale* in Prague (another half-century would pass before the actual univer-sity was created in 1348). The king's devotion, according to Peter, was so great that

> he received this unique privilege of love as a free gift from the Virgin's Son: namely, he arranged that the Mass of the Blessed Virgin and especially the *Rorate caeli desuper* ["Drop dew, ye heavens, from above"], that is, the Office of the Annunciation, might be performed in his presence not only on Saturdays but every day—if not solemnly chanted, then at least read for him privately—because in this mystery of the divine Incarnation, Mary's name and praises are frequently uttered. He was accustomed to attend this Office with great devotion, and whenever the venerable name of Mary was pronounced, he used to hear it joyfully, with his eyes and hands raised toward heaven and the ears of his devout heart wide open. For he said that any Mass in which the sweet name of Mary, impressed upon his mind, did not sound in his ears, would have less savor to his soul.[21]

Amazingly, Peter says the king once admitted that for Mary's sake, he could even forget Christ—a theological faux pas that the chronicler excuses as stemming from a "spirit of fervor, not error." At any rate, if Frauenlob spent his formative years as a singer at King Wenceslas's court, he would have had ample occasion to experience the full panoply of Marian worship. Christoph März, following Bertau, even speculates that the *Marienleich* could have been com-posed as a "deluxe private office" for the royal chapel.[22]

Whether or not the liturgical matrix of the *leich* extended to its performance, it explains a great deal of its theology. Frauenlob did not have to decide, individually and idiosyncratically, that the mother of Jesus, the woman clothed with the sun, the Bride of the Canticle, and the

21. Peter von Zittau, *Chronicon Aulae Regiae*, chap. 58, *Fontes rerum bohemicarum* 4 (Prague, 1884), 69; cited in März, *Frauenlobs Marienleich*, 53–56.

22. März, *Frauenlobs Marienleich*, 59.

all-creating Wisdom of God should be the same person, because the church through its liturgists had already made that decision. The development of a sapiential liturgy for Marian feasts had been a slow, gradual process, beginning as early as the seventh century, but it was complete by 1200 and firmly established by 1250.[23] The Song commentators, in fact, were not so much innovating as articulating and rationalizing a theology that was already implicit in the liturgy itself.[24] In the braided biblical texts that Frauenlob inherited from the Divine Office, the youthful mother of Luke's Gospel was already the eternal partner of God from Proverbs 8, and the invitation of divine Wisdom in Ecclesiasticus 24 had already fused with the apocalyptic summons of the Spirit and the Bride:

> Transite ad me, omnes qui concupiscitis me,
> Et a generationibus meis implemini.
>> (Ecclus. 24:26)

> [Come to me, all you who desire me,
> And take your fill of my produce.]

> komt alle zu mir, die min gern.
> ich wil, ich kan, ich muz gewern.
>> (I.12.9–10)

> [Come to me, all you who desire me!
> I will, I can, I must content you.]

> Et spiritus et sponsa dicunt: Veni.
> Et qui audit, dicat: Veni.
> Et qui sitit, veniat:
> et qui vult, accipiat aquam vitae, gratis.
>> (Apoc. 22:17)

> [The Spirit and the Bride say: Come.
> And let whoever hears say: Come.
> And let whoever thirsts, come:
> and whoever will, take the water of life without price.]

23. Paula Seethaler, "Die Weisheitstexte in der Marienliturgie," Benediktinische Monatschrift 34 (1958), 111–20; Étienne Catta, "Sedes Sapientiae," in Hubert du Manoir, ed., Maria: Études sur la sainte Vierge, 8 vols. (Paris: Beauchesne, 1949–71), 6:689–866; Rachel Fulton, "'Quae est ista quae ascendit sicut aurora consurgens?' The Song of Songs as the Historia for the Office of the Assumption," Mediaeval Studies 60 (1998), 55–122; Newman, God and the Goddesses, 194–206.

24. Fulton, From Judgment to Passion, 244–88 (on Honorius Augustodunensis); eadem, "Mimetic Devotion, Marian Exegesis, and the Historical Sense of the Song of Songs," Viator 27 (1996): 85–116.

Yet another liturgical (or paraliturgical) source for Frauenlob's learning would have been the so-called Marian Psalters, a genre of devotional texts closely linked with the origins of the rosary. Beginning in the twelfth century, the Marian Psalter emerged as a lay surrogate for the Divine Office chanted by monks and nuns—a simplified spiritual exercise deemed suitable for lay brothers and other devout men and women. It consisted of fifty or 150 Ave Marias (based on the number of psalms), interspersed with short rhyming verses that adapted or substituted for the traditional monastic antiphons. By Frauenlob's time such texts were available in both German and Latin. Each verse normally began with a salutation to the Virgin ("Ave Maria," "Ave rosa," "Ich grûze dich," "Wis gegrüezet") followed by standard epithets of praise. Poetically simpler than the Latin Office hymns, Marian Psalters had a litany-like character that influenced the vernacular *Marienlob* discussed below.[25]

In addition to biblical lessons, psalm antiphons, and litanies, the liturgy included some more poetically ambitious texts, especially the votive Marian antiphons and the sequences chanted between the Alleluia and the Gospel at mass. Diehl has shrewdly characterized the *Marienleich* as "a fitting climax to a specifically German sequence tradition beginning with certain poems by Notker in the ninth century, continuing through Hermannus Contractus (eleventh century) and Hildegard of Bingen (twelfth century)."[26] In the case of Notker and Hermann, Frauenlob's debt is a formal one, for Notker was a pioneer and Hermann a master of the classical sequence, a form that provided a key structural model for the German *leich*. Hermann the Lame, a learned abbot of Reichenau (d. 1054), is sometimes credited with the famous antiphon "Alma Redemptoris Mater," but one sequence he certainly composed is "Ave praeclara maris stella," a piece Frauenlob knew.[27] This text provides a fine illustration of the classical sequence form. Its versicles are arranged in the pattern X AA BB CC DD EE Y, with the first and last sections unique and the intervening versicles metrically and melodically paired. Rhyme is a frequent but not a mandatory ornament; more important is the exact syllabic match between corresponding lines of text and music. Here are two paired versicles from "Ave praeclara":[28]

Te, plenam fide,	The fathers of old
virgam almae stirpis Iesse,	and prophets longed for you,
nascituram	faithful branch,
priores	to come forth at last
desideraverant	from the generous
patres et prophetae.	stock of Jesse.

25. Anne Winston-Allen, *Stories of the Rose: The Making of the Rosary in the Middle Ages* (University Park: The Pennsylvania State University Press, 1997), 15–22, 148–49; Peter Appelhans, *Untersuchungen zur spätmittelalterlichen Mariendichtung: Die rhythmischen mittelhochdeutschen Mariengrüsse* (Heidelberg: Carl Winter, 1970), 35–40.

26. Diehl, *Medieval European Religious Lyric*, 97.

27. Burghart Wachinger, "Frauenlobs Cantica canticorum," in Walter Haug and Burghart Wachinger, eds., *Literatur, Artes und Philosophie* (Tübingen: Niemeyer, 1992), 23–43, at 24.

28. Hermannus Contractus, "Ave praeclara maris stella" (sequence for the Assumption), in Clemens Blume and Guido Dreves, eds., *Analecta Hymnica Medii Aevi*, 55 vols. (New York: Johnson Reprint Corp., 1961), 50:313–15.

<table>
<tr><td>

Te, lignum vitae,
sancto rorante pneumate
parituram
divini
floris amygdalum
signavit Gabriel.

</td><td>

Gabriel revealed
that from you, tree of life,
moist with the
Holy Spirit's dew,
God's divine almond
blossom would bloom.

</td></tr>
</table>

This delicate form had some influence on vernacular poetry before Frauenlob: two twelfth-century German sequences are extant, both loosely based on "Ave praeclara."[29] But of all the thirteenth- and fourteenth-century *leichs*, Frauenlob's *Marienleich* is the one most clearly modeled on the classical sequence and, as we shall see in Chapter 4, the most regular and exacting in its observance of strophic response.

Hildegard, a liturgical composer quite different from Hermann, would scarcely have impressed Frauenlob with her virtuosity, for she wrote sequences in an archaic style with neither rhyme nor meter. Yet there is a remarkable affinity between her religious temperament and Frauenlob's. Both express what Christoph Huber has aptly termed a "Platonic creation-Mariology"[30] Creation and Incarnation appear as parallel acts in the same drama, linked by the divine Feminine through the composite figure of Sapientia/Maria. Hildegard's *feminea forma* is an abstract, cosmic principle of fertility much like Frauenlob's joy-bestowing *vrouwe*, and what she calls *viriditas* ("greening power," *élan vital*) is a divine life-force akin to Caritas and the Holy Spirit—in effect, the same power that Frauenlob calls sometimes Minne and sometimes Natura.[31] One of Hildegard's Marian sequences praises the Virgin by praising Adam as the source of Eve—an essentializing of Woman that Frauenlob would repeat in almost identical terms in one of his *Sprüche*:

<table>
<tr><td>

O quam magnum est
in viribus suis latus viri,
de quo Deus formam mulieris produxit,

quam fecit speculum
omnis ornamenti sui
et amplexionem
omnis creature sue.[32]

</td><td>

O how great
in its strength is the side of man,
from which God produced the form of
    woman.
He made her the mirror
of all his beauty
and the embrace
of his whole creation.

</td></tr>
</table>

29. Sayce, *Medieval German Lyric*, 370–71.

30. Huber, "*Gepartiret und geschrenket*," 47.

31. Finckh, *Minor Mundus Homo*, 421. See also Newman, *Sister of Wisdom*, and Constant Mews, "Religious Thinker: 'A Frail Human Being' on Fiery Life," in Barbara Newman, ed., *Voice of*

the *Living Light: Hildegard of Bingen and Her World* (Berkeley and Los Angeles: University of California Press, 1998), 52–69.

32. Hildegard of Bingen, "O virga ac diadema" 4a, *Symphonia armonie celestium revelationum* 20, ed. and trans. Barbara Newman, 2nd ed. (Ithaca: Cornell University Press, 1998), 130.

Lop si dir, Adam, durch din bein,   Praise to you, Adam, for your bone
von dem erschein   from which the form of woman
uns wibes bilde! lop la dir sin rein,   appeared to us! Let your praise be pure—
lop immer lop, lob hoher sedel!   praise, ever praise, O throne on high!

(VIII.18.8–11)

Both poets strongly assert the Virgin's eternal presence before the face of God:

Tu candidum lilium   You are the shining lily
quod Deus ante omnem creaturam   on which God gazed
inspexit.[33]   before all creation.

O virga, floriditatem tuam   O branch, God foresaw
Deus in prima die   your blossoming
creature sue previderat.[34]   on the first day of his creation.

ich binz ein spiegel der vil klaren reinekeit,
da got von erst sich inne ersach.
ich was mit im, do er entwarf gar alle schepfenunge,
er sach mich stetes an in siner ewiclichen ger.

(I.12.3–6)

[I am the mirror of great purity
in which God saw himself from the beginning.
I was with him when he formed the whole creation,
he gazed at me always with desire unceasing.]

Like the *Marienleich,* Hildegard's lyrics present the Virgin not only as the mother of Christ and of all Christians but also as birth-giver of a redeemed and recreated nature. For the abbess, Eve is the *prima materia* of creation, and Mary is the *aurea* or *lucida materia* of the renewed creation:

. . . es tu illa lucida materia   you are that luminous matter
per quam hoc ipsum Verbum exspiravit   through which the Word breathed forth
omnes virtutes,   all virtues,
ut eduxit in prima materia   as in the primal matter
omnes creaturas.[35]   he brought forth all creatures.

33. Hildegard, "Ave generosa," stanza 3, *Symphonia* 17, p. 122.
34. Hildegard, "O virga ac diadema" 3a, *Symphonia* 20, p. 128.

35. Hildegard, "O splendidissima gemma," lines 12–16, *Symphonia* 10, p. 114. Mary is called *aurea materia* ("golden matter") in "O virga ac diadema" 3b.

The Maria/Sapientia of Frauenlob's *leich* makes a similar assertion, presenting herself as both the *materia* and the creative agent:

Zwar ich binz aller tugent nature	I am every virtue's nature
und der materjen nachgebure.	and primal matter's neighbor.
swaz ich in dem sinne mure,	Whatever I design in will,
speher bilde ich vil behure.	I decorate with joyful skill.

(I.17.16–19)

Such parallels could be extended. In Hildegard's "O viridissima virga," for instance, Mary is both a verdant, blossoming tree and a lush, richly watered field that brings forth wheat for the eucharistic bread. The same imagery occurs in *Marienleich* 12b. Obviously, these were not the only poets to adopt this theme from the virtually unlimited repertoire of Marian symbols.[36] But as a matter of emphasis, they stand out from the rest for their blend of sapiential Mariology with an extraordinary vitalism. Their lyrics are also difficult in comparable ways, for both draw on the full range of motifs offered by the exegetical tradition, without troubling to erect the allegorical scaffolding that most poets assembled for the reader's convenience. Instead, they let one image bleed into the next, conflating multiple symbolic registers to produce an allusive, elliptical, and frequently esoteric text rather than an easily legible one. In a study of Hildegard's poetry, I once contrasted the dense and often bewildering texture of her lyrics with the more transparent sequences of her contemporary, Adam of Saint-Victor: they treat parallel themes in radically different styles.[37] As we shall see, a similar contrast can be drawn between Frauenlob and his admired precursor, Konrad von Würzburg.

Given these affinities, I cannot resist asking whether Frauenlob could have known of Hildegard's work, especially since he spent his last years in Mainz, the diocesan center of her cult. It would be most satisfying to locate at least one concrete woman in intellectual proximity to this champion of Woman in the abstract. But how well was Hildegard remembered in Mainz at the turn of the fourteenth century? Abbot Trithemius of Sponheim writes that Clement V, the first Avignon pope (1305–16), reopened her abortive canonization process, which had been stalled since 1233.[38] Since his papacy coincided with Frauenlob's sojourn in Mainz, the cathedral's

36. See Anselm Salzer, *Die Sinnbilder und Beiworte Mariens in der deutschen Literatur und lateinischen Hymnenpoesie des Mittelalters* (1897; repr. Darmstadt: Wissenschaftliche Buchgesellschaft, 1967).

37. Introduction to Hildegard, *Symphonia*, 33–34. On Hildegard's poetic style, see also Peter Dronke, "Hildegard of Bingen as Poetess and Dramatist," in *Poetic Individuality in the Middle Ages: New Departures in Poetry, 1000–1150* (Oxford: Clarendon, 1970), 150–79; Barbara Newman, "Poet: 'Where the Living Majesty Utters Mysteries,'" in *Voice of the Living Light,* 176–92.

38. Trithemius of Sponheim, *Annales Hirsaugiensis* 2 (St. Gallen, 1690), 142; cited in Helmut Hinkel, "St. Hildegards Verehrung im Bistum Mainz," in Anton Brück, ed., *Hildegard von Bingen, 1179–1979: Festschrift zum 800. Todestag der Heiligen* (Mainz: Gesellschaft für Mittelrheinische Kirchengeschichte, 1979), 385–411, at 387. See also Stephanus Hilpisch, "Der Kult der hl. Hildegard," *Pastor bonus* 45 (1934): 118–33; Ludwig Berg, "Die Mainzer Kirche und die heilige Hildegard," *Archiv für mittelrheinische Kirchengeschichte* 27 (1975): 49–70; Josef Krasenbrink, "Die 'inoffizielle' Heilige: Zur Verehrung Hildegards diesseits und jenseits des Rheins," in Edeltraud Forster, ed., *Hildegard von Bingen, Prophetin durch die Zeiten: Zum 900. Geburtstag* (Freiburg: Herder, 1997), 496–513.

artist-in-residence could scarcely have failed to hear about the matter. Unfortunately, though, no contemporary source confirms Trithemius's fifteenth-century report, and he is not always the most reliable of witnesses. More solid evidence is provided by a papal letter to the Rupertsberg nuns in 1324, granting forty days' indulgence to pilgrims visiting their chapel on certain feast days, including Hildegard's. The brief was confirmed by the current archbishop of Mainz.[39] Although these events took place a few years after Frauenlob's death, the nuns' request presupposes a pilgrimage of many years' standing. The evidence of thirteenth-century relic distribution, artworks depicting Hildegard with nimbus, and at least six chronicles referring to her as *sancta* confirm that her cult was fairly well known, so it is in fact likely that Frauenlob learned of her during his stay in Mainz, if not earlier. But even in the Rhineland, Hildegard was more revered than read. The manuscript transmission of her works ends abruptly in the early thirteenth century, and no manuscript extant today can be traced to Mainz during Frauenlob's lifetime.[40] So in all probability, we must reckon with kindred spirits using common sources rather than direct literary influence.

TWELFTH-CENTURY PLATONISTS AND THE LIBERAL ARTS TRADITION

As with many vernacular writers, we find a certain time lag between the poet and his most important Latin sources. His main vernacular influences were near-contemporary works, dating not before 1250, while the Latin authors who most inspired him belonged to the twelfth century. One reason for the time lag is that most of them were French—Peter Abelard, William of Conches, Bernard Silvestris, Alan of Lille—and the diffusion of their works into German lands was not immediate.[41] It is interesting that most of these figures were, like Hildegard, poet-theologians. It stands to reason that an intellectual poet like Frauenlob should have been attracted to Latin writers with similar aims, writers who aspired to convey complex philosophical thought through the medium of elegant verse. But in Latin that was a twelfth-century ideal; after 1200 one finds few philosophical poems on the scale of Bernard's *Cosmographia* or Alan's *Anticlaudianus*. In fact, twelfth-century humanists were already lamenting "the decline of the humanities," observing the relentless march of logic and narrow specialist learning at the expense of rhetoric and poetry.[42] (It is telling that Robert Grosseteste, an English poet-theologian of the thirteenth century, used Latin for his theological and scientific writings but Anglo-Norman for

39. Hinkel, "St. Hildegards Verehrung," 389.

40. Albert Derolez, "The Manuscript Transmission of Hildegard of Bingen's Writings: The State of the Problem," in Charles Burnett and Peter Dronke, eds., *Hildegard of Bingen: The Context of Her Thought and Art* (London: Warburg Institute, 1998), 17–27. Considering that the archbishop of Mainz had excommunicated Hildegard and placed her nuns under interdict during the last year of her life, it is hardly surprising that the city was not a center for the dissemination of her works.

41. It has been argued that the Flemish-born Alan of Lille spent much of his career not in Paris but in England. A recent study by Françoise Hudry revives the old hypothesis that the famous *magister* was identical with the monk Alan of Canterbury, later abbot of Tewkesbury. Alain de Lille (?), *Lettres Familières (1167–1170)*, ed. Françoise Hudry (Paris: J. Vrin, 2003). For Alan's German reception, see Huber, *Aufnahme und Verarbeitung*.

42. C. Stephen Jaeger, "Pessimism in the Twelfth-Century 'Renaissance,'" *Speculum* 78 (2003): 1151–83; Willemien Otten, *From Paradise to Paradigm: A Study of Twelfth-Century Humanism* (Leiden: Brill, 2004).

his verse.) In addition to the aureate style of a writer like Alan of Lille, Frauenlob admired twelfth-century Christian Platonism, as we saw apropos of his *Minneleich* and *Minne und Welt*. The second half of the *Marienleich* is awash in Platonizing cosmology. Conflating several goddess-figures—Alan's Natura, the biblical Sapientia, and Minne or Caritas—in the person of Mary, Frauenlob lets her speak as Lady of the universe and *anima mundi*:

werden und unwerden brechen	Becoming and unbecoming
mit geburt, ob ich sol sprechen,	start with birth, so I may say,
daz ich der bin ein beginne.	for I am their beginning—
swie des geistes worchtlich minne	as the active love of the Spirit
mit der liebe und mit der lüste	ebbs and flows with desire
enget, witet ane unküste:	and pleasure, without falsehood.[43]
ich binz aller formen forme,	I am the Form of all forms,
abgenomen nach des innern sinnes	drawn from the inner meaning's norm
norme,	
die durchblümet was und ist und immer	which was and is and ever must be
muz ane ende sin.	blooming without end.
(I.17.7–15)	

In this context, the "active love of the Spirit" that "ebbs and flows with desire and pleasure" is not "supernatural grace" but the life-force of nature, the process of generation and corruption (*werden und unwerden*) through which the world is ceaselessly renewed. Plato had called this force the world soul, or *anima mundi,* and in their enthusiastic reception of his *Timaeus,* William of Conches and Peter Abelard identified it as one aspect of the Holy Spirit. According to William's Boethius commentary, "the world soul is a natural energy (*vigor*) by which certain things possess movement alone, others growth, others sensation, others discernment. But it is asked what this natural energy is. It seems to me that this natural energy is the Holy Spirit— that is, a divine and gracious harmony—because by divine love and concord all things possess being, movement, life, growth, sensation, and discernment. It is aptly called a natural energy, because by divine love (*amore*) all things grow and thrive. It is aptly called the world soul, because, by divine love and charity alone, all living things in the world possess life."[44] Similarly, Abelard wrote in his *Theologia christiana* that Plato "rightly posited the Holy Spirit (the world soul) as the life of the universe, because in the goodness of God all things have a kind of life. . . . The apostle's teaching seems not unsuitably to agree with what some ancient philosophers are reported to have said, namely, that in God 'we live, move, and have our being,' as if by the world soul they understood God himself" (Acts 17:28).[45]

43. See Commentary, strophe 17, on the ambiguous punctuation of this passage.

44. William of Conches, *Glosae super Boetium,* III m. 9, ed. Lodi Nauta, CCCM 158 (Turnhout: Brepols, 1999), 169–70.

45. Peter Abelard, *Theologia christiana* 1.72, in *Opera theologica,* ed. Eligius Buytaert, CCCM 12 (Turnhout: Brepols, 1969), 101–2; same text in *Theologia "scholarium"* 1.128, CCCM 13:370.

Frauenlob knew Abelard's *Theologia* in one of its versions, as we saw in our analysis of the *Kreuzleich,* so that text could have been his source for the idea of the world soul—although he might just as easily have learned it from William of Conches's Boethius commentary, which remained in use as a textbook throughout the thirteenth century. Other sources for the *anima mundi* doctrine would have included William's *Philosophia mundi* and *Timaeus* commentary, as well as works by Thierry of Chartres, Arnold of Bonneval, Robert of Melun, and John of Salisbury. Despite a fierce critique of the *anima mundi* by William of St.-Thierry and Bernard of Clairvaux, who found the idea dangerously pantheistic and procured Abelard's condemnation for heresy in 1141, it nonetheless remained in circulation.[46] Even though Abelard was remembered in the later Middle Ages as a notorious heretic, thanks to the Cistercian propaganda machine, his thought continued to exercise an influence, partly through the teaching of his students, partly through Peter Lombard's *Sentences.* But neither Abelard nor William of Conches can be held to account for the Mariological spin Frauenlob gives the world soul, extending even to the Lady's self-designation as *forma formarum* ("aller formen forme"). In Aristotelian theology this is a term for God. As Burghart Wachinger remarks, "Frauenlob seems to mean that the Holy Spirit as world soul acts through Mary throughout the cosmic process of becoming and passing away. But this would be precisely the conception condemned as heretical by the Council of Sens [in 1141], only exacerbated through the insertion of Mary. Was Frauenlob aware that he was moving on the margin of heresy?"[47] Probably not; he betrays no self-conception as other than orthodox, and many of his *Sprüche* express deep respect for the priesthood. As I have argued elsewhere, a vernacular poet would scarcely have risked prosecution for heresy in any case.[48] But that is just as well for Frauenlob, since this is one of several points at which his Mariology skirts the far edges of the permissible.

In the *Minneleich,* as we saw, Alan of Lille's goddess Natura is upheld as a type of the ideal *Vrouwe* before being folded into the composite Lady of the *Marienleich.* Another facet of Alan's influence comes to the fore in strophes 16–18, where Frauenlob represents the Virgin by means of the seven liberal arts. In this case, he does not so much follow Alan of Lille as offer a deliberately revisionist account of his material. Alan had composed his *Anticlaudianus* as a textbook of the arts to replace Martianus Capella's beloved but hopelessly dated *Marriage of Philology and Mercury.* Like the late antique work, the *Anticlaudianus* frames its encyclopedic instruction in an allegorical narrative, which concerns the collective efforts of Natura, Prudentia, the arts, and the virtues to produce a *novus homo,* or Perfect Man. But since only God can create a soul, Prudentia and her entourage must journey to his celestial throne to ask this favor of him. When they arrive, Prudentia, accompanied by Theology and Faith, marvels at the sight of Mary, whose divine motherhood confounds all reason:

---

46. Steinmetz, *Liebe als universales Prinzip,* 49–50. On the revised dating of Abelard's condemnation, see Constant J. Mews, "The Council of Sens (1141): Abelard, Bernard, and the Fear of Social Upheaval," *Speculum* 77 (2002): 342–82.

47. Wachinger, "Frauenlobs Cantica canticorum," 40.
48. Newman, *God and the Goddesses,* 305–9.

Ista tamen racio nutat, cum uirgine matrem
Inuenit et logices uidet argumenta iacere.
Amplius admirans, magis hesitat, amplius herens,
Inquirit quo iure poli, qua lege beata
Nata patrem, terrena Deum, casura manentem,
Flos cedrum, sidus solem, scintilla caminum
Proferat, et mellis desudet petra liquorem.

[Reason herself staggers when she finds a virgin
a mother, and sees the arguments of logic overthrown.
Marvelling further, she hesitates, comes to a standstill,
asks by what heavenly rule, what blessed law
a daughter brings forth the Father, perishable earth
gives birth to abiding God, a flower bears a cedar, a star the sun,
a spark the furnace, and honey exudes from a rock.]

Theology advises her that Reason can never solve this problem because it lies beyond the domain of Nature:

. . . Ubi nulla potestas
Illius, sed cuncta silent decreta, pauescunt
Leges, iura stupent, ubi regnat sola uoluntas
Artificis summi.[49]

[Here Nature has no power,
but all her decrees are silent, her laws take fright,
her rules are stunned, where the supreme
Architect's will alone prevails.]

Alan's epic maintains that Natura, impressive though she is, has clear limits: the Incarnation is a strictly miraculous event that neither she nor her protégés, the liberal arts, can comprehend. He elaborates on this theme in a famous lyric, the "Rhythmus de Incarnatione Christi." Taking each art in turn, Alan shows how the paradox of the Incarnation confounded its axioms, thus demonstrating the inadequacy of all human knowledge in the face of divine mystery. For example, the stanza on Geometry declares:

---

49. Alain de Lille, *Anticlaudianus* 6.155–61, 174–77, ed.
Bossuat, 145–46. Cf. 5.478–79: "Hic natura silet, logice uis
exulat, omnis / Rethorice perit arbitrium racioque uacillat."

Sue artis in censura	The geometer is deceived
Geometra fallitur,	in the judgment of his art
Dum immensus sub mensura	when the Immeasurable One appears
Terrenorum sistitur,	beneath an earthly measure;
In directum curvatura	the curvature of the circle
Circuli convertitur,	is transformed into a straight line;
Speram claudit quadratura	the square contains the sphere
Et sub ipsa clauditur.	and yet is contained within it.
In hac Verbi copula	In this coupling of the Word
Stupet omnis regula.[50]	every rule is stupefied.

Alan's supernaturalism broke with the older twelfth-century traditions of Thierry of Chartres and William of Conches, for whom the arts curriculum led the student by stages "through knowledge of creation to knowledge of the Creator." Thierry, himself the author of an *artes* textbook, served as chancellor to the bishop of Chartres in the 1140s—the same decade that the celebrated arts portal in the west façade of Chartres Cathedral was carved, perhaps under his patronage.[51] In the south tympanum, seven allegorical women representing the liberal arts appear as handmaids to Mary, Throne of Wisdom. Frauenlob, an heir to this "Chartrain" humanism, not only rejected Alan's supernaturalist stance but also devoted three strophes of his *leich* to rebuttal of it, defending the Virgin's patronage of the *artes*. Since Mary in his *leich* subsumes Nature, Nature cannot be silenced by her.[52] Since she is also Wisdom, she does not stupefy but justifies human learning, being herself the embodiment of all knowledge. Thus the Incarnation, for all its paradoxes, represents less the downfall than the culmination of grammar, rhetoric, and so forth. Grammar, for instance, is vindicated when the eternal Verb (*verbum* or *wort*) becomes a Noun (*nomen* or *name*) in Mary's womb; the relationship between eternal and temporal, divine and human, can be qualified as a relationship between parts of speech. Of Geometry the Lady says, echoing Ephesians 3:18 and Wisdom 11:21:

> wite, lenge, tiufe, höhe
>
> winkelmezic miner lust sich nicht entflöhe!
>
> zal der dinge mit den sachen ligen in der gehügde min. (I.17.28–30)

50. Marie-Thérèse d'Alverny, "Alain de Lille et la 'Theologia,'" in *L'Homme devant Dieu: Mélanges offerts au Père Henri de Lubac*, 3 vols. (Paris: Aubier, 1964), 2:111–28.

51. Michael Stolz, "Maria und die Artes liberales: Aspekte einer mittelalterlichen Zuordnung," in Claudia Opitz, Hedwig Röckelein, Gabriela Signori, and Guy Marchal, eds., *Maria in der Welt: Marienverehrung im Kontext der Sozialgeschichte 10.–18. Jahrhundert* (Zurich: Chronos, 1993), 95–120, at 98.

52. "Mary is Minne in the dual sense of Natura and the biblical Sapientia, she who at the same time fulfills and surpasses nature. She is the one 'through whom all women are honored'; through her, divine love is mirrored in every relationship of love. . . . But precisely because she presides over the laws and powers of nature, it is also through her that nature can be transcended." Rudolf Krayer, *Frauenlob und die Natur-Allegorese* (Heidelberg: Carl Winter, 1960), 178.

[I need no compass to delight
in breadth and length and depth and height.
In my mind all causes lie, and all things' reckoning.]

Among the liberal arts was logic or dialectic, which in the eyes of Alan of Lille (and hymnodists generally) was undone by the paradoxes of a virgin mother and a God-man. Frauenlob, however, sets out to prove what might be called the rationality of the Incarnation by showing how it can be analyzed in terms of Aristotle's ten *praedicamenta* (categories) and five *praedicabilia* (universals). Strophe 16, a *tour de force* of philosophical translation, not only relates each of these concepts to Mary but also coins a whole new vernacular lexicon for them. Applying the five universals or predicables—genus, species, specific difference, individual property, and accident—he has the Virgin Mother declare:

sin art, die mac man von mir sagen
und min gestalt in sinen jagen.

welch underscheit mac daz geclagen?

die menscheit unser eigen immer muz
    betagen,

kein zuschicht noch kein abeschicht er
    mac getragen,

ern si ein got den ich gebar.

His genus can be predicated of me
and my species sought in his.

What distinction can prove this wrong?

Humanity must always remain our own;

He can suffer neither addition nor
    subtraction—

unless he is a God that I bore.

(I.16.8–13)

The theological point seems to be that Mother and Son are consubstantial, belonging to the same *genus* or *art* (animal) and *species* or *gestalt* (human), with no difference or distinguishing mark (*underscheit*) between them. This human nature is their shared *proprietas* (*unser eigen*), with Christ suffering no *accidens* (*zuschicht, abeschicht*) that would make him more or less than fully human—unless, of course, he is also divine! These Aristotelian terms are not used in the precise technical senses that Frauenlob's follower, Heinrich von Mügeln, would give them a generation later in his own poem about Mary and the arts, entitled *Der meide kranz* (The Virgin's Garland).[53] This is because Frauenlob was an erudite poet, but not a didactic one. Unlike Alan of Lille or Heinrich von Mügeln, he aimed in this passage neither to teach logic nor to expose its limits, but to enthrone the Virgin at the pinnacle of yet another discourse—to craft yet another language for her praise.[54]

53. Heinrich von Mügeln, *Der meide kranz*: text, English translation, and commentary by Annette Volfing (Tübingen: Niemeyer, 1997). See pp. 73–85 on the speech of Loica (Logic), which adapts the vocabulary crafted by Frauenlob.

54. Cf. Kern, *Trinität, Maria, Inkarnation*, 229.

As a vernacular poet, Frauenlob mediated his Latin learning to readers and hearers at some distance, but he stood in a more direct relationship to his German sources, which can be grouped in three broad categories. Closest to the poet are the other *Spruchdichter* whose works he knew well and quoted frequently—Konrad von Würzburg, Reinmar von Zweter, and at a greater remove, Walther von der Vogelweide, Wolfram von Eschenbach, and Friedrich von Sonnenburg. In the middle distance stands a tradition of largely anonymous *Marienlob* ("Marian praise"), represented by such poems as the twelfth-century *Melker Marienlied* and the later *Rheinisches Marienlob*. All these provide an aural and conceptual context in which listeners would have heard the *Marienleich*. Finally, the poem can and should be read alongside certain twelfth- and thirteenth-century mystical works, such as the *St. Trudperter Hohelied*, Lamprecht von Regenburg's *Tochter Syon* (Daughter of Zion), and Mechthild von Magdeburg's *Das fliessende Licht der Gottheit* (The Flowing Light of the Godhead). Though these texts of *Brautmystik* may not have been known to Frauenlob, they belong to the same affective and devotional world as the *Marienleich*. All are saturated with the Song of Songs and vibrant with the same currents of erotic spirituality, the same impulse to celebrate and experience the love of God as *hohe Minne* or, in Susanne Köbele's words, *hochste Minne*.[55]

The *Marienlob* genre originated in the twelfth century as a transposition of Latin hymnody into the vernacular, but it gradually developed toward a more self-consciously aesthetic, courtly style.[56] The early thirteenth-century *Rheinisches Marienlob*, a comprehensive praise-poem, typifies the older exegetical mode. To introduce his verse homily of more than five thousand lines, the Low German poet reviews Mary's most important attributes: she is heaven and earth, garden enclosed and fountain sealed, New Eve, radiant moon; her name, *Maria*, means both "star of the sea" (*stella maris*) and "bitter" (*amara*), because of her sufferings at the Passion. At this point the poet inserts her first-person lament (*klage*) in a strophic form distinct from his own verse in couplets—a precedent for the lengthy discourse that Frauenlob's Lady speaks in her own voice.[57] The *Marienlob* continues with Mary's five joys, her exaltation above the nine orders of angels, and her celestial beauty, ending with an elaborate account of the gems in her robe and crown. It is no coincidence that the *Marienleich* concludes with the same motif, though Frauenlob is enigmatic where the Rhenish poet is excruciatingly clear. The *Marienlob* also includes a vision of the woman clothed with the sun (Apoc. 12), with which Frauenlob's *leich* begins—but stylistically the treatments are poles apart. Here is the *Rheinisches Marienlob*:

55. Köbele, *Frauenlobs Lieder*, 240.

56. See Schäfer, *Untersuchungen*, and the more succinct account of Karl Stackmann, "Magd und Königin," in Jens Haustein, ed., *Frauenlob, Heinrich von Mügeln und ihre Nachfolger* (Göttingen: Wallstein, 2002), 9–33.

57. Adolf Bach, ed., *Das Rheinische Marienlob: Eine deutsche Dichtung des 13. Jahrhunderts*, lines 897–1313 (Leipzig: Hiersemann, 1934), 28–41. Cf. Commentary under strophe 8. The *klage Mariens* was an independent lyric genre also found in Latin (as *planctus Mariae*) and other vernaculars.

He sach ein vrow in himelriche,	[St. John] saw a lady in heaven
der schin was schöne sunderliche:	whose appearance was of rare beauty:
si was lövelich ind walgedan,	she was laudable and well-attired.
he sac die sunn' si gar ümbvan,	He saw her wholly clothed in the sun,
under irn vuezen stuont de man,	beneath her feet stood the moon,
hinave schein die walgedan.	well-dressed she appeared on high.
Dis vrowe schön ind süverlich,	This fair and immaculate lady
schön vrowe, si bezeichent dich.[58]	signifies you, fair Lady.

Lest anyone miss the point, the poet goes on to explain that the sun stands for Christ, the moon for the communion of saints, and so forth—not caring that in eight lines he has used *vrowe* and *schön* three times each and rhymed *walgedan* twice. In contrast, Frauenlob not only varies the diction and eschews the commentary, but also defamiliarizes the vision by breaking it into two parts, both presented in the first person. The poet-seer, speaking for John the Divine, proclaims his vision with stunned immediacy.

Ei, ich sach in dem trone	Look! I saw upon the throne
ein vrouwen, die was swanger.	a Lady who was pregnant.
die trug ein wunderkrone	She wore a wondrous crown
vor miner ougen anger.	before the pasture of my eyes.

(I.1.1–4)

Only nine strophes later does the Lady flaunt her cosmic attire, as usual asserting divine agency of herself:

der sunnen glesten ist min kleit,	The shining sun is my garment:
dar in so han ich mich gebriset und gereit.	I have clad and laced myself within it
so hat der mane sich geleit	so the moon has laid itself down
zu minen füzen.	at my feet.

(I.10.10–13)

In the course of time, as Gert Hübner has shown, Marian poets increasingly cut familiar exegetical predicates loose from their moorings, converting them into pure *Lobblumen,* or "flowers of praise." Explicit allegory becomes implicit; typological relationships are assumed rather than asserted; figurative speech evolves from simile ("You are like a rose") to metaphor ("You are a rose") to apostrophe ("You rose" or simply "Rose!").[59] Biblical images persist, newly supplemented

58. *Das Rheinische Marienlob*, lines 4225–32, p. 125.   59. Hübner, *Lobblumen*, 164–65.

by courtly ones: Mary is still the enclosed garden and the well of life, but she is also the music of stringed instruments (*seitenclanc*), the flying arrow of love (*minneschuz*), the throne of princes (*fürstenstuol*). The most privileged repertoires of imagery—flowers, gemstones, spring scenes— are at home in both realms. Sigeher's *Marienlied,* a poem contemporary with Frauenlob's *leich,* begins in this vein:

Maria, muoter unde meit,	Mary, mother and maiden,
du hast den hohsten pris bejeit,	you have earned the highest praise,
der tugende keiserinne.	O empress of virtues.
Du süeze ob aller süezecheit,	You are sweet above all sweetness—
din süeze ist al der werlde bereit,	your sweetness is for all the world,
heilberndiu küniginne.	salvation-bearing queen.
Du cederwaz, du balsemsmac,	You cedar vessel, scent of balsam,
du richiu liljenouwe,	meadow rich in lilies,
du himelstraz, du saeldentac,	you road to heaven, day of blessings,
gote liebiu spiegelschouwe.[60]	lovely mirror-image of God.

Sensual imagery and high diction are coupled with simple, transparent syntax and undemanding thought. Sigeher no longer explains *how* Mary resembles cedar (an incorruptible wood), balsam (a healing ointment), or lilies (an emblem of virginity), but why should he? Everyone knew by now. Praise-poems of this genre, which had been circulating for a century by the time Frauenlob composed his *leich,* form part of its unspoken background. He too sings of sweetness and virtues; he too links the Virgin with cedar, balsam, lilies, and mirrors. But if he does not share the Rhenish poet's exegetical zeal, neither is he content with Sigeher's purely ornamental Mary: he will insist on theology, but he makes the reader do the glossing that earlier, less hermetic poets did for themselves.

KONRAD VON WÜRZBURG AND *DIE GOLDENE SCHMIEDE*

The consummate heir to the *Marienlob* tradition was Konrad von Würzburg (d. 1287), a poet whose reputation has been steadily rising.[61] We have already heard Frauenlob's extravagant praise for his "violet-blossomed art" and the "star-spangled heaven of his skill."[62] Max Wehrli's literary history describes Konrad's verse, in terms just slightly less florid, as possessed of "a weightless and, perhaps for that very reason, somewhat melancholy beauty"—so fraught with

---

60. Sigeher, *Marienlied* 1, ed. Hübner, *Lobblumen,* 173.

61. For recent research, see Horst Brunner, ed., *Konrad von Würzburg: Seine Zeit, sein Werk, seine Wirkung. Tagung Würzburg 1987* (Marbach: Oswald von Wolkenstein-Gesellschaft, 1988).

62. See Chapter 1, pp. 56–57.

echoes, correspondences, and ornamental rhymes as to stand "on the boundary of the bearable, even sometimes beyond it."[63] *Die goldene Schmiede* (The Golden Forge) delighted the poet's contemporaries with its elegant *meisterschaft*, while restoring the overt commentary of poems like the *Rheinisches Marienlob* in a much more graceful fashion. Konrad's Mary, as Hübner observes, is once again "an intelligible Mary, situated within salvation history and mediating salvation—not a sensually mediated, joy-bringing courtly lady," as in Sigeher's *Marienlied*.[64] In his spacious poem of two thousand lines (less than half the length of the *Rheinisches Marienlob* but almost four times that of Frauenlob's *leich*), Konrad artfully interweaves clusters of imagery with allegories and prayers. All the standard theological tropes are present (New Eve, bride of the Trinity, vessel of grace, vanquisher of Satan), along with the full range of scriptural types and a wide array of secular ones, including the mystical unicorn hunt and others from the *Physiologus* tradition. Stackmann is surely right to argue that the *Marienleich* originated in Frauenlob's artistic conversation with Konrad—competition being, for *Spruchdichter*, the sincerest form of flattery.[65] In my quest for the *Marienleich*'s sources and analogues, I have identified no fewer than twenty allusions to *Die goldene Schmiede* (adding several to Stackmann's list)—compared with eight to Reinmar von Zweter's *Leich*, two to Walther's, one to Gottfried, and possibly one to Friedrich von Sonnenburg. Strophe 12 alone contains eight echoes of Konrad.

But Frauenlob did not simply borrow; he condensed, recombined images, suppressed explanations, and translated praise in the second person to proclamation in the first. Hence "obscurities of meaning, caused by radical abridgment of the image [in Frauenlob], disappear when we take a look at the corresponding passage in Konrad's poem."[66] As these parallels are spelled out in the Commentary, one example here can serve for many. In *Marienleich* I.9.14 the Lady utters a more than usually cryptic line: "Den slangen beiz min harm, ich wisel" ("My ermine bit the snake; I [am a] weasel"). On first reading this makes little or no sense, for the image is hardly a common one. But a look at the much lengthier allegory in *Die goldene Schmiede* makes it clear:

der hellebasiliscus	The basilisk of hell
schaden vil von dir begreif:	took great injury from you:
din tugent schuof daz uf in sleif	your virtue showered him
des todes hagel und sin risel.	with the rain and hail of death.
bi dir bezeichent ist diu wisel	You are signified by the weasel
diu daz hermelin gebar,	that bore the ermine
daz den slangen eitervar	that bit the venomous snake
ze tode an siner crefte beiz,	to death in his power

63. Wehrli, *Geschichte der deutschen Literatur*, 1:449–50.
64. Hübner, *Lobblumen*, 189. On this poem, see also Peter Ganz, "'Nur eine schöne Kunstfigur': Zur 'Goldenen Schmiede' Konrads von Würzburg," *Germanisch-Romanische Monatsschrift* 29 (1979): 27–45.
65. Stackmann, "Magd und Königin," 22–27.
66. Stackmann, "Bild und Bedeutung," 449.

und sinen bluotvarwen sweiz	and sweated bloody sweat
rerte durch ir beider sturm.	in their mighty struggle.
do Lucifer der hellewurm	When Lucifer, the worm of hell,
uns den aphel eẓẓen sach,	saw us eat the apple
davon ẓe sterben uns geschach,	from which death came upon us,
do quam uns din geburt ẓe staten,	then your childbearing relieved us
und warf uns an der wünne schaten	and cast us into joyful shade
uẓ bitterlicher noete warm.	out of hot and bitter torments.
Crist der hohe himelharm	Christ, the high ermine of heaven,
slouf in der tiefen helle tunc,	crept into the dark depths of hell
und beiẓ den mortgitigen unc	and bit the lethal serpent
ẓe tode an aller siner maht.[67]	to death in all his might.

Even Konrad's account makes a few assumptions: the reader must know that the ermine, whose heraldic fur signified royalty, is a species of weasel, a creature with the ability to kill poisonous snakes. Though not actually true of European weasels, this bit of bestiary lore stemmed from a garbled knowledge of the Indian mongoose, which resembles a weasel and does in fact kill cobras.[68] Where Konrad spells out the beast's *significatio* in full, Frauenlob reduces it to a single line embedded in a dense web of allusions (strophe 9b) that also includes leprosy in hell, dew with the strength to shatter rocks, a divining rod without a fork, a palm tree that turns scarlet when spoken to, and an economic metaphor about interest and debt.[69] Presented with this daunting metaphorical display, a listener who happened to know *Die goldene Schmiede* would have a distinct advantage.

BRAUTMYSTIK AND EROTIC SPIRITUALITY

Finally we turn to a textual realm, not ordinarily linked with *Spruchdichtung,* that shows marked affinities with the *Marienleich.* This is the sphere of vernacular *Brautmystik*—texts of erotic spirituality written for and occasionally by consecrated women. The earliest of these is the *St. Trudperter Hohelied,* also known as *Ein lêre der minneclichen gotes erkennüsse* (A Teaching of the Loving Knowledge of God)—the first vernacular commentary on the Song of Songs.[70]

67. Konrad, *Die goldene Schmiede,* lines 156–75.

68. Albertus Magnus says in *De animalibus* 25.13 that weasels can kill basilisks: *On Animals: A Medieval Summa Zoologica,* trans. Kenneth Kitchell Jr. and I. M. Resnick, 2 vols. (Baltimore: Johns Hopkins University Press, 1999), 2:1721.

69. For a fuller comparison of these passages, see Hartmut Freytag, "Beobachtungen zu Konrads von Würzburg 'Goldener Schmiede' und Frauenlobs Marienleich," in Brunner, ed., *Konrad von Würzburg,* 185–88.

70. Ohly, ed., *Das St. Trudperter Hohelied;* see also Bernard McGinn, *The Growth of Mysticism: Gregory the Great Through the Twelfth Century* (New York: Crossroad, 1994), 347–52; Hans-Jörg Spitz, "'*Ez ist sanc aller sange*': Das 'St. Trudperter Hohelied' zwischen Kommentar und Dichtung," in Volker Honemann and Tomas Tomasek, eds., *Germanistische Mediävistik* (Münster: Lit, 1999), 61–88; Keller, *My Secret Is Mine,* 110–12 and passim.

Ascribed to a monastic priest writing for the nuns of Admont, the text dates from the early 1160s, which would place it three or four decades after Rupert's Song commentary and at least a decade before Alan's. The writer deftly combines Marian with mystical and ecclesial interpretations of the Bride, presenting the Virgin as the unique beloved of God but also as a model for every prospective bride. One intriguing feature of this text is its inclusion of songlike interludes, much like the later romances with interpolated lyrics.[71] These mini-poems would have heightened the work's affective power and helped its audience commit the salient points to memory. They are often structured around lists—three theological virtues, seven gifts of the Holy Spirit, three faculties of the soul—using anaphora to create a litany-like effect. The Bride praises the Bridegroom, for instance, with reference to the seven gifts of Isaiah 11:2:

> you are the brightness of eternal Wisdom (*wîstuomes / sapientia*),
> you are the living fountain of holy Understanding (*vernunste / intellectus*),
> you are the messenger of the eternal Counsel (*râtes / consilium*),
> you are the champion of holy Strength (*sterke / fortitudo*),
> you are the ordering of holy Knowledge (*gewizzedes / scientia*),
> you are the donor of holy Goodness (*güete / pietas*),
> you are the strong judge on the Last Day of the Fear of God (*vorhte / timor*).[72]

In one of the more gnomic passages of the *Marienleich*, Frauenlob uses the same style and the same list to praise the Virgin as embodiment of these gifts:

du minne, wisheit was dir kunt,	You are Love; Wisdom was known to you;
du senftekeit, du künste funt,	you are Gentleness, you the source of arts,
du rat, din sterke bleib gesunt,	you are Counsel, your Strength was sound,
din vorchte entsloz den grozen bunt.	your Fear of God unlocked the great bond.
	(I.6.13–16)

Four of the seven gifts are conveyed by the same or similar terms (*wisheit, rat, sterke, vorchte*), and even the divergences stem from a common interpretive tradition. In the *Hohelied*, Christ is the "ordering" (*ordenunge*) of knowledge, suggesting a curriculum; similarly, Frauenlob's Lady is the source of the liberal arts (*künste funt*), anticipating the *artes* strophes later in the poem. Both

---

71. There is a similar work in French, *Les Cantiques Salemon*—a versified commentary on the Song composed for a beguine audience around 1300. Although the *Cantiques* is written entirely in stanzaic verse, it also contains eight interpolated *chansons*, some of them based on preexisting trouvère lyrics. Unlike the *St. Trudperter Hohelied*, the *Cantiques* includes a section on the *artes* as "the King's storerooms" (Cant. 1:3). See Tony Hunt, ed., *Les Cantiques Salemon: The Song of Songs in MS Paris BNF fr. 14966* (Turnhout: Brepols, 2006).

72. *St. Trudperter Hohelied*, 70–72: "Dû bist ein schim des êwigen wîstuomes, / dû bist ein lebender brunne der heiligen vernunste, / dû bist ein bote des êwigen râtes, / dû bist ein kempfe der heiligen sterke, / dû bist ein ordenunge des heiligen gewizzedes, / dû bist ein spendaere der heiligen güete, / dû bist ein starker rihtaere an deme iüngesten tage der gotes vorhte."

texts also imply an eschatological reading of *timor Dei*: Christ will be judge on the Last Day, Mary through her fear of God unlocked the chains of hell. Typical of Frauenlob is his replacement of *intellectus* with *minne* as the first and greatest gift.[73]

Like the *Marienleich*, the *Hohelied* is grounded in the liturgy and freely blends the Song of Songs with the sapiential books, asserting the eternal predestination of Mary. Apropos of Canticle 4:1 (*quam pulchra es, amica mea*), the writer links this praise of the Bride's beauty with the Annunciation, and that in turn with the Atonement:

> your beauty was perceived by the wisdom of the Eternal Father: then you stood as advocate for your ancestors, Adam and Eve. God gazed on your beautiful countenance when you lay among other children in Adam's loins and Eve's womb.

> There you had mercy on the holy goodness,
> there God's vengeance was restrained,
> there the wrath of power was stilled,
> there justice was silenced,
> there atonement was made for the sake of your beauty.
> There you were ordained as
> daughter of God,
> mother of Christ,
> and bride of the Holy Spirit.[74]

Commenting on Canticle 8:10, "I am a wall, and my breasts like a tower," the writer again links Mary's virtues with the Trinity (understood in Abelardian terms as *potentia, sapientia, bonitas*). She is a wall to shelter all the redeemed because:

> The hand of Wisdom built her,
> the finger of the holy Goodness plastered her,
> the power of the eternal Father dried her.
> She was whitewashed with holy chastity,
> strengthened with ramparts of holy virtues,
> established on a foundation of holy humility,
> fortified with strong silver towers—her innocent life and pure knowledge.[75]

73. For further discussion, see Commentary, strophe 6.

74. *St. Trudperter Hohelied*, 126: "Dîn schoene wart gesehen von deme wîstuome des êwigen vater. dô wegetest dû dînen vorderen Âdâme unde Êven. dô sach got dîn schoene antlütze, dâ dû laege under anderen kinden in Âdâmes lanken unde in Êven wambe. / dâ erbarmtest dû die heilige güete, / dâ wart diu gotes râche enthabet, / dâ wart der zorn der magenkrefte gestillet, / dâ wart daz reht gesweiget, / dâ wart durch dîne schoene diu süene geschaffen, / dâ wurde dû geordenet / ein tohter gotes unde / ein muoter Christes unde / ein brût des heiligen geistes."

75. *St. Trudperter Hohelied*, 294–96: "Die diu hant des wîstuomes geworht hât, / die der vinger der heiligen güete geebenet hât, / die der gewalt des êwigen vater getruckenet hât. / diu dâ gewîzet ist mit der heiligen kiusche, / diu dâ gezinnet ist mit den

Though Frauenlob avoids such overt allegorizing, it lies just beneath the surface of passages like the following, where the "towers" and "ramparts" suggest much the same meaning as in the *Hohelied*, with the white lilies figuring chastity:

Ich bin erkennig, nennig, kurc,	I am famed, acclaimed, elect,
des höchsten küneges sedelburg.	the palace of the highest king.
min türne nieman kan gewinnen.	My towers none can storm.
min zinnen	Without, within,
uz und innen	white lilies trim
sint mit liljen wiz gepinset.	my ramparts strong.

(I.10.1–6)

Once again, an effective reading of the *Marienleich* depends on a kind of learned ignorance—knowing exegetical texts as if not knowing them. The submerged presence of allegorical sub-texts, whether imported from the St. *Trudperter Hohelied,* Alan of Lille's *Elucidatio,* or *Die goldene Schmiede,* gives the poem much of its depth, while their visible absence gives it much of its power.

Frauenlob himself may or may not have known the *Hohelied,* but his older contemporary, Mechthild of Magdeburg, is quite likely to have been familiar with it.[76] The lyrical episodes in her own book, *The Flowing Light of the Godhead,* are written in much the same style, with the added ornament of rhyme—but that literary relationship, interesting though it is, cannot detain us now. Completed perhaps twenty years before the *Marienleich, Das fliessende Licht* deserves mention here for two reasons. First, it provides a near-contemporary example of speculative Mariology comparable to Frauenlob's, worked out in a context of personal reflection and vision-narrative rather than exegesis or formal theology.[77] Second, Mechthild's skillful techniques of impersonation and dramatic dialogue shed some light on the performative aspect of the *leich,* itself the most sustained piece of impersonation in the Marian repertoire.

The dynamics of salvation in Mechthild's work are deployed to a tricky rhythm of "three against two." On one level, her book is suffused with Trinitarian thought. Sometimes the visionary designates the three Persons by their standard names, though more often they are

---

heiligen tugenden, / diu dâ gegruntvestet ist mit der heiligen diemüete, / diu dâ werehaft ist mit den vesten silberînen türnen. / daz ist ir unschuldigez leben unde ir lûterez gewizzede."

76. The *Hohelied* had a modest but lasting currency in several dialects; the latest manuscript copy dates from 1509. Traces of eight manuscripts written before or during Mechthild's lifetime are known. Ohly, *St. Trudperter Hohelied,* 336–37.

77. On Mechthild, see Kurt Ruh, "Beginenmystik: Hadewijch, Mechthild von Magdeburg, Marguerite Porete," *Zeitschrift für deutsches Altertum* 106 (1977): 265–77; Margot Schmidt, "'Die spilende minnevluot': Der Eros als Sein und Wirkkraft in

der Trinität bei Mechthild von Magdeburg," in Margot Schmidt and Dieter Bauer, eds., *"Eine Höhe, über die nichts geht": Spezielle Glaubenserfahrung in der Frauenmystik?* (Stuttgart-Bad Cannstatt: Frommann-Holzboog, 1986), 71–133; Amy Hollywood, *The Soul as Virgin Wife: Mechthild of Magdeburg, Marguerite Porete, and Meister Eckhart* (Notre Dame, Ind.: University of Notre Dame Press, 1995), 57–86; Bernard McGinn, *The Flowering of Mysticism: Men and Women in the New Mysticism (1200–1350)* (New York: Crossroad, 1998), 222–44; Keller, *My Secret Is Mine,* 107–10 and passim.

presented as Divinity, Humanity, and Spirit, while at times they stand iconically for three stages of life (aged and dignified Father, handsome and virile Son, playful and childlike Spirit). Against this triple rhythm, a second theme plays out in double time: the motif of God and his Bride.[78] The Three and the Two mesh in a variety of ways: the Bridegroom can be either the whole Trinity or any member of it, while the Bride is either Mary, the Church, or the "noble soul"—or Mechthild herself as a specially chosen soul. In this way the varied possibilities offered by the exegetical tradition take on new and parallel lives, ultimately yielding Mechthild's own, distinctively erotic chronicle of salvation history.

Humankind is created in the first place because the Trinity is lonely—or better, bursting with desire. So the Father vows to "make a bride for myself who shall greet me with her mouth and wound me with her beauty" as their love begins; the Holy Spirit offers to bring her to the Father's bed, and the Son promises that he will die for love.[79] The divine act of creation, however, produces not one couple but two: first, Adam with Eve, his "refined, noble, and delicate virgin," and second, the heavenly Bridegroom with the human soul/bride. No sooner is the soul created than the impatient Father plights his troth, declaring, "I am God of all gods; you are Goddess of all creatures, and I give you my solemn vow that I shall never forsake you."[80] But the Bride tragically withholds her consent to this marriage, falling at once into sin. In a separate vignette, the celestial Virgin reveals to Mechthild that she, together with Eternal Wisdom, had to "intercept" the Father's anger at the Fall. At that time, she adds, "The Father chose me for his bride—that he might have something to love; for his darling bride, the noble soul, was dead. The Son chose me to be his mother, and the Holy Spirit received me as his beloved. Then I alone was the bride of the Holy Trinity."[81] But if bride, then also goddess. On seeing Mary enthroned in heaven, Mechthild exclaims, "Her Son is God and she Goddess. No one can be compared to her!"[82] As an immortal being, the virgin goddess transcends time; thus, she explains, her breasts will be full until the Last Judgment because she is the universal mother of mankind. From on high she nursed the prophets and sages "even before I was born," suckled Jesus himself "in my childhood," and "later, in my youth, I suckled God's bride, Holy Christendom."[83] Here we see multiple brides overlapping: Eternal Wisdom, the historical Mary, and

78. Barbara Newman, *From Virile Woman to WomanChrist: Studies in Medieval Religion and Literature* (Philadelphia: University of Pennsylvania Press, 1995), 151.

79. "Ich wil mir selben machen ein brut, dú sol mich mit irem munde gruessen und mit irem ansehen verwunden; denne erste gat es an ein minnen!" Mechthild von Magdeburg, *Das fliessende Licht der Gottheit*, 3.9, ed. Gisela Vollmann-Profe (Frankfurt am Main: Deutscher Klassiker Verlag, 2003), 176. I have used the translation by Frank Tobin, *The Flowing Light of the Godhead* (New York: Paulist, 1998), with slight changes.

80. "Ich bin got aller goetten, du bist aller creaturen goettinne und ich gibe dir mine hanttrúwe, das ich dich niemer verkiese." Mechthild von Magdeburg, *Das fliessende Licht*, 178.

81. "Do erwelte mich der vatter zuo einer brut, das er etwas ze minnende hette, wand sin liebú brut was tot, die edel sele; und do kos mich der sun zuo einer muoter und do enpfieng mich der helig geist ze einer trútinne. Do was ich alleine brut der heligen drivaltekeit." Ibid., 1.22, pp. 40–42.

82. "Ir sun ist got und si goettinne; es mag ir nieman gliche gewinnen." Ibid., 3.1, p. 150.

83. "Do ich also muoter was maniges ellenden kindes, do wurden mine brúste also vol der reinen unbewollener milch der waren milten barmherzekeit, das ich soegete die propheten und die wissagen, e denne ich geborn wart. Dar nach in miner kintheit soegete ich Jhesum; fúrbas in miner jugent soegete ich gottes brut, die heligen cristanheit, bi dem crútze." Ibid., 1.22, p. 42.

"Holy Christendom," the Church, are now distinguished and now identified. Even though Mary's maternity and brideship are eternal, her marriage is also consummated in earthly time— at the moment of the Annunciation. Upon pronouncing her *fiat mihi* to Gabriel, the Virgin becomes God's mother and bride not only in spirit, but also in the flesh: "Then the whole Holy Trinity, with the power of the Godhead, the good will of the Manhood, and the noble delicacy of the Holy Spirit, passed through her whole virginal body into the fiery soul of her good will, placed itself in the open heart of her most pure flesh, and united itself with all that it found in her."[84] Although this carnal union had a beginning, it will have no end, for in heaven the three Persons in their unity still "flow joyously toward Mary's countenance in full flood, undivided in a single beam of light," greeting her heart with such ineffable glory that her face becomes a mirror of the Trinity and reflects God's glory on all heaven.[85]

This scenario is not recounted in a single narrative, but scattered piecemeal through the text. Sometimes Mary reveals her own mysteries, sometimes Mechthild writes in the third person, and sometimes the divine Three speak among themselves in counsel as if she were a secretary recording their minutes. Both formally and theologically, *Das fliessende Licht* is a most original book, a unique blend of genres including vision, prophecy, homily, prayer, litany, allegorical dialogue, and more. Yet in some ways, Mechthild's Mariology provides the closest analogue to Frauenlob's *leich* that we have. To be sure, both the idea of Mary as bride of the Trinity and her assimilation to eternal Wisdom were common theological currency of the age. But Frauenlob, like Mechthild, places exceptional emphasis on these motifs, developing them with an unabashed eroticism that betrays the same double vision of the Divine: on the one hand, the Trinity as creator and redeemer of the world; on the other, the divine Couple as archetype and end. Even within the Song of Songs tradition, the sheer amorous intensity that Frauenlob confers on the love affair of God and Mary is found more often in works of personal *Brautmystik* like *Das fliessende Licht* than in the tradition of *Marienlob*. (It is not to be found in *Die goldene Schmiede*, for instance, despite that poem's stress on the Trinity and on Mary's preexistence as Sapientia.) Here are two of Mary's expressions of union with the Trinity in the *Marienleich*:

min schepfer und min vriedel der vil alte,	My Creator and my ancient Lover
der sich zu mir nach siner kust in drin	by his art enfolded himself in me in
personen valte.	Persons three:
des selben mutermeit bin ich.	maiden-mother of the same am I.

(I.13.38–40)

84. "Do trat dú ganze helige drivaltekeit mit der gewalt der gotheit und mit dem guoten willen der menscheit und mit der edelen gevuogheit des heligen geistes dur den ganzen lichamen ires magtuomes in die vúrigen sele irs guoten willen und saste sich in das offen herze ires allerreinosten vleisches und vereinete sich mit allem dem, das er an ir vant." Ibid., 5.23, p. 364.

85. "Si vliessent gegen Marien antlize wunnenklich in eime strame ungescheiden mit voller vluot in milter gabe mit clarem schine der himelschen eren. Mit unsprechlicher gruosse rueret er ir herze, das si schinet und lúhtet, also das der hohe gegenblik der heligen drivaltekeit vor únser frovwen antlize entstet." Ibid,. 6.39, p. 512.

die wechter miner bürge zwar   The watchmen of my turrets
der tougen wurden nie gewar,   never knew my secrets—
wie got in mich sin kint gebar,   how God in me begot his child,
daz ich gebar fürbaz al dar.   the One I then brought forth for all.
die süze miner sele nar   The sweet nourishment of my soul
gebar den geist, ich menschen clar.   bore the divine Spirit; I, the manhood
     pure.

sust vater, sun, heiliger geist in mich sich   Thus Father, Son, and Holy Spirit spun
     span.   themselves within me.

                                           (I.15.24–30)

This theology culminates in two remarkable assertions. Just after the halfway point of the poem the Lady declares, *Ich got, sie got, er got*—"I am God, they are God, he is God" (I.12.33)—presumably of herself, the Trinity, and her Son.[86] And just before the end of the *leich* she asserts, *Alsust ich menschlich gotlich wart*: "thus I, human, became divine" (I.20.30).

No matter how thoroughly divinized the medieval Virgin was in practice, whether in hymnody, iconography, or devotion, the *explicit* proclamation of her divinity was heterodox and therefore extremely rare. Mary was the Mother of God: *Theotokos*, neither *theos* (except in Frauenlob) nor *thea* (except in Mechthild). But the pressures contributing to her divinization were intense. From the twelfth century onward, poets and commentators felt the need to remark that Mary was *not* the fourth person of the Trinity, a sign that others assumed she was precisely that.[87] Yet before Frauenlob, I have found no one but Mechthild who openly and unapologetically applies the language of deity to the Virgin. In the absence of direct literary influence, which is unlikely,[88] what might have led these two very different authors in the same direction? It may be that both articulate what Köbele has described as a "vernacular Marian theology, relatively independent of Latin, on the other side of traditional dogmatic Mariology."[89] But more specific factors are also at work. The most obvious of these is a highly gendered, eroticized vision of ultimate reality shared by the beguine and the minstrel, both alike galvanized by the cult of Frau Minne who crossed—and all but effaced—the otherwise well-guarded boundary between sacred and secular love. Mechthild's famous courtly idioms are matched by Frauenlob's

---

86. See Chapter 4, p. 126, and Commentary, strophe 12.

87. Newman, *God and the Goddesses*, 254–55. For other explorations of Mary as goddess, see E. Ann Matter, "The Virgin Mary: A Goddess?" in Carl Olson, ed., *The Book of the Goddess, Past and Present* (New York: Crossroad, 1983), 80–96; David Kinsley, "Mary: Virgin, Mother, and Queen," in *The Goddesses' Mirror: Visions of the Divine from East and West* (Albany, N.Y.: SUNY Press, 1989), 215–60; Andrew Harvey and Anne Baring, "Queen of Heaven," in *The Divine Feminine: Exploring the Feminine Face of God Around the World* (Berkeley, Calif.: Conari Press, 1996), 102–19;

Francis X. Clooney, *Divine Mother, Blessed Mother: Hindu Goddesses and the Virgin Mary* (New York: Oxford, 2005).

88. For Mechthild's influence, see Sara S. Poor, *Mechthild of Magdeburg and Her Book: Gender and the Making of Textual Authority* (Philadelphia: University of Pennsylvania Press, 2004). All surviving manuscripts of *Das fliessende Licht*, both Latin and German, postdate Frauenlob (pp. 205–7). Mechthild's original Low German text has not survived.

89. Köbele, "Umbesetzungen," 222.

allusions to the Grail quest, to secret love intrigues, to Christ as Mary's *friedel* (sweetheart) or *amis curtois* (courtly lover, I.11.22). A second shared habit is the tendency to interpret doctrine through the lens of poetic imagination, without imposing the usual filters that more circumspect writers, especially in Latin, used to keep their *fabula* distinct from their dogma.

Recent literature on beguine spirituality has emphasized its performative nature,[90] and Mechthild is nothing if not a dramatic writer. In the opening scenes of *Das fliessende Licht*, she represents the Soul in dramatic dialogues with Frau Minne, the body, the senses, the heavenly Bridegroom, the Virgin, and God—and this is only the first book. Many more allegorical figures appear onstage in books 2 through 7. The character of the Soul is one of many devices that Mechthild (like other women mystics) uses to distance her artistic representations of the Divine from her direct personal experience. In addition, she "herself" speaks in many voices, including those of the ecstatic bride, the wretched sinner, the preacher, the compassionate intercessor, and the prophet. Frauenlob too speaks in many voices. *Minne und Welt* is of course a debate between two goddess-figures. The *Minneleich* begins as a dialogue between the poet and Herr Sinn (Sir Thought) before launching into a lengthy apostrophe to the *Vrouwe*, who is invited to speak its climactic line (III.32.6); and in the first few strophes of the *Kreuzleich*, all three Persons of the Trinity come onstage as speakers, in addition to the prophet David and the patriarch Isaac. In the *Marienleich*, the poet-seer begins by impersonating Saint John the Divine. Even in the first eight strophes, before the Virgin's monologue begins, the speaking "I" is unstable, oscillating among third-person description, direct address in the intimate *du*, and a more courtly address in the formal *ir*.[91] The Lady herself speaks in the voices of innocent child-bride, mother, passionate lover, confidante, eternal Wisdom, world soul, and celestial goddess. Once she even speaks of herself in the third person (I.15.9), and once the poet's voice interrupts her discourse to hope that no one in his audience will be offended (I.11.15–16).

In order to stage her divine love affair convincingly for readers, Mechthild had to imagine and compose not only the female parts, such as the Soul and Frau Minne, but also the male parts assigned to her decidedly masculine God. In the *Marienleich*, Frauenlob similarly composed in a woman's voice—or, we might even say, *the* Woman's voice. Such attempts in lyric poetry were not wholly new, for we find "women's songs" composed and performed by men in the repertoire of minnesang, and we hear the Virgin lamenting in works like the *Rheinisches Marienlob*. But Frauenlob's experiment is distant from both modes, and more ambitious than either. The reality of oral performance also inflects his project. While Mechthild performed the scenes of her spiritual drama on the page, Frauenlob performed his onstage—and, unlike the ensemble Sequentia,

90. See for example Mary Suydam, "Visionaries in the Public Eye: Beguine Literature as Performance," in Ellen Kittell and Mary Suydam, eds., *The Texture of Society: Medieval Women in the Southern Low Countries* (New York: Palgrave Macmillan, 2004), 131–52; Mary Suydam and Joanna Ziegler, eds., *Performance and Transformation: New Approaches to Late Medieval Spirituality* (New York: St. Martin's, 1999).

91. Nigel Palmer, "Duzen und Ihrzen in Frauenlobs *Marienleich* und in der mittelhochdeutschen Mariendichtung," in Schröder, ed., *Wolfram-Studien* 10:87–104.

he did not have the option of using female voices for the last twelve strophes. In all likelihood, he not only composed the Virgin's part but also sang and acted it—a cross-gender performance that is, alas, irretrievably lost to us. Yet reading a more obviously dramatic and dialogical work like *The Flowing Light of the Godhead* can give us some inkling of the effect. What Mechthild finally offers is not a model of "the female mystical voice" that a male author might imitate but something considerably more complicated: a model of dramatic impersonation that enables both the powerful expression and the artistic distancing of spiritual experience.[92] Because that experience is also erotic, the performance is necessarily gendered. Like *Das fliessende Licht*, like the Song of Songs itself and its commentaries, the *Marienleich* is not only a vehement declaration of desire but also a profound meditation on it. Its shimmering texture is, in one of Frauenlob's favorite metaphors, braided from many voices—male and female, human and divine, sacred and secular voices that ceaselessly summon, answer, echo, and impersonate one another as they perform their circular and therefore unending dialogue of love.

92. For a poignant theoretical reflection on these themes, see Nicholas Watson, Afterword to "Desire for the Past," in Louise D'Arcens and Juanita Feros Ruys, eds., *Maistresse of My Wit: Medieval Women, Modern Scholars* (Turnhout: Brepols, 2004), 185–88.

4

THE MARIENLEICH AS A WORK OF ART

Thus far I have analyzed the *Marienleich* in terms of content, reading it against the rest of Frauenlob's oeuvre and pertinent Latin and vernacular contexts. In this chapter I shall discuss the composition's formal structure, both poetic and musical, and make some observations on its style.

MUSICAL STRUCTURE AND POETIC FORM

Every *leich* employs structural repetition or echoing in some form, as this is a defining trait of the genre. But the *Marienleich* represents a novelty in its strict use of strophic responsion, a principle borrowed from the classical Latin sequence developed by Notker. In the paired versicles from Hermann the Lame's Marian sequence, "Ave praeclara maris stella" (Chapter 3, pp. 100–101), we saw an illustration of this principle. Each strophe is made up of two melodically and metrically identical half-strophes, but no two pairs in the poem are alike. Frauenlob used the same compositional structure, except that he omitted the unpaired opening and closing verses typical of the sequence form. Since the *Marienleich* has twenty strophes, it consists of "twenty large, songlike unities," each sung exactly twice.[1] Each strophe is, in effect, an independent *Ton* comparable to the nine *Spruchtöne* in which Frauenlob composed his short strophic poems (Chapter 2, pp. 85–86). Within this basic structure, we find overarching principles of unity on the macro-level and extreme variety on the micro-level.

The most important unifying principle is the tonal organization of the music, which is intertwined with the poem's metrical structure.[2] Frauenlob arranged the melodies of his *leich* according to the cycle of eight modes or scales used in plainchant, composing the first strophe in the first mode, the second in the second mode, and so forth. Musicologists characterize these eight modes in a variety of ways according to their ancient Greek names, their "final" (the note on which a melody ends), and their tonality (authentic or plagal, roughly analogous to the later distinction between major and minor keys). After Frauenlob concludes his first cycle of modes (or *cursus*) with the eighth strophe, he begins anew in the ninth and completes a second *cursus* running through the sixteenth. Thus the composition as a whole employs a "double *cursus*" pattern, with a third half-*cursus* informing strophes seventeen through twenty. The following table illustrates this pattern:[3]

D	1st tone	First authentic	Dorian	Strophes 1, 9, 17
D	2nd tone	First plagal	Hypodorian	Strophes 2, 10, 18
E	3rd tone	Second authentic	Phrygian	Strophes 3, 11, 19
E	4th tone	Second plagal	Hypophrygian	Strophes 4, 12, 20
F	5th tone	Third authentic	Lydian	Strophes 5, 13
F	6th tone	Third plagal	Hypolydian	Strophes 6, 14
G	7th tone	Fourth authentic	Mixolydian	Strophes 7, 15
G	8th tone	Fourth plagal	Hypomixolydian	Strophes 8, 16

The double *cursus* structure was not invented by Frauenlob but borrowed from a particular type of liturgical office, developed in the twelfth century and composed in vast numbers in the thirteenth. This is the rhymed office, typically written to honor new and local saints, but especially the Virgin Mary. Some thousand such offices appear in the *Analecta hymnica*. In rhymed offices for Matins (the longest of the canonical hours, sung before dawn), it was customary to chant the first psalm with its antiphon in the first mode and the second in the second mode, continuing through the full sequence of eight. Although the rhymed offices themselves were purged in the

1. Michael Shields, "Zum melodischen Aufbau des Marienleichs," in Schröder, ed., *Wolfram-Studien* 10:117–24, at 117.

2. I follow the very helpful analysis of März, *Frauenlobs Marienleich*.

3. Adapted from März, *Frauenlobs Marienleich*, 6.

liturgical reforms of Trent, their musical *cursus* pattern—that is, the numerical sequence of melodies following the eight modes—can still be seen in the Matins for Corpus Christi in the *Liber Usualis*, the standard pre–Vatican II compendium of plainchant.[4] Frauenlob's debt to liturgical chant is indicated by the *differentiae* or cadences marked at the end of most strophes. These are melodic formulas set to the closing syllables of the doxology ("seculorum, amen," customarily abbreviated to the vowels EVOVAE), written to show the mode in which an antiphon ought to be sung. Outside of Frauenlob's work, they are found only in liturgical manuscripts.[5]

One consequence of the *Marienleich*'s double *cursus* structure is that, musically speaking, the work contains two significant breaks following strophes 8 and 16. The first of these reinforces its most important textual break. At the end of strophe 8, the poet-seer ends his introduction by inviting the Lady to speak ("vil schöne ob allen vrouwen, sprich," 8.24), and she begins her discourse with a rhyming line sung to the same melody ("der schönen liebe ein muter ich," 8.25). From this point on, the rest of the *leich* is performed in her first-person voice. While there is no comparable caesura at the end of the second *cursus*, strophe 17 begins with the exclamation *ei*, the same expression of wonder that opens the first strophe. This repetition creates at least a weak link between the beginnings of the first *cursus* and the final half-*cursus*.[6]

Another structuring principle is numerology, a pan-European device beloved of learned medieval poets.[7] Dante, a contemporary of Frauenlob, used elaborate numerical symbolism to structure his *Commedia*. Another contemporary, Jean de Meun—hardly known for his structural elegance—nonetheless inserted his "signature" and poetic credo at the numerical centerpoint of the sprawling *Roman de la Rose*. The anonymous fourteenth-century English poet of *Pearl* and *Sir Gawain and the Green Knight* carried numerology to extraordinary lengths. In German poetry, Hartmann von Aue before Frauenlob and Heinrich von Mügeln after him used the device extensively. So it would be surprising if such a formalist work as the *Marienleich* were not composed "according to the numbers." On the micro-level, it is easy to find examples of numerical structuring. The seventh strophe, for instance, allegorizes the seven lampstands of the Apocalypse as seven virtues of Mary, while the eighteenth (twice nine) has nine lines in each half and treats the nine choirs of angels and their song. The three Persons of the Trinity are mentioned three times (lines 11.8, 13.39, and 16.3), while a total of seven sevens are named: lampstands, churches, angels, gifts of the Holy Spirit, virtues, sacraments, and horns on the head of the Lamb (strophes 2a, 6, 7, 11a, and 13b). The twelve gems in the Lady's crown are introduced in the first stro-

---

4. Gärtner, "Das Hohelied," 107; "In Festo SS. Corporis Christi," *Liber Usualis Missae et Officii*, ed. monks of Solesmes (Tournai, Belgium: Desclée, 1953), 917–39.

5. März, *Frauenlobs Marienleich*, 2. *Differentiae* also appear in the music for the *Kreuzleich* and even the secular *Minneleich*, though only the *Marienleich* ends with a sung "amen."

6. März, *Frauenlobs Marienleich*, 96.

7. Vincent Hopper, *Medieval Number Symbolism: Its Sources, Meaning, and Influence on Thought and Expression* (New York:

Columbia University Press, 1938); E. R. Curtius, "Numerical Composition," in *European Literature and the Latin Middle Ages*, trans. Willard Trask (Princeton: Princeton University Press, 1953), 501–9; John Guzzardo, *Dante: Numerological Studies* (New York: Peter Lang, 1987); Robert Surles, ed., *Medieval Numerology: A Book of Essays* (New York: Garland, 1993); Edward Condren, *The Numerical Universe of the "Gawain-Pearl" Poet: Beyond "Phi"* (Gainesville: University Press of Florida, 2002).

phe but not fully elaborated until the last, giving the *leich* a pleasingly circular form. In strophe 19a the poet sets an exegetical riddle: the Lady proclaims herself to be the bed of Solomon, guarded by sixty strong men (Cant. 3:7). This number is then broken down to signify the saints encircling her throne: twenty-four elders, twelve apostles, nine angelic orders, three patriarchs, four evangelists, and a mysterious eight more to make up the sum of sixty.[8]

On the macro-level, Frauenlob's numerical design is more elusive. One would expect to find a symbolic number of either strophes or lines. Twenty (the number of strophes) is a satisfying round figure, yet it bears no obvious symbolic relationship to the content. The number of lines (508) does not seem to be significant either. But since the line lengths in this poem are so irregular and variable, Christoph März has proposed that its numerical proportions should be sought instead in the number of feet or bars (*tactus*). If we count the *tactus* per half-strophe, the total number in the first *cursus* is 296, while the number in the second is 592, exactly twice as many. Adding the 312 stresses in the final half-*cursus*, we reach a total of 1,200.[9] This number is indeed symbolic, representing the sacred twelve—the number of apostles, jewels in the Lady's crown, and gates of the celestial city (Apoc. 21:12–21)—multiplied by the perfect square 100, signifying perfection. It also happens to be the number of Solomon's *pacifici* ("those who find peace with God") at the end of the Song of Songs (8:12), a biblical text cited no fewer than sixty times in the poem. Finally, the proportions yielded by these figures are aesthetically harmonious, since the first, second, and third *cursus* turn out to be related in an approximate ratio of 1:2:1. (The Sequentia recording corroborates these figures; if we omit the two instrumental interludes composed by the ensemble, the first *cursus* takes about fifteen minutes to perform, the second thirty minutes, and the third again fifteen.) We also discover that the Lady's climactic assertion, the startling if not scandalous *ich got* ("I am God"), occurs at the numerical midpoint of the work in strophe 12b, giving it extra prominence.

These large-scale symmetries are offset by the *leich*'s exuberant variety at the level of individual strophes. Frauenlob described his own compositional methods in one of his *Sprüche* by comparing himself to a carpenter. First the craftsman establishes the shape and proportions of the whole structure, using mathematical guidelines, and only then does he set to work on the details:

> Ja tun ich als ein wercman, der sin winkelmaz
> ane unterlaz
> zu sinen werken richtet,
> uz der fuge tichtet
> die höhe und lenge: wit und breit,   alse ist ez geschichtet;
> und swenne er hat daz winkelrecht   nach sinem willen gezirket,
> Darnach er danne wirket, als man wirken kan.

$$(V.13.1-7)$$

8. For further discussion, see Commentary, strophe 19.   9. März, *Frauenlobs Marienleich*, 73–76.

["Indeed, I act like a workman who guides his work with his carpenter's square without interruption. By his skill he shapes its height and length, as wide and broad as he means to structure it; and once he has encompassed it at right angles according to his desire, then he works on it as best he can."]

Following this method, Frauenlob presumably determined the overall proportions of his *leich*—the musical *cursus* structure and the numerological symmetries—before designing the pattern of each strophe.

PROSODY

The *Marienleich* is both heterostrophic and heterometric; that is, each strophe is unlike any other, and within each strophe the lines may differ widely in length and rhythm. Most regular verse in English is isometric, but some of the great technical innovators of the nineteenth and twentieth centuries, especially those influenced by classical or medieval poetry, experimented with forms reminiscent of Frauenlob's. A few well-known English examples may help the anglophone reader to appreciate this largely unfamiliar prosody. In "The Shield of Achilles," W. H. Auden intermingled trimeter with pentameter stanzas to portray contrasting visions of peace and war. Dylan Thomas's "Fern Hill" employs a lilting mixed stanza that, like Frauenlob's stophes, combines long pentameter and hexameter lines with short ones in trimeter and tetrameter. In "Goblin Market," Christina Rossetti used heterostrophic stanzas of varying lengths and rhyme schemes, with lines that are also of unequal length:

Laura turned cold as stone	(Trimeter)
To find her sister heard that cry alone,	(Pentameter)
That goblin cry,	(Dimeter)
"Come buy our fruits, come buy."	(Trimeter)
Must she then buy no more such dainty fruit?	(Pentameter)
Must she no more such succous pasture find,	(Pentameter)
Gone deaf and blind?[10]	(Dimeter)

But the most spectacular example of heterometric verse in English is undoubtedly the "sprung rhythm" of Gerard Manley Hopkins, a poet whom Frauenlob would have admired. Here is the penultimate stanza of "The Wreck of the Deutschland," with its heavy stresses, alliterations, and oscillating rhythms that culminate in a thunderous hexameter:

10. Christina Rossetti, "Goblin Market," lines 253–59, in *Complete Poems*, ed. R. W. Crump (London: Penguin, 2001), 11–12.

> Now burn, new born to the world,
> Double-naturèd name,
> The heaven-flung, heart-fleshed, maiden-furled
> Miracle-in-Mary-of-flame,
> Mid-numberèd he in three of the thunder-throne!
> Not a dooms-day dazzle in his coming nor dark as he came;
> Kind, but royally reclaiming his own;
> A released shower, let flash to the shire, not a lightning of fire hard-hurled.[11]

Unlike these English poets, who wrote for the eye as well as the ear, Frauenlob could not have expected his audience to see his compositions on the page—and even if they had, they would have seen them written in unbroken lines, indistinguishable from prose, to save parchment. Instead, he composed his verse to be sung, and in this case the music makes a crucial difference to the prosody. If read apart from his melodic lines, Frauenlob's text often sounds iambic because many of his verses begin with a weak syllable (anacrusis or *Auftakt*). For musical reasons, however, this syllable is lengthened and counts as a foot or bar unto itself, so that every sung line begins with a stress. The consequences for prosody are best explained by none other than G. M. Hopkins, in the author's preface to his own collected poems:

> For purposes of scanning it is a great convenience to follow the example of music and take the stress always first, as the accent or the chief accent always comes first in a musical bar. If this is done there will be in common English verse only two possible feet—the so-called accentual Trochee and Dactyl, and correspondingly only two possible uniform rhythms, the so-called Trochaic and Dactylic. But they may be mixed and then what the Greeks called a Logaoedic Rhythm arises. . . . Sprung Rhythm, as used in this book, is measured by feet of from one to four syllables. . . . It has one stress, which falls on the only syllable, if there is only one, or, if there are more, then scanning as above, on the first, and so gives rise to four sorts of feet, a monosyllable and the so-called accentual Trochee, Dactyl, and the First Paeon [with more than two weak syllables following the stress]. . . . nominally the feet are mixed and any one may follow any other. . . . In Sprung Rhythm, as in logaoedic rhythm generally, the feet are assumed to be equally long or strong and their seeming inequality is made up by pause or stressing.[12]

This turns out to be a fairly precise description of Frauenlob's rhythms, which are basically trochaic with an intermixture of monosyllabic feet and (rarely) dactyls, and the first syllable in every line is stressed. In the examples that follow, I have based my scansion on the bars or *tactus*

11. Gerard Manley Hopkins, "The Wreck of the Deutschland," stanza 34, in *The Poems of Gerard Manley Hopkins*, 4th ed., ed. W. H. Gardner and N. H. MacKenzie (London: Oxford University Press, 1967), 62.

12. Hopkins, "Author's Preface," in *Poems*, 45–48.

as they appear in Karl Bertau's transcription of the music (facing Karl Stackmann's text) in the Göttingen edition. Where the scansion appears counterintuitive, then, it is for musical reasons.

Frauenlob's strophic patterns show an almost bewildering variety, which is belied by the simplicity of the first half-strophe. The sign "/" indicates the division of *tactus*:

> Ei, / ich sach / in dem / trone
> ein / vrouwen, / die was / swanger.
> die / trug ein / wunder- / krone
> vor / miner / ougen / anger.
>
> (1.1–4)

We can diagram this quatrain with the simple formula:

> 4' 4' 4' 4'
> a b a b

where the 4 denotes the number of *tactus* (feet or bars) per line, the sign ' marks a feminine ending, and the letters abab denote the rhyme scheme.[13] This four-bar (or tetrameter) line sets a basic metrical norm, though it is usually observed in the breach: the line can be shrunk to two bars or expanded to six, eight, or even ten. Lines of three, five, and seven bars also occur, though less frequently.

Strophe 4 reveals a more complex pattern, making use of caesuras (marked by the sign ‖) with Frauenlob's characteristically jagged alternation of long and short lines:

> Nu / lougen / nicht ‖ durch / icht ‖ der / schicht, ‖ daz / dich / ‖ sunder- / lich
> der / künig in / sinen / keler / furte.
> dich / rurte
> sin / grüzen.
> 5 wie / nu, ver / meit, hat / ir iuch / wol ver- / sunnen?
> wir / gunnen
> der / wunnen
> iu / wol, daz / ir den / win / habt ge- / trunken
> [pause] mit der / milch ‖ so / süzen.
>
> (4.1–9)

The formal scheme of this strophe is indicated by the following diagram, with f' and g' denoting rhymes across the two halves of the strophe:

13. My diagrams of prosody are based on the method used by Horst Brunner in "Die Spruchtöne Frauenlobs."

2‖1‖1‖1‖3 5' 2' 2' 6' 2' 2' 6' 2‖1'
a ⁻a ⁻a ⁻b ⁻b c c d e e e f' g'⁻d

Here the first, long line consists of eight feet marked by four caesuras and five internal rhymes.[14] The short lines 3, 4, 6, and 7 are all sung to the same three-note tune but distinguished by their rhymes: line 3 points backward (*rurte / furte*), line 4 anticipates the end of the strophe (*grüzen / süzen*), and lines 6 and 7 form a couplet (*gunnen / wunnen*) echoing line 5 (*versunnen*). Line 8 rhymes only with its counterpart in the second half-strophe (*getrunken / durchsunken*), as does the first half of line 9 (*milch / drilch*).

Two contrasting examples of Frauenlob's metrical virtuosity can be seen in strophes 6 and 12. Strophe 6 uses the ornament of monorhyme: nine successive lines rhyme on the same syllable without repetition, while the concluding lines rhyme across the two halves of the strophe (*geiste / meiste*). Within Frauenlob's musical *cursus* structure, strophe 6 is composed in the third plagal or Hypolydian mode. This mode does not return until strophe 14 in the second *cursus,* and with it the same closing rhymes also recur, but modified and in reverse order (*meister / geister*).[15] These echoes are among the many subtle devices the poet-composer uses to achieve harmony within complexity.

Strophe 12, for which the melody is lost,[16] reveals one of the most elaborate rhyme schemes in the piece.

    Ich / binz ein / zucker⁻ / süzer / brunne
    des / lebens / und der / bernden / wunne.
    ich / binz ein / spiegel / der vil / klaren / reine⁻ / keit,
    da / got von / erst sich / inne er⁻ / sach.
  5 Ich / was mit / im, do / er ent⁻ / warf gar / alle / schepfe⁻ / nunge,
    er / sach mich / stetes / an in / siner / ewic⁻ / lichen / ger.
    wie / rechte / wol ich / tet im / in den / ougen,
    ich / zarter, / wolge⁻ / muter / rosen⁻ / garte!
    komt / alle zu / mir, / die min / gern.
 1 0 Ich / wil, ich / kan, ich / muz ge⁻ / wern.
    ich / binz der / lebende / leite⁻ / stern,
    des / nieman / sol noch / mag en⁻ / bern.
    min / mut / ‖   gut   / ‖ frut   / ‖ tut.
    ich / binz die / stimme, / do der / alte / leo / lut
 1 5 die / sinen / kint uf / von des / alten / todes / flut.

1 4. The a and b syllables (*nicht* and *dich*) are considered not off-rhymes but two distinct rhyming sounds, as indicated by their counterparts (*wol* and *munt*) in strophe 4b.

1 5. Shields, "Zum melodischen Aufbau," 1 2 2.

1 6. The melody of the *Marienleich* has been reassembled from multiple manuscript sources, all of them fragmentary. Strophe 1 2, with parts of strophes 1 1 and 1 3, falls into a gap not covered by any of the extant musical manuscripts. The music sung by Sequentia was reconstructed by the ensemble on the basis of the *cursus* pattern and other melodic motifs and formulas characteristic of the piece.

Ich / binz die / glut,
da / der / alte / fenix / inne / sich er- / jungen / wolte.
ich / binz des / edel- / en / tiuren / peli- / kanes / blut
und / han daz / allez / wol be- / hut. (1 2.1–1 9)

Two lines employ the ornament of "chain rhyme" in which a series of adjacent words are rhymed: *min mut gut frut tut* (1 2.1 3) with its counterpart in 1 2b, *min schar gar clar var* (1 2.3 2). In contrast, lines 3–8 of strophe 1 2a appear to be unrhymed, until we hear the sequence of rhymes echoing them in 1 2b, lines 2 2–2 7. The overall pattern is as follows:

5' 5' 7 5 8' 8 6' 6' 5 5 5 5 2‖1‖1‖1 7 7 3 8' 8 5
a a b' c' d' e' f' g' h h h h i i i i i i i j' i i

Here ten different rhyme sounds are used in a half-strophe of nineteen lines: the a-rhyme is heard twice, the h-rhyme four times, and the i-rhyme as many as nine times (including internal rhymes), while the remaining seven rhyme syllables link the two parallel halves of the strophe. The line lengths vary from three to eight feet, with eight distinct verse types (masculine and feminine endings count as separate types). The frequency of rhyme—within single lines, within the half-strophe, and across the strophic pair—gives an impression of sonic unity, while the extremely heterometric verse forms create a counterbalancing dissonance, making the meter unpredictable and continually surprising.[17] To put it differently, the lines within a strophe may be linked in any of three ways—by rhyme, by identical verse type, and by melodic repetition. The formal linkages created by these means sometimes coincide and sometimes diverge, heightening the impression of extraordinarily intricate verse.

Once again, the qualities of the *Marienleich* can be set in sharp relief by comparison with *Die goldene Schmiede*, for the long list of Frauenlob's borrowings makes these two closely related poems sound much more similar than they are. In fact, the differences between the poets' imagistic techniques are mirrored by an equally strong contrast in their formal choices (see the excerpts from Konrad on pp. 56 and 1 1 3–1 4, above). *Die goldene Schmiede*, a poem meant for recitation or private reading rather than singing, is written in octosyllabic rhymed couplets (give or take a syllable or two), adapting the French verse form already used with such skill by Hartmann von Aue and Gottfried von Strassburg. Konrad's elegant couplets, like his neatly dovetailed allegorical images, give his work great clarity and fluency.[18] By contrast, Frauenlob's ferociously acrobatic verse matches his web of teasingly enigmatic allusions. The *leich* is forever calling attention to its

17. According to Shields, "Zum melodischen Aufbau," the music of the *leich* reveals a similar interplay between the recurrence of melodic formulas across tonally related strophes and a countervailing tendency toward independence, which gives the piece as a whole a "through-composed" aura.

18. Konrad, of course, was a versatile poet who also composed *leichs* and *Sprüche*. I am comparing the *Marienleich* only with *Die goldene Schmiede*, not with Konrad's poetry in general.

own technique; it does not yield its secrets easily, but it demands concentrated study. In short, it is the kind of piece that has always repelled readers who prefer an aesthetic of transparency, spontaneity, or understatement, while prompting its admirers to either futile imitation or academic commentary—both temptations to which the present volume succumbs.

GEBLÜMTER STIL

This observation brings us back to the *geblümter Stil,* a term that has become almost as contested in German literary criticism as *amour courtois* is in French. Gert Hübner, in the most comprehensive study of the mode to date, characterizes it as a feature less of specific authors, epochs, or genres than of a particular *function,* namely, praise.[19] The *blüemen* correspond in part to Latin *flores rhetorici,* verbal ornaments of any kind, but with a special emphasis on hyperbole. The object of praise may be an epic hero, a beloved lady, a patron, or—most especially—the Virgin; but here we must demur, for in the eyes of Konrad, Frauenlob, and other medieval poets, hyperbole directed toward God or Mary would be by definition impossible since their worth exceeds all human capacity. In traditional *Marienlob,* therefore, praise must be offset by the topoi of ineffability on the one hand and poetic modesty on the other, lest the singer offend by claiming that he has extolled the incomparable Virgin as she deserves.[20]

Frauenlob, however, finds a novel way to elude this paradox by placing the praise in Mary's own mouth, making the conventional modesty preface both unnecessary and impossible. "Maria blümt ihr eigenes Lob": she adorns her own praises.[21] Thus the *leich* contains only two overt statements of artistic self-consciousness. In the first, the poet-seer merely expresses his goal of superlative praise: "min munt / dich mizzet uf daz beste und uf daz meiste" ("My speech measures you above the best and greatest," 6.19–20). In the second, disconcertingly, he interrupts the Lady's own account of her love-idyll to say:

> swie züchtig stolzer meide rum ich schalle,
> doch hoffe ich, daz ez ieman missevalle.
>
> (11.15–16)

[No matter how irreproachably I sing the proud Maid's praise,
I hope that it will not displease anyone.]

Although Stackmann ascribes this parenthetical speech to Mary herself,[22] it seems more likely to be an apologia on Frauenlob's part. The Virgin has, after all, just uttered her bold *ich slief bi drin*

---

19. Hübner, *Lobblumen,* 4–6.
20. Schnyder, "Eine Poetik des Marienlobs."

21. Hübner, *Lobblumen,* 191, 200.
22. Stackmann and Haustein, *Wörterbuch,* 304 (*schallen*).

("I slept with Three," 11.8), so one might say that *zucht*—self-restraint or modesty—is not the most obvious feature of her speech. Further, although *stolz* can have the connotations of "magnificent" and "splendid," its primary meaning is "proud," so it is very far from being a standard epithet for God's lowly handmaid (Luke 1:38, 48). It seems, therefore, that Frauenlob is here acknowledging the audacity of his nontraditional praise in a belated *captatio benevolentiae*.

The most frequently discussed aspects of *geblümter Stil* in this poem are its eroticism, aestheticism, and hermeticism. Of the first I have already spoken. Although any poem in the Song of Songs tradition is bound to be erotic, I have argued that Frauenlob's unusual brand of "crossover" poetry, his seamless fusion of the sacred and the sensual, is a matter not so much of style as of religious conviction and sensibility. But concerning the other two, more needs to be said. Some critics have seen Frauenlob as anticipating the nineteenth-century aesthetic of "art for art's sake," while others have characterized him as a "baroque" or "mannerist" poet.[23] Jörg Schaefer, adopting E. R. Curtius's distinction between classicism and mannerism, represented Walther as a prime specimen of the first, Frauenlob of the second. The picture he paints is not a flattering one: Schaefer finds in Frauenlob's art an odd mix of the rigid and the hectic, the monotonous and the sensational—or, at best, a difficult beauty purchased at the price of all balance.[24] This evaluation stands in the long tradition of Ludwig Pfannmüller, whose 1913 edition of the *Marienleich* deplored the "bizarre, abstruse, often laughable erudition" with which Frauenlob adorns his heroine, even as his futile attempts at *hohe Minne* drag her through the basest mud of *niedere Minne*.[25]

As we saw in Chapter 1, Frauenlob was controversial from the moment he appeared on the scene. Hermann Damen, Regenbogen, and other anonymous critics already found much to ridicule in a style that struck them as pretentious and needlessly opaque. Even Konrad von Würzburg, whom I have presented as a model of clarity beside Frauenlob, provoked similar critiques. Konrad was probably the target of this satirical passage from *Der Renner* by Hugo von Trimberg (ca. 1230–ca. 1315), another poet from the region of Würzburg. Even though Hugo was a schoolteacher and the author of several Latin works, he reacted vigorously against displays of erudition in German verse:

Got minnet slehte einveltikeit,   God loves plain simplicity—
Der wênic ist in der kristenheit.   Of which there is little in Christendom.
Swer gerne swenden wölle sîn hirne,   He who would gladly strain his brain
Daz er tiefiu wort ûz kirne   To churn deep words out of it
Und durch breche tiefen sin,   And force profound thoughts

---

23. Stackmann, "Bild und Bedeutung," 459–60; Köbele, *Frauenlobs Lieder*, 229–40. Stackmann is skeptical about the mannerist label, while Köbele rejects the characterization of Frauenlob as an apostle of *l'art pour l'art*. See also Chapter 5, below.

24. Jörg Schaefer, *Walther von der Vogelweide und Frauenlob: Beispiele klassischer und manieristischer Lyrik im Mittelalter* (Tübingen: Niemeyer, 1966), 327–29.

25. Pfannmüller, *Frauenlobs Marienleich*, 27.

| Der neme hie lop vür dort gewin | May win praise here, but gets nothing there, |
| Und smelze sin hirne in sorgen tegel.[26] | And melts his brain in the crucible of care. |

Hugo's critique of the nascent *geblümter Stil* and Pfannmüller's attack on its ripest fruit have one point in common: both come out in favor of "plain simplicity" over "abstruse erudition," though they themselves were erudite men. In fact, their distaste reacts less to erudition as such than to its jarring presence where they felt it did not belong—in vernacular poetry. By Frauen- lob's time, the German language already had a rich heritage of lyric, epic, and romance. But it had as yet no tradition of learned or philosophical writing, much less a defense of "vernacular eloquence," such as Dante's *De vulgari eloquentia* (which, tellingly, he had to write in Latin, as if to prove that he could). The distinction between Latin and vernacular was one that held true, *mutatis mutandis,* all over Europe: Latin was "the tongue of the fathers," suitable for high cul- ture, theology, philosophy, and humanistic verse, while the "mother tongue" was an oral lan- guage, capable of refinements yet valued because its "plain simplicity" made it accessible to all. Recent work in Middle English, based on the study of literary prefaces to texts in all genres, has shown that whether the vernacular was praised or damned, it was understood to be simple, "common," and "natural." Middle English in all its roughness could be contrasted with either the polished sophistication or the pretentious affectation of Latin; it was the inherently base metal that could be transmuted to alchemical gold. As the mother tongue (a phrase also used by Dante), the vernacular was "a language with immediate access to people's feelings and easily comprehensible—as Latin is not, even to those who can understand it." For this reason, it could also "*signify* clarity and open access and do so even in texts whose projected audience [was] rel- atively narrow."[27]

If a similar aesthetic prevailed in Germanic lands—and the contemporary critiques of Frauenlob suggest that it did—then it is easy to see why his new ideal of vernacular *meister- schaft* aroused such opposition. The novel poetics of Konrad von Würzburg and (*a fortiori*) Frauenlob challenged a linguistic distinction that made sense to Latin and German speakers alike, insofar as these two mavericks aimed to create in German the kind of ostentatiously learned poetry (*tiefiu wort, tiefen sin*) that many believed only Latin could support. In a poetic cul- ture based on oral performance, such a distinction was all the more necessary. Whatever else it does, the *Marienleich* does not signify—or afford—clarity and open access. "Tolmetsche, ver- nimz!" mocks Regenbogen. "Wilt du uns tiutsch vertolken?" ("Interpreter, listen! Will you

26. Hugo von Trimberg, *Der Renner,* lines 23501–7, ed. Gustav Ehrismann, 4 vols. (Tübingen: Litterarischer Verein, 1908–11), 3:269. See also Stackmann, "Bild und Bedeutung," 450–51.

27. Ruth Evans, Andrew Taylor, Nicholas Watson, and Joce- lyn Wogan-Browne, "The Notion of Vernacular Theory," in *The*

Idea of the Vernacular: An Anthology of Middle English Literary Theory, 1280–1520, ed. Wogan-Browne et al. (The Pennsylvania State University Press, 1999), 314–30; quotations, p. 325.

translate that into German for us?" V.117G.2–3). Frauenlob's exotic German bewilders the casual or unprepared listener while beckoning to an elite, whether the learned King Wenceslas II and his courtiers, the archbishop of Mainz and his clerics, or some other audience of connoisseurs. I suspect there were few women among them. Yet the project of forging a learned idiom in the vernacular could be fraught with peril on many fronts. While Frauenlob was busy cultivating an elite with his hermetic style, his contemporary, Meister Eckhart, succeeded all too well in making Latin theological learning accessible to the masses. Women flocked to hear his German preaching, much to the dismay of more conservative clergy; and it was on the basis of his vernacular sermons, not his Latin ones, that the mystic was charged with heresy. It is interesting that Eckhartian language is echoed at a few points in the *Marienleich,* notably the distinction between *gotheit* and *got* (that is, *divinitas* and *deus*) in strophe 12b.

Frauenlob's vaunted difficulties can be grouped under two headings. First, there are those of the matter itself. As Hübner observes, the poet's hermeticism—his choice of learned and arcane subject matter—is an issue distinct from his style, for the *geblümter Stil* as such is always ornate but need not always be difficult.[28] This hermeticism is a willed and self-conscious choice. No listener in Frauenlob's own day—and no reader now—can comprehend the German terms he devised for the concepts of Aristotelian logic (strophe 16a) unless he or she first understands the Latin categories. Strophe 16b requires some knowledge of grammar, rhetoric, and dialectic; 17a of metaphysics (critics are still baffled by its mixture of Platonic and Aristotelian elements); 17b of the technical terms of astronomy; 18a of music theory; and 20 of gems and their properties. Strophe 14 proposes the riddling allegory of a tailor, two garments, and a "mirror-vessel" (perhaps alchemical) without explanation, while 19a assumes familiarity with symbolic numbers and arithmetical sequences. In 9b, 11b, and 12a, animal symbolism from the *Physiologus* tradition is evoked much more succinctly and elusively than is normal. Strophe 11b features a teasing allusion to the Grail myth, and 12b presents Mary and Christ under the still-mysterious guise of Adelheit and Engelmar. Underlying all these more or less esoteric allusions is the pervasive presence of the Bible. Without a thorough acquaintance with the Song of Songs and related texts from the Marian liturgy, the entire piece will remain opaque.

A second and stylistically more interesting source of difficulty is the language itself. Frauenlob's syntax is sometimes tangled to meet the demands of his rhyme schemes, and he was inordinately fond of the grammatical construction linguists call "genitive paraphrase" (*Genitivumschreibung*), in which a noun in the genitive case precedes the noun on which it depends:

sunder valles wan (6.4): "with no intention of fall[ing]"
der grundelosen güte ein endelose mugend (13.27): "an infinite potentiality of unfathomable
    goodness" (Eckhart again!)

28. Hübner, *Lobblumen,* 189–201.

der ersten sache kint (16.1): "child of the First Cause" (Aristotelian)
des herten vluches adamas (20.17): "the diamond of the hard curse" (with pun on Adam /
   adamant)

Also characteristic is Frauenlob's penchant for neologisms—the *tiefiu wort* that bothered such critics as Hugo von Trimberg. Some of these are intriguing compounds: the *lewenberge*, or "lion-mountain," of the Song of Songs (3.11 and Cant. 4:8); the Virgin's hips as golden clasps purified by fire (*viurguldin fürspan*, 5.12); and Mary as the Father's mother (*vatermuter*), just as God is the father of Mary's mother (*mutervater*, 12.34). Christ is represented as *der jungalte*, "the Young-Old One" (7.5), and "Engelmar," a personal name probably derived from "angel's tidings" (12.38).

The poet was especially partial to verbs intensified with *durch*, a prefix he used to convey the all-pervading grace of God or Mary. The Virgin *durchschönet* all the thrones of heaven (beautifies them through and through with her own beauty, 8.4); the sweet taste of balsam *durchgümet* (pierces to the heart's palate) anyone who utters her name (10.9); as *forma formarum* or *anima mundi*, Maria/Sophia eternally *durchblümet* (blossoms always and everywhere, 17.15); divinized, she is *durchswummen* (suffused through and through, like a fish in water) with the power of the Godhead (20.4). The last of these coinages recalls Mechthild's comparison of the soul plunged into the divine fire to a fish in its native sea.[29] In all these verbs, the *durch-* prefix underlines a theological tenet central to the *leich*: the universal immanence, through the feminine Divine, of the transcendent Godhead.

Frauenlob also liked to form verbs from other parts of speech, such as nouns and adjectives. The Virgin and her divine Lover *merzen, meien, lenzen* (19.25): they behave like March, like May, like the spring. In taking on finite *qualitas* through the Incarnation, the three divine Persons are "whiched": *gewelchet sint die dri* (16.2–3). In a freshly coined adjective, the distressed heart is *jachandine*, like a jacinth (20.22)—a semi-opaque gem until it is held up to the sunlight, where it "catches fire" like a heart newly kindled by love. Remarkably, two more jewels transformed into verbs describe the courtship of the holy couple: after God's *topasieren* ("topazing") came to Mary in pure desire, she modestly *calcedonete* ("chalcedoned") to him (20.23–24). Quirky as this passage is, it too serves a theological function, for the second idiosyncratic verb evokes not only the gem called chalcedony but also the fifth-century Council of Chalcedon, at which the two natures of Christ were formally defined. Mary's *caldedonete* leads into the final lines of the *Marienleich*, where she ends her long address by proclaiming her own two natures: *ich menschlich gotlich wart* ("I, human, became divine," 20.30).[30] Precious to the end, the *leich* draws attention to a last doctrinal surprise with a final linguistic one.

In sum, the *Marienleich* is in all respects an experimental piece, very nearly *sui generis*. As Burghart Wachinger remarks, Frauenlob "condenses images from biblical and other traditions,

29. Mechthild, *Das fliessende Licht*, 1.44, ed. Vollmann-Profe, 62.   30. For fuller discussion, see Commentary, strophe 20.

combines them on the one hand to the point of incomprehensibility, and heightens them on the other to a new, almost aggressive sensuality."[31] Offering a calculated provocation to poetic convention as to orthodox piety, he opened himself to—and received—scathing criticism on both fronts, lasting from his day to ours. But to those who welcomed the challenge of this exceptional work, it offered endless possibilities for imitation and amazement. I turn in the next chapter to the checkered history of its reception.

31. Wachinger, "Frauenlobs Cantica canticorum," 43.

5

RECEPTION AND INFLUENCE

Paradoxically, the same factors that make it so difficult to assess Frauenlob's oeuvre bear witness to his profound and lasting influence. Despite the herculean labors of Karl Stackmann and his predecessor, Helmuth Thomas (who died in 1957 without completing the edition on which he had worked for years), it is still impossible to say with certainty which *Sprüche* are Frauenlob's and which were produced by his disciples and admirers.[1] If imitation is the sincerest form of flattery, it is also the most frustrating to a textual editor. Nonetheless, a bewildering array of manuscripts and works by other writers, known and anonymous, testify to the stellar reputation Frauenlob enjoyed for two centuries after his death. In this chapter I shall pay particular attention to the fourteenth-century evidence, looking more briefly at his influence on the fifteenth-century meistersingers. I shall also consider the

---

1. Karl Stackmann, "Frauenlob (Heinrich von Meissen)— eine Bilanz," in Karl Stackmann and Jens Haustein, eds., *Frauenlob,* *Heinrich von Mügeln und ihre Nachfolger* (Göttingen: Wallstein, 2002), 34–89, at 37.

afterlife of the *Marienleich*'s most remarkable features, such as its linkage of Mary with the seven arts, its proclamation of her double nature, and its representation of the Trinity as her "three lovers." Finally, I glance at Frauenlob's reception by the Romantics, the nineteenth-century collapse of his critical reputation, and the hesitant revival it has experienced in recent years.

THE EARLY MANUSCRIPTS AND THE LATIN *MARIENLEICH*

Any study of a medieval writer's influence must begin with the manuscripts. In Frauenlob's case, these are too numerous to permit an account of every available witness. Stackmann's detailed discussion includes twenty-three principal manuscripts, ten fragments, and three lost manuscripts.[2] Over half the witnesses stem from the fourteenth century and the remainder from the fifteenth, with the latest dated circa 1470. All areas and dialects of the German-speaking world are represented, including the present-day Netherlands, Lower Saxony, the Rhineland, Franconia, Silesia, Bavaria, Prussia, Austria, Swabia, and Switzerland. Five anthologies are especially significant, conveying a sense of the varied contexts in which posterity saw fit to enshrine the master's work. In order of age, these are the Manesse Codex (C) from circa 1300–1340, whose illustrations we have already considered; the mid-fourteenth-century Jena Liederhandschrift (J); the Vienna Leichhandschrift (W), also from the fourteenth century; the Weimar Frauenlob manuscript (F), dated circa 1455–75; and the Colmar manuscript (t) compiled by the meistersingers of Mainz around 1470.

The Manesse Codex (Heidelberg, Universitätsbibliothek Cod. pal. germ. 848) is probably the most famous of all medieval German manuscripts.[3] Compiled in Zurich under the patronage of Rüdiger Manesse, his son Johannes, and the local *Spruchdichter* Johannes Hadlaub, this enormous and lavish manuscript consists of 426 folios, featuring no less than 140 poets and 137 full-page illustrations. A collaborative and cross-generational production, it includes the work of at least six scribes and four artists. Although the bulk of the entries were completed around the year 1300, the editors left space for additions and sewed or stuck in many new leaves. The earlier poets are arranged hierarchically in order of social status, as in analogous French manuscripts, followed by about thirty later poets, including Frauenlob, added by 1340. Among the anthologized figures are *Spruchdichter* as well as minnesingers (including Frauenlob's patron, King Wenceslas of Bohemia). "Meister Heinrich Vrouwenlob" appears on fols. 399r through 404r, a few pages after Konrad von Würzburg and just before Friedrich von Sonnenburg. It is interesting that the amount of space allotted to each poet in this fourteenth-century canon more

2. My account is drawn from GA 1:20–168 and from the summary in Stackmann, "Frauenlob," *Verfasserlexikon*, 869–70.

3. There is a complete, high-resolution facsimile on the internet at http://digi.ub.uni-heidelberg.de/cpg848. For discussions of the manuscript, see Jammers, *Königliche Liederbuch*; Sayce, *Medieval German Lyric*, 51–73; *Codex Manesse: Katalog*; and Frühmorgen-Voss, "Bildtypen."

or less closely mirrors the level of critical prestige he still enjoys. With eleven pages to his name, Frauenlob ranks quite high. Ahead of him stand Walther von der Vogelweide with 43 pages, Reinmar von Zweter with 30, Ulrich von Winterstetten (22 pages), Ulrich von Lichtenstein (21), Reinmar der Alte (21), the patron Hadlaub (20), Konrad von Würzburg (17), Neidhart (16), and Der Marner (12). Of these, all were minnesingers except for Konrad and Reinmar von Zweter, the two *Spruchdichter* whom Frauenlob himself most esteemed, with the patron Hadlaub and the influential Marner. Frauenlob's archenemy, Regenbogen, gets only a portrait and a single text page.

If we accept the consensus that Frauenlob is the debating partner shown in Regenbogen's portrait (fig. 2), he may be the only poet in the manuscript who is visually depicted twice. On the reverse of his *Singschule* illustration (fig. 1), his canon begins with a complete, untitled text of the *Marienleich*. Around its initial E an artist has drawn a charming indication of the poem's subject (fig. 3): Mary, holding the Christ Child, appears above the initial as *mulier amicta sole* with the moon beneath her feet, while below, the poet-seer stands gazing with his hand to his eyes, to show that he is seeing a vision. These figures illustrate the first strophe of the *leich*: "ey, ich sach in dem trone / eine vrowen." The full composition fills nine columns without music, each strophe marked off by a blue decorated initial. The pages reveal signs of considerable wear, rendering parts of the text barely legible. Following the *Marienleich* are thirty more strophes ascribed to Frauenlob, including another Marian poem, the notorious boast of his prowess with counterattacks (ascribed in the margins to Regenbogen), and further poems in the Langer Ton, the Kurzer Ton, and the Grüner Ton. After these we find five blank pages, as if the compilers had hoped to insert more texts by Frauenlob but were unable to find them. Produced two decades at most after the composer's death, his entry in the Manesse Codex reveals several key elements of his reputation already in place: the tradition of his *Singschule*, the prestige of the *Marienleich*, and his celebrated *Sängerkrieg* with Regenbogen, who was remembered for little else. In fact, the oldest canon of the meistersingers' "twelve old masters" (ca. 1340) includes a commemorative line:

> Der regenboge den vrouwenlop bestunt gelicher wer.[4]
> Regenbogen gave Frauenlob as good as he got!

The Jena manuscript (Jena, Universitätsbibliothek, Ms. El. f. 101) was completed before 1350, not long after the last entries in the Manesse Codex.[5] Unlike the famous Swiss production, this sumptuous manuscript from northern Germany contains almost no minnesang, only *Spruchdichtung*, testifying to more contemporary tastes. Prepared for a noble patron, possibly

---

4. Lupold Hornburg, catalogue strophe from the *Hausbuch* of Michael de Leone; cited in Henkel, "Die zwölf alten Meister," 378.

5. See the facsimile *Die Jenaer Liederhandschrift*, ed. Helmut Tervooren and Ulrich Müller (Göppingen: A. Kümmerle, 1972).

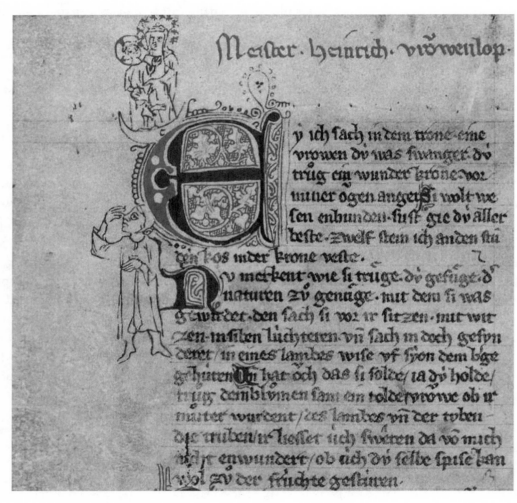

FIG. 3   Initial "E" with drawing of Virgin and seer. Codex Manesse, CPG 848, fol. 399v

Duke Rudolf I of Saxony (1298–1356), J is a crucial source for musicologists, since it is the most important collection of *Sangsprüche* to include their melodies. It is interesting to note that the pieces are arranged not by author but by *Ton,* that is, by strophic form and melody, with pieces in the borrowed *Töne* of an older composer listed after that poet's original canon. Among the twenty-six named composers are Bruder Werner, Wild Alexander, Friedrich von Sonnenburg, Hermann Damen, Konrad von Würzburg, Kelin, Rubin, Spervogel, Der Meissner, Der Unverzagte, Singuf, and Rumelant, along with the fictional poetic competition known as the *Wartburgkrieg.* Frauenlob and another of his patrons, Prince Wizlav of Rügen (d. 1325), are the most recent poets to be included. This anthology transmits more than eighty Frauenlob strophes in the Langer Ton, Flugton, Grüner Ton, and Zarter Ton, but lacks the *Marienleich.*

In contrast, the unusual Vienna Leichhandschrift (Vienna, Österreichische Nationalbibliothek Cod. Vind. 2701) is specially devoted to the *leich* as a genre.[6] Written in the Silesian dialect, this manuscript of unknown provenance consists of fifty folios in three fascicles by different scribes, all created in the fourteenth century and probably bound together not long after their production. They may indeed have been compiled as part of a common project. Unfortunately, the manuscript is damaged and its first leaf is missing, so it contains only strophes 14 through 20 of the *Marienleich* (with music), ending with the colophon "Expliciunt cantica canticorum vrowenlobiz." Figure 4 illustrates the text and neumes of strophe 14a from this manuscript. The *leich* is followed by a fragmentary Latin translation of the piece ("latinum super cantica canticorum"), which breaks off in the middle of strophe 12a so that, in this manuscript at least, there is no overlap between the German and the Latin texts. The second fascicle of W contains Reinmar von Zweter's *Leich,* which Frauenlob knew and admired, as well as *Sprüche* by both poets. In the third fascicle are the *Kreuzleich* and the *Minneleich* (both without attribution), a *leich* by Wild Alexander, and a few more strophic poems.

We must say more about the Latin *Marienleich,* for this is one of the most astonishing lyrical translations produced anywhere in medieval Europe.[7] It was far more common for texts to be translated from Latin into the vernacular than vice versa, although other important German works—including Mechthild von Magdeburg's *Flowing Light of the Godhead*—also received the honor of Latin translations. In the mid-fourteenth century, to take another example, Henry Suso produced a much-revised and expanded Latin version of his own *Büchlein der ewigen Weisheit,* giving it the new title *Horologium Sapientiae.*[8] From the Latin this work was translated into nine other European vernaculars and still survives in many hundreds of manuscripts. In fact, it became the most widely read devotional text of the fourteenth century, known all the way from Sweden to Bohemia. Clearly, any author seeking a pan-European audience for a vernacular

6. Facsimile ed. Heinrich Rietsch, *Gesänge von Frauenlob, Reinmar von Zweter und Alexander* (Vienna, 1913; repr. Graz: Akademische Druck- und Verlagsanstalt, 1960).

7. Text in GA 1:284–90; see also Udo Kühne, "*Latinum super cantica canticorum:* Die lateinische Übertragung von Frauenlobs Marienleich," in Haustein and Steinmetz, ed., *Studien zu Frauenlob und Heinrich von Mügeln,* 1–14.

8. On this text and its influence, see Newman, *God and the Goddesses,* 206–22.

FIG. 4   Music from the *Marienleich*, strophe 14. Vienna, Österreichische Nationalbibliothek, Cod. 2701, fol. 2.

work would have done well to commission or produce a Latin version. But this can hardly have been the motivation for the Latin *Marienleich,* which is transmitted only in the W fragment. Instead, it seems that the translator was indulging in a purely aesthetic exercise of a high order. Lyric verse in general was seldom translated because its complex strophic forms are more difficult to reproduce than the rhyming couplets of epic or romance. The Latin *Marienleich,* however, is not only a translation, and a fairly accurate one at that. It is also a *contrafactum,* reproducing the fiendishly complex meters and rhyme schemes of the original so that it can be sung to the same melody. A few other Latin *contrafacta* to Middle High German strophes are known, but they are not normally translations and rarely appear in the same manuscripts as their originals.[9]

Here is the first strophe of the Latin *Marienleich* alongside the German:

Ey in superno trono	Ei, ich sach in dem trone
heram uidi pregnantem,	ein vrouwen, die was swanger.
stupor est cunctis, cono	die trug ein wunderkrone
aureolam gestantem.	vor miner ougen anger.
Hyans abonerari	Sie wolte wesen enbunden,
processit summe bona,	sust gie die allerbeste,
gemmas bis sex ut fari	zwelf steine ich zu den stunden
gestauit in corona.	kos in der krone veste.

Even these few lines suffice to reveal the quality of the whole. Not only are they metrically flawless, but they also show a remarkable facility for capturing the nuances of the original. *Heram* (*vrouwen*) means "Lady" as a title of address for a goddess, echoing the Greek name of Hera, wife of Zeus and queen of heaven. *Stupor est cunctis* ("to the amazement of all") replaces *vor miner ougen anger,* an analogous phrase expressing visionary wonder; while *abonerari* ("to be unburdened") is a freshly coined, precise equivalent for *wesen enbunden.* Vernacular courtly allusions elsewhere in the poem are replaced by appropriate biblical analogues in Latin. The translator shows a flair for Greek vocabulary, neologisms, and rare nonce words (*florizans, predulcorizans*). He refers to God as both *theos* and *Adonay*[10] and even—for the sake of rhyme and meter—uses the archaic genitive forms *mis* and *tis* in place of *mei* and *tui.* Although these forms could be learned from ancient grammars, such as Donatus's *Ars minor,* they were already archaic in classical Latin and formed no part of the normal working lexicon of medieval poets.

9. Kühne, "*Latinum*"; see also Christoph März, "Walthers Leich und das Carmen Buranum 60/60a: Überlegungen zu einer Kontrafaktur," in Cyril Edwards, Ernst Hellgardt, and Norbert Ott, eds., *Lied im deutschen Mittelalter: Überlieferung, Typen, Gebrauch. Chiemsee-Colloquium 1991* (Tübingen: Niemeyer, 1996), 43–56; Udo Kühne, "Deutsch und Latein als Sprachen der Lyrik in den 'Carmina Burana,'" *Beiträge zur Geschichte der deutschen Sprache und Literatur* 122 (2000), 57–73.

10. See Frauenlob's strophes XII.1–3 in the Goldener Ton, which use a variety of Greek and Hebrew names for God: *fürste Sabaoth, alpha et o, Adonai, Ischiros* (Almighty), *Tetragrammaton, Atanatos* (Immortal), *Messias, o Theos* (GA 1:538–39).

As the German text becomes more virtuosic, so too does the translation:

Contra na -	Nu merket,
ture iura	wie sie trüge,
uirgo pura	die gefüge,
en quem erat paritura	der naturen zu genüge:
quem ymmo quem gestauit	mit dem sie was gebürdet,
pre se uidit sedere, lucere	den sach sie vor ir sitzen mit witzen
in septem lucernis	in siben liuchteren
uidit ta-	und sach in
men diuisum	doch besundert
hunc agni sub figura	in eines lammes wise
florigero Syon in monte.	uf Sion, dem berge gehiuren.

Here the translator resorts to word division for the sake of meter, a device the meistersingers would sometimes use as they developed ever more complicated rhyme schemes. The Latin even seems to contradict the German text at one point by replacing *der naturen zu genüge* ("to satisfy nature") with its opposite, the stock phrase *contra nature iura* ("against the laws of nature"). But since the *leich* goes on to assert that the Virgin conceived *gein der naturen* ("against nature," 10.28), the translation does not so much contradict as simplify and clarify a paradox in the German.[11] Whoever the translator was, he possessed a profound understanding of the *Marienleich*, a store of arcane knowledge, lexical ingenuity, and amazing technical wizardry. It is hard to imagine who could have achieved this feat other than Frauenlob himself. Unless a more complete copy of the translation should materialize with an attribution, my conjecture cannot be proven—but it was last ventured by the poem's previous translator, A. E. Kroeger, in 1877.[12] If indeed Frauenlob was, like Suso, his own translator, he might have worked for his own pleasure, at the request of a patron, or even—why not?—on the dare of a fellow minstrel. In any case, this virtuoso version stands alongside a few of the *Carmina burana* as a rare monument to the learned, bilingual environment of high medieval German poetry.[13]

One lesser manuscript from this period is of interest for the company Frauenlob keeps. In Ms. L (Berlin, Stiftung Preussischer Kulturbesitz, Ms. germ. oct. 403), a collection of three fascicles from the early to mid-fourteenth century, the *Marienleich* finds itself sandwiched between a collection of sermons by the Franciscan Berthold von Regensburg and an allegory of mystical love, *Tochter Syon*, by his colleague Lamprecht. Berthold (d. 1272), an immensely successful preacher, was known for his scathing attacks on poet-minstrels, whom he denounced as "apostate

---

11. For fuller discussion, see Commentary, strophe 2.
12. Kroeger, trans., *Lay of Our Lady*, introduction.

13. März, "Walthers Leich," 55–56. März notes that Marner also composed in Latin as well as German.

devils"—even going so far as to claim that anyone who gave them money would have to answer to God at the Last Judgment for those sinful gifts.[14] The *Spruchdichter*, among them Frauenlob in the next generation, responded with polemics in kind. As Hannes Kästner explains, there was no love lost between mendicants and minstrels because the two groups stood in direct competition: the mendicant preachers were moral counselors compelled to attract notice with entertaining performances, while the minstrels were performers who sought to gain respectability by giving moral counsel, as both competed for alms from the same lords and burghers.[15] Lamprecht von Regensburg, a Franciscan of a different stripe, found his vocation as a spiritual director of nuns, whom he urged along the way of bridal mysticism with his divine romance, *Tochter Syon* (Daughter of Zion). This allegory, written around 1250, features a divinized Minne (also called Karitas) as matchmaker in a love affair between God and the soul and thus promotes the same conflation of erotic and spiritual love that we have seen in the *Marienleich*.[16] At some point in the fifteenth century, a book owner who happened to possess all three works decided that they belonged between the same set of covers.

FOURTEENTH-CENTURY WRITERS

Other fourteenth-century witnesses confirm Frauenlob's impact on the Latin as well as the German tradition. For instance, his enthusiastic reception of Alan of Lille sparked a wider interest in that twelfth-century author among the learned. In the early fourteenth century, while Frauenlob was still living, the Viennese physician Heinrich von Neustadt wrote *Von Gottes Zukunft* ("On the Advent of God"), a poem based on a Latin paraphrase of Alan called the *Compendium Anticlaudiani*.[17] That thirteenth-century Cistercian text not only abridges Alan's *Anticlaudianus* but also radically changes its meaning. In the original poem, Natura's quest to create a perfect man in collaboration with the Virtues is a secular, humanistic project, whereas in the *Compendium* it becomes an allegory of the Incarnation, as it is for Heinrich von Neustadt. *Gottes Zukunft* concerns us here because it contains the earliest known citation of the *Marienleich*: Heinrich borrows Frauenlob's designation of Christ as "Engelmar" (12.38).[18] Unfortunately, we cannot

14. Dobozy, *Re-Membering the Present*, 116–17.

15. Hannes Kästner, "'Sermo Vulgaris' oder 'Hövischer Sanc': Der Wettstreit zwischen Mendikantenpredigern und Wanderdichtern um die Gunst des Laienpublikums und seine Folgen für die mittelhochdeutsche Sangspruchdichtung des 13. Jahrhunderts (Am Beispiel Bertholds von Regensburg und Friedrichs von Sonnenburg)," in Michael Schilling and Peter Strohschneider, eds., *Wechselspiele, Kommunikationsformen und Gattungsinterferenzen mittelhochdeutscher Lyrik* (Heidelberg: Carl Winter, 1996), 209–43. See also Dobozy, *Re-Membering the Present*, 227–38.

16. On Lamprecht's work, see Keller, *My Secret Is Mine*, 112–15 and passim.

17. Peter Ochsenbein, ed., "Das *Compendium Anticlaudiani*," *Zeitschrift für deutsches Altertum und deutsche Literatur* 98 (1969): 80–109; Christel Meier, "Die Rezeption des *Anticlaudianus* Alans von Lille in Textkommentierung und Illustration," in Christel Meier and Uwe Ruberg, eds., *Text und Bild: Aspekte des Zusammenwirkens zweier Künste in Mittelalter und früher Neuzeit* (Wiesbaden: Reichert, 1980), 408–549.

18. Heinrich von Neustadt, *Gottes Zukunft*, 2280, ed. Samuel Singer (Berlin: Weidmann, 1906), 365.

date *Gottes Zukunft*; if we could, we would have a firm *terminus ad quem* for the *Marienleich*. Christoph Huber conjectures that Heinrich's poem was written "circa 1300."[19] Others say 1312, but this date is based on no more than a document that names Heinrich as practicing medicine in Vienna at that time.

   Around 1330, the *scholasticus* Franko von Meschede composed a Latin *Marienlob* that some manuscripts name *Aurea fabrica* in homage to Konrad's *Goldene Schmiede*.[20] The edition in the *Analecta hymnica* calls it a "Carmen Magistrale," which it certainly is.[21] Ferociously learned and aureate, Franko's poem emulates a *leich* by deploying a variety of stanza forms in its thirteen sections. Part 9 is clearly indebted to the *Marienleich,* beginning with an allusion to Frauenlob's "smith from the high country" (strophe 11):

Tu incus tu metalleus	You are the anvil, you the metal
Es huius fabri malleus,	hammer of that smith
Auroram atque solem	who welds together the dawn
Qui fabricans conglutinat	and the sun in his forge
Et in statera trutinat	and weighs in the balance
Totius orbis molem.	the mass of the whole world.

(11.14)

The section continues with an *artes* cycle modeled on Frauenlob's strophes 16 through 18, in which each learned craft and science turns its skill to the Virgin's praise:

Te praedicat theologus,	The theologian preaches you,
Te praefert physiologus,	the zoologist displays you [in types],
Te medicus, legista,	the physician, the civil lawyer,
Te naturalis physicus,	the natural scientist,
Miratur metaphysicus,	and the metaphysician marvel,
Extollit canonista.	the canonist extols you.

(11.21)

Grammar, according to Franko, represents Mary as a "perfect and fitting locution," while logic distinguishes truth from falsehood through her; the rhetorician extols her in brilliantly colored *flores*; the geometer circumscribes her in figures; astrologers interpret her signs in heaven; and music exalts her with instruments and song—not to mention the naiads, dryads, and Pleiades! The section culminates in a paean to Mary as the Wisdom of God:

---

19. Huber, *Aufnahme und Verarbeitung*, 202. On Heinrich's poem, see 214–36.

20. See Kurt Gärtner, "Franko von Meschede," *Verfasserlexikon*, 2nd ed., 2:829–34.

21. Franko von Meschede, "Carmen Magistrale de beata Maria Virgine," *Analecta Hymnica* 29:185–204.

Idcirco, virgo pia,	Rejoice therefore, most kind
Maria,	Maria,
Gaude,	Maiden
Dei mater, dia	Mother of God, divine
Sophia,	Sophia:
[Tu] pia, plaude.	Most gracious, be glad.

                                                      (12.1)

Throughout this poem the Mother of God is elevated, in Michael Stolz's words, to "a feminine principle pervading the whole creation," very much as in Frauenlob's *leich*.[22]

The next witness to our author's fourteenth-century reputation attests again to his popularity in humanist circles. Albrecht von Strassburg's chronicle (a continuation of Mathias von Neuenburg's) was probably written soon after 1350. As we saw in Chapter 1, Albrecht gives a remarkable account of Frauenlob's burial in 1318, an event he could not personally have witnessed: "Women carried him from his lodgings to the sepulchre with loud lamentation and great mourning, on account of the infinite praises that he heaped on the whole feminine sex in his poems. Moreover, such copious libations of wine were poured on his tomb that it overflowed through the whole cloister of the church."[23] This romantic account inspired the carving of a new tombstone for Frauenlob in 1783, but it has long puzzled those familiar with medieval funeral customs. Pouring libations of wine on graves was a pagan, not Christian, practice and it is hard to imagine such a scene taking place at a burial in a cathedral cloister with the archbishop himself presiding. More likely, as Uwe Ruberg writes, "the chronicler's insistence on the excessive overflowing of the libation . . . serves to predestine the tomb in the cloister as a special cultic location for Frauenlob's memory."[24] For that purpose, it did not hurt that a massive wine cellar lay (and still lies) beneath the school and chapter house next to the monument. More important, the chronicler's choice of imagery is a classicizing touch, not unlike the Italian humanists' revival of the custom of crowning poets with laurel wreaths. In effect, Albrecht dignifies Frauenlob by giving him the kind of burial he might have imagined for Horace or Virgil. Like Boccaccio's contemporary life of Dante, Albrecht's memorial notice elevates a vernacular poet's stature by surrounding him with symbols that befit a celebrated classical one.

John of Neumarkt, another mid-century humanist, had a similar agenda. In a letter composed around 1364, he translated one of Frauenlob's political strophes into Latin prose for the benefit of his correspondent, a Bohemian bishop, to showcase the rhetorical brilliance the German tongue could achieve. "The prince of vernacular eloquence," he wrote, "Master Johannes [*sic*],

---

22. Stolz, "Maria und die Artes liberales," 102.

23. *Chronik des Mathias von Neuenburg,* ed. Hofmeister, MGH.SS., n.s. 4, fasc. 1, 312; and see Chapter 1, above, p. 43.

24. Ruberg, "Frauenlob-Gedenken," 83.

called Frauenlob, who has adorned the German language with a dewy sprinkling of eloquence and graced it with charming rhetorical flowers, composed such a remarkable and famous poem in elegiac style, lamenting the exile of justice, that, since it has come to my knowledge, I would have judged it a great crime if, through my negligence, my lord were to remain ignorant of the sweetness of so great a song."[25] Although the strophe in question is lost, Herbert Thoma has ingeniously retranslated enough of John's Latin into Middle High German to show that it fits neatly into Frauenlob's Langer Ton[26]—an index that for every spurious poem ascribed to the master an authentic one may be lost.

In a later epistle to Emperor Charles IV (ca. 1376), John quotes a long speech of Natura from Alan of Lille's *De planctu,* a work apparently unknown in Germany before Frauenlob cited it in the *Minneleich.*[27] John's letters, like the poem *Gottes Zukunft,* suggest that Alan of Lille's new-found popularity and Frauenlob's were mutually reinforcing. It is significant, though, that the speech in question marks a wide gulf between Alan's perspective and Frauenlob's. Natura in this key discourse underlines her inferiority to God: his work is sufficient and hers deficient; he is omnipotent, she nearly impotent. Although she bears responsibility for all earthly births, she can understand neither the Incarnation nor the supernatural birth by which man is reborn to eternal life. For this, one must "consult the authority of the theological faculty."[28] So in Alan's later *Anticlaudianus* it will be Theology alone, with Faith, who accompanies the heroine Prudentia to the throne of God, where Reason and the arts cannot follow. Much as Frauenlob admired Alan, his own naturalism as expressed in *Minne und Welt* and the *Marienleich* stands at some distance from Alan's supernaturalism.

This discrepancy emerges all the more sharply when we compare the *Marienleich* with the most important poem influenced by it—*Der meide kranz* (The Virgin's Garland), written by Heinrich von Mügeln around 1355. This work of nearly 2,600 lines, composed (like *Die gold-ene Schmiede*) in octosyllabic couplets, features a debate among the seven liberal arts, supple-mented by Philosophy, Medicine, Alchemy, Metaphysics, and Theology, at the court of Charles IV in Prague. Each art gives a speech outlining her discipline, then stating how she can best glorify the Virgin; the one who proves herself supreme is to hold the place of honor as a jewel in Mary's crown. The role of judge is diplomatically reserved for the imperial patron— the same to whom John of Neumarkt would address his Natura letter. A monarch with strong humanist leanings and cultural ambitions, Charles had founded the University of Prague in 1348 when he was still king of Bohemia, so it is not surprising that such learned works were directed to him. Von Mügeln's debate poem also follows in the wake of Guillaume de

25. "Vulgaris eloquencie princeps, qui facundi roris aspergine linguam adornauit theutunicam et venusto florum germine deco-rauit, magister Johannes dictus Frawenlob, condolens exulanti iusticie tam notabile tamque famosum carmen elegiaco stilo in materia tali composuit, quod, dum ad mei perueniret noticiam, scelus arbitrabar eximium, si ex negligencia mea dominus meus tanti carminis dulcedinem ignoraret." Piur, ed., *Briefe Johanns von Neumarkt,* no. 121, pp. 178–79.

26. Thoma, "John of Neumarkt and Heinrich Frauenlob."

27. *Briefe Johanns von Neumarkt,* no. 48, pp. 79–83.

28. Alan, *De planctu Naturae* 6, ed. Häring, 829.

Machaut's *Jugement du roi de Behaigne*, a courtly love debate composed only a few years earlier for Charles's father, the Bohemian king John of Luxembourg. With exemplary courtesy, the fictional Heinrich von Mügeln, asked for advice within his own text, expresses a mild preference for Philosophy but defers to the emperor, who instead chooses Theology as victor. All twelve arts are nevertheless allowed to adorn the Virgin's garland. In Part 2 of the poem, Theology herself judges a quarrel between Nature and the Virtues, who have offended the goddess by denying her authority over them. After each virtue has declared her own praise and offered advice to the prince, Theology decrees that all virtues come from God rather than Nature, who in turn "nam ir nar / uss gotes tugent" ("derived her nourishment from God's virtue").[29]

In his imperial verdict, Charles stresses the inadequacy of each art in comparison with theological truth, which is embodied in Mary. Philosophy teaches the doctrine of generation and corruption, but the virgin birth transcends that law. Grammar understands the properties of all words except the One who became flesh in Mary. Arithmetic can count and measure everything but the infinite wounds of Christ. Metaphysics teaches about the eight spheres and the angelic intelligences that guide them, but theology reveals a numberless host of angels—and so forth.[30] Although Heinrich's idea of organizing an arts competition around the praise of Mary was probably inspired by the *Marienleich,* his final judgment follows not Frauenlob's or Franko von Meschede's positive assessment of the *artes,* but Alan's supernaturalist view, expressed in the "Rhythmus de incarnatione" as well as the *Anticlaudianus.* Annette Volfing, in fact, judges Heinrich to be even more pessimistic than Alan on this score: the arts, as disciples of Natura, stand powerless before the mystery of grace.[31] Far from subsuming Natura and vindicating the study of the *artes,* it is Mary who ultimately defeats them all.

Despite this antihumanist stance, Heinrich approaches Frauenlob more closely in part 2 when he crafts the speech of Libe (Love)—giving the theological virtue this relatively innocuous name instead of the more evocative Minne, under whose aegis divine and erotic love so often met. Yet Libe's self-conception turns out to be very much like that of Minne in Frauenlob's *Minne und Welt:* she identifies herself as at once the principle of sexual desire and the goal of all virtues. Moreover, she claims, it is she who "seduced" God into becoming incarnate:

> er klam durch libe her zutal,
> das er min wirken möchte sen.
> gütlich min ougen liss ich bren
> und gap im manchen süssen blik,
> die wil ich span der salden strik,

29. Heinrich von Mügeln, *Der meide kranz,* vv. 2270–71, ed. and trans. Volfing, 332. My discussion draws on Volfing's excellent commentary and on Stolz, "Maria und die Artes liberales," 102–4.

30. Heinrich, *Der meide kranz,* vv. 719–864, ed. and trans. Volfing, 183–86.

31. Volfing, *Der meide kranz,* 371–72.

das er nicht mochte kummen dann.
ein fremde forme zoch er an,
das er bi mir bleip ungemelt:
ein meit in furt in ir gezelt
und druckt in an irs herzen brust:
darzu gab ich min ware lust,
so das der keiser hoher art
da mit der meit getruwet wart;
sie sneit im an ein rich gewant,
davon er bleip gar unbekant.

["He climbed down here because of love (*libe*), in order to see my activities. I let my eyes shine kindly and gave him many sweet glances, while I spun the snare of blessedness, so that he would not be able to escape. He assumed an alien form, so that his presence with me was not made known: a maiden led him into her tent and pressed him to the breast over her heart: I added my true desire (*lust*), so that the emperor of noble descent thereby became betrothed to the maiden. She cut for him a rich garment, so that he remained unrecognised."][32]

The eroticism of this passage betrays the same intentional ambiguity as the *Marienleich,* albeit in mitigated form. Love, playing temptress and matchmaker, beguiles the divine emperor into a virgin's tent, where he disguises himself to contract a clandestine marriage with her. As in Frauenlob, Love to some extent doubles the role of the seductive maiden. The *rich gewant* cut for Christ by his mother-bride may echo *Marienleich* 14, with its famous allegory of the tailor, though in Frauenlob's more paradoxical strophe it is God who first cuts a garment for Mary, then cuts his own clothing out of hers.

In addition to *Der meide kranz,* Heinrich von Mügeln composed a *geblümtes Marienlob* with the odd title of *Tum.*[33] (The word is probably a variant of *Dom,* "cathedral.")[34] The poem consists of seventy-two strophes representing the seventy-two languages of the world, each honoring the

---

32. Heinrich, *Der meide kranz,* vv. 2040–54, ed. and trans. Volfing, 311.

33. *Die kleineren Dichtungen Heinrichs von Mügeln,* 3 vols., ed. Karl Stackmann (Berlin: Akademie-Verlag, 1959), 2:147–219.

34. Michael Stolz, *"Tum"-Studien: Zur dichterischen Gestaltung im Marienpreis Heinrichs von Mügeln* (Tübingen: Francke, 1996), 376. As a suffix, *tum* also means "office" or "dignity," as in *richtum* ("kingdom"), *bischtum* ("episcopate"), or *magetum* ("virginity"). Strophe 67 reads, "Diss buch, das heisst der tum, / in dem der blünden sprüche blum / man fint gestrout in lobes rum / der hochsten himels keiserin, / die gotes ein genas / und spist uss ires herzen fass. / des sie ein tum der tugende was / und unsers heiles bilderin" (p. 215). "This book is called the *Cathedral* (?), in which the reader will find flowers of blossoming poetry strewn in praise of the empress of highest heaven, who alone refreshed God and fed him from the vessel of her heart. Therefore, she was a cathedral of virtues and the fashioner of our salvation."

Virgin under the form of a biblical type or some other image. This work stands in a long tradition stretching back to the twelfth century, but portions of it quote freely from the *Marienleich*. Here, for example, is the twentieth strophe, which echoes Frauenlob's strophes 12 and 14:

Du brunn und heiles mar,
   in dem des himels adelar
sich jungt und sin gefider gar
   (und bleib doch in der ersten art),

uss diner wat er sneit
   im wat und liess doch sunder leit
die wat und diner küsche kleit,
   wie er von dir gekleidet wart.

blick in den spiegel, maget, diner truwe
   und kleid uns mit der tugent wete nuwe.
strass zu des himels buwe
   an dich kein ouge finden kan.[35]

You fount and sea of salvation,
   in which the eagle of heaven
rejuvenated himself and his plumage
   and yet remained as he was before:

out of your clothing he cut clothes
   for himself, yet left your clothing
and the robe of your chastity unharmed
   just as he was clothed by you.

Look, Virgin, into the mirror of your loyalty
   and clothe us with new robes of virtue.
Without you, no eye can find the way
   to heaven's dwelling.

Despite such borrowings—and there are many—von Mügeln distances himself from what is most original and striking in Frauenlob's work. He employs the traditional third-person idiom of praise, rather than the unsettling self-proclamation of the *leich*; he makes his allegory more explicit, specifying, for example, that the Virgin's undamaged robe is her chastity; and he ends many of his strophes with prayer, a conventional gesture that Frauenlob's impersonation of Mary disallows.[36]

From the century's end comes a final witness to the reach of the *geblümter Stil*. Bruder Hans, a poet and lay brother of the Devotio Moderna, had perhaps been a merchant before his conversion. A native of the Lower Rhineland (he called himself a *niderlender*), he seems to have traveled widely, for his dialect includes both Middle Dutch and High German borrowings. Among his literary influences are Latin exegesis, mystical writings such as the revelations of Saint Birgitta, and vernacular poets including Wolfram, Neidhart, Konrad von Würzburg, and Frauenlob.[37] In his famous *Marienlieder,* composed in the 1390s, self-conscious virtuosity reaches a new zenith (or nadir, depending on the critic's feelings about "mannerism"). "If I had Solomon's wisdom," Bruder Hans tells the Virgin, "and if I were as resourceful (*vundich*) a poet as Frauenlob,"

35. Heinrich von Mügeln, *Die kleineren Dichtungen,* 167.
36. See Köbele, "Umbesetzungen," for similar examples.
37. Susanne Fritsch-Starr, "Bruder Hans: Spiegel spätmittelalterlicher Frauenlobrezeption am Niederrhein," *Jahrbuch der* *Oswald von Wolkenstein Gesellschaft* 10 (1998): 139–51; Hartmut Beckers, "Die volkssprachige Literatur des Mittelalters am Niederrhein," *Digitale bibliotheek voor de Nederlandse letteren,* 157–58 (http://www.dbnl.org).

then I would truly praise you as you deserve![38] His paraphrase of the tailor image from *Marien-leich* 14, which seems to have been everyone's favorite *blüeme,* shows tendencies similar to Heinrich von Mügeln's: he translates the passage into the third person, simplifies, and de-eroticizes it.[39] But direct borrowing may be the least significant aspect of Frauenlob's effect on Bruder Hans, for the historical dynamic of the *geblümter Stil*—or any artistic mode that strives self-consciously for novelty, for a "mannered" extreme rather than classical balance—must nec-essarily entail a quest to outdo its own past achievements. This striving stems less from a Bloom-ian anxiety of influence than from a need to create ever more daring, outrageous, and provoca-tive works to impress an ever more jaded audience—a stylistic trajectory familiar enough from the history of high modernism. Frauenlob's style was already exotic and audacious enough to set a high mark for would-be outdoers, but Bruder Hans found at least one way to surpass the master at his own tricks. How else to explain the first of his *Marienlieder,* an "Ave Maria" acros-tic that rhymes and scans in four languages?

Ave alpha du stercher god!	Hail, Alpha, thou mighty God!
Je diroy volentiers un mot	I would gladly say a word
Of that swete ladi deer,	About that sweet, dear Lady
Cuius venter te portavit.	Whose womb carried thee.
Ich meyn miin vrou dye alrebest,	I mean my Lady, the best of all,
Qui dam de toutes dammes est.	who is the Lady of all ladies.
Thye in yr blisset woomb shy beer	She bore thee in her blessed womb
Et te dulci lacte pavit	And fed thee with sweet milk
Et tam ardenter te amavit,	And so ardently loved thee
Daʒ ir myn dich cund neder ʒeen.	That my song can scarcely tell of her.
Their thu ars kinc schol se bi queen,	Where thou art king, she shall be queen—
La noble fillie dou roye Davit.[40]	The noble daughter of King David.

This is the *ne plus ultra* of a certain kind of brilliance. If Bruder Hans has not succeeded in say-ing anything new about the Virgin, he has at least said it in an unforgettably new way—and his ʒeal to be as *vundich* as Frauenlob must bear some of the credit.

38. "Weer mir Salmons wiisheit cundich, / Al dinc ʒu dinen lob untbund ich; / Und weer ich dichtens alʒo vundich, / Als her was der Vrouwenlop." *Bruder Hansens Marienlieder,* 4092–95, ed. Michael Batts (Tübingen: Niemeyer, 1963), 182.

39. *Bruder Hansens Marienlieder,* 3729–44, p. 169. The pas-sage begins: "Eyn snider woende in ueberlant. / Der was geheyssen und ghenant / Die beste meyster, die men vant, / Von alre consten die man wist" ("There lived a tailor in the high country, who was called and named the best master men could find in all the arts they knew").

40. *Bruder Hansens Marienlieder,* 1–12, p. 1. Subsequent stro-phes begin with the words "Maria," "Gracia," "Plena," and so forth. The sequence of languages is fixed—a part of the *Ton,* so to speak—and the rhyme scheme is aabc ddbc ceec. Thus German rhymes with French, English with itself and German, Latin with itself and French.

THE MEISTERSINGERS AND THE FIFTEENTH CENTURY

Bruder Hansens Marienlieder suggest the dominant trend in Frauenlob's fifteenth-century reception: his defining influence on the meistersingers and their fascination with complex form. Returning to the manuscripts, we find that the major fifteenth-century collections of Frauenlob's work, both redacted by meistersingers, differ greatly from those closer to the poet's lifetime. The mid-fifteenth-century manuscript F (Weimar, Zentralbibliothek der deutschen Klassik, Q 564) was once thought to have been an autograph by Hans Sachs (1494–1576), the hero of Wagner's *Die Meistersinger,* but it actually predates him. Written in Nuremberg, F contains by far the largest collection of the poet's works: the first hundred of its 142 leaves are devoted almost entirely to Frauenlob, including all three *leichs,* our only copy of *Minne und Welt,* seven *Minnelieder,* and some 242 strophes in all nine of his tones. These are followed by a few other poets—Walther von der Vogelweide, Friedrich von Husen, Regenbogen, Konrad von Würzburg—and miscellaneous texts including a *Fastnachtspiel* or carnival play. As in J, the texts are grouped according to their *Töne,* two of which (the Neuer Ton and the Vergessener Ton) are not attested before this manuscript. Such a large anthology testifies to a vigorous interest in Frauenlob, whose songs must have been collected from far and wide via oral tradition and now-lost textual sources. One hundred and fifty years of oral transmission can easily explain why many texts found only in F have been "corrupted almost to unintelligibility."[41] Although the tight formal structure of their *Töne* would have afforded some protection against random variants, even art songs, like folksongs, could be expected to change over the course of a long performance history. Despite their weak transmission and textual problems, Stackmann accepts most of these songs as authentic on the basis of thematic and stylistic affinities with better-attested poems.[42] F therefore is the base manuscript for a great many texts in the Göttingen edition.

The second late collection, t (Munich, Bayerische Staatsbibliothek Cod. germ. mon. 4997), has been a source of persistent confusion. Compiled around 1470 by the meistersingers of Mainz, its early history is obscure. But after 1546 the book belonged to the meistersingers' guild at Colmar, where for a half-century its fame was such that visitors came from all over Germany to see it, and it was borrowed by other singers' guilds on festive occasions—as we know from entries in the manuscript itself. After a period of waning interest, the book was rediscovered at the shoemakers' guildhall in 1789, disappeared again after its prospective editor went blind, and finally resurfaced in 1857, at which time the Royal Library in Munich purchased it from a dealer in Basel. A first edition was published by Karl Bartsch in 1862.[43] The Colmar manuscript contains more than one thousand strophes in various tones ascribed to Frauenlob, of

---

41. Stackmann, "Frauenlob (Heinrich von Meissen)—eine Bilanz," 39.
42. GA 1:169–72.

43. Karl Bartsch, ed., *Meisterlieder der Kolmarer Handschrift* (Stuttgart: Litterarischer Verein, 1862).

which Stackmann accepted only thirty-seven as authentic, as well as the *Marienleich* and the *Kreuzleich*, the latter implausibly ascribed to Regenbogen. In addition to the nine *Spruchtöne* accepted as genuine because they occur in F or earlier manuscripts, t credits Frauenlob with a Forest Tune (*Tannton*), a Crowned Tune (*Gekrönter Ton*), a Frog Melody (*Froschweise*), a Dog Melody (*Hundweise*), a Mirror Melody (*Spiegelweise*), a Knights' Melody (*Ritterweise*), and many more. The manuscript also contains lyrics of earlier and contemporary poets (Walther, Wolfram, Tannhäuser, Marner, Reinmar von Zweter, Konrad von Würzburg, Regenbogen), as well as later ones (Heinrich von Mügeln, Peter von Reichenbach, the Monk of Salzburg, Suchensinn, Muskatblut), and anonymous meistersinger songs.

   If Frauenlob's fame suffered eclipse in the eighteenth and nineteenth centuries, the meistersingers fared even worse. In fact, their poetry has been little studied because their critical reputation is so poor: They tend to be dismissed as pretentious epigones maniacally obsessed with form at the expense of substance, and (like Frauenlob himself) "pious" and "bourgeois" in the pejorative sense of both terms.[44] It is interesting that the fifteenth century has also had a bad press in French, English, and Netherlandish literature. Ever since Johan Huizinga deplored the decadence of the late medieval imagination, the period has been seen as an age of excess or stagnation marking time between the creative flourishing of the High Middle Ages and the Renaissance. But now that English medievalists have found new and interesting questions to ask of Lydgate, Hoccleve, and other once-despised authors, it may be time to take a fresh look at the late *Spruchdichter* and early meistersingers too. These itinerant poets—many of them well educated and widely traveled, all of them uncensored and untrammeled—were lay vernacular theologians singing of ethical, devotional, and speculative themes in direct competition with the mendicant preachers. Yet, having by no means renounced the world, they continued to craft political, amorous, and satirical songs as well as sacred ones. By aesthetic criteria, their huge output is of course uneven. But without a better knowledge of these influential shapers of public opinion, large gaps will remain in our understanding of medieval German culture.[45] Such a reassessment far exceeds the scope of this volume, but it should be made easier by the recent publication of Haustein and Stackmann's supplement to the Göttingen edition—a new critical text of "pseudo-Frauenlob" songs in the master's authentic tones, edited chiefly from the Colmar manuscript.[46] Most of these are religious, and a great many are Marian. Collectively they confirm Stackmann's judgment that Frauenlob's influence on early *meistersang* "was amazingly great" if still largely unstudied.[47] I will here ignore the meistersingers' ubiquitous pastiche of

44. Krayer, *Frauenlob und die Natur-Allegorese*, 16.

45. The foundational work is Frieder Schanze, *Meisterliche Liedkunst zwischen Heinrich von Mügeln und Hans Sachs*, 2 vols. (Munich: Artemis, 1983–84). See also Bert Nagel, ed., *Der deutsche Meistersang* (Darmstadt: Wissenschaftliche Buchgesellschaft, 1967); Walter Blank and Günter Kochendörfer, *Mittelhochdeutsche Spruchdichtung, früher Meistersang: Der Codex Palatinus Germanicus 350 der Universitätsbibliothek Heidelberg*, 3 vols. (Wiesbaden:

Reichert, 1974); Alwine Edelmann-Ginkel, *Das Loblied auf Maria im Meistersang* (Göppingen: Kümmerle, 1978).

46. Jens Haustein and Karl Stackmann, eds., *Sangsprüche in Tönen Frauenlobs: Supplement zur Göttinger Frauenlob-Ausgabe*, 2 vols. (Göttingen: Vandenhoeck & Ruprecht, 2000).

47. Stackmann, "Frauenlob (Heinrich von Meissen)—eine Bilanz," 37.

his style to concentrate on two Colmar poems of particular interest, the *Taugenhort* and the *Krieg von Würzburg*.

The *Taugenhort* (Treasury of Mysteries) attributed to Frauenlob in t is a verse paraphrase and commentary on the *Marienleich*.[48] (The *hort* was a generic successor to the *leich*, a long poem in which each strophe has a different tune and metrical form.)[49] Considerably longer than its original, the *Taugenhort* differs from other imitations in retaining Mary's distinctive *ich bin* speech, but it resembles them in seeking to expand where Frauenlob compresses, to explain where he mystifies, and to assert where he only suggests. The Song-based sensuality of the *leich* is played down, while its Trinitarian theology is played up. Although the fifteenth-century poet still teaches that the Virgin "possessed" and "wove together" all three persons of the Trinity (lines 77–79), he is so convinced of the orthodoxy of this doctrine that he takes several lines to condemn Trinitarian heretics to hell (65–76). Mary's sapiential nature is clarified through a direct paraphrase of Wisdom's self-praise in Proverbs 8:22–30. Thus it is to Solomon, the Virgin's prophet, that these lines are ascribed:

er sprach: got mich besezzen hât	He said: God possessed me
vor aller dinge beginne	before the beginning of all things
in sîner werden majestât:	in his noble majesty:
ich bin sîn gotlîch minne.	I am his divine love.
ich bin der gotheit spiegel clâr.	I am the bright mirror of divinity.
ich bin sîn freud sîn wünne,	I am his joy, his gladness,
ich bin sîn wesen, sîn senfte nar,	I am his essence, his gentle food,
ich bin sîn saelic künne.	I am his blessed nature.
ich bin ouch sîn werder trôn,	I am also his noble throne,
ich bin sîn ougenweide,	I am the delight of his eyes.
ich bin der gotheit girlich crôn,	I am the Godhead's crown of desire
wan ich mich mit im cleide.	for I clothe myself with him.

(123–34)

The poet adds numerous Old Testament types omitted by Frauenlob, including Judith, Esther, the widow of Sarepta, and the queen of Sheba. Since the queen came from afar to test Solomon's wisdom, she provides a useful pretext to discuss the relationship between Maria/Sapientia and the Trinity:

sîn wîsheit got in mir verbarc,	God concealed his wisdom in me
dô er sîn kint verslôz in mînen sarc.	when he enclosed his child in my shrine.

---

48. "Diz ist Frouwenlobes tougen hort," in Bartsch, *Meister-lieder*, 204–31.

49. Archer Taylor, *The Literary History of Meistergesang* (London: Oxford, 1937), 28, 61.

daz worhte er mit des geistes flamme.	This he wrought by the Spirit's flame.
der lewe verwandelt sich ze lamme.	The lion changed himself into a lamb.
dô verlasch des zornes glamme:	Then the spark of wrath was quenched:
diu menscheit fuogt sich zuo der gotheit frône.	Humanity united itself to the Lord's divinity.
got was got, bleip got ungemeilet,	God was God, remained God undefiled;
got von got schiet got ungeteilet,	God split God from God undivided:
got in dem trône, got in mînem lîbe,	God on the throne, God in my body,
got drîlich wonet in mir schône,	The threefold God dwells in me splendidly.
die drî ein, dar inn ich beclîbe:	The three are one, in whom I abide;
sîn wîsheit lerne ich, des bin ich gezieret.	I learn his wisdom, which makes me lovely.
	(461–72)

Much of the *Taugenhort* reads like a gloss on obscure parts of the *Marienleich*. Where Frauenlob has the Virgin proclaim "Ich binz die groze gotes stat" ("I am the great City of God," 15.3), the *Taugenhort* lets her identify herself as Jerusalem ("peace") and Bethlehem ("house of bread"). Her invitation, "Komt alle zu mir, die min gern" ("Come to me, all who desire me," 12.9), is expanded accordingly: "kumt alle zuo mir, nemt daz brôt / daz in mir ist beslozzen" ("Come to me, all of you, take the bread that is enclosed in me," 220–21). An enigmatic passage like the following—

swaz die propheten alle kunden	Whatever all the prophets proclaim—
—ir wort, ir rede sie uf mich bunden—	their words, their speech refer to me—
ich bir, niur himel minen friunden.	I bring only heaven to my friends.
gein mir so lan die ingesigel alle ir rigel,	Against me locks lose all their bolts,
swie vaste er sie behalte,	however fast he binds them—
	(13.33–37)

is doubly expanded. On the one hand, the poet gives a full list of twenty-four biblical prophets, and on the other, he clarifies the metaphor of locks and seals:

Ich bin des himels creftic ingesigel,	I am the mighty seal of heaven,
ich stoere ich breche der helle bant, ir rigel,	I destroy, I break hell's bonds, its bolts,
ich binde den vint mit sîner craft:	I bind the fiend with his might:
sîn gewalt der muoz sich vor mir smiegen.	his power must yield before me.
	(613–16)

In short, the *Taugenhort* is not just another paraphrase of the *Marienleich*, but an intelligent fifteenth-century reader's interpretation—an act of criticism in poetic form. The most daring passages are omitted (*ich got; ich slief bi drin*), while a bit of morality is added:

der welte gnâde ist trügenhaft,	the grace of the world is deceiving,
ir schoene zierde ein îtelschaft,	its lovely adornment a vanity;
ir vinster lieht nicht liuhtet.	its dark light does not illumine.

(677–79)

Rather poignantly, the pseudonymous singer makes a refrain out of Frauenlob's plea that no one will be offended: "doch hoffe ich, daz ez ieman missevalle" (11.16):

wem mac daz missevallen	Who could be displeased
daz sie sô schône ist mit gote vereinet?	that she is so beautifully united with God?

(117–18; cf. 403, 885)

Is this sheer irony, or does it suggest that some who knew the *leich* actually did take offense? It would be useful to know.

Der Krieg von Würzburg (The Battle of Würzburg) is a quite different kind of poem—a fictional *Sängerkrieg* between Frauenlob and Regenbogen, perhaps read by posterity as an actual debate.[50] Although it does not imitate Frauenlob's style, as the *Taugenhort* does, its author shows considerable familiarity with his work. In the fiction, Frauenlob travels up and down the Rhine, looking for the best singers, until he arrives in Würzburg—perhaps another homage to Konrad. There he challenges all comers to a tournament of song, hanging a floral crown as the prize. Regenbogen accepts the challenge, alluding to a famous knightly combat:

bistuz her Gâwîn, sô bin ichz her Parzifâl.
lâ sehen wer under uns ersinge hie den Grâl.
(50–51)

[If you are Sir Gawain, I will be Sir Parzival.
Let us see which of us here achieves the Grail of song!]

When Frauenlob announces his signature theme—the praise of ladies—Regenbogen takes up the opposing side: he will argue that man is the original and superior sex, "alz ez die wisen

---

50. "Der kriec von Wirzburc, XXIII lieder," in Bartsch, *Meisterlieder*, 351–62.

pfaffen in den buochen lesen" ("as wise priests read in books," 81). The poem thus positions itself as part of the *querelle des femmes,* a literary parlor game that flourished throughout Europe in the late Middle Ages and early modern period. Unlike some specimens of the genre, *Der Krieg* is remarkably chivalrous. Regenbogen, who in a Manesse Codex song calls Frauenlob a "brag-gart, nitwit, fool, idiot," now insists on courtesy (Gawain and Parzival were friends, after all); and even as he makes his case for male preeminence, he scrupulously avoids misogyny. It appears at first that the debate will be a clash between courtly and clerical perspectives: Frauen-lob takes his stand "for the sake of his love" (*durch mînes liebes willen*) and "for the honor of ladies" (*durch frouwen êre*), while Regenbogen appeals to priestly texts. This is deceptive, how-ever, for it soon becomes clear that both minstrels mean to argue on theological grounds.

It may be an index of the real Frauenlob's influence that this poem reverses the normal pre-suppositions of the genre. Ordinarily, the question under debate is whether women as such are good or bad. Misogyny presents itself as the norm—the "affirmative," as it were—so the pro-woman cause must be cast in the form of a defense, refuting slurs about the sin of Eve, feminine lust and greed, weakness and mendacity, before any positive case can be made.[51] This is the method of Christine de Pizan's *Book of the City of Ladies* (1405), the most ambitious and indis-putably serious work in this vein before the sixteenth century. But in the more lighthearted *Krieg von Würzburg,* it is Frauenlob who initiates the debate and states the theme, so the praise of women is normative and the pro-masculine case must be argued, for once, by the underdog. Hence there is no discussion of Adam and Eve, of responsibility for the Fall, or of the alleged vices of women. Instead, the entire debate hinges on Christ and Mary, whom both parties implicitly take to be representative of their genders.

Regenbogen opens with the standard claim that man is the origin of the human race, which might seem in biblical terms to be unimpeachable. Normally it scored a debating point for the male side—but not in Frauenlob's theology! As he sees it, God created man in time, yet woman in Mary is eternal: "Got kam zuo ir ê Adam was geschafen" ("God came to her before Adam was created," 126). When Regenbogen fails to take his point, he elaborates:

> Her Regenboge, ir sullent rehte mich verstân.
> ê got geschuof ie crêâtiure, wîp noch man,
> dô sach er dise maget under ougen an
> die er ze muoter hete erkorn, der cristenheit ze trôste. (170–73)

> [Sir Regenbogen, you should understand me correctly!
> Before God created any creature, woman or man,
> already he saw before his eyes this virgin
> whom he had chosen as mother, for the comfort of Christendom.]

51. Alcuin Blamires, *The Case for Women in Medieval Culture* (Oxford: Clarendon, 1997).

Against the exaltation of the female sex in Mary, Regenbogen sets the awesome power of the male clergy:

> Mannes name ist aller tugende ein ursprinc
> und ist sô hôch erhoehet über alle dinc.
> sît du mit dînre maht in einen kleinen rinc
> betwingest got daz er sich gibet under priesters hende. . . .
> Daz kan allez mannes nam zuo bringen.
> solicher wirde ein ieglîch frouwe muoz enbern. (131–40)

> [Man is the origin of all virtues
> and is so high exalted above all things,
> since you (man) compel God by your power
> to give himself in a little circle in the hands of a priest. . . .
> Any man is able to achieve this;
> every woman must lack this dignity.]

The alarming priestly power to "compel" God in the Eucharist was a favorite meistersinger theme, which the fictional Frauenlob counters by asking where the mass would be without the Incarnation, which could not have occurred without Mary (178–80). Hence one can ask, "Wâ wart ie man gewaltic gotes als sie was?" ("Wherever did a man have so much power over God as she did?" 201). Suchensinn, a fourteenth-century admirer of Frauenlob, composed a similar debate between a woman and a priest as to which exercises more sway over God. The woman wins, because it was she who first "divided the Godhead into three Persons without resistance" when she separated the Son from the Father and the Holy Spirit in the Incarnation. If not for her, the priest would have no mass to offer; so even the gift in the priest's hands "came from a woman's heart."[52]

In the *Krieg*, Regenbogen parries with the claim that although God's mother was a woman, God himself was incarnate as a man, and it is therefore a man who created all things and whom heaven and earth obey (239–40). The debate, like most of its genre, finally ends in a truce:

> dar umbe zimt uns kristen wol daz wir sie êren beide,
> Die werden man und ouch die reinen frouwen. (294–95)

> [Therefore it is most fitting for us Christians
> to honor both—worthy men and pure women alike.]

52. "Sie hât geteilt die gotheit eben / in drî persôn ân wider-streben"; "die gâb, die dir [Priester] got selber gît, / die kam ûsz wibes hertzen." Emil Pflug, ed., *Suchensinn und seine Dichtungen,* 1.36–37 and 2.33–34 (Hildesheim: Olms, 1908); cited in Kern, *Trinität, Maria, Inkarnation,* 142.

For all its lightness of touch, *Der Krieg von Würzburg* was not without consequences. The German *querelle des femmes* began in earnest about sixty years after the Colmar manuscript was written, with the 1529 publication of Heinrich Cornelius Agrippa's *Declamation on the Nobility and Preeminence of the Female Sex.*[53] Agrippa, a Renaissance humanist and occultist, aimed at least as much to shock and entertain as to make a serious case for the superiority of women, but his case, such as it is, depends largely on esoteric theology.[54] A century later, as the flood of pro- and anti-woman pamphlets continued in full spate, one "Johann Frawenlob" published a 1631 tract entitled "Die lobwürdige Gesellschafft der gelehrten Weiber" ("The Laudable Company of Learned Women").[55] Frawenlob's pamphlet supplied a long, alphabetical list of learned and distinguished women, both ancient and modern—including such medieval writers as Hrotswitha, Hildegard of Bingen, Elisabeth of Schönau, Mechthild of Magdeburg, Catherine of Siena, and Birgitta of Sweden—to support his arguments for female education. This feminist writer adopted his pseudonym in homage to the still-famous *Spruchdichter* Frauenlob—whom, interestingly enough, John of Neumarkt had also known by the name of "Johannes Frauenlob." Could the pseudonymous Frawenlob have been familiar with the fictional Frauenlob of *Der Krieg von Würzburg,* a chivalrous champion of female superiority? Given the celebrity of the Colmar manuscript, it is certainly possible; and if he did know that text, he would probably have taken it as authentic. It is by such wayward and roundabout paths that the minstrel from Meissen's abstract, theological praise of Woman finally converged with a concrete feminist argument.

Returning to the Colmar manuscript, we find countless instances of Frauenlob's theological as well as stylistic influence. In the corpus of *meistersang,* ideas that had been radical and extreme by the standards of late thirteenth-century theology became almost normal by the mid-fifteenth. Peter Kern's still-unsurpassed study of the meistersingers' religious songs suggests the theological dynamics underlying this development. Frauenlob and other high medieval authors took pains to present the Incarnation as an *opus Trinitatis,* a work of the undivided Trinity, and this emphasis led their successors to insist ever more vehemently on Mary as bride and mother of the whole Godhead. In other words, if Jesus is God, and God is the Trinity, then in bearing Jesus, Mary must have contained the whole Trinity within her womb—a belief that was dramatically and ubiquitously displayed in the popular Shrine Madonnas (or *vierges ouvrantes*).[56] Similarly, the emphasis on her eternal preexistence as Sapientia encouraged belief in a true quaternity of divine persons: Father, Son, Spirit, and Mother. Frauenlob's influence of course represents only one aspect of a much broader development in religious thought; nor are these tendencies found

53. Heinrich Agrippa von Nettesheim, *De nobilitate et praecellentia foeminei sexus: lateinischer Text und deutsche Übersetzung in Prosa,* ed. and trans. Otto Schönberger (Würzburg: Königshausen & Neumann, 1997); Henricus Cornelius Agrippa, *Declamation on the Nobility and Preeminence of the Female Sex,* trans. Albert Rabil Jr. (Chicago: University of Chicago Press, 1996).

54. Barbara Newman, "Renaissance Feminism and Esoteric Theology: The Case of Cornelius Agrippa," in *From Virile Woman to WomanChrist,* 224–43.

55. Johann Frawenlob, "Die lobwürdige Gesellschafft der gelehrten Weiber," in Elisabeth Gössmann, ed., *Eva, Gottes Meisterwerk* (Munich: Iudicium, 1985), 46–83.

56. Kern, *Trinität, Maria, Inkarnation,* 48–65, 128–38; Newman, *God and the Goddesses,* 269–73.

uniquely in German literature. But within the specific context of *meistersang,* we should not underestimate the provocative power of his expressions. One factor at work in this poetry was a lack of precision among singers who admired, but could not match, Frauenlob's theological learning. Another is the same impulse to outdo an already flamboyant master that we have seen in the stylistic extremes of a Franko von Meschede or a Bruder Hans. Yet, as Krayer wrote, "the throng of his imitators proved how inimitable he was."[57]

In reading these songs, it becomes extremely hard to distinguish deliberately over-the-top expressions of orthodox belief from outright if unintentional heterodoxy. What to make of this Colmar *meisterlied,* for example?

Ich wil von vier personen singen	I will sing of four persons
die waren ee wan fiat ye gesprochen wart	who existed before the *fiat* was ever spoken,
ee es wart dag all oder nacht	before there was any day or night;
do waren sy by got in siner czesen.[58]	they were with God then at his right hand.

The Monk of Salzburg (ca. 1400) has Gabriel bid farewell to Mary after the Annunciation, saying:

Behüet dich got, trawt schöns junkfrewlein,	God keep you, dear, lovely Virgin:
enphangen hast du dy namen drey,	you have conceived the three Persons,
Got vater, sun, den heyligen geist,	God the Father, Son, and Holy Spirit.
wie pilleich du Gotes mueter haist	How aptly you are called God's mother
in der ewikaite fron.[59]	in the Lord's eternity!

Conversely, a poet might try to avoid this theological error by asserting the contrary. Far from conceiving the entire Trinity, Mary had such power over the Godhead that she "split" the undivided Trinity into three Persons and took one alone as her portion. This topos, which we have already seen in Suchensinn, seems yet again to have been Frauenlob's invention. In a peculiar strophe about God's lopsided victory over Nature, he declares:

Wan got sie bestunt selbvierde,	When God opposed her as a quaternity—
er ein und ouch sin ewicheit	he alone, with his Eternity
und sin majestas, wirde.	and his noble Majesty,
dar zu so half die reine,	they were helped by the pure maid

---

57. Krayer, *Frauenlob und die Natur-Allegorese,* 15.
58. Kern, *Trinität, Maria, Inkarnation,* 87.

59. Kern, *Trinität, Maria, Inkarnation,* 200.

Maria, vleisches bleiche vri:	Mary, free of all fleshly taint:
sie spielt uz ein personen dri.	she divided three Persons out of one:
vier mochten me dan nature alterseine.	Four could do more than Nature alone.[60]

(VII.3.13–19)

Another of the Colmar songs echoes this motif:

Maria kunigynne	Mary the Queen—
wa wart ie macht so hoher craft	wherever was might of such high power?—
herdacht mit richem synne	thought with potent intellect
daz sich die gotheit spilt in dry	that the Godhead split itself in three:
din sun wart dir zu teil.[61]	Your Son was given you as your share.

The prolific fifteenth-century poet Michel Beheim, who had a knack for offbeat allegories, found a way to improve on Frauenlob's *ich slief bi drin*.[62] In his "Exempel von der hailgen drivaltikait," three suitors—a hunter, a fisherman, and a falconer—all fall in love with the same girl, so they compete for her hand with a demonstration of their arts. But the maiden is equally impressed with them all and refuses to make a choice:

Mich dunket sicherlich	It seems to me indeed
eür dreier wesen ains.	that you three are one being:
fur war, ich kan ir kains	truly I can in no way
geschaiden van dem andern.	distinguish you from each other,
an euch ist kain verwandern,	there is no difference among you—
ich sol euch han all drei.[63]	I shall have all three of you!

In another of Beheim's allegories, a virgin finds three roses blooming on one stalk and plucks them to weave a garland for the dance, which she wears for the forty weeks of her pregnancy. The roses turn out to be the three Persons, and their stem, the divine essence.[64] Still stranger is Heinrich von Mügeln's version of this allegory, perhaps inspired by Frauenlob's promiscuous mingling of bestiary images. The speaker addresses Mary with a prodigiously mixed metaphor:

60. For God, his Eternity, and his Majesty as the three Persons, compare *Kreuzleich* II.4.6–10.

61. Kern, *Trinität, Maria, Inkarnation*, 141.

62. For an interesting study of this late *Spruchdichter*, see William C. McDonald, *Whose Bread I Eat: The Song-Poetry of Michel Beheim* (Göppingen: Kümmerle, 1981).

63. Michel Beheim, "Exempel von der hailgen drivaltikait," 51–56, in *Die Gedichte des Michel Beheim*, 300.51–56, ed. Hans

Gille and Ingeborg Spriewald, 3 vols. (Berlin: Akademie-Verlag, 1968–72), 2:557–59. See also Kern, *Trinität, Maria, Inkarnation*, 113–16.

64. Beheim, *Gedichte* 306, vol. 2:591–92. According to its title, this poem was occasioned by King Ladislav of Bohemia (reg. 1440–57), who gave the minstrel three roses and challenged him to compose a song about them.

Durch diner küsche stam	From your chaste stalk
wuchs adelar, louw unde lamm,	grew an eagle, a lion, and a lamb:
davon sich brach des fluches tam.	by them the dam of the curse was broken.
die dri ein wesen gar besloss.[65]	A single essence enclosed the Three.

Even Latin hymnody eventually yielded to the outright divinization of the Virgin. The so-called "Marian Te Deum" from the Dominican monastery at Pettau, circa 1440, begins with the surprising proclamation "Te deam digne laudibus / et dominam fatemur" ("We acknowledge thee with fitting praise as Goddess and Lady"), continuing in that vein for thirty stanzas.[66]

Artistic statements of the quaternity motif are legion. I have written elsewhere about the Coronation of the Virgin by the Trinity, a favorite fifteenth-century subject that introduces Mary into full membership in the divine family,[67] so I present here only one more little-known example (fig. 5). The carved retable at the parish church of St. Nicholas, Eggenfelden (Bavaria), is ascribed to the sculptor Heinrich Helmschrott, circa 1480.[68] It differs from most comparable images in that here all three Persons of the Trinity are represented anthropomorphically. Instead of the usual dove, the Holy Spirit appears at right as a beardless figure with long, curly blond locks. The tradition of correlating the three divine Persons with stages of human life—the Father as an old man, the Son in his vigorous prime, and the Spirit as a child or adolescent—dates back at least to the thirteenth century; Mechthild von Magdeburg alludes to it in *The Flowing Light*.[69] There may even be a remote link with the Joachite idea of the "age of the Holy Spirit" as the third and final *status* of salvation history. But only in the fifteenth century did the motif take widespread pictorial form. In the Eggenfelden quaternity, it results in a striking physical resemblance between the Spirit and the Virgin, who in the *Marienleich* share the role of *anima mundi* ("des geistes worchtlich minne," 17.10). Instead of replacing the Holy Spirit as she so often does in such compositions, Mary seems here to share her identity.[70]

But we need not seek obscure provincial works to find evidence for the triumph of Frauenlob's Mariology, for his double-natured Virgin gazes out from one of the most canonical works of late medieval art—the Isenheim Altarpiece by Master Matthias of Würzburg, called Grünewald (fig. 6). This monumental work was completed around 1515, originally for a hospital at Isenheim staffed by the Order of Saint Anthony, but it now stands in the former Dominican convent of Unterlinden in Colmar. In the "intermediate" opening of the great polyptych—the panels representing the joyful mysteries—we see, from left to right, the Annunciation; an

65. Heinrich von Mügeln, *Die kleineren Dichtungen*, 185.1–4, vol 2:225.

66. "'Te Deum' Marianum," *Analecta Hymnica* 31:212–14. The manuscript is Graz, Universitätsbibliothek, Cod. graecen. 347, fols. 102r–103v.

67. Newman, *God and the Goddesses*, 256–61.

68. The work has been restored and repainted; its neo-Gothic architectural frame dates from 1875. "Eggenfelden: Pfarrkirche und Nebenkirchen," pamphlet issued by the Katholisches Stadtpfarramt Eggenfelden, 2004.

69. Mechthild, *Das fliessende Licht*, 7.3, ed. Vollmann-Profe, 538.

70. Another feminine Holy Spirit, possibly meant to represent a boy, can be seen in the late fourteenth-century Urschalling Trinity near Prien-am-Chiemsee, Bavaria. For a photograph and discussion, see Newman, *From Virile Woman to WomanChrist*, 198–203.

FIG. 5 "Marian quaternity." Retable ascribed to Heinrich Helmschrott, Church of St. Nicholas, Eggenfelden, Bavaria, ca. 1480

angelic concert; the Nativity; and the Resurrection. Mary is depicted in this sequence three times. Between the Virgin Annunciate on the left and the Madonna and Child in the third panel, a mysterious *Virgo gloriosa* kneels on the threshold of the heavenly tabernacle, gesturing toward the earthly Madonna. Interpretations of the second panel have varied widely, but it is generally agreed that the elaborate Gothic structure around the music-making angels represents not only heaven but also the Jerusalem Temple or the Old Testament. Its pillars and arches are bedecked with luxuriously flowering vines; on top of its two slender, golden columns, prophets gesticulate vehemently; and on the small tympanum at right, a son kneels to receive his father's blessing, probably an emblem of Christ before God the Father. The Virgin on the threshold, who is clothed with the sun and crowned with a diadem of flames, has been variously described as *Maria aeterna, Maria expectans,* Maria-Sophia, Maria-Ecclesia, *Maria coronata,* and *mulier amicta sole.*[71] The gold and red aureole around her head mirrors the luminous sphere surrounding the risen Christ, and within it her auburn hair is transfigured, like his, to pure gold. One commentator describes her as "the most luminous and ideal figure in Master Matthias's work."[72] Together, the Madonna and the eternal Virgin define two sides of an isosceles triangle whose pinnacle is God the Father, veiled by excess of light within a cloud.

Here, unmistakably, we see the double-natured Virgin of *Marienleich* 20, at once *gotlich* as Maria-Sophia and *menschlich* as the Madonna. There is no need to decide whether Grünewald's luminous Virgin represents Mary before her earthly life or after it, for the two coincide: she is both preexistent and glorified, both the eternally predestined Bride and the crowned Queen of Heaven—or, in the words of the *Marienleich*:

> ich binz ein spiegel der vil klaren reinekeit,
> da got von erst sich inne ersach.
> ich was mit im, do er entwarf gar alle schepfenunge,
> er sach mich stetes an in siner ewiclichen ger.
>
> . . . .
>
> ich binz der tron, dem nie entweich
> die gotheit, sit got in mich sleich.
> min schar   gar   clar   var:
> ich got, sie got, er got, daz ich vor nieman spar.
>
> (12.3–6 and 30–33)

> [I am the mirror of great purity
> in which God saw himself from the beginning.

71. For summaries of these interpretations, see Thomas Schipflinger, *Sophia—Maria: A Holistic Vision of Creation,* trans. James Morgante (York Beach, Maine: Samuel Weiser, 1998), 170–83, and Georg Scheja, *The Isenheim Altarpiece,* trans. Robert E. Wolf (New York: H. N. Abrams, 1969).

72. Lucien Sittler, *Der Isenheimer Altar des Meisters Mathis genannt Grünewald* (Colmar: Alsatia, 1957), 19.

FIG. 6   Double nature of Mary: the Madonna and the Eternal Virgin. Matthias Grünewald, Isenheim Altarpiece, 1515

I was with him when he formed the whole creation,
he gazed at me always with desire unceasing.

. . . .

I am the throne the Godhead
never fled—since God slipped inside.
Strong the throng where I belong!
I am God, they are God, he is God: this I will hide from none.]

THE ROMANTICS AND MODERN CRITICS

With the decay and eventual demise of the meistersinger guilds, Frauenlob's reputation faded.
Yet if he was still remembered in 1630 as a champion of women, his legacy may have persisted
elsewhere even when his name was forgotten. In 1960, Rudolf Krayer made a provocative case
for Frauenlob as a missing link between the twelfth-century cult of the goddess Natura and its
revival and transformation by the German Romantics.[73] It was largely through Frauenlob's
influence, as we saw, that Alan of Lille was discovered by his fellow poets and humanists,
whose preoccupation with Natura remained strong even to the time of Hans Sachs, the last and
greatest of the meistersingers. Although Goethe did not read Alan or (apparently) Frauenlob, he
did read Sachs. In his 1776 poem "Hans Sachsens poetische Sendung," he works "Nature's
Genius" (a figure invented by Alan in *De planctu Naturae*) into a nostalgic evocation of the wan-
dering minstrels' ethos:

Sollst halten über Ehr und Recht,	Uphold Justice and worthy Fame,
In allem Ding seyn schlicht und schlecht,	In everything be simple and plain.
Frummkeit und Tugend bieder preisen,	Praise Piety and Virtue honestly,
Das Böse mit seinem Nahmen heissen.	Call Evil and its partisans by name.
Nichts verlindert und nichts verwitzelt,	Let nothing be softened, nothing shamed,
Nichts verzierlicht und nichts verkritzelt;	Nothing prettified, nothing defamed;
Sondern die Welt soll vor dir stehn,	But let the world stand before you
Wie Albrecht Dürer sie hat gesehn,	As Albrecht Dürer saw it—
Ihr festes Leben und Männlichkeit,	Its solid life and virility,
Ihre innre Kraft und Ständigkeit.	Its inner strength and stability.
Der Natur Genius an der Hand	The Genius of Nature at your hand
Soll dich führen durch alle Land,	Shall lead you throughout every land,
Soll dir zeigen alles Leben.[74]	Shall show you all there is of life.

73. Krayer, *Frauenlob und die Natur-Allegorese*, 38–40.
74. Johann Wolfgang von Goethe, "Erklärung eines alten
Holzschnittes vorstellend Hans Sachsens poetische Sendung,"
lines 47–59, in *Sämtliche Werke*, 27 vols. (Frankfurt am Main:
Deutscher Klassiker Verlag, 1987–99), 1:358.

On Krayer's telling, it is Frauenlob who, through his oblique influence on Goethe, links medieval Platonic naturalism with high Romanticism. He would thus occupy a position in German poetry analogous to Jean de Meun's in French letters. Such a claim, too far-reaching to investigate here, deserves attention from specialists. What is certain, though, is that Frauenlob would have appreciated the famous ending of Goethe's *Faust,* with its unexpected prayer to Mary as *Jungfrau, Mutter, Königin, Göttin* ("Virgin, Mother, Queen, Goddess"), and the Chorus Mysticus that follows:

Alles Vergängliche	All that is transient
Ist nur ein Gleichnis;	But as symbol is sent;
Das Unzulängliche	The insufficient
Hier wird's Ereignis;	Becomes here event;
Das Unbeschreibliche	The indescribable—
Hier ist es getan;	Here it is done;
Das Ewig-Weibliche	Woman Eternal
Zieht uns hinan.[75]	Leads upward and on.

In these celebrated lines we meet once more not the Virgin of everyday piety but the exalted Lady of the *Marienleich.* Frauenlob of course would have interpreted the abstract Sublime of Goethe's Chorus Mysticus as an account—hardly more veiled than his own—of the Incarnation.

Another facet of the Romantic movement, its enthusiasm for the medieval past, sparked a revival of interest in the minnesingers and, to some degree, Frauenlob. The city of Mainz saw fit to honor the poet's memory by naming a street, a square, a city gate, a school, and a choir after him; and in 1783 his medieval monument, destroyed in a recent building project, was restored and enhanced. The effigy that now appears in the cathedral cloister (fig. 7), though badly weathered, depicts a bust of Frauenlob with his long hair bound in a coronet of lilies, following an antiquarian's description of the original stone: "caput corona, seu potius serto cinctum, collum et humeri floribus ornati" ("a head girded with a crown or rather a garland, the neck and shoulders adorned with flowers"). Beneath this stone is another carved in the late eighteenth century depicting the funeral scene recounted by Albrecht von Strassburg: mourning women carry the poet's bier, surmounted by three crowns, to his burial place. According to a recent chronicler, flowers still appear from time to time beneath the stone.[76]

But antiquarian fondness is one thing, scholarship another, and Frauenlob fared badly with nineteenth-century critics. When a first edition of his collected works was published by Ludwig Ettmüller in 1843, including numerous inauthentic songs from the Colmar manuscript, most

---

75. Goethe, *Faust* 2, act 5, 12104–11, *Sämtliche Werke* 7, pt. 1:464. The superb translation is not mine, but I have been unable to discover its source.

76. Ruberg, "Frauenlob-Gedenken," 83. See also Rudolf Kautzsch and Ernst Neeb, *Die Kunstdenkmäler der Stadt und des Kreises Mainz,* Bd. 2, Teil 1, *Der Dom zu Mainz* (Darmstadt: Hessische Staatsverlag, 1919), 451–53.

FIG. 7   Frauenlob's tombstone. Mainz Cathedral cloister, 1783

literary historians were unenthusiastic.[77] They tended to see him as either a late, decadent representative of minnesang or a baneful harbinger of meistersang.[78] But some of the late Romantics, like their precursors a century before, found reason to admire the extravagant poet. A. E. Kroeger, whose translation of the *Marienleich* I cite in the Preface of this book, called Frauenlob "the Algernon Swinburne of his time"—not a bad analogy in some ways, although Swinburne's still-unknown contemporary, Gerard Manley Hopkins, would have been a better one. (Kroeger published his *Lay of Our Lady* in 1877, only two years after Hopkins wrote "The Wreck of the Deutschland.") The translator goes on to observe that Frauenlob stands to the early minnesingers much as Wagner does to Mozart or Beethoven.[79] Again, his analogy has merit, especially when we consider that the medieval German poems still most widely known today—*Tristan, Parzival*, the *Nibelungenlied*—are those of the Wagner canon.

Frauenlob found another admirer in the esoteric, experimental poet Stefan George (1866–1933), whose lofty ideas about the nobility of art and principled resistance to modernity made him a cult figure. During his symbolist phase, when he was much influenced by Mallarmé's aesthetic of *l'art pour l'art*, George published his *Buch der Sagen und Sänge* (1895), which includes the poem "Frauenlob." Composed in a deliberately archaic style, this elegy evokes the dying poet as he bids farewell to the ladies—proud patricians' daughters, "mighty and unmoved" in their bright, loose-fitting robes—and then the funeral so memorably described by the medieval chronicler:

> Bei der glocke klage folgen jungfraun und bräute sacht
> Einem sarg in düstrer tracht.
> Nur zarte hände reine und hehre
> Dürfen ihn zum münster tragen zum gewölb und grab
> Mit königlicher ehre
> Den toten priester ihrer schönheit zu verklären.
> Mädchen und mütter unter den zähren
> Gemeinsamer witwenschaft giessen edle weine
> Blumen und edelsteine
> Fromm in die gruft hinab.[80]

> [Softly in somber garb, virgins and brides
> Follow his bier as the bells lament.
> Only tender hands, exalted, pure,
> May bear him to the minster, to vault and grave,

77. Frauenlob, *Leiche, Sprüche, Streitgedichte und Lieder*, ed. Ludwig Ettmüller (Leipzig, 1843; repr. Amsterdam: Rodopi, 1966).

78. See Krayer, *Frauenlob und die Natur-Allegorese*, 13–21, for a summary.

79. Kroeger, *Lay of Our Lady*, introduction.

80. Stefan George, "Frauenlob," 29–38, in *Sämtliche Werke*, 18 vols. (Stuttgart: Klett-Cotta, 1991), 3:46–47.

To transfigure with kingly rites
The dead priest of their beauty.
Maidens and mothers amid tears
Of a common widowhood pour noble wines,
Blossoms and gems
With devotion into the tomb.]

Despite this pre-Raphaelite tribute, it would be a long while before Frauenlob's critical rep-
utation improved. Ludwig Pfannmüller's edition of the *Marienleich* (1913) included the first seri-
ous critical study of the poem, and much in it is still valuable. But the editor made no attempt
to conceal his distaste for the author. Inspired by his teacher Gustav Roethe, the editor of Rein-
mar von Zweter, Pfannmüller set out to shed some light on the "still unsolved problem" of
Frauenlob, only to find himself deeply offended by what he perceived as the poet's Mariolatry,
pretentious and overwrought style, pompous display of learning, and willed eccentricity. As a
good rationalist, Pfannmüller was especially troubled by Frauenlob's unsystematic blurring of
boundaries between image and image, concept and concept—the same phenomenon that
Susanne Köbele has more recently and sympathetically characterized as *Ineinander,* in contrast to
the *Nebeneinander* of Konrad von Würzburg or Heinrich von Mügeln.[81] In a revealing compari-
son, Pfannmüller presents Frauenlob's relation to his precursors in the same way that Heinrich
Denifle understood Eckhart's relation to Thomas Aquinas, as one of distortion and
corruption—yet he concedes that in such cases a friendly critic might perceive development or
legitimate difference where an unfriendly one sees only misunderstanding.[82] Quite possibly,
Pfannmüller himself did not misunderstand Frauenlob; he just lacked all sympathy with him.
In a plaintive preface, he even lamented the *sacrificium intellectus* required of anyone who would
faithfully seek to reconstruct "all the ideas and mental associations of a not fully normal
brain."[83] One can only pity the young scholar, squandering so much energy on an intellectual
mismatch before his own life was snuffed out in the supreme irrationality of World War I.

Twentieth-century critics largely shared Pfannmüller's views, even if they seldom expressed
them so candidly. Rather than citing a long litany of similar remarks, I shall compare only two of
the most important literary histories, those of Gustav Ehrismann (1935) and Max Wehrli (1980),
to suggest the critical shift that has now begun. Ehrismann tried hard to do Frauenlob justice.
Though put off by his notorious literary boast, whose authenticity has now been challenged, the
scholar acknowledged that Frauenlob possessed "a great virtuosity and an astonishing amount of
knowledge." His was a poetry not of feeling but of intellect, an *ars* in the true medieval sense of
ars rhetorica. Both his achievement and his flaws can be summed up in the term *Superklugheit,*
"brilliance" in a rather pejorative sense. As the apotheosis of the *geblümter Stil,* Frauenlob's

---

81. See Chapter 2, above, p. 88.
82. Pfannmüller, *Frauenlobs Marienleich,* 20.

83. Pfannmüller, *Frauenlobs Marienleich,* vii–viii.

poetry is mannered, florid, baroque, though in his *leichs* he produced works of genuine verbal magic. Yet Ehrismann cannot altogether approve, for this kind of poetry represents "the consummation of an unwholesome, extravagant, expressionistic tendency in thirteenth-century lyric, a tendency that viewed dark whispering as high knowledge and wordplay as art." Moreover, the *Marienleich* is morally offensive, for it "lets the love of God and the Virgin degenerate into erotic sensuality."[84] Instead of exalting eros to the level of spiritual love in the manner of the *dolce stil nuovo,* the *leich* merely drags what is sacred down to the human level. Ehrismann, of course, was neither the first nor the last Protestant to take offense at the ambivalence of late medieval Minne.

Writing forty-five years later, with the benefit of Krayer's important study and Stackmann's 1972 manifesto, "Bild und Bedeutung bei Frauenlob," Max Wehrli is more sympathetic. The relatively new category of *Spruchdichtung* enables him to distinguish Frauenlob and his fellow wandering poets more clearly from the courtly minnesingers and the urban meistersingers.[85] He characterizes these minstrels' songs as virtuosic and "learned," for theirs is an art marked by recherché metaphors, verbal enigmas, foreign loan words, intense musicality, and a marked preference for scientific and (especially) theological subject matter. Even though "all this has nothing to do with lyric in the modern sense," *Spruchdichtung* had its own distinctive aesthetic within which individual voices can be discerned. Wehrli expresses particular admiration for Reinmar von Zweter, Wild Alexander, and Konrad von Würzburg. In Frauenlob, however, all the characteristic tendencies of *Spruchdichtung*—its artistic boldness, hermetic obscurity, and mannered torture of the German language—"attain their clearest, most convincing form and find a genuine poetic solution."[86] Wehrli notes that not all of Frauenlob's poetry is obscure or *geblümt;* many of his *Sprüche* are perfectly clear and accessible. The three *leichs,* on the other hand, are extreme and demanding masterpieces, unequaled in their verbal and melodic complexity. In the *Minneleich,* that "astonishingly calculated orgy of language," verbal acrobatics at times get in the way of meaning. Yet the intellectual and aural excitement of that piece, as of the "daring" *Marienleich,* is unmistakable. Wehrli concludes that, given the contemporary state of research, it is still hard to reach a final assessment of Frauenlob, which will in any case be a matter of taste. Yet, once again, he alludes to the parallel case of his contemporary, Meister Eckhart. With Frauenlob as with Eckhart, the more nervous and experimental the language, the more profoundly "aestheticized," the more too it expresses a secret quest and longing for the ineffable.[87]

Frauenlob will never be a poet for all seasons, a universal genius like Dante or Chaucer, whose immense variety has something to offer every taste. Yet for connoisseurs who enjoy "the fascination of what's difficult," who find his ideas appealing and his language intoxicating, who may even (for all things are possible) share his predilection for *das Ewig-Weibliche,* his is a voice like no other.

84. Gustav Ehrismann, *Geschichte der deutschen Literatur bis zum Ausgang des Mittelalters,* 2 vols. (Munich: Beck, 1935), 2:301–4; quotations, 303.

85. Max Wehrli, "Fahrende und Meister (Spruchdichtung)," in *Geschichte der deutschen Literatur vom frühen Mittelalter bis zum Ende des 16. Jahrhunderts,* vol. 1 (Stuttgart: Philipp Reclam, 1980), 439–54.

86. Wehrli, *Geschichte,* 450.

87. Wehrli, *Geschichte,* 454.

COMMENTARY ON THE *MARIENLEICH*

This commentary is based on the Middle High German text. It supplies literal translations for all passages cited, rather than my facing-page verse translations, which often diverge from strict equivalence for the sake of rhyme, meter, and poetic effect. All references to Frauenlob's poetry are from the Göttingen edition (GA) by Stackmann and Bertau, cited by section, strophe, and line numbers. I have made ample use throughout of Stackmann's notes to the *Marienleich* (GA, pp. 613–59), as well as his *Wörterbuch zur Göttinger Frauenlob-Ausgabe,* prepared in collaboration with Jens Haustein (Göttingen: Vandenhoeck & Ruprecht, 1990). The poet's allusions to the Vulgate are cited comprehensively,[1] as are his echoes of Reinmar von Zweter's *Leich* and Konrad von Würzburg's Marian poem, *Die goldene Schmiede* (with line numbers given in parentheses). Other "sources and analogues" represent a suggestive rather than exhaustive listing.

1. For a full register of biblical citations, see Gärtner, "Das Hohelied in Frauenlobs Marienleich," in Schröder, ed., *Wolfram-Studien* 10:113–16. I have added a few allusions to Gärtner's list, while omitting others that I found less convincing.

Strophe 1

The *leich* begins in the first-person voice of a seer-prophet modeled on Saint John the Divine. This "I," who does not necessarily represent the poet as an individual, speaks for the first eight strophes. His opening words at once declare that the subject of the poem is a vision, for the rhetorical gesture *ei, ich sach* parallels the prophetic *vidi* of the Vulgate and contemporary mystics.[2] *Vor miner ougen anger* ("before the meadow of my eyes") in 1.4 is a more florid way of presenting a visionary experience, but the phrase also echoes a convention of minnesang and anticipates the imagery of blossoms and fruitfulness that will pervade the poem.[3]

What the speaker sees is the *mulier amicta sole* of Apocalypse 12, but Frauenlob chooses only a few details, and not the most usual ones. The Lady is enthroned and pregnant and wears a crown of twelve stars, here identified with the twelve jewels of the New Jerusalem. These gems and their virtues will be fully enumerated in the final strophe, giving the poem an elegant circularity as its end returns to its beginning. Other details of the apocalyptic vision ("clothed with the sun, with the moon beneath her feet") are not mentioned here because they are reserved for the Lady's own speech in strophe 10a. The seer perceives that she "wishe[s] to be delivered" (*wolte wesen enbunden*)—a considerable softening of the biblical text, where she cries out in her labor pangs—but according to a long-standing theological tradition, the Virgin's childbearing was without pain because her conception was without sin.

It is significant that the Lady is nowhere explicitly named as Mary, nor is her Son ever named as Jesus. The meaning of this restraint becomes clear once awareness has dawned on the reader or listener: while the poem's feminine speaker is indeed Mary, the mother of Christ, she is also a divine, eternal being whose full identity is revealed only gradually. In the meantime, the poet's initial use of the title *vrouwe*, "lady" (rather than *maget* or virgin), is itself significant. *Vrouwe* corresponds to the Latin *domina*, the Virgin Mary's most common devotional title, but this term also played a key role in the so-called *wip-vrouwe* debate between Frauenlob and some of his contemporaries.[4] Alone among medieval German poets, he defined *vrouwe* as signifying first of all a mother, rather than a lady in either the social or the moral sense. Deriving the word etymologically from *vro* plus *we* (the joy of fertility and the pain of childbirth) in his strophe V.112, he praised the *vrouwe* as the noblest of the three degrees of womanhood, superior to the virginal *maget* as well as the sexually initiated *wip*, because of her fruitfulness (V.102).

Sources and analogues: By 1300 the woman clothed with the sun, interpreted by the earliest Christian exegetes as a figure of the church, had come to be frequently identified with Mary. It would be pointless to seek all the parallels, but here as elsewhere, Frauenlob most closely echoes *Die goldene Schmiede* (1833–39): "din crone luter glestet, / got der hat dich gegestet / mit

---

2. Barbara Newman, "What Did It Mean to Say 'I Saw'? The Clash Between Theory and Practice in Medieval Visionary Culture," *Speculum* 80 (2005): 1–43.

3. Köbele, "Umbesetzungen," 213–35. Frauenlob's fourth Minnelied (XIV.16.1) begins with the line "Ahi, wie blut der anger miner ougen" ("Ah, how the meadow of my eyes is blooming!").

4. See Chapter 2, above, pp. 64–67.

einem liehten cranze: / zwelf sternen mit ir glanze / din houbet zierent schone, / die siht man dir ze lone / da brehen unde schinen" ("Your bright crown is glistening; God has bedecked you with a radiant garland. Twelve stars with their splendor beautifully adorn your head. We see them glitter and shine there as your reward").

Strophe 2

The words *Nu merket* echo the Latin *nota bene,* as if to annotate the vision—an index of the learned commentary tradition in which this poem is rooted. Mary is represented as *die gefüge,* probably "the obedient or compliant one" (as in modern *fügsam*),[5] although a Latin gloss in one manuscript translates this term as *tenera, gracilis* ("delicate"). The Virgin is "obedient" insofar as she carries her divine Child for nine months *der naturen zu genüge,* "to satisfy Nature." Although her miraculous conception defies Nature's laws (10.28), her normal pregnancy fulfills them—a paradox noted as early as Ambrose's discussion of her virginal maternity.[6] The word *nature* itself rarely occurs in the poem, but its significance is great, for Natura is prominent among the many goddesses subsumed in the poem's *vrouwe.*

Just as the poet announced his own vision in the first strophe, so here he announces the Lady's vision. While still pregnant with her Son she already "sees" him *mit witzen* (2.6)—with her mind's eye—in two symbolic forms. Both of these allude again to the Apocalypse: he is the One enthroned amid seven candlesticks (Apoc. 1:12–13; cf. strophe 7) and also the Lamb on Mount Zion (Apoc. 14:1; see 13.31–32). The Lady's vision is not a question of prophecy or foreseeing the future so much as a glimpse into eternity: her own childbearing and the Lamb's enthronement constitute two moments in an eternal, simultaneous present.

The second half-strophe introduces the ubiquitous floral theme in a characteristically condensed and synaesthetic way. Mary bears her flower *sam ein tolde,* "like a treetop," perhaps alluding to the iconography of Jesus as the flower atop the genealogical Tree of Jesse (cf. 18.13). Christ is at once blossom and fruit, and the same fruit whose weight Mary bears in her womb is the cluster of grapes that made her fruitful, for God is both her lover and her son. These grapes also suggest the wine of the Eucharist; they are mentioned again in strophe 19b. Mary's complex relationship to the Trinity is introduced by the reference to her as Mother of both the Lamb and the Dove—symbols of the divine Son and the Holy Spirit. Elsewhere she speaks of the whole Trinity as "folded" or "spun" within her (13.39; 15.30). Mary in late medieval hymnody was frequently represented as "Mother of the Trinity," and she is graphically depicted as such in the late medieval sculptural type known as the Shrine Madonna, or *vierge ouvrante.*[7]

---

5. Schäfer, *Untersuchungen zur deutschsprachigen Marienlyrik,* 86.

6. "Multaque in eodem et secundum naturam invenies, et ultra naturam. Secundum conditionem etenim corporis in utero fuit, natus est, lactatus est, in praesepio est collocatus, sed supra conditionem Virgo concepit, Virgo generavit: ut crederes quia Deus erat, qui novabat naturam; et homo erat, qui secundum naturam nascebatur ab homine." Ambrose, *De incarnationis Dominicae sacramento,* 6.54 (PL 16:832b). This contrast between natural and supernatural aspects of the Virgin's maternity was often cited.

7. For an exhaustive catalogue of these images, see Christoph Baumer, "Die Schreinmadonna," *Marian Library Studies* 9 (1977): 239–72.

Mary's personal virtue (*sie tet rechte / als sie solde,* "she did just as she should") will be the theme of strophes 6 and 7. A similar phrase recurs in 12.36, *ich warb, als ich do solde* ("then I behaved as I should"). In her maternity, nature and grace, virtue and miracle, are inseparably intertwined.

At 2.16 the poet-seer begins to address the Virgin directly in the second person. He uses the unexpected polite form *ir*, characteristic of courtly literature, rather than the familiar *du* of Christian hymnody and prayer—an almost unprecedented gesture in *Marienlob*. With strophe 3, however, the perspective shifts to become more intimate, with Mary now addressed as *du*. These two forms continue to oscillate until 8.25, where the Lady's own discourse finally begins. This instability in address typifies, even on the semantic level, the iridescent and ever-shifting points of view that make the *Marienleich* so remarkable.[8]

Sources and analogues: In *Die goldene Schmiede* 1298, Mary is addressed as *erentrube* ("honored cluster of grapes"). Several critics have seen a typological allusion to Numbers 13:24, where Moses' spies carry a cluster of grapes back from the promised land to the Israelite camp.

Strophe 3

In this strophe Frauenlob introduces the second of the three biblical repertoires from which he draws most of his imagery. From the Song of Songs comes this strophe's springtime idyll: winter's rains are over, the voice of the turtledove is heard in the land, and the vineyards are in blossom (Cant. 2:11–13), prompting the young lovers to arrange their tryst on the "mountain of myrrh" (Cant. 4:6). In 3.11 some manuscripts read *lewenberge* ("mountain of lions"), while others have *libanberge* ("Mount Lebanon"), both alike from Canticle 4:8: "veni de Libano, sponsa, . . . de cubilibus leonum, de montibus pardorum" ("Come out of Lebanon, my bride, . . . from the dens of lions, from the mountains of panthers").

The poet modifies this biblical imagery in the directions of both *hohe Minne* and Christian typology. Mary is a "fertile maiden" (*bernde meit*) and an "honorable lady" (*eren riche vrouwe*) whose lover calls her to a meeting in the rose garden. *Friedel* (3.8) is a favorite courtly term equivalent to the Latin *dilectus* or *sponsus* of the Song of Songs. The *locus amenus* of the tryst is a vineyard for the production of sacred wine, recalling the fertile grapes of strophe 2; and the Lady herself is both vineyard and garden. It is "the great dew of heaven" (*himeltouwe*), a symbol of the Holy Spirit, that has made her so fruitful. *Arten* in 3.8 is a notorious crux; two possibilities are an adjective, "of noble birth," and a verb, "to cultivate or dwell in the land." The second of these options would yield the reading: "your lover is calling you, tender one, to dwell in the garden that bears the sacred wine" (cf. Cant. 7:11–12).

Strophe 3 also rehearses the numerous roles that Mary fills vis-à-vis the Divine: she is "daughter, mother, maid" (3.14) as well as courtly lover. Speaking as a fatherly guide, the poet

8. Palmer, "Duzen und Ihrzen," *Wolfram-Studien* 10:87–104.

instructs the virgin daughter not to fear literally or metaphorically "going astray" (*irren*, 3.11) when she accepts this invitation to a tryst.

Sources and analogues: The strophe echoes a Song of Songs paraphrase in Konrad's *Goldene Schmiede* (216–21): "in sines vater lande / wil er dich lazen warten, / ob in dem wingarten / blüejen noch die truben, / und ob die türteltuben / ir stimme lazen hoeren" ("He wants to let you wait in his Father's land, [to see] whether the grapes have blossomed yet in the vineyard, and whether the turtledoves let their voices be heard").

Strophe 4

The love tryst initiated in strophe 3 has now taken place: the king has allured the beloved maiden into his intoxicating wine cellar (Cant. 1:3, 2:4). There his "greeting" (*grüzen*, 4.4) has "touched" her, a courtly euphemism for sexual initiation that also evokes the angelic *ave* of the Annunciation. Marian poets and mystics often played on the double sense of this *grüzen*. Mechthild of Magdeburg described her mystical experience as a "true greeting, coming from the heavenly flood out of the spring of the flowing Trinity," lifting the soul out of her body into erotic and ecstatic union.[9] In the king's cellar the Lady drinks the wine of union along with the "milk so sweet" that betokens her motherhood (Cant. 5:1). Here for the first time the poet speaks in the first person plural (4.6): his "we" represents the daughters of Jerusalem, who constitute a chorus in the Song of Songs, but also the "we" of the Christian community. The Lady will address this audience of friends and well-wishers several times in her own discourse. Here they express a mildly voyeuristic pleasure, free of envy, in her consummated love affair with God. *Ver meit* in 4.5 is an enclitic or shortened form of *vrouwe meit*, "maiden Lady"—a highly deferential form of address that pinpoints the moment of Mary's conception. She is still a virgin but has now also become a *vrouwe*, an expectant mother.

The second half-strophe is more difficult. Immediately after a tryst, the bride in the Song of Songs is seized by the "watchmen of the walls" (*custodes, murehüter*), who strike her, wound her, and rob her of her mantle (*pallium* or *mandel*). A lyrical interlude gives way to a scandalous tale in which a virgin is overpowered in a dark alley by three assailants who strip her naked and brutally attack her.[10] Exegetes gave this mysterious episode a variety of interpretations, but Frauenlob's is closest to the Song commentary of Alan of Lille. For Alan, these watchmen are not enemies but friends. He interprets the verse "tulerunt pallium meum mihi custodes murorum" (Cant. 5:7) to mean "abstulerunt a me velamen ignorantiae patriarchae et prophetae" ("the patriarchs and prophets snatched from me the veil of ignorance").[11] Frauenlob goes one step further.

---

9. Mechthild von Magdeburg, *Das fliessende Licht*, 1.2, ed. Vollmann-Profe, 20; trans. Tobin, *Flowing Light of the Godhead*, 40.

10. Wachinger, "Frauenlobs Cantica canticorum," 29.

11. Alan of Lille, *Elucidatio in Cantica canticorum* ad 5:7 (PL 210:87b); Schäfer, *Untersuchungen*, 92. On this commentary, see John Trout, "Alan of Lille's Commentary on the Song of Songs: A Preliminary Study," *Cistercian Studies* 8 (1973): 25–36; Astell, *Song of Songs*, 60–72; Matter, *Voice of My Beloved*, 164–67; and Turner, *Eros and Allegory*, 291–307 (partial translation).

As we learn clearly only at the end of the poem (20.27–29), these watchmen or "robbers" are none other than the three Persons of the Trinity. Enlightened by her divine union, the Lady has entered into knowledge of the eternal mystery of the Incarnation, which was foreshadowed by Old Testament figures but is now revealed to her directly by her lover's own mouth. This knowledge is the "toll" (zol, 4.10) she pays for her erotic initiation.

In lines 14–18 the watchmen seize the beloved maiden and wound her. *Drilch* (4.18) is triplicity or threeness, here referring to the three divine Persons who have "sunk transformation (*wandel*) deep in your wounds."[12] Mary has been transformed by the divine union, which inflicts the wound of mystical love, but God too is transformed, having become incarnate at the moment of Mary's conception.

Sources and analogues: Frauenlob's use of *wandel* here contrasts with that of Konrad, who describes Mary after childbearing as *wandels frie* ("free of change," 1724) to denote her perpetual virginity.

Strophe 5

Here the Lady is identified with the bride at another moment in the Song of Songs, where she "comes up through the desert like a pillar of smoke, with the perfumes of myrrh and frankincense" (Cant. 3:6). Turning to the learned language of dialectic, the poet "proves" that Mary has become a royal bride by referring to the paradox of her perpetual virginity. Although the king, her husband, can enter and leave her "gates" (*pforten*) at his pleasure, they remain forever closed to all others "in all places of honor" (5.6). The imagery is borrowed from Ezekiel 44:2–3, where the prophet proclaims that the east gate of the Jerusalem Temple must remain closed to all men "because the Lord God of Israel has entered through it" and "the prince himself will sit in it to eat bread before the Lord." This passage was taken by the church fathers as a prefiguration of Mary's virginal maternity, and it is among the standard Old Testament lessons read on her feast days.

"David" in strophe 5b is the psalmist, identifying Mary as the golden-robed queen standing at the king's right hand on her wedding day (Ps. 44:10). The theme of marriage leads back once more to the Song of Songs with its frankly sexual celebration of the bride's beauty: the locks of her hair dance like gazelles (cf. Cant. 4:1) and her thighs are like gold purified by fire (Cant. 7:1 compares them to "necklaces fashioned by an artist's hand"). The last sentence has a contrasting didactic or proverbial tone: "The chaste woman's clothes (literally 'skirts') become her well." This verse looks forward to the symbolic celebration of Mary's clothing in strophe 14 and underlines the paradox once more: despite her consummated marriage, the Lady remains forever chaste (*kiusche*).

Sources and analogues: The exegetical gesture of 5.3, *daz prüfe ich*, also occurs in *Die goldene Schmiede* (lines 399, 1142). Two passages from Walther von der Vogelweide's *leich* may have

---

12. Wachinger interestingly interprets *den wandel* in 4.18 as *das Vergängliche*. On his speculative reading, the Trinity (*sin drilch*) has stamped its pervasive imprint on (*durchsunken*) the mutable, sublunary world (*den wandel*) through the wounds of Mary. "Frauenlobs Cantica canticorum," 29 n. 16.

provided models for lines 5.4–6. In 2.b1 Walther addresses the Virgin as "Ezechîeles porte, diu nie wart ûf getân, / dur die der künic hêrlîche wart ûz und în gelân" ("Ezekiel's gate which was never opened, through which the king passed in and out in majesty"). The same rhyme words occur in 3.1: "Ein wort ob allen worten / beslôz dînr ôren porten, / daz süeze ob allen orten / dich hât gesüezet, süeze himelfrowe" ("A word above all words sealed the portals of your ears; the absolute Sweetness has sweetened you, sweet Lady of heaven").[13]

Strophe 6

In this strophe Frauenlob returns from the Song of Songs to the Apocalypse, from Mary's personal union with her Beloved to her universal significance as a figure of the church and of divine Wisdom. The apostle John wrote to the seven churches of Asia Minor (Apoc. 1:11) with moral exhortations and promises; each church had its own "angel" or guardian spirit to symbolize its collective identity (Apoc. 1:20). In the exegetical tradition, these seven angels or spirits (Apoc. 4:5) were often linked with the seven gifts of the Holy Spirit enumerated in Isaiah 11:2. Such schemes of sevens, twelves, and other numbered lists were popular as mnemonic devices in manuals of instruction throughout the Middle Ages.[14] As a *figura* of the universal Church, Mary can also typify the seven local churches, their angels, and their spiritual gifts as she does here. The poet addresses her directly, explaining that since her own "form" or body enclosed "the One who can create all forms" (6.8–9), the creative power of the sevenfold Spirit is and was always at work in her.

Strophe 6b enumerates the seven gifts possessed by Mary as the "fertile ground" (*bernder grunt*) of the Incarnation. Most of these correspond with the seven gifts named by the prophet Isaiah. The Lady possesses—or, better, is identified with—wisdom (*sapientia, wisheit*), counsel (*consilium, rat*), strength (*fortitudo, sterke*), gentleness (*pietas, senftekeit*), and fear of the Lord (*timor Domini, vorchte*). In place of knowledge (*scientia*), the poet interestingly describes Mary as *künste funt,* the source of the seven liberal arts, which constituted the curriculum of human as opposed to divine or theological learning. This phrase anticipates the lengthy development of strophes 16–18a, in which the Lady will be systematically linked with the arts of the trivium (grammar, rhetoric, dialectic) and the quadrivium (astronomy, geometry, arithmetic, and music).

The one missing gift is understanding (*intellectus*), which perhaps overlaps too much with wisdom and knowledge to need repetition. So Frauenlob replaces it with another quality of immense importance to him, *minne* or love. Hartmut Freytag notes that the famous Cistercian axiom *amor ipse intellectus est* ("love itself is understanding") may have suggested this substitution.[15]

13. Walther von der Vogelweide, *Leich* 2.b1 and 3.1, in *Leich, Lieder, Sangsprüche,* ed. Cormeau, 14th ed., 4, 6; first passage trans. Sayce, *Medieval German Lyric,* 390.

14. Mary Carruthers, *The Book of Memory: A Study of Memory in Medieval Culture* (Cambridge: Cambridge University Press, 1990), 80–107.

15. William of St.-Thierry, *Expositio altera super Cantica canticorum* 1 (PL 180:491d); Hartmut Freytag, "Zu den Strophen 6 und 7 von Frauenlobs Marienleich," in *Wolfram-Studien* 10:74.

In any case, *du minne* (6.13) is one of several passages identifying Mary explicitly or implicitly with Love—not just the stylized courtly love of minnesang but the eternal, cosmic, creative force that, according to Frauenlob's debate poem *Minne und Welt*, effects union and fertility in every realm. This theme will be further developed in strophe 17a. *Bernder grunt*, here used of Mary (6.12), is also one of the epithets of the World (a version of the goddess Natura) in the debate poem (IV.2.10). As Ralf-Henning Steinmetz demonstrated, Frauenlob's Lady unites both partners in the debate—Minne standing for the immaterial power of Love, and the World for its material matrix—since it is Mary who gave God his physical, tangible form.[16]

Line 6.16 may have a double sense; the "great bond" (*grozen bunt*) unlocked by Mary's reverential fear of God could be either the symbolic meaning of the Old Testament or, more likely, the bond of hell and Adam's curse, to which the Lady will refer several times (9.23; 11.34; 19.31; 20.17).[17] The last line of the strophe is one of two self-referential passages in which the poet justifies his own song. The other is 11.15–16, where he more jarringly interrupts the Lady's own speech to do so.

Strophe 7

With his characteristic respect for numerology, Frauenlob continues the motif of sevens in his seventh strophe. We have already seen the Lady linked with seven churches, seven angels, and the seven gifts of the Holy Spirit. Here the poet returns to the seven lampstands of the Apocalypse (Apoc. 1:12–13) and the Lady's original vision. In strophe 2 the pregnant Mary saw her still unborn Son "sitting before her" (*vor ir sitzen*) among the lampstands, which represent the seven early Christian churches as in strophe 6. Now the seven burning candles become seven lanterns (*siben liecht lucerne*, 7.2) or seven stars, signifying the virtues of Mary's soul. These are the virtues of a good Christian but also of a courtly lover: self-discipline or modesty (*zucht*) and chastity (*kiusche*); loyalty (*triuwe*) and constancy (*stete*); faith or fidelity (*geloube*); goodness or kindness (*güte*); and humility (*diemut*), which paradoxically "ascends to heaven" by seeking the lowest place. The last line sums up Mary's constellation of virtues: *so bleip din wille an alle swere* ("thus your will remained free of all heaviness" or "all sorrow"). Frauenlob refers to Mary's freedom from original sin on account of her immaculate conception. But *wille* can also mean "sexual desire" as in 9.2. The Latin translation renders this as *paris maris expers tumore*, "you give birth without the turgescence of the male"—expressing this freedom from sin in the context of her virginal pregnancy.

Lines 7.5–7 introduce the mysterious motif of *der jungalte*, "the young-old one." The oxymoron recalls the apocalyptic identification of Christ as *primus et novissimus*, "the first and the last" (Apoc. 2:8). In strophe 11a the Lady will say that when her "ancient lover" kissed her, she "gazed at him [and] he became young," and in 12.16–17 she calls herself the fire in which the

---

16. Steinmetz, *Liebe als universales Prinzip*, 58–65.

17. Freytag, "Zu den Strophen 6 und 7," 78 n. 35. Stackmann reads 6.16 as "unlocked the bonds of hell," while Gerhard

Schäfer, drawing on the exegetical tradition, prefers "opened the great covenant." GA 621; Schäfer, *Untersuchungen*, 94.

aged but immortal phoenix renews its youth. An ancient Christian text, unknown to Frauen-lob, eloquently expresses the idea he refashions here: "This is he who was from the beginning, who appeared new and was found to be old, and is ever born young in the hearts of the saints. This is the eternal one, who today is accounted a Son."[18]

Line 7.8 echoes Zechariah 2:10, "rejoice, O daughter of Zion." Here, Mary is to rejoice at the tidings (*mere*) of the angel Gabriel. This verse was more often applied to the church or the Christian soul.

Strophe 8

In this strophe, the last spoken in his own voice, the seer-poet represents a scene in heaven, evoking the assumption and coronation of the Virgin. The heavenly "thrones" (*tröne*, 8.4), con-stituting one of the nine angelic choirs, demand Mary's coronation as queen because it is fitting for one so beautiful to reign at the king's right hand (Ps. 44:10). "The apple that she bears begins to ripen" (8.9), a symbol with many meanings. Most obvious is that the apple is her child, the "fruit of her womb," but it also evokes the orb of world rule shown as an icono-graphic attribute of kings and, by extension, of God.[19] And the Virgin's apple at least fleetingly evokes the fruit of Eden, which is no longer forbidden in this new paradise. The laughing flow-ers, rendered almost capable of speech to welcome their queen, suggest the Edenic innocence of the scene but also recall the apparition of the goddess Natura in Alan's *De planctu*. When the goddess first manifests herself in the twelfth-century poet's vision, all creation greets her joy-fully with a fresh outburst of fertile life.

Returning to the Song of Songs in 8b, the poet compares Mary's navel—a euphemism for her womb—to a rich drinking vessel fit for kings (Cant. 7:2). The jacinths adorning the vessel derive from the *hyacinthis* mentioned in Canticle 5:14. This name was given to a variety of gem-stones in the Middle Ages, but the most pertinent in this context seems to be the translucent blue gem reflecting the color of heaven and thus symbolizing celestial desire.[20] In this jeweled vessel, which is "the chalice of the Son," Christ has "brought his Father down to us," another example of Frauenlob's very freewheeling treatment of the Trinity. This is one of many passages where he suggests that in bearing Christ, Mary in a fuller sense contains the entire triune God-head. The familial imagery extends from Father and Son to the "tender Daughter" in 8.22, introducing an unexpected chess metaphor: the disastrous fall of the "Old One" (Adam) put all humanity in check, presumably in a game of chess with Death—much as in Ingmar Bergman's film, *The Seventh Seal*. But Adam's (or God's) wise daughter Mary "considered carefully" (*wol sich bedachte*) until she discovered the perfect move to save the game. This move should proba-bly be understood as her answer to Gabriel, *Fiat mihi secundum verbum tuum* (Luke 1:38).

18. *Epistle to Diognetus*, chap. 11 (2nd century), in Cyril Richardson et al., ed. and trans., *Early Christian Fathers* (New York: Macmillan, 1970), 222.

19. Schäfer, *Untersuchungen*, 96–97.

20. Rabanus Maurus, *De universo* 17.7 (PL 111:469d–470a). On the jacinth (also called hyacinth or jachant), see Salzer, *Die Sinnbilder und Beiworte Mariens*, 229–34; and below under strophe 20.

Concluding his long introduction, the poet at last asks Mary, the "fairest among women" (Cant. 5:9), to speak for herself. Her discourse will occupy the remaining two-thirds of the poem. Following the allusion to Solomon's wisdom,[21] she opens with a line adapted from Wisdom's self-praise in Ecclesiasticus 24:24, one of several books ascribed to that king. The verse was read liturgically on the feast of the Assumption: "I am the mother of fair love (*der schönen liebe*) and of fear, of knowledge, and of holy hope (*der heilicheit ein hoffenunge*)." Lines 8.24 and 8.25 are sung to the same melody, creating a musical as well as verbal rhyme to mark this caesura, which divides the *leich* into its two main portions.

Sources and analogues: Strophe 8a recalls the scene of Mary's coronation in *Die goldene Schmiede* (228–33): "zuo der zeswen hende sin / solt du sitzen ane zil, / da der himel seitenspil / in din ore clinget, / und dir ze lobe singet / der engel samenunge" ("At his right hand you should sit without end, while the music of heaven's strings sounds in your ears, and the assembly of angels sings your praise").

The jacinth (8.18), among other properties, was said to be transparent in fair weather and opaque on a cloudy day. According to Jacobus de Voragine, just as the jacinth is neither the brightest nor the dullest of stones, so Mary occupies an intermediate place between the infinite radiance of God and the opacity of humankind. She also possesses this gem's intrinsic virtues of dispelling sadness and protecting against enemies.[22]

The chess metaphor recalls Frauenlob's account of erotic chess (*der minnen schach*), a familiar courtly image, in his strophe VIII.15. There it is the pleasure of a kiss that "puts the lover in check" and leads ultimately to his checkmate, which is the total triumph of Minne.[23]

The shift from third-person to first-person speech is almost unprecedented in Marian poetry, save for one passage in the thirteenth-century *Rheinisches Marienlob*. The anonymous poet interrupts himself by asking Mary to voice her own lament at Christ's passion, since her speech would be more moving than his: "klag self din rüen, maget reine! / din klag mach alle herzen brechen. / ich wen, du möchtes alsus sprechen"[24] ("Lament your own sorrow, pure Virgin! Your lamentation could break all hearts. I imagine that you might speak like this"). The Virgin's lament, which follows this invitation, is distinguished by its strophic form from the poet's narrative in couplets.

Strophe 9

The Lady's discourse begins with a scene of intense, vivid eroticism in strophe 9a, balanced by the difficult allegory of 9b. She first presents herself as the "great one" chosen for her role by an

---

21. *Selch* in 8.14 is a crux that has never been resolved. The Manesse Codex (C) reads *selig*, which yields good sense ("blessed in wisdom") but fails to supply the necessary rhyme. See GA 624.

22. Jacobus de Voragine, *Mariale*, Sermo 1, cited in Salzer, *Die Sinnbilder*, 233.

23. Thomas Bein, "*Liep unde Lust*: Beobachtungen zu einem 'Minneprinzip' Frauenlobs unter besonderer Berücksichtigung von VII,38–40," in *Wolfram-Studien* 10:166. A *Livre des Echecs amoureux* was written circa 1400 by Evrart de Conty.

24. *Das Rheinische Marienlob*, ed. Bach, 28.

eternal, divine decree: "elegit eam Deus et praeelegit eam," as the liturgy puts it.[25] Her *wille*—sexual desire, but also free will or *liberum arbitrium*—is both strong and tender (*kreftig und ouch mür*, 9.2). Mary takes on the bride's active role as presented in the Song of Songs, rising to open the door to her Beloved, who gazes in through the window (Cant. 2:9), his body wet with the dew of the night (Cant. 5:2), and they make love: "my Beloved put his hand through the opening, and my womb trembled at his touch" (Cant. 5:4). Their tryst is sweet as honey, she says: *comedi favum cum melle meo*, "I have eaten my honeycomb with my honey" (Cant. 5:1). Insouciant after lovemaking, she says almost defiantly, "It did me good! What's the harm in this? (*waz wirret daz*? 9.13). The Latin version translates the last phrase as *quid errat, dic!* For all his insistence on Mary's virginity, Frauenlob will have no squeamishness about her passionate encounter with God. Following such twelfth-century exegetes as Rupert of Deutz and Philip of Harvengt, he assumes that the Virgin's purity only intensified her pleasure.[26]

As a consequence she becomes pregnant, and Frauenlob evokes her state in 9b with a dense cluster of allegorical images from various sources. In bestiary lore, the weasel was thought to possess instinctive knowledge of an herb that can revive the dead. The same creature and its close relative, the ermine, were credited with the ability to kill snakes. Here Mary as "weasel" gives birth to the royal ermine (Jesus), who slays the venomous serpent (Satan) with his bite. The next four lines convey two loosely related images inspired by Exodus 17:5–6, where God commands Moses to strike a rock with his staff and draw miraculous water for the Israelites to drink. Mary is the "sweet morning dew" (*morgenrisel*, 9.15) that splits the rock of Adam's curse, providing a wholesome spring of water. But she is also Moses' staff, teasingly called a "divining rod without a fork" (9.17) because rods used to dowse for water normally *are* forked. The straightness of the rod may denote Mary's integrity: serpents' tongues are forked, but she is not. The passage can be interpreted with the help of *Die goldene Schmiede*, which as usual presents the allegory in clearer form (664–67): "du bist diu wünschelgerte / da mite uz eime steine / wart ein wazzer reine / geslagen in der wüeste" ("you are the divining rod with which a stream of pure water was struck out of a stone in the desert"). Without pausing to expound this metaphor, Frauenlob characteristically moves on at once to another. Mary's staff not only drew water from the rock but also "scraped off the leprosy (*misel*) of black hell" (9.18). The Virgin Mother cleanses as she nourishes.

Lines 9.19–20 are still more condensed and confusing.[27] "Then the palm tree to which my greeting came," says the Lady, "was reddened without dye." (*Prisel* is a scarlet dye made from brazil wood.) In Canticle 7:7 the bridegroom compares the bride to a date palm, and her breasts

25. According to the last pre–Vatican II breviary, this versicle was still used in the third nocturn of Matins on all feasts of the Virgin Mary, as well as in the hours of Sext and None in her Saturday office. The liturgical response is "In tabernaculo suo habitare facit eam." *The Hours of the Divine Office in English and Latin* (Collegeville, Minn.: Liturgical Press, 1964).

26. Astell, *Song of Songs*, 62–63; Fulton, *From Judgment to Passion*, chaps. 6–7. Part 2 of Fulton's work is the fullest study of Marian Song commentaries to date.

27. For a range of interpretations, see GA, 627 n. 20.

to its clusters of fruit. Frauenlob's verses perhaps conflate this simile with an allusion to the cross, a "tree" reddened by the blood of Christ at his Passion. In the devotional lyrics known as *planctus Mariae*, Mary often "greets" the cross by reproaching it for her son's sufferings. Another possible interpretation rests on an apocryphal legend best known to anglophone readers through the Cherry Tree Carol. During the Holy Family's flight into Egypt, Mary becomes hungry and asks Joseph to pluck her some fruit, but he lashes out in anger and says she should ask the father of her child for help. Thereupon Jesus himself speaks to the tree, which bows low so that Mary can pick her fill. In some versions of the tale, which after all is set in Egypt, the tree in question is a palm, not a cherry. Yet another pertinent palm is that of Ecclesiasticus 24:18, where Wisdom declares, "I am exalted like a palm tree in Cades."[28]

In the last six lines Mary appeals to her "wise friend" Adam, calling him to bear witness to his deliverance. She uses a commercial metaphor: her maternity has earned enough profit or interest (*gesuch*, 9.22) to pay off the debt of his curse, so now he is free.

Strophe 9b first introduces a disconcerting linguistic feature that will characterize the Lady's speech throughout the *leich*. Ludwig Pfannmüller called it the "I/my displacement": instead of letting Mary say "I am the morning dew," "I am the divining rod," and so forth, Frauenlob varies her speech by representing these symbols as objects that belong to her: "my morning dew," "my divining rod."[29] The displacement enhances the Virgin's agency: instead of appearing as a glorious but passive object on whom laudatory epithets are heaped, as in much Marian poetry, she represents her own direct, salvific action with a great variety of images.

Sources and analogues: The Lady's evocative "waz wirret daz?" (9.13), spoken after her draught of honeyed love, is the same question Îsôt asks Brangaene after drinking the fateful potion in Gottfried's *Tristan*—adding a still further dimension to the eroticism of this strophe.[30] At the same time, the Lady's words echo the most famous question in medieval German literature. In Wolfram's *Parzival*, the hero finally heals the Grail king Anfortas when he asks the Compassionate Question, *Oeheim, waz wirret dir?* ("Uncle, what ails you?").[31] Frauenlob's Lady will later say she herself is the Grail that healed the suffering king (11.30–31).

The lore of the weasel, the ermine, and the serpent existed in various forms; Isidore of Seville describes a creature he calls *enhydros*, a kind of water-serpent that is a natural enemy of the crocodile.[32] But Frauenlob's immediate source is once again Konrad von Würzburg (160–63): "bi dir bezeichent ist diu wisel / diu daz hermelin gebar, / daz den slangen eitervar / ze tode an

28. Richard of St.-Laurent's *De laudibus beatae Mariae*, 12.6.5.2, says that a palm tree bears red fruit when it is one hundred years old, just as Mary—"young in age, yet ancient in figures and prophecies"—bore the blood-red fruit of the Crucified. This thirteenth-century work, formerly ascribed to Albertus Magnus, is printed in *Alberti Magni Opera omnia*, ed. Auguste and Émile Borgnet, vol. 36 (Paris: Louis Vivès, 1898), 746.

29. Pfannmüller, ed., *Frauenlobs Marienleich*, 16.

30. Gottfried von Strassburg, *Tristan*, line 12490, ed. Reinhold Bechstein and Peter Ganz, 2 vols. (Wiesbaden: Brockhaus, 1978), 2:83.

31. Wolfram von Eschenbach, *Parzival*, sec. 795, line 29, ed. Karl Lachmann, 6th ed. (Berlin: Walter de Gruyter, 1999), 404.

32. Isidore of Seville, *Etymologiae* 12.2.36 (PL 82:439bc); Nikolaus Henkel, *Studien zum Physiologus im Mittelalter* (Tübingen: Niemeyer, 1976), 171–72.

siner crefte beiz" ("You [Mary] are signified by the weasel that bore the ermine, which bit the venomous serpent to death in its power").[33]

Strophe 10

In the first lines of strophe 10 the Lady compares herself to the mighty fortress (*sedelburg*) of the King, echoing Canticle 8:10: "I am a wall, and my breasts like a tower." Her ramparts, painted white with the lilies of chastity, are impregnable to corruption. Once again flowers line her streets, and her name is sweet as balsam (Ecclus. 24:21) to all who call on her (10.8–9). The royal household, perhaps even "the throne itself" (*des trones wesen*), pays tribute (*zinset*) to the noble queen (10.7). From this unusual image, with its reminiscences of the Temple and the New Jerusalem, the poem returns to its initial figure of the woman clothed with the sun (Apoc. 12:1), refreshing it with some new and startling verbs. The Lady has "laced" (*gebriset*) herself in the solar rays, while the moon has—voluntarily, it seems—"laid itself down" at her feet (10.12–13). Allegorically, sun and moon in medieval poetry often stand for Christ and the church, but Frauenlob's lines more likely have a cosmological sense. In medieval cosmology, the orbit of the moon marked the boundary between Nature's corruptible, sublunary realm and the changeless celestial spheres. Isis, a "natural" cosmic goddess who presides over birth, is *crowned* with the moon, while the moon beneath Mary's feet (*luna sub pedibus eius*) indicates that she transcends the natural realm even as she governs it.[34]

Despite the poet's praise of the Lady's modesty and humility in 7b, her rhetoric of self-glorification is the unabashed speech of a goddess. In 10.15 she avows that the divine Spirit itself "praises" her for relieving mortal sin and sorrow (*swere*). Burghart Wachinger takes this grammatically ambiguous line to mean "God in praising me calls me 'Spirit,'" because Mary shares in the Holy Spirit's mission as Comforter or Paraclete.[35] An alternative reading in the imperative mood is possible but even more audacious: "praise me therefore as the Spirit of God."[36]

In 10b Frauenlob juxtaposes the cosmic goddess of sun and moon with the child bride of the Song of Songs, a girl betrothed so young that she "has no breasts" (Cant. 8:8) "on the day she is spoken for," that is, sought in marriage. Line 10.16 alludes to the bridegroom's repeated words of endearment, *soror mea sponsa* (Cant. 4:9–12); *vester* may be taken as either an adjective ("strong, steadfast") or an adverb ("still more boldly").[37] The nubile maiden is portrayed as *brunen* (brown) in 10.23, echoing Canticle 1:4: *nigra sum sed formosa* ("I am black, but beautiful"). Frauenlob now revisits the love-tryst of 9a from a very different angle. Instead of a passionate union between two consenting adults, we see an older lover who uses cunning stratagems

---

33. Cf. Chapter 3, above, pp. 113–14.
34. Krayer, *Frauenlob und die Natur-Allegorese*, 67.
35. Wachinger, "Frauenlobs Cantica canticorum," 33 n. 21.

36. GA 629 n. 15. On early Christian and medieval treatments of Mary as a double for the Holy Spirit, see Newman, *From Virile Woman to WomanChrist*, 198–209.
37. GA 629–30 n. 16; Wachinger, "Frauenlobs Cantica canticorum," 33.

to consummate his marriage with an innocent virgin, still practically a child. After giving his young bride mandrakes (Cant. 7:13) as an aphrodisiac, he waits until she is lulled into slumber, then takes her sleeping. This presentation may have been inspired by Canticle 5:2, "I sleep and my heart wakes"—a favorite verse of contemplative writers, who used it to characterize mystical ecstasy. In this dreamlike union, the Bride says, he "must have woven and braided my pleasure." (*Behuren* in 10.29 is obscure and could also derive from a verb "to acquire."[38]) This representation of Mary as totally passive is surprising and somewhat uncharacteristic, but it emphasizes the miraculous nature of her experience. Unlike her childbearing, which takes place in accord with the ordinary laws of nature (2.4), her conception in this strophe occurs "against nature" (*gein der naturen*, 10.28) and therefore without her active cooperation, though certainly not against her will.

Sources and analogues: The most important analogues for 10b may be negative ones, pointing to the exceptional character of Frauenlob's *leich*. His use of the mandrakes (*alrunen*, 10.24) is a case in point. In the Song of Songs, the Bride invites her lover to an alfresco tryst: "Come, my beloved, let us go out into the field and lodge in the villages! In the morning let us go up to the vineyards and see if the vines have blossomed, if the flowers have yielded their fruit, if the pomegranates are blooming. There I will give you my breasts! The mandrakes have put forth fragrance in our gates. For you, my beloved, I have kept all the fruits both new and old" (Cant. 7:11–13). Frauenlob modifies this scenario, giving the initiative to the male lover instead of his girl-bride and making the scene even more explicitly erotic, but he preserves its overall character. The mandrakes, both narcotic and aphrodisiac, lend an exotic quality to the lovers' drowsy idyll. Alan of Lille, on the other hand, says these mandrakes symbolize "the perfection of the glorious Virgin's virtues," while the influential Marian treatise of Richard of St.-Laurent (often ascribed to Albertus Magnus) says Mary is denoted by the mandrake because, like that plant, she is cold and dry through virginity, fragrant through a reputation for virtue, deeply rooted through contemplation and love, and so forth.[39] Although Frauenlob praises Mary's virtues elsewhere in the *leich,* this kind of explicit allegoresis is precisely what he does *not* do.[40] The powerful effect of strophe 10b depends on its vivid imagining of the "literal sense," offset by only a single allegorical marker, *gein der naturen* ("against nature"), in 10.28.

Strophe 11

In this, the most famous strophe of the poem, Frauenlob names the evocative "smith from the high country" as Mary's lover. Earlier critics took this as a reminiscence of pagan lore, seeing

38. Stackmann gives several possibilities (GA 630–31 n. 29). Wachinger interprets *behuren* as *gehiure machen,* "to make pleasing," and the phrase *min behuren* as the object of the verbs *vlechten* and *ziunen.* On his reading, the whole sentence (10.27–30) would mean "While I slept, he must have beautified me with a braided hedge against nature," that is, prepared and adorned the still-too-young bride for her wedding night. The "braided hedge"

would represent the silver battlements or bulwarks (*propugnacula*) of Canticle 8:9. "Frauenlobs Cantica canticorum," 33 n. 22.

39. Alan of Lille, *Elucidatio ad* 7:13 (PL 210:103a); Richard of St.-Laurent, *De laudibus beatae Mariae* 12.4.41, in *Alberti Magni Opera* 36:673; Salzer, *Die Sinnbilder* 172 n. 2.

40. Cf. Jackson, "Erotische Metaphorik und geistliche Dichtung," in *Wolfram-Studien* 10:80–86.

the smith as Thor or Zeus, and his hammer as the thunderbolt of the sky-god who fructifies the earth-goddess. A more obvious point of reference is Alan of Lille, who in *De planctu Naturae* deploys hammer and anvil as symbols of the male and female genitals. Alan's goddess Natura entrusts Venus (unwisely) with the responsibility for supervising their proper use.[41] More recently, Tobias Kemper has pointed to a source in the exegetical tradition. In Matthew's Gospel, scoffers in Jesus' home town mock his pretensions to work miracles by asking, "Nonne hic est fabri filius? Nonne mater eius dicitur Maria?" ("Is not this the craftsman's son? Is not his mother called Mary?" Matt. 13:55). Kemper shows that *faber*, which translates the Greek τέκτων ("craftsman"), was understood in antiquity as it now is to mean a carpenter; but in the Middle Ages, *faber* was routinely interpreted as "smith" (*smit*). So Jesus appears in several early Christian and medieval commentaries as "son of the smith"—not of Joseph, as the unbelievers implied, but of the divine *faber* who forged heaven and earth with fire and Spirit.[42] The cosmological and sexual connotations of the hammer are balanced by Jeremiah 23:29: "Are not my words like fire, says the Lord, and like a hammer crushing rock?" And Wisdom 18:15 represents the Incarnation as a great leap down from "the high country": "your almighty Word leapt out of heaven, from the royal throne . . . into the midst of the earth." Whatever Frauenlob may have intended, the dense conflation of pagan and Christian symbolism gives this image an exceptional resonance.

By carrying "the one who carries heaven and earth" in her virgin womb, Mary—or the celestial smith—forges "seven holy things," probably the seven sacraments.[43] The notion that Christ left his mother's body "without labor" (*sunder arebeit*, 11.6) harks back to the ancient motif of Mary's freedom from original sin: since labor pangs belong to the curse of Eve (Gen. 3:16), the New Eve was exempt from them. *Mit sicherheit* (11.7) is polysemous: it can mean either "certainly," without a doubt, or "securely," without loss of virginity. Timothy Jackson proposes emending the punctuation to place a comma after *arebeit* and a full stop after *sicherheit*, attaching the qualifier to Mary's painless childbirth rather than her conception.[44]

The Lady proclaims in 11.8 that she "slept with Three" (*slief bi drin*)—another instance of Frauenlob's tendency to treat her as mother and bride of the whole Trinity. Such deliberately risqué language underlines the paradox of a pure virgin who seems to boast of her promiscuity. But in 11.11 she speaks of her lover in the singular. Although he is "ancient," her gaze makes him young again—indeed, he becomes the paradoxical *jungalte* of 7.5. The ancient lover's "kiss" (Cant. 1:1) is the Incarnation, and at the Nativity that follows, the eternal God is

---

41. For a compendium of these readings, see Krayer, *Frauenlob und die Natur-Allegorese*, 124–74.

42. Tobias Kemper, "*Der smit von oberlande*: Zu Frauenlobs Marienleich 11.1f. und verwandten Stellen," *Beiträge der deutschen Sprache und Literatur* 121 (1999): 201–13, citing Bede, *In Lucae Evangelium Expositio* 2.4.22, CCSL 120, p. 105: "pater Christi igne operatur et spiritu. Unde et de ipso tamquam de fabri filio praecursor suus ait: Ipse vos baptizabit in spiritu sancto et igni."

43. Stackmann's text *ich worchte* is based on the readings of manuscript fragments K and L. His base MS C has *und worchte*, which Peter Kern prefers on theological grounds, as cited in Stackmann, "Frauenlob (Heinrich von Meissen)—eine Bilanz," in Stackmann and Haustein, eds., *Frauenlob, Heinrich von Mügeln und ihre Nachfolger*, 54. My translation agrees with Kern on this point.

44. Jackson, "Erotische Metaphorik," 84.

revealed as a tiny babe surrounded by a joyous host of angels singing *Gloria in altissimis Deo* (Luke 2:1 3–1 4). Like so many passages in the *leich,* line 11.1 3 is double-coded, with both secular and sacred referents. Mary alone transforms the Ancient of Days into an infant, but it was also a convention of minnesang that love has the power to rejuvenate old men. The twelfth-century *Kaiserchronik,* for example, observes, "swer rehte wirt innen / frumer wibe minne, / ist er siech, er wirt gesunt, / ist er alt, er wirt junc"[45] ("Whoever is truly in love with a virtuous woman—if he is sick, he is made well, and if he is old, he becomes young"). Reinmar von Zweter's *leich,* well known to Frauenlob, already combines the two senses: "Durch minne wart der alde junc, / der ie was alt ân ende: / von himel tet er einen sprunc / her ab in diz ellende, / ein Got unt dri genende / Enphienc von einer meide jugent, / daz geschach durch minne"[46] ("Through love the Old One became young, he who was forever ancient without end: from heaven he leapt down below, into this exile. One God and three persons received youth from a maiden! It was through love that this happened").

The parenthetical lines 11.15–16 mark the poet's second and final interruption of his song. He expresses a hope that no one will be offended by his praise of the "proud" (*stolzer*)—not humble—Virgin. It is hard to know if this is a mere rhetorical gesture or if Frauenlob actually heard, or at any rate feared, objections from some of his audience to the poem's intense eroticism and somewhat heterodox Mariology. A number of modern critics have indeed taken offense, as did some of the poet's contemporaries, but so far as we know, contemporary objections touched on Frauenlob's style rather than on any supposed doctrinal aberrations.[47] Somewhat jarringly, the Bride's voice immediately resumes her own praise with a verse from the Song of Songs (Cant. 4:10): "he said my breasts were sweeter than wine." In this context, the image refers simultaneously to food and desire, maternal nursing and erotic longing.[48]

Strophe 11b rings changes on the theme of Mary as a chamber where God is hidden, both as lover and as child. In 11.20 he is firmly "locked" (*versloz*) in her womb as an unborn babe. But in 11.22 he is the courtly lover (*amis curtois*) who secretly steals into the "valley of lilies" for a tryst: the Bridegroom of the Song "pastures among the lilies" (Cant. 2:16), and the Bride calls herself a *lilium convallium* (Cant. 2:1). The ostentatious French loan-words, *amis curtois,* point unmistakably to the secular love tradition from which thirteenth-century devotional literature borrowed not only numerous motifs but also a whole ethos celebrating God's relationship with the Virgin (and the soul) as a passionate, even clandestine affair.[49]

In the third spatial image of the strophe, amorous rhetoric gives way to a legal trope. Mary is now the courtroom (*sal,* 11.23) where the "case of Eve's fall" was tried, echoing earlier and later

45. *Die Kaiserchronik eines Regensburger Geistlichen,* 4609–1 2, ed. Edward Schröder, MGH Script. vernac. 1 (Hannover: Hahn, 1892), 166.

46. *Leich,* 51–57, in *Die Gedichte Reinmars von Zweter,* ed. Roethe, 403. Frauenlob also uses the line "ein got unt dri genende" to describe the Trinity in his strophe V.4.19.

47. See Chapter 1, above, pp. 57–60. For modern allegations of heresy, see Chapter 3, p. 106.

48. Jackson, "Erotic Imagery in Medieval Spiritual Poetry," in Debatin et al., eds., *Metaphor and Rational Discourse,* 120.

49. Keller, *My Secret Is Mine;* Newman, *God and the Goddesses,* chap. 4.

passages where she is the means of undoing Adam's curse. This metaphor alludes to the allegory of the Four Daughters of God (Mercy, Truth, Justice, and Peace), a mini-drama rooted in the exegesis of Psalm 84:11 and frequently illustrated. Bernard of Clairvaux, Hugh of St.-Victor, and other twelfth-century commentators adapted what had begun as a Talmudic debate on the desirability of God's creating man to develop a Christian debate on the redeemability of fallen man. The four allegorical sisters argue whether Adam and Eve can ever be saved, until finally their brother Christ ends the debate by promising to take man's punishment on himself and thus satisfy the rival claims of Mercy and Justice. In Robert Grosseteste's Anglo-Norman version of the allegory, *Le Château d'Amour,* the resolution of this debate leads immediately to the scene of the Annunciation, with Christ keeping his promise by taking flesh in Mary, his "castle of love."[50] Reinmar von Zweter represents God as acting in accord with the counsels of Love and Mercy in this world, whereas Justice will prevail hereafter.[51]

The aurora, or dawn (*morgenröte,* 11.27), is a familiar Marian symbol from the Song of Songs and the liturgy: "who is this that comes forth like the rising dawn?" (Cant. 6:9). As the sunrise of Christ, the *sol justitiae,* Mary awakens "lofty song" to celebrate a new day after the ancient night of sin—or perhaps "the night of the elders" (*nox seniorum*), as the Latin translation has it.

Line 11.30 marks a transition back to courtly literature as the Lady rather startlingly announces, "I am the Grail." This is traditionally the chalice used at the Last Supper, in which Joseph of Arimathea caught the Savior's dripping blood on the Cross. According to legend, it was then secretly preserved by a lineage of Grail keepers as a sacred vessel of healing and plenty. In Frauenlob's day the best-known Grail romance in Germany would have been Wolfram von Eschenbach's *Parzival,* in which the Grail is not a chalice but a magic stone, kept in the custody of a radiant virgin named Repanse de Schoye ("spreading of joy"). However, Frauenlob's allusion might point instead to a late thirteenth-century sequel by Albrecht von Scharfenberg, *Der Jüngere Titurel,* which restores the normative vessel with its sacramental connotations.[52] In both the German and the better-known French and English versions, the accomplishment of the Grail quest by a chosen knight heals an ancient, suffering, impotent king—usually called the Fisher King—of his age-old malady (11.31). The French *Queste del saint Graal* (ca. 1220) supplies the explicit allegory which Frauenlob merely implies: the ailing

---

50. Hugh of St.-Victor, *Adnotationes elucidatoriae in quosdam Psalmos David,* c. 63 (PL 177:623–25); Bernard of Clairvaux, *Sermo 1 in Annuntiatione Dominica,* in *Sancti Bernardi Opera,* ed. Jean Leclercq, Henri Rochais, and C. H. Talbot, 5 vols. (Rome: Editiones Cistercienses, 1957–77), 5:13–29; Robert Grosseteste, *Le Château d'Amour,* ed. J. Murray (Paris: Champion, 1918). For German versions of the *consilium Trinitatis* with the four daughters of God, see Kern, *Trinität, Maria, Inkarnation,* 70–80.

51. *Leich,* 214–23, in *Gedichte Reinmars,* 409: "Dâ hât diu Minne den gewalt, / daz si unt der Barmunge rât / vor Gote sint sô manicvalt, / daz er durch si tuot unde lât, / unz disiu werlt ein ende hât. / Dar nâch sô gât diu Rehtikeit / mit vil gelîcher wâge vür: / ez sî uns liep, ez sî uns leit, / si bringet mir ir willekür / si zwei in unser sünden spür" ("Here Love has the power; the counsels of Love and Mercy are so multiplied before God that he acts and suffers in accord with them until this world comes to an end. Afterwards Justice will go forth with evenly balanced scales. Whether we like it or not, she will bring them with their free judgment to bear on the traces of our sins").

52. Stackmann, "Frauenlob und Wolfram von Eschenbach," in Gärtner and Heinzle, eds., *Studien zu Wolfram von Eschenbach,* 78. See also Richard Barber, *The Holy Grail: Imagination and Belief* (Cambridge: Harvard University Press, 2004), esp. pp. 192–97, on *Der Jüngere Titurel.*

king is Adam, his malady is original sin, and the healing mystery of the Grail is the Eucharist. As mother of Christ, Mary is mother of this sacrament as well—a theme that Frauenlob will further develop in strophe 12b.

Biblical allegory and chivalric imagery converge in 11.32–33. The Lady says her milk nurtured "the child (or hero) from the violet vale," which is probably the same place as the "valley of lilies" in 11.21. Although the violet is not biblical, this lowly flower was said to yield its fragrance most fully when trampled and thus affords a ubiquitous symbol of humility in monastic writings. In humbling himself to infancy, Christ could aptly be called a child from the field of violets. The grammatical construction employing the definite article without a noun, followed by an indication of place (*den von violvelde*), was common shorthand for naming chivalric heroes as well as poets. Thus it inserts Christ once again into the world of courtly romance and lyric.

The hero's mother states that, as her reward, she was given "the antlers of a stag" (*hirzgewige*, 11.33)—a rather pagan-sounding gift that evokes memories of Diana the virgin huntress, but is more directly rooted in the bestiary lore of *Physiologus*. The stag is a symbol of longing for God (Ps. 41:2), but like the ermine of strophe 9b it was reputed to kill snakes with its antlers, so it fittingly symbolizes the victory of the Woman over the serpent (Gen. 3:15). The stag in 11b is also connected with the rejuvenation theme of 11a: Frauenlob has separated two motifs that are closely linked in his source, *Die goldene Schmiede* (1378–89). Konrad writes: "der sich erjungen wolte sit / in diner tugende walde, / alsam ein hirz der balde / ze holze und in gedürne / verreret sin gehürne / und sich erniuwet schone. / der geschefte sin ze lone / der schepher sich erfrischte / do sich diu jugent mischte / ze sinen jaren manecfalt; / do hiez er beide junc und alt, / do von dir wart sin lip geborn" ("[God] wanted to rejuvenate himself afterward in the forest of your virtue, like a stag that hastens to the wood and sheds his antlers amid the thorns and beautifully renews himself. To reward his own creature, the Creator renewed himself when youth was mingled with his countless years. When his body was born of you, he was called both young and old").

With the stag's discarded antlers, says the Lady, she "drove the curse out of the tent," or tabernacle (11.34), yet another way of celebrating her reversal of Adam's curse. Thus Mary, whether as the Grail itself or as mother of the promised Grail knight, "undid the ancient law" (*enbant die alten recht*, 11.35), a phrase that closely parallels "unlocked the great curse" (*entsloz den grozen bunt*) in 6.16. The last line of the strophe glances at Psalm 123:7, "the snare is broken and we have escaped."

Sources and analogues: The motif of the Virgin's three lovers dates back at least to a set of sermons composed by the twelfth-century monks and nuns of Admont.[53] "Ich slief bi drin" (11.8)

---

53. "Amatores habuit Rahab sui similes, injustos homines et peccatores, quibus corpus suum prostituit; amatores habuit et Maria, Patrem et Filium et Spiritum sanctum, quibus virginei corporis sui integritatem consecravit." *Homiliae festivales* 77 (PL 174:1025c). An early editor ascribed these anonymous sermons without warrant to the twelfth-century abbot Godfrey of Admont. On their authorship, see Alison Beach, "Listening for the Voices of Admont's Twelfth-Century Nuns," in Linda Olson and Kathryn Kerby-Fulton, eds., *Voices in Dialogue: Reading Women in the Middle Ages* (Notre Dame, Ind.: University of Notre Dame Press, 2005), 187–98.

recalls a suggestive passage in a poem ascribed to Frauenlob's contemporary, the thirteenth-century poet Boppe: "si hat dri vriedel minniklich: / so gar mit eime ein ander magt benueget" ("She has three paramours in love; every other maid is content with one"). But this strophe is among those rejected as inauthentic by Boppe's recent editor and may reflect Frauenlob's own influence on the meistersingers, whose songs were often transmitted pseudonymously.[54]

For *der stric des valles* ("the snare of the Fall," 11.36), cf. *Die goldene Schmiede*, 1100–101.

Strophe 12

After the Apocalypse and the Song of Songs, the third major biblical font of the *Marienleich* is the wisdom literature. In strophe 12a Frauenlob turns to Proverbs, Ecclesiasticus, and the Wisdom of Solomon, and the Lady begins to speak at length in the voice of Sapientia. Hitherto she has appeared as the mother of an eternal Son and as the human bride of God, either ardent and amorous or bashful and maidenly. Now she appears as his divine bride, so to speak—a goddess/consort who was present at the creation (12.5; Prov. 8:30). She is the fountain of life (Cant. 4:15), the joyful fertility of nature (*der bernden wunne*, 12.2), and the pure mirror in which God beheld his perfection from before the foundation of the world (12.3–4; Wisd. 7:26). In 11.13 we saw the virgin bride gazing at her ancient lover (*ich sach in an*) to make him young; in 12.6 he gazes at her without ceasing (*er sach mich stetes an*) in everlasting desire. We might say that Mary's assent to the Incarnation is her way of returning this gaze of divine desire. God and his Wisdom are lovers in eternity as father and daughter; Mary and Christ are lovers in time as mother and son. Viewed *sub specie aeternitatis*, the Incarnation is both a temporal manifestation of an eternal union and a pivotal moment in which that union is turned inside out and upside down, so to speak. The Ancient of Days becomes a newborn child, while the tender maid enters into timeless divinity.

It is as the bestower rather than the recipient of grace that Mary issues Wisdom's invitation from Ecclesiasticus 24:26: "Come to me, all you who desire me" (12.9). The biblical passage continues, "and take your fill of my fruit," so—in a tour de force of Frauenlob's prosody—the Lady declares with quadruple rhyme, *min mut gut frut tut* (12.13): "my mind (or spirit) bears good fruit."[55] *Mut* embraces all the human mental faculties: thought, feeling, and will. The Virgin further identifies herself as the "living lodestar" (12.11) or *stella maris*, star of the sea, echoing a famous pun by Bernard of Clairvaux. Without her guidance, no one can navigate the storm-tossed sea of mortal life.[56]

The last three images of 12a come from the *Physiologus* tradition. The lion and the pelican are figures of Christ because they resurrect their young: the lion by arousing its stillborn cub to life

54. Friedrich von der Hagen, ed., *Minnesinger: Deutsche Liederdichter des zwölften, dreizehnten und vierzehnten Jahrhunderts*, 5 vols. (Leipzig: J. A. Barth, 1838–56): 3, 138; Kern, *Trinität, Maria, Inkarnation*, 105; Heidrun Alex, ed., *Der Spruchdichter Boppe: Edition, Übersetzung, Kommentar* (Tübingen: Niemeyer, 1998).

55. This ornament is known as *Kettenreim*, or "chain rhyme." Sayce, *Medieval German Lyric*, 481.

56. Bernard of Clairvaux, *Homiliae super "missus est" in laudibus Virginis Matris*, 2.17, in *Opera* 4:34–35.

with a roar,[57] the mother pelican by piercing her own breast to feed her chicks with life-sustaining blood. The phoenix symbolizes immortality: only one exists in the universe, and when it has grown old and frail, it kindles a fire, burns itself to a crisp, and is reborn from its own ashes. This image recalls the *jungalte* motif: Mary is the fire in which her ancient but immortal lover makes himself young again. The other animal figures likewise suggest the Lady's intimate identification with her Son. She is not the lion itself but its voice (*stimme*), not the pelican but its blood (*blut*)—in each case, the operative, life-giving element.

This strophe is the first to feature what will henceforth be the Lady's most distinctive speech-act: *ich binz* with the indefinite article. Modeled on the biblical discourses of Sapientia and the Johannine Jesus, this rhetorical mode is emphatic and unexpected, calling the greatest possible attention to the speaker's self-revelation. It might be paraphrased, "This is what I am: a sugar-sweet well of life" (12.1–2). For the anglophone reader, the closest analogue is the series of "I it am" statements made by Christ in Julian of Norwich's *Revelation of Love*: "I it am that is highest. I it am that thou lovest. I it am that thou likest. I it am that thou servest." And so forth.[58]

Frauenlob's strophe 12b turns from the animal to the plant kingdom, renewing the themes of strophe 3. Mary is a field richly planted with spices, so fertile that her "flowers are all pregnant" (*swanger,* 12.21) with nourishing fruit. Like the Garden of Eden she is a source of ever-flowing streams (Gen. 2:6, 10; Isa. 58:11). In a more specific application, her golden-yellow crop becomes the wheat used to bake sacramental bread (see Cant. 7:2, "your belly is like a heap of wheat"). Frauenlob anticipates the motif of the Mystical Mill common in fifteenth-century art, where Mary is shown pouring grain into a mill; its crank is turned by the apostles, who grind the wheat to produce eucharistic Hosts.[59] Here it is the Lady herself who not only grows the sacred wheat but threshes it, mills it, and bakes the bread, keeping it soft and tender with a spread of olive oil—probably designating the human nature of Christ.

The second half of 12b evokes Mary as shrine of the Trinity. Frauenlob makes a distinction reminiscent of Meister Eckhart between God (*got*) and the Godhead (*gotheit,* equivalent to Latin *divinitas*). The former can stand for any one of the divine Persons, each of whom is individually God, while the Godhead signifies the divine nature or essence shared by the Three.[60] Hence, since the day of the Incarnation when the second person of the Trinity "slipped" into the Virgin's

---

57. The presumed verb *lut* in 12.14 is problematic; it may derive from either *lüejen,* "to roar," or *laden,* "to invite." But in the parallel from *Die goldene Schmiede,* 502–5, *luten* is an adjective: "du bist des lewen muoter, / der siniu toten welfelin / mit der luten stimme sin / lebende machet schone" ("You are the mother of the lion, who with his loud voice beautifully brings his dead cub to life").

58. Julian of Norwich, *A Revelation of Love,* chap. 26, in Nicholas Watson and Jacqueline Jenkins, ed., *The Writings of Julian of Norwich* (University Park: The Pennsylvania State University Press, 2006), 207.

59. Caroline Walker Bynum, *Holy Feast and Holy Fast: The Religious Significance of Food to Medieval Women* (Berkeley and Los Angeles: University of California Press, 1987), 285 and plate 1.

60. Although other thirteenth-century German poets make the same distinction, it was most widely diffused through Eckhart's works. See the "Glossary of Eckhartian Terms" in Bernard McGinn, ed., *Meister Eckhart: Teacher and Preacher* (New York: Paulist, 1986): 388–405; Kurt Ruh, "Die trinitarische Spekulation in deutscher Mystik und Scholastik," *Zeitschrift für deutsche Philologie* 72 (1953): 24–53; John Caputo, "Fundamental Themes of Meister Eckhart's Mysticism," *The Thomist* 42 (1978): 197–225; Nigel Palmer, "Frauenlob and Meister Eckhart," in Helen Watanabe-O'Kelly, ed., *The Cambridge History of German Literature* (Cambridge: Cambridge University Press, 1997), 82–85.

body, the divine nature as such has never departed from her (12.30–31). As throne of the triple Godhead, Mary can proclaim *min schar gar clar var* (12.32), metrically and musically echoing *min mut gut frut tut* in 12.13. The line is enigmatic, but I accept Stackmann's view that her "very noble throng" refers to the three Persons of the Trinity, now her inseparable companions.[61] The same rhymes recur in an interesting Marian passage from the *Kreuzleich*: "Der blumen glanz gar sunder schranz belibet, / swie wite ir smac, ir süz bejag, sich tribet. / Jeremias, der schribet: / sie bar gar clar den rat ob aller engel schar, / meit, werlich ungewibet" ("The flower's brightness remains quite undiminished no matter how far its fragrance, its sweet attainment, spreads abroad. Jeremiah writes that she bore most purely the Counselor above all hosts of angels, a maiden truly undefiled," II.12.1–5).

Lines 12.33–34 proclaim the Lady's divine status in even bolder tones. "I [am] God, they [are] God, he [is] God," she announces, without clarifying the persons to whom these pronouns might refer. I would read as follows: the Lady herself "is God" because her union with the Trinity has divinized her; "they," the Father and the Holy Spirit, are also God;[62] and finally "he," her son Jesus, is God.[63] In short, the Trinity has become a quaternity, as it will visually appear in fifteenth-century depictions of the Coronation and other "Marian Trinities."[64] Stackmann rightly observes that in declaring *ich got*, Mary "unites herself with the Father of her Son and with the Son himself in a single essence, merges in the last analysis with whatever humankind can rationally grasp of God."[65]

The mysterious coinages *vatermuter* and *mutervater* (12.34) are best read as possessives: "I am the Father's mother, he is my mother's father." The first half of this claim presumes the absolute inseparability of the divine Persons: in giving birth to the Son, Mary has in some sense become "the Father's mother" as well. Alternatively, Christ *qua* God is Mary's creator, so, in an extended sense, he is both her father and her "mother's father" because he is the parent of all humanity. Medieval hymnody delighted in the familial paradoxes generated by Mary's complex and multiple roles as mother, daughter, and bride of God.

The last three lines are perplexing in a different way, since they suggest an exchange of roles between Christ and Mary. *She* came to earth, suffered, and overcame death (*brach den tot*), then ascended into heaven like an eagle, while *he* "did not suffer" (*er leit do nicht*, 12.38).[66] Mary is

61. I cannot agree with Burghart Wachinger, who interprets the *schar* as the twenty-four elders of the Apocalypse, much less with Ludwig Pfannmüller, who reads it as "plowshare." Wachinger, "Frauenlobs Cantica canticorum," 42; Pfannmüller, *Frauenlobs Marienleich*, 102.

62. *Sie got* could also be translated "she is God," but since Mary is the speaker it is difficult to see what other feminine figure could be intended. A distinction between the human Mary and the divine Sapientia would be out of keeping with the whole tenor of the *leich*, which aims to synthesize rather than distinguish these figures.

63. Wachinger's reading of this line is ingenious but unconvincing. He punctuates "ich, got: si-got, er-got" and translates "I and God: feminine God and masculine God." This seems, to say the least, anachronistic. "Frauenlobs Cantica canticorum," 42 n. 33.

64. Newman, *God and the Goddesses*, 254–73.

65. Stackmann, "Magd und Königin," in Stackmann and Haustein, eds., *Frauenlob, Heinrich von Mügeln und ihre Nachfolger*, 25–26.

66. The phrase *brach den tot* echoes Konrad, *Die goldene Schmiede*, 508: "do brach des todes bant enzwei" ("Then he [Christ, not Mary!] broke the bond of death in two").

active, Christ is passive—a polarity that will be reversed in 16.6. But the same verbs could also be interpreted to denote Mary's full participation in her Son's fate: her suffering would then represent her *compassio* at the foot of the Cross, while her "breaking death" and heavenly ascent would signify her bodily assumption. In that case we could read *er leit do nicht* as "he was not sorry then." A third possibility is that Mary identifies herself as or with Christ's humanity, noting that his divinity—his "angelic" aspect—did not suffer in the Passion. In the *Kreuzleich*, Frauenlob similarly addresses the Cross as an altar of sacrifice: "uf dir der tot / brach sin brot. / daz tet die menscheit, sam die gotheit ir gebot, / sie leit aber do kein not" (On you Death broke his bread. The humanity did this as the Godhead commanded it, but [the Godhead] suffered no pain then," II.18.3–6).

The proper names Adelheit and Engelmar (12.37–38) have long puzzled critics, as they are not linked in romance or any other context.[67] Most likely these names recommended themselves to the poet because of their etymologies: "Adelheit" derives from *adel* ("nobility") and is related to *adelar,* another term for "eagle,"[68] while "Engelmar" comes from *engel* ("angel") and *maere* ("tidings"), with a glance at the Annunciation.

Sources and analogues: The eternal preexistence of the Virgin receives a fuller but more cautious statement in *Die goldene Schmiede* (716–27): "sit daz er künftec wunder weiz, / so weste er ouch benamen ie, / daz du soldest werden hie / sin muoter ane widerstrit: / davon du lebtest alle zit / vor siner claren angesiht. / ob du da liphaft waere niht, / so was doch ie mit hoher state / din bilde und diner sele schate / vor sime antlitze swebende, / vil schone was ie lebende / din forme in der gehügede sin" ("Since [God] knows future miracles, so too he knew by name forever that you should here become his mother without resistance. Therefore you have lived at all times before his radiant countenance. Although you did not yet exist in the body, your image and the shadow of your soul hovered in exalted state before his face forever. Your form has always been most beautifully alive within his mind").

Konrad also presents an elegant account of the Incarnation as *opus Trinitatis,* expressing wonder at the paradox while avoiding the dogmatically dangerous formulations that Frauenlob deliberately courted (328–41).[69] "Got, in der einekeite drilch / und einlich in der trinitat, / gewürket sich ze menschen hat / von sime werke uf erden. / wie möhte ouch iemer werden / kein dinc so wilde wunderhaft, / so daz den schepfer sin geschaft / menschlichen an die werlt gebar, / und sich in einem libe war / kint under vater underein: / und sich da stricte zuo den zwein / der frone geist enzwischen, / so daz ir drier mischen / was niht wan der eine got" ("God—three in the Unity and one in the Trinity—wrought himself as a human being from his work on earth. How could anything so wild and wonderful as this ever happen? His own creature

---

67. In Neidhart's first *Winterlied,* "Engelmar" keeps warm in his chamber on a cold winter day, while "Adelber" is one of several peasant girls at a dance. *Die Lieder Neidharts,* ed. Siegfried Beyschlag (Darmstadt: Wissenschaftliche Buchgesellschaft, 1975), 110.

68. For Mary as an eagle (*aquila, ar, adelar*), see Salzer, *Die Sinnbilder,* 418, 506–7, and Konrad, *Die goldene Schmiede,* 1052–67.

69. Kern, *Trinität, Maria, Inkarnation,* 27–80; Wachinger, "Frauenlobs Cantica canticorum," 40–42.

gave birth to the Creator as a man in the world, and he was child and father alike in a single body; and then the Holy Spirit of both bound himself to the Two, so that the mingling of those Three was nothing other than the One God").

For the *leitestern* or *stella maris* of 12.11, see the hymn "Ave maris stella"[70] and Konrad, *Die goldene Schmiede*, 828: "du glanzer leitesterne."

The lion, the eagle, and the phoenix (together with the unicorn) appear again in a strophe of the *Minneleich* (III.17.1–4), where they provide similes for the sweetness of woman's love. Frauenlob could have learned about these animals and their allegorical meanings directly from the Latin *Physiologus* or its German translation, but also from sources as diverse as Isidore's *Etymologies*, Peter Abelard's Easter hymns, Hildegard of Bingen's *Physica*, Jacques de Vitry's *Historia orientalis*, Vincent of Beauvais's *Speculum naturale*, Albertus Magnus's *De animalibus*, Wolfram von Eschenbach's *Parzival*, or—closest to home—*Die goldene Schmiede*.[71] Konrad explains the phoenix exemplum at greater length (364–69): "du bist ein fiur des lebetagen, / da sich der fenix inne / von altem ungewinne / ze fröuden wider muzete: / wie sanfte er bi dir luzete / biz daz er wart erjunget wol!" ("You are a fire of renewal, in which the phoenix returned from the misery of old age to joy again. How gently he lay within you until he was thoroughly rejuvenated!"). The symbolic lion, phoenix, and pelican were all represented frequently in sacred art.[72]

For parallels to Frauenlob's explicit divinization of the Virgin see Chapter 3, pp. 118–20, and Chapter 5, pp. 162–65.

Strophe 13

Strophe 13, with its forty lines, is the longest in the *leich*. The intensely biblical 13a combines images from the Song of Songs, the wisdom books, and the Gospel of Luke. Uniting strength with beauty, the Lady boasts of her dread power: "I am as terrifying as a man who builds castles on mountaintops" (13.2). It is presumably the devil whom she frightens, as in standard interpretations of Canticle 6:3, where the Bride is called "terrible as an army arrayed for battle." She next compares herself to the magnificent cedar and cypress trees of Ecclesiasticus 24:17, echoing the self-presentation of divine Wisdom. Merely naming her is a source of sweetness to her devotees (13.5; compare 10.8–9 and Cant. 1:2, "Your name is like oil poured out").

Line 13.6 evokes Mary's experience in Luke 1:39, where she hastens across the mountains to visit her cousin Elizabeth, but here her intention is only "to speak to my love." She travels in the litter of King Solomon (Cant. 3:9–10); this is the chariot or *wagen* fashioned by the "wise man" (*der wise*) out of precious wood (*von holze . . . zu prise*), the cedars of Lebanon evoked in 13.3. Some of the rare and puzzling nouns in this passage represent Frauenlob's translations from the Latin: the posts (*columnas, siulen*) of the king's litter are fashioned of silver, its seat (*reclinatorium,*

---

70. The well-known early medieval hymn sung at the office of Vespers on Marian feasts begins with the verse "Ave maris stella, / Dei Mater alma, / atque semper Virgo, / felix caeli porta." See also Salzer, *Die Sinnbilder*, 400.

71. Henkel, *Studien zum Physiologus*, 166–67, 194–96, 202–3; Salzer, *Die Sinnbilder*, 58–63, 538.

72. Cf. *Die goldene Schmiede*, 468–75, on the pelican.

anelein) and window-ledges (*simz*) of gold,[73] and its steps (*ascensum, ufganc*) of royal purple, while "true love" (*die were minne*) is strewn within it (*media caritate constravit propter filias Hierusalem*). When King Solomon rides through Jerusalem in this litter, he wears "the diadem with which his mother crowned him on his wedding day, on the day of the gladness of his heart" (Cant. 3:11)—an event understood prophetically as the Incarnation, the day of God's marriage to the human race. Therefore "of all this," Mary says, "I am the beginning" (13.15). She is like the bride in Psalm 44:3, another royal wedding song: "grace is poured out upon [her] lips," and Wisdom opened her mouth when her tongue "tasted the gentleness of the angelic hosts" (*der ordenunge*), a reference to Gabriel's greeting at the Annunciation. Hence her devotees or dear ones (*lieben*) are invited to greet her in turn with their songs of praise.

Strophe 13b invokes Mary as the fulfillment of Old Testament prophecy. The symbolic visions of the patriarchs, such as Jacob's ladder and Aaron's blossoming rod, all prefigured her, as did the later discourse of the prophets (13.33–34). This was a commonplace that would have evoked for the medieval reader such figures as Gideon's fleece (Judg. 6:36–40), the closed gate of the Temple (Ezek. 44:2), the prophecy concerning Bethlehem (Mic. 5:2–3), and of course the Virgin who conceives (Isa. 7:14). The Lady's declaration that no nature in all the world has ever been so fine and pure as hers (13.22–23) belongs to a more abstract realm reminiscent of the *novus homo* in Alan of Lille's *Anticlaudianus*, created as a new beginning for humankind by a fresh covenant between God and Nature. She is taught by divine Wisdom (13.18; Wisd. 7:21) but also personifies her when she "cries out and . . . utters her voice" (13.28; Prov. 8:1), ready to heal and comfort all who turn to her because her mind is free of wrath (*zornes*) and struggle (*ernste*). Eckhartian language recurs in 13.27: the Lady represents the infinite potentiality (*ende-lose mugend*) of the abyss of God's goodness (*der grundelosen güte*).

The "seven horns" of 13.31 are those of the Lamb who was slain (Apoc. 5:6), standing for the "seven spirits of God sent out into all the earth." Frauenlob's imagery here recalls strophes 6 and 7, where these spirits are linked with the seven churches of the Apocalypse, the seven gifts of the Holy Spirit (Isa. 11:2), and the seven virtues of Mary's soul. But the horns of the Lamb seem also to be drinking horns: as the Virgin has supplied wheat for the eucharistic bread, so too she pours the sacramental wine.

The last lines are enigmatic and beautiful. Mary brings "only heaven" (*niur himel*) to her friends, swinging wide its portals long shut because of sin, for in the face of her power all locks fly open, all bolts are helpless. The strophe ends with another allusion to her divine maternity: she is "maiden-mother" (*mutermeit*) of the Trinity, her "Creator and [her] ancient lover" (13.38), who "enfolded" the three divine persons in her body. Just as Mary became the lover of the whole Trinity in 11.8 (*ich slief bi drin*), here she becomes mother of all three Persons. Although this teaching is not strictly orthodox, it is nonetheless implied by such phrases as *triclinium Trinitatis*

---

73. *Simz* and *anelein* in 13.11 have puzzled both scribes and philologists; the manuscripts have a variety of readings. See   Pfannmüller, *Frauenlobs Marienleich*, 103–4, and GA 638 n. 11 for possibilities.

("banqueting hall of the Trinity") in Latin hymns and by sculptural types like the Shrine Madonna. A thirteenth-century Latin sequence on the Annunciation states the same idea: "Tres personas trinitatis, / Unum ens divinitatis / Venter claudit virginis" ("The Virgin's womb enclosed the three Persons of the Trinity, the one being of the Godhead").[74]

Sources and analogues: For 13.3–4 compare *Die goldene Schmiede* (182–85): "du bist erhoehet, frouwe, / sam in Sion der cyprian / und als der ceder in Liban, / der sich ʒe berge leichet" ("You are exalted, Lady, like the cypress in Zion, and like the cedar in Lebanon that climbs up the mountain").

The mysterious *kefse* of 13.16 is probably a ciborium or eucharistic vessel, as in Frauenlob's Marian strophe IX.1.13–14: "Die kefse din besloʒʒen hete / die ewigen gotheit" ("your ciborium enclosed the eternal Godhead").[75]

Lines 13.39–40 are indebted to Reinmar von Zweter. *Mutermeit* is his coinage, and he also speaks of God "folding" himself into Mary's heart: "Er Got der minne, er minnenschenke, / in tet diu minne alsô gelenke, / daʒ er sich in dîn herʒe vielt, / der aller elementen wielt"[76] ("He is the God of love, he is the gift of love; love made him so supple that he who wields all the elements enfolded himself in your heart").

Strophe 14

Strophe 14 is unique in that it develops a single metaphor throughout, instead of piling on a profusion of images, as Frauenlob usually does. The figure of the tailor (*snider*), which is not biblical, derives from the *assumptus homo* Christology common to many patristic and medieval theologians.[77] In this metaphor for the Incarnation, the divine Logos "assumed" or "put on" human nature in Mary's womb, clothing himself in flesh and blood as in a garment, with no change to his eternal divinity. But Frauenlob has complicated the metaphor, rendering it deeply paradoxical. The tailor, like the smith in 11.1, is the divine craftsman whose intelligence and skill the poem so often praises. Making good on the promise of 5.12 ("the chaste woman's clothes become her well"), this celestial tailor fashions an exceptionally beautiful robe for the Lady, taking pleasure in her fine array like a lover admiring his mistress. Line 14.4 (*er sach mich an*) echoes 12.6 (*er sach mich stetes an*): just as God gazed with eternal desire at Lady Wisdom, he now gazes with wise admiration at Mary. The verb *gebriset* ("laced") in 14.3 recalls the same verb in 10.11 where the Lady's garment is the sun itself: she is the *mulier amicta sole* of Apocalypse 12:1. In this strophe, Mary's *cleider* are not the solar rays but her radiant feminine charms. Frauenlob hints at the Lady's own "incarnation": divine Wisdom, the cosmic goddess, takes flesh in Mary just as the divine Logos does in Jesus. But this aspect of the metaphor can also be read more

74. *Analecta Hymnica* 34, no. 79, 3b. See also Kern, *Trinität, Maria, Inkarnation*, 128–38.

75. On this poem, see Stackmann, "Bild und Bedeutung," 446–53.

76. *Leich*, 107–10, in *Gedichte Reinmars*, 405. Cf. "muotermeit Marie," *Leich*, 117.

77. Krayer, *Frauenlob und die Natur-Allegorese*, 41–49.

conventionally to celebrate the Virgin as "fairest among women" (Cant. 5:9), the masterpiece of God's creative skill.

For all Mary's beauty, the truly artful (*spehe*) miracle wrought by the divine tailor is the Incarnation itself. While she still wears the splendid attire he fashioned for her, he cuts his own garments out of his Mother's without damaging her finery in any way. In short, she gives him birth, yet her virginity remains intact. Because of this miracle, *der meister heizet meister* (14.14): well and truly is the Master called a master! His "wondrous robe"—the human body of Jesus—is broad enough to contain all the fullness of the Godhead, "the Great One who holds heaven and earth in his hands" (14.18). This language again echoes 11.4: "I carried him who carries heaven and earth." There is also a reminiscence of the *tunica inconsutilis* in John 19:23, the seamless robe of Christ, traditionally said to have been woven by his mother and interpreted as a symbol of the Church.

Lines 14.19–28 are more difficult. Unlike Mary's garment, which remains immaculate, Christ's robe is "torn to pieces" on him (*verschroten*), a reference to his violent death on the Cross. Most critics interpret the *spehez spiegelvaz* ("artful mirror-vessel") of 14.20 as Mary's body once again—a double for the *wunderliche cleit*. The mirror-vessel, made of reflecting glass, may have magical or alchemical connotations, but it also recalls the mirror of eternal Wisdom in 12.3. Like Christ's robe of human flesh, the *spiegelvaz* is large enough to contain all God's greatness, but like Mary's inviolate robe, it is indestructible. Christ sits down within this marvelous vessel (14.21) until he is ready to "blossom forth" from it like a flowering branch (14.24) or a ripening fruit (14.26), leaving the vessel itself—his mother's virginity—intact (14.27). Yet an alternative reading is possible, and in fact required by the temporal narrative of this strophe. It was after the destruction of Christ's human flesh that he sat down in the *spiegelvaz* and *aventiurte meisterschaft von vremder craft* (14.22): "he staked his mastery against an alien power," like a knight jousting in disguise against his enemy or a master craftsman competing with a dangerous rival. In this context the mirror-vessel can denote Christ's tomb, which was often compared typologically with Mary's womb: just as he left her body at birth without breaking the seal of her maidenhood, so in rising from death he left his sealed tomb with the grave clothes intact. The second half of the strophe thus celebrates Christ's resurrection as well as his birth.

In the Easter liturgy and in countless artistic and dramatic representations, the three days between Good Friday and Easter figured as an epic struggle between Christ and Satan, culminating in the defeat of the demonic hosts and the liberation of their captives—an event known as the harrowing of hell. Hence the triumphant closing line, *sust ich verwant die geister*: "thus I overcame the spirits" (that is, the demons). Yet it is not Christ but Mary who speaks. As in 12.36, where she says it was she who suffered passion and shattered the power of death (*ich leit, ich brach den tot*), the Mother is so totally identified with the Son that she claims full participation and credit for his victory.

An index of Frauenlob's own *meisterschaft* can be gauged from the final rhyme-words. *Meister* and *geister,* linking 14a to 14b, echo the end-rhymes *geiste* and *meiste* connecting 6a and 6b. But strophes 6 and 14 also correspond in the elaborate double-*cursus* structure of the music, whereby the first eight strophes of the *leich* run in order through the cycle of eight liturgical modes, which are then repeated in the same order in strophes 9–16. Thus strophes 6 and 14 are both composed in the sixth mode, the so-called Hypolydian or third plagal.[78]

Sources and analogues: Line 14.22 obliquely echoes a passage in *Die goldene Schmiede,* 702–3: "din sun der hat gewundert / an dir mit fremder meisterschaft" ("Your Son marveled at you with wondrous, magisterial skill"). The context is Mary's eternal preexistence *qua* Sapientia: Konrad seems to mean that the eternal Word, foreseeing the miracle of his Incarnation, was himself awed by his mother-to-be and the wonder that he would perform through her. But the text is, for once, almost as enigmatic as Frauenlob.

Strophe 15

After the seamless metaphorical narrative of Christ's birth, death, and resurrection in strophe 14, Frauenlob returns to his more typical strategy of juxtaposition. The "star of Jacob" (15.1), reminiscent of the *leitestern* in 12.11, comes from a messianic prophecy ascribed to Balaam in Numbers 24:17: "a star shall come forth out of Jacob, and a scepter shall rise out of Israel." More ambitious and startling is the Lady's self-designation as "the great city of God" (15.3), about which Saint Augustine wrote in his classic *De civitate Dei.* For Augustine, the city of God celebrated in Psalm 86:3 ("gloriosa dicta sunt de te, civitas Dei") is the eternal, universal Church incorporating all the redeemed, whether living, departed, or still to be born. While the psalm verse seldom received a Marian interpretation, the city of God is already feminized in one of Frauenlob's main scriptural sources: "I saw the holy city, the New Jerusalem, coming down out of heaven from God, prepared like a bride adorned for her husband" (Apoc. 21:2). If Mary *qua* bride of God is a type of the Church, this parallel can also be extended to the City. We have already seen Mary linked with the seven churches of the Apocalypse in strophe 6, and in the culminating strophe 20, she will be fully identified with the twelve-gated, gem-studded New Jerusalem.

The rest of 15a is built from two interlocking but contrasting erotic scenarios. In the first, Mary is again the perpetual virgin whose gates are sealed to all comers except her Beloved (cf. 5.4–6), who comes to "help [her] bear" the child of their love-tryst (15.6–7). The meaning of this "help" is explained at the end of 15b where Mary says that the "sweet nourishment of [her] soul" (15.28), that is, the "power of the Most High" that overshadowed her at the Annunciation (Luke 1:35), bore Christ's divinity (*den geist*), while she in her humanity bore a pure

---

78. Shields, "Zum melodischen Aufbau des Marienleichs," in
Wolfram-Studien 10: 122; Märzt, *Frauenlobs Marienleich,* 69. See
also Chapter 4, above, pp. 124–25.

human being (*menschen clar*). Frauenlob here is surprisingly precise about the two distinct natures of Christ, divinity and humanity, which were united in the single person of the God-Man—as formally defined by the Council of Chalcedon in 451. Yet that council would certainly not have assented to the statement that follows, typical of Frauenlob's loose treatment of the Trinity: "Thus Father, Son, and Holy Spirit spun themselves within me" (15.30). The verb *span* is singular, indicating that the Trinity is to be understood as a single subject acting on Mary.[79]

Returning to 15a, a second erotic scenario begins at 15.9. The Lady says that her lover, caught "with a beautiful maiden, was denounced (*überseit*) before his Father." When their subversive love affair was made known, the father harshly punished the son by disinheriting him and sentencing him to exile (*ellende*) and hard labor (*arebeit*). Although the son bore this exile patiently (*gutlich*), he nonetheless fought—with success—to regain his lost heritage (*sin erbe erstreit*). So Mary concludes triumphantly, "How fortunate it was that ever I began the affair!" (15.15). This miniature romance is indeed puzzling because it casts the mystique of a forbidden love around the Incarnation, which hitherto has been presented as an erotic but not transgressive event. On one level, the "beautiful maiden" must be Mary herself. Because of his liaison with her, Christ was exiled from heaven to earth and compelled to endure the *arebeit* of his Passion. Yet in the end he rose from the dead and regained his celestial heritage, along with all nations (Ps. 2:7–8), so the Lady can rejoice that all was for the best. But several features of the allegory remain perplexing. Nowhere else in the poem does Mary speak of herself in the third person (*einer schönen meit*) as she does here; and nowhere else is there a suggestion of anger or even distance between the divine Father and his Son. Moreover, it is odd for the Virgin (even as *praeelecta*) to describe herself as the one who *initiated* her love affair with God. Some of these difficulties can be relieved if we read the passage as double-coded: the illicit lovers are indeed Christ and Mary, but on a different level they are also Adam and Eve—much as in Julian of Norwich's parable of the lord and the servant, where the latter simultaneously represents Christ and Adam.[80] On this submerged level, Adam and his lovely bride are exiled from Paradise for their sin and driven to the hard labor of this world (Gen. 3:19: "in the sweat of your brow you shall eat bread"). But Christ himself takes on the punishment of Adam, atones for his sin, and so regains the inheritance "from which his father banished him" (15.14). On this reading, the *schönen meit* may be Eve or perhaps the feminine soul (*anima*), a collective figure of the human race for whose sake Christ undergoes his trials. The speaker of 15.15 could then be Mary in her role as the New Eve, at the same time celebrating the *felix culpa* and rejoicing that she began the work of redemption.

In 15b the Lady speaks once again as a clandestine lover, addressing her friends (*vil lieben*) as confidantes. Her seducer, "the divine thief of love" (15.17), has slipped secretly into her soul (see 12.31) just as he entered her closed virginal body, wounding her with the "sweetness" of

---

79. Kern, *Trinität, Maria, Inkarnation*, 199.   80. Julian, *Revelation of Love*, chap. 51.

his love (see 11.10). Suffused by this sweetness, her human nature is ennobled and enabled to bear "the greeting of the great Greeting" (15.21)—Gabriel's *ave* at which the Word became flesh. In the deep secrecy of a courtly love-tryst, which is also the secrecy of God's ineffable wisdom, Mary conceives his child, while the "watchmen of [her] city" (Cant. 3:3) remain none the wiser (15.24–25). These ignorant watchmen (*vigiles, wechter*) are distinct from the violent guards (*custodes, murehüter, röuber*) of Canticle 5:7 and strophes 4b and 20b, who despoil the Virgin of her mantle. Unlike most clandestine affairs, this one brings only love and pleasure, not woe and sorrow (15.23), because the sinless Mary is exempt from Eve's curse of painful childbirth. *Nie we* may be a translation of the Latin *a vae*, "without woe," a common explanation of Gabriel's *ave*.

Sources and analogues: The opening lines of strophe 15 echo the *leich* of Reinmar von Zweter: "si ist ein sterne von Jâcop, / an ir lit aller engel lop" ("She is a star of Jacob; on her rests all the angels' praise").[81] Frauenlob's reference to Mary's "burden," which her lover helps her carry (15.6–7), recalls another passage in Reinmar: "Minnenbürde sunder swaere, / minnenbürde sünden lêre / unt doch rehtiu minnenbürde / Wart getragen von dir al einer, / dû vil reine unt er vil reiner, / mit dem dû gebürdet würde"[82] ("The burden of love without heaviness, devoid of sin, yet truly a burden of love, was carried by you alone—you most pure and he most pure, with whom you were burdened").

For Mary as city of God, see Konrad von Würzburg (580–81): "du bist ein lebendigiu stat / der eweclichen gotheit" ("you are a living city of the eternal Godhead").[83]

The "scandalous" tone of 15.9–15 recalls a strophe by Friedrich von Sonnenburg that presents the Incarnation as a courtly love affair, with the poet in the role of *merker*—the typically malicious spy who threatens to blackmail the lovers. In this poem he warns the Queen that unless she gives him a reward, he will tell of her love affair with a nobleman by whom she has become pregnant—and, worse yet, reveal that she has promised her favor to three different lovers (the Trinity) by means of her secret messenger Gabriel.[84]

For the distinction of natures in Christ (15.28–29), compare Frauenlob's strophe VI.1.8–9 in the Flugton: "durch die geburt / gotheit tet gein der menscheit ein buhurt" ("through birth, [Christ's] divinity rode a *bohort* against the humanity"). A *bohort* is an equestrian game in which two lines of knights ride against each other with shields and blunted weapons; in this case, a mock joust is implied, suggesting both the tension and the harmony between Christ's two natures. Even closer to *Marienleich* 15.28–30 is strophe X.3.11–13 in the Vergessener Ton: "got vater sun mit geiste, / ir ieglichez was, da sie gebar den waren got / und waren menschen"

81. Reinmar, *Leich*, 77–78, p. 404; Behr, *Literatur als Machtlegitimation*, 238. Behr is unduly skeptical about Frauenlob's knowledge of Reinmar.

82. Reinmar, *Leich*, 101–6, p. 405. Cf. *Marienleich* 2.5: "mit dem sie was gebürdet."

83. In lines 514–15 Konrad compares the Virgin "zer obersten Jerusalem" ("to the Jerusalem above").

84. *Die Sprüche Friedrichs von Sonnenburg*, 62, ed. Achim Masser (Tübingen: Niemeyer, 1979), 43; Kern, *Trinität, Maria, Inkarnation*, 102–4.

("God is Father, Son, and Spirit: each of them was present when [Mary] bore the true God and true man"). Konrad von Würzburg has, as usual, a plainer and theologically clearer statement of the idea (282–85): "der sun der vater und der geist / haeten an dir, frouwe trut, / ir kint ir muoter unde ir brut / vor mangen ziten uz erkorn" ("The Son, the Father, and the Spirit had chosen you, beloved Lady, before the ages as their child, their mother, and their bride").

Strophe 16

Strophes 16–18a systematically present the Lady in terms of the seven liberal arts, fulfilling the promise of 6.14, where she is called *künste funt*, the source or fountain of all arts and sciences.[85] From the twelfth century onward, Sapientia and Philosophia often appear in art as feminine figures from whose breasts the liberal arts proceed in the form of seven streams or allegorical maidens.[86] Thus in 16–18a Frauenlob's Lady is implicitly identified with Sapientia as well as Natura. In strophe 16a the arena of discourse is Aristotelian metaphysics and *Sprachlogik*, and 16b deals with the three verbal arts of the trivium—grammar, rhetoric, and dialectic. Strophe 17a treats physics and metaphysics from a more Platonizing stance, while 17b is primarily about astronomy, but concludes with brief allusions to geometry and arithmetic. These three arts along with music, the subject of 18a, comprised the quadrivium or mathematical portion of the medieval arts curriculum. Frauenlob's strophes on the *artes liberales* reverse Alan of Lille's perspective in the "Rhythmus de Incarnatione Christi," a poem in which he "sang most ingeniously of how that divine work spurned all the rules of the liberal arts."[87] Where Alan presents the defeat of the arts in the face of Mary's divine motherhood, Frauenlob prefers to show their fulfillment.

In 16a the Lady speaks of herself, her Son, and the Trinity in Aristotelian terms, using the poet's original vernacular translations for the Philosopher's ten *praedicamenta* (categories) and five *praedicabilia* (universals). The categories are substance, quality, quantity, relation, action, passion, time, place, position, and condition, while the universals—in descending order from the broadest to the most particular—are genus, species, difference (defining trait of a species), individual property, and accident.[88] The best way to make sense of 16a is to begin by retranslating these technical terms into Latin. Thus the Mother of God would say: "I am the child of the First Cause (*prima causa; der ersten sache*). I am the substance (*substantia; understant*) in which the Three took on qualities (*qualitas; gewelchet sint*), yet they will never be known through quantity

85. On Mary and the liberal arts, see Schreiner, *Maria: Jungfrau, Mutter, Herrscherin*, 133–35, and Stolz, "Maria und die Artes liberales," 95–120. For a German prose translation and commentary on strophes 16–18a, see Wachinger, "Frauenlobs Cantica canticorum," 36–39.

86. For examples, see Newman, *God and the Goddesses*, 74, 80, 215.

87. Alan of Lille, "Rhythmus de Incarnatione Christi," PL 210:577–80 (with scribal inscription); d'Alverny, "Alain de Lille et la 'Theologia,'" in *L'Homme devant Dieu*, 2:126–28;

Stolz, "Maria und die Artes liberales," 100–101. See Chapter 3, above, pp. 106–9.

88. The *praedicamenta* are discussed in Aristotle's *Categories* and the *praedicabilia* in his *Topics* 1.4–5, a section expounded more clearly in Porphyry's *Isagoge* or introduction. The *Categories* and *Isagoge*, together with the commentaries of Boethius, belonged to what was known in the thirteenth century as the *logica vetus*, while the more recently introduced *Topics* belonged to the *logica nova*. To these technical terms of logic must be added the metaphysical concepts of *esse* (*wesen*) and *prima causa* (*erste sache*).

(*quantitas; mazheftic*). He is my essence (*esse; wesen*) and I am his, good Son, he the child and I the mother (*relatio*). He acted (*actio; tet*); I suffered (*passio; leit*). I am the occasion (*situs; gelegenheit*) of every "when" (*quando; wenne*) and "where" (*ubi; wa*) and state or condition (*habitus; habens*). His *genus* (*art*) can be predicated of me, and my *species* (*gestalt*) can be sought in his. What distinction (*differentia; underscheit*) can prove this wrong? Human nature must always remain our own (*proprium; unser eigen*). He—the one I bore—can admit neither addition nor substraction (*accidentia; zuschicht, abeschicht*), unless he is a God."

Speaking as the "substance" or material matrix of the Trinity, the Lady announces her first paradox: in becoming the Mother of God she has given finite qualities to the Infinite. Yet even though the divine Persons can be numbered (as *die dri*), they cannot be known through number or measure. God remains what Alan called "immensus sub mensura terrenorum." But since this Infinite One is now contained in the body of a mother, Mary herself becomes a cosmic entity: all time, space, and particular qualities and relationships find their "place" in her since their metaphysical location is God, the First Cause, and God's physical location is Mary. (Alternatively, the Lady may be speaking in 16.7 as Sapientia, the divine Mind, which could also be called the *gelegenheit* of time, space, and condition.) Mary then posits both identity and reciprocity between herself and Christ. Although the two are related reciprocally as child to mother and active partner to passive, yet they are identical in *esse, genus,* and *species*; no formal distinction (*differentia*) can come between them. Hence whatever can be predicated of the Son can be predicated of the Mother and *vice versa*—a key concept for Frauenlob's poetics in the *Marienleich*. Since human nature (*die menscheit*) is precisely this shared essence common to both Mother and Son (*unser eigen*), it follows that the substance of his humanity can suffer no "accidents," no additions or substractions that would change the nature he inherits from his mother. But then she adds an exception clause: *ern si ein got den ich gebar* (16.13)—"unless he is a God whom I bore." The theological point is that insofar as his humanity is concerned, Christ's nature is in no way different from or greater than Mary's, but insofar as he is God, he possesses a divine *esse* or *wesen* in addition to hers.

The two natures of Christ are more fully explored in 16b. Mary refers to Christ's divinity as "the Word" (Logos, *wort*), which came down from heaven and in her body "became" a blessed Name (Jesus). Jesus is indeed the proper name of the God-Man.[89] As a human being he did not always exist, whereas the divine Word was eternal and "without becoming" (*ane werden,* 16.16); the terms *name* and *wort* are parallel to *mensch* and *geist* in 15.29. Since the liberal art at issue here is grammar, Frauenlob is also playing on the difference between a verb (*verbum* or *wort*, the divine Word) and a noun (*name*, the Name of Jesus).[90] A verb is active as befits the Creator, while a noun *qua* creature is the subject of action. Frauenlob's distinction gains a further dimension from the Johannine prologue, which proclaims that the *Verbum* "was in the beginning

89. The word *name* in MHG could also mean "person" and was often used to translate *persona* in the liturgical creeds. Kern, *Trinität, Maria, Inkarnation,* 184.

90. See further Hübner, *Lobblumen,* 201 n. 124.

with God" (John 1:1–2) but that after he became flesh (1:14) he gave power to all "who believe in his name" (1:12).

Mary now modulates to the art of rhetoric, stating that from this convergence of divine Word and human Name was woven a speech (*rede, oratio*) that her mind or senses (*witze*) were able to grasp (16.17–18). This speech or discourse had a meaning (*meinen*) that she "debated" (*disputirete*) with God's messenger, signaling the art of dialectic. Mary's dialogue with the angel could loosely be termed a "debate" because she was initially "disturbed" by his appearance and, after hearing his message, asked, "How can this be?" (Luke 1:34). This is indeed her question in 16.22, but Gabriel's answer is not the one he gives in the Gospel. Instead he spreads before her a "net of true sayings" (*warer sprüche vach*) about the Son she will bear.[91] Although the terms are somewhat obscure, the point is that Christ is Lord of all three realms of the universe: the ground of the underworld (hell), the goal or boundary of the middle realm (earth), and the "roof" or summit of heaven (16.25). The master of all these, says Mary, she nursed with the *bernder künste*, or "fertile arts," over which she presides. This theme has further iconographic resonance, for in a handful of esoteric manuscripts, Philosophia or Sapientia is shown nursing philosophers at her breasts, just as Mary nursed the Christ Child.[92] Once again we see the human mother converging with the cosmic goddess Natura and the scholars' goddess of wisdom.

Sources and analogues: In one of his strophes on the Incarnation, Frauenlob describes Christ as "die erste ursache . . . aller creatiuren" ("the first cause of all creatures," X.1.10–11). Strophe VII.9 in the Grüner Ton, a cosmological riddle about the macrocosm and microcosm, begins with the lines "Sache einen knoten stricte / mit underscheidener dinge kraft" ("The [First] Cause tied a knot with the power of different things," VII.9.1–2). The description of Nature's three realms in 16.25 recalls another strophe in the same tone, summarizing the argument of Alan's *De planctu Naturae:* "Nature ist als ein frouwe, / und swaz ie wart und immer ist / und swaz zukunft beschouwe, / des waldet sie gemeine. / swaz unden ist und ouch darobe / und mitten durch naturen cloben, / sie trübet nicht, niur menschen lust unreine" ("Nature is like a Lady, and whatever has been and always is, and whatever the future may reveal, she rules them altogether. Whatever is below, above, and in between, bound by Nature's bonds, troubles her not—only the impure desires of humans," VII.5.13–19).

For the influence of Frauenlob's *artes* strophes on later Marian poetry, see Chapter 5, pp. 148–51.

Strophe 17

This difficult, much-discussed strophe is inspired by the cosmology of the twelfth-century Platonists.[93] Taking his cue from Bernard Silvestris's *Cosmographia* and Alan of Lille's *Anticlaudianus,*

---

91. *Sprüche* could also mean "proverbs" or—perhaps more to the point—"poems."

92. Newman, *God and the Goddesses,* 237–38.

93. For extended readings, see Krayer, *Frauenlob und die Natur-Allegorese,* 94–123; Wachinger, "Frauenlobs Cantica canticorum," 38–41; Huber, *Aufnahme und Verarbeitung,* 180–83; Steinmetz, *Liebe als universales Prinzip,* 62–65.

Frauenlob represents the cosmogonic process in metaphysical terms, with the Lady initially filling the role of the goddess Natura. Critics disagree about the precise meaning of "what is mixed" (*waz sich mischet*), "what is unmixed," and "what is threshed from the mixture," but these appear to represent three different states of the primal matter or world-stuff, the *materje* of 17.17. The "unmixed" most likely stands for the primeval chaos, the undifferentiated *prima materia* as it existed before creation, corresponding to the Greek *hyle* or Latin *silva* (personified in Bernard Silvestris's prose-poem as a dishevelled female longing for form and beauty).[94] If this is the case, the "mixing" (*daz mischen*) would represent the separation of the four elements—earth, air, fire, and water—by a creative deity to enable their reassemblage in the orderly combinations that constitute individual beings. Every living creature comes into being when an eternal form impresses itself on unformed matter and gives its elements the distinctive shape that belongs to that particular being. In Bernard Silvestris, this cosmological process is the work of Natura, a daughter of the divine Mind (Noys), and it is in Natura's voice that the Lady declares, "daz ich der bin ein beginne" (17.9). The great creative act of Nature "rejuvenates the source," turns chaos into cosmos, gives the world meaning and beauty.[95]

The "becoming and unbecoming" (*werden und unwerden*) of 17.7 correspond to Aristotle's "generation and corruption." One could say that both these processes begin (*brechen*) with birth, since to be born is to enter into the world of becoming and change, which inevitably leads to death—though another possible meaning for *brechen* is "part company." As Natura, the Lady of the poem is the origin of birth, death, and rebirth, for every death is only a parting between form and matter. After the *unwerden* or death of a living creature, its matter relapses into formlessness until it is eventually subsumed in new individuals, while the eternally virgin form returns to its pristine purity. Frauenlob Christianizes this Platonic cosmology with his reference to the "creative love of the Spirit" (*des geistes worchtlich minne*) in 17.10. Still following the twelfth-century Platonists, he seems to conflate the Holy Spirit (as *caritas* or *minne*) with the *anima mundi*, the world soul that pervades and quickens all creation. The identity of the Holy Spirit with the Platonic world soul was posited in the early twelfth century by William of Conches and Peter Abelard, though the hypothesis was quickly withdrawn when it raised charges of pantheism from such critics as William of Saint-Thierry, a friend of Saint Bernard.[96] These critics objected to precisely the sort of inference that Frauenlob draws from the identification, namely, that the Holy Spirit *qua* world soul is the divine force animating all that lives *mit der liebe und mit der lüste* (17.11), that is, with erotic love, in an act of continuous creation.

The word *liebe*, denoting first joy and secondarily love, has ethical and courtly connotations, while its overlapping counterpart, *lüste*, signifies sexual desire and pleasure. Variants of the

94. Bernardus Silvestris, *Cosmographia* 1.1, ed. Peter Dronke (Leiden: Brill, 1978); trans. Winthrop Wetherbee, *The "Cosmographia" of Bernardus Silvestris* (New York: Columbia University Press, 1973).

95. Compare the extravagant reading of Krayer, who describes Mary in this role as "the primal goddess, bent over the cauldron of the world-stuff, watching it with Nornlike gaze" while she utters the magic formulas of creation. *Frauenlob und die Natur-Allegorese*, 106.

96. Huber, *Aufnahme*, 174–79; Steinmetz, *Liebe*, 37–50.

phrase *lieb und lust* occur often in Frauenlob's oeuvre, but this alliterative pair was by no means standard. In fact, the word *lust* is found nowhere else in the corpus of MHG love lyric.[97] Its frequency in Frauenlob testifies to the poet's unusually positive evaluation of sexuality, even here in the exceptional context of Marian praise. The meaning of this passage is clarified by a parallel in *Minne und Welt,* which states that "all things long to be diminished and increased (*geminnert und gemeret*) according to Love's counsel" (IV.1.8).[98] *Enget* and *witet* in *Marienleich* 17.12 are analogous to *geminnert und gemeret* in *Minne und Welt*: all beings in the universe ebb and flow, wax and wane, in accord with the will of Love and her helpers, desire and pleasure.

The Lady's relationship to Minne is not altogether clear. If we accept the editors' punctuation, lines 17.10–14 can be rendered as follows: "Just as the creative love of the Spirit ebbs and flows with desire and pleasure, without falsehood, I am the Form of all forms, drawn from the inner meaning's norm."[99] The Lady may be identifying herself as the world soul, which could be called *forma formarum* insofar as the *anima mundi* is the form of the material world, which in turn contains the forms of all other creatures. In that case, Frauenlob would be making a distinction after all between the universal love of the Holy Spirit (*des geistes worchtlich minne*) and the world soul (*aller formen forme*), only to draw a parallel between them. On the other hand, it might make better sense to place a comma after *beginne* (17.9) and a full stop after *unküste* (17.12). If 17.13 begins a new sentence, the Lady would be speaking less as *anima mundi* than as Sapientia, the role she resumes in 17b. The creative, "ever-blooming" Wisdom of God (17.15) can be characterized as "Form of all forms" in a different sense, since in Christian Platonism the mind of God is the repository of all created forms before they come into existence as empirical beings.[100] Yet whichever divine mediatrix we take as providing the closest model for the Lady at this point, the overarching sense is unmistakable.

In 17b the Lady's identity modulates gradually from the extrabiblical Natura back to the biblical Sapientia. She identifies herself as "the nature of all virtues" (17.16) either because she possesses them all (as in strophes 6–7) or, more likely, because all are gifts of God *secundum naturam.* She is also the "neighbor" of primal matter as the divine force that gives it form and life. As the creative, world-fashioning goddess of 17.18–19, she could be either Natura or Sapientia. But biblical references return with 17.20. In the Wisdom of Solomon 7:17–19, Sapientia declares, "For [God] has given me true knowledge of the things that are, that I might know the disposition of the earth and the powers of the elements, . . . the seasons of the year and the arrangement of the stars." And in Ecclesiasticus 24:5–8 she says, "I am the firstborn before all creation; I

97. Bein, "*Liep unde Lust.*"

98. See Chapter 2, above, p. 75.

99. *Norme* and *forme* are related as *Urbild* and *Abbild,* or original and copy. Kern, *Trinität, Maria, Inkarnation,* 201 n. 79.

100. Krayer suggests "ever-virgin" as a possible meaning of *durchblümet* (17.15), since the Forms do not perish or decay when

they are parted from their material substrates. *Frauenlob und die Natur-Allegorese,* 114–15, citing *Anticlaudianus,* lines 476–77: "Subiecti senio non deflorata iuuentus / Formarum, formas semper facit esse puellas," ed. Bossuat, 71. Wachinger, on the other hand, reads *durchblümet* as "eternally praised," playing on the rhetorical meaning of *geblümt.* "Frauenlobs Cantica canticorum," 38.

made a never-setting light to rise in the heavens . . . I dwelt in the heights, and my throne is in a pillar of cloud. I circled the vault of heaven alone." This rhetoric of divine self-praise, adapted from earlier hymns to Isis as queen of heaven, justifies Frauenlob's presentation of his Lady as goddess of the stars. At this point in his poem she stands at the furthest possible remove from the historical Mary, yet there has been no change in the poetic "I," for goddess and woman are ultimately one.

Strophe 17b is again filled with technical terms, this time from astronomy, as Frauenlob returns to his scheme of the seven liberal arts. In a fairly literal paraphrase of 17.20–27, the Lady declares, "I am the measure of all the heavens and whatever their swift motion (*snelle*) has enclosed. How the fixed stars (*sterne*) are set within the firmament, this I determine, and how the paths of the wandering planets (*irre*) cross one another (*sich werren*), their forward and reverse motions (*inguz, wandel*), and their proximity and distance from the earth (*nehe, virre*). I have set all the spheres on their axis, both their standing still (*hemmen*) and their retrograde motion (*keren*)."[101] Surpassing even the high praise of Wisdom in Scripture, the Lady ascribes to herself what is clearly to be understood as divine activity.

The last lines of 17b pay homage to the quadrivial arts of geometry (17.28–29) and arithmetic (17.30). In 17.28 the Lady comprehends the "breadth and length and depth and height" of the cosmos (Eph. 3:18), taking pleasure in all its dimensions just as Sapientia delights to play in God's world (Prov. 8:31). The enigmatic lines 17.28–29 recall a strophe in the Langer Ton, in which Frauenlob compares himself to a craftsman working with square and compass: "Ja tun ich als ein wercman, der sin winkelmaz / ane unterlaz / zu sinen werken richtet, / uz der fuge tichtet / die höhe und lenge: wit und breit, alse ist ez geschichtet; / und swenne er hat das winkelrecht nach sinem willen gezirket, / Darnach er danne wirket, als man wirken kan" ("Indeed, I act like a workman who guides his work with his carpenter's square without interruption. By his skill he shapes its height and length, as wide and broad as he means to structure it; and once he has encompassed it at right angles according to his desire, then he works on it as best he can." V.13.1–7). The poet establishes the coordinates of his artistic space much as the Lady maps the dimensions of cosmic space. In 17.30 she echoes Wisdom 11:21, an oft-cited verse on the cosmic order, which proclaims that God or Sapientia has "ordered all things according to measure, number, and weight." The Lady claims divine omniscience in that "the number of things with their causes" all lie within her memory. *Zal* (number) is the keyword meant to evoke arithmetic, just as the problematic *winkelmezic* ("at right angles") in 17.29 evokes geometry.[102]

101. These technical terms were first interpreted by Johannes Siebert, "Die Astronomie in den Gedichten des Kanzlers und Frauenlobs," *Zeitschrift für deutsches Altertum* 75 (1938): 1–23; see also Krayer, *Frauenlob und die Natur-Allegorese*, 120–21. The terms appear to be Frauenlob's original vernacular translations from the Astronomy section of Alan's *Anticlaudianus*.

102. Wachinger reads 17.28–29 as "May nothing with measurable dimensions elude my loving desire." "Frauenlobs Cantica canticorum," 39.

In the formal structure of Frauenlob's music, strophe 17 opens the final half-*cursus* as the cycle of eight modes begins for a third time. This structural division may be signaled by the opening gesture *ei,* which echoes the first word of the *leich*.[103]

Sources and analogues: The cosmology of 17a is succinctly reprised in a strophe in the Zarter Ton: "materje gert der formen mit der mische / und ouch darzu des höchsten zirkels frische" ("Matter longs for form by means of mixing, and thereby also the renewal of the highest vault of heaven," VIII.23.15–16).

Mary's identification with Natura in strophe 17 bears comparison with the much-discussed passage from the *Minneleich* (III.4–7) where Woman is compared to the *feie,* or "fairy," who appears in Alan of Lille's vision, *De planctu Naturae*.[104] Although the *Minneleich* goes on to praise love and women in secular terms, the Lady of the *Marienleich* can be understood, in part, as a further development of this impulse to link human motherhood with the world-sustaining goddess.

Mary as Sapientia—goddess of the three realms and the four elements—also appears in *Die goldene Schmiede* (689–99): "du bist diu frone wisheit / von der uns Salomon da seit / und alle die propheten. / die zirkel der planeten, / sunn unde manen bilde, / wint regen doner wilde, / wazzer fiur erd unde luft, / der himel kor, der helle gruft, / und alle creatiure / von diner helfe stiure / geschephet unde gordent sint" (You are the Lord's Wisdom, of whom Salomon and all the prophets told us. The circle of the planets, the forms of the sun and moon, wind, rain, wild thunder, water, fire, earth and air, the choir of heaven, the abyss of hell, and all creatures were created and ordered with your help and support").

Strophe 18

In 18a Frauenlob concludes his catalogue of the seven liberal arts with music. His primary reference is to the music of the spheres, here linked with the nine choirs of angels (18.6) whose rising and falling melodies (*steige, velle*) modulate "thrice three" times (*dries drien*) in honor of the Trinity. Drawing on numerology, Frauenlob not only points out with this phrase that the angelic nine is the square of the divine Three, but also deliberately incorporates his discussion of music into strophe 18, representing twice nine. This heavenly music is indestructible: "no one can destroy its resonance" (18.7). But the tones (*döne*) pouring out their "beautiful rewards" (*löne schöne*) in 18.1 also suggest earthly music, for the compositions of Frauenlob and his contemporaries were classified according to their shared *Töne*. This term, derived ultimately from the modes of plainchant, denotes not only the melodic structure of a piece (its "tune") but also its corresponding patterns of rhyme and meter.[105]

With 18.8 Frauenlob returns at last to the human Mary, long eclipsed in the poem by the cosmic goddess. This celestial music, she proclaims, was composed by her sweetheart, her

---

103. März, *Frauenlobs Marienleich,* 96.
104. See Chapter 2, pp. 68–69.

105. Frauenlob's strophes of *Spruchdichtung* fall into nine musical/poetic patterns of his own composition. See Chapter 2, above, pp. 85–86.

vriedel—and with this word we are back in the domain of the Song of Songs. "Crown me, enthrone me," the imperious Queen of Heaven demands (18.10), echoing the angels' plea in 8.5, but also "give me a kiss"—alluding to the first verse of the Song, *osculetur me osculo oris sui* ("let him kiss me with the kiss of his mouth"). Christ's epithet *sun der gerten* ("son of the branch," 18.11) translates the Latin *filius virgae,* Mary herself being the *virga,* or branch of Jesse, from which the divine flower blossomed (Isa. 11:1). Enigmatically, she adds that the "shield-companions of [her] humanity" (18.12) tore her from King Jesse, that is, from the royal lineage of David. But this verse is a crux because *dem künige Jesse* is in the dative, so the literal sense would be that the shield companions (an epic term for comrades in battle) dragged Mary *before* King Jesse by force, like a prisoner of war being led to the victor for ransom. It is difficult to assign a credible meaning to this image. Stackmann surmises: "my ancestors led me with irresistible force to King Jesse, that is, they made him my forebear."[106]

The last lines allude once again to the Song, this time to Canticle 8:5: "under the apple tree I awakened you; there your mother was corrupted, there she who bore you was violated." But Mary, as the new and innocent Eve, is awakened "sweetly" beneath the Tree of Knowledge by her son and lover. Apples have already been mentioned in 8.9 and 14.26, both times referring to Christ as the fruit of the Virgin's flowering branch. Frauenlob will treat the allegory of Eden more fully in strophe 19.

Sources and analogues: Frauenlob's association of his Lady with the nine musical heavens and the square of the Trinity is strikingly reminiscent of a passage in Dante's *Vita Nuova,* a work contemporary with the *Marienleich:* "Since, according to Ptolemy and according to Christian truth, there are nine heavens that move, and since, according to widespread astrological opinion, these heavens affect the earth below according to the relations they have to one another, this number was in harmony with [Beatrice] to make it understood that at her birth all nine of the moving heavens were in perfect relationship to one another. . . . [Further,] if three is the sole factor of nine, and the sole factor of miracles is three, that is, Father, Son, and Holy Spirit, who are Three in One, then this lady was accompanied by the number nine so that it might be understood that she was a nine, or a miracle, whose root, namely that of the miracle, is the miraculous Trinity itself."[107]

Strophe 19

This strophe introduces the story of Genesis as if it were a fairy tale (*hübsches meres*). God may be the "old gardener" (Gen. 2:8) whose son grafted the fatal tree on which he would eventually die; in the resurrection story, Mary Magdalene mistakes the risen Christ for a gardener (John 20:15). On the other hand, we see here another example of double-coding, for under a different aspect, the gardener is Adam. Frauenlob alludes to the legend of the True Cross, which specifies that when Adam lay dying, he sent his son Seth back to Paradise for a remedy. Versions of the

106. Stackmann and Haustein, *Wörterbuch,* 177, under "Jesse."

107. Dante, *Vita Nuova,* chap. 29, trans. Mark Musa (Bloomington: Indiana University Press, 1973), 62.

legend differ, but according to one known to Frauenlob, Seth returned too late with a seed or sprout from the Tree of Knowledge and placed it in his dead father's mouth, so that an offshoot of the paradisal tree grew out of Adam's grave. Centuries later, it was revealed to the Queen of Sheba that the Savior of the world would be crucified on this tree, which she revered. She then disclosed the prophecy to King Solomon, who incorporated the wood into the Jerusalem Temple, whence in due time it yielded the cross on which Christ died. Thus the tree of the original sin and the tree of redemption were one and the same.[108] Mary can therefore say that Eve—"my mother in humanity" (19.5)—was "violently broken" beneath this tree (*violata est*, Cant. 8:5), whereas her own "child of life" behaved in his Father's fashion, remaining free of sin.

The *nu secht (nota bene!)* of 19.7 announces an exegetical puzzle for readers to solve. The Lady calls herself the "bed of Solomon" guarded by sixty of Israel's strongest warriors (Cant. 3:7), a number that Frauenlob breaks down into its components:

$$60 = 24 + 12 + 9 + 3 + 4 + 8.$$

If this equation is divided into two numerical series, the first descending (24, 12, 9) and the second ascending (3, 4, 8), a mathematically interesting relationship obtains between them: divide each number in the first sequence by three and it will yield the corresponding number in the second sequence in reverse order.[109] Thus the sacred number of the Trinity is again brought to the fore—while sixty divided by three yields twenty, the number of strophes in the *Marien-leich*. The "strong men" themselves signify Mary's companions, the citizens of heaven: twenty-four elders (Apoc. 4:4), twelve apostles, nine angelic orders, three patriarchs, four evangelists—plus the mysterious "eight" whom the Lady exhorts to "guard [her] fruitful praise" since that is their nature (*slachte*). If the first part of the riddle is arithmetical, the second lies in the identification of these eight. By analogy with the seven spiritual gifts of strophe 6 and the seven virtues of strophe 7, they may stand for the eight beatitudes (Matt. 5:3–10), all of which were held to be embodied in the Virgin.

Strophe 19b opens with a bravura play on the word *blume* (flower), forms of which appear no fewer than ten times in the first six lines, and once more in 19.33. This kind of ornament, oppressive to modern taste, was such a notable feature of the *geblümter Stil* that the *blume* may well be self-referential, in addition to summing up a Marian motif introduced as early as 2.15. The Bride evokes Canticle 2:5 (*fulcite me floribus*), asking that her chamber be strewn with the lilies of chastity and the roses of love to honor her blossoming. Christ is not only a figurative

108. For other versions of this pan-European legend, see Arthur S. Napier, ed., *History of the Holy Rood-Tree: A Twelfth-Century Version of the Cross-Legend*, EETS o.s. 103 (London: K. Paul, Trench, Trübner & Co., 1894); Mariane Overgaard, ed., *The History of the Cross-Tree Down to Christ's Passion: Icelandic Legend Versions* (Copenhagen: Munksgaard, 1968); Michael Podrot, *Piero della Francesca's Legend of the True Cross* (Newcastle upon Tyne: University of Newcastle, 1974); *The Stavelot Triptych: Mosan Art and the Legend of the True Cross* (New York: Pierpont Morgan Library, 1980).

109. Karl Bertau, "Untersuchungen zur geistlichen Dichtung Frauenlobs" (dissertation, Göttingen, 1954), 127, cited in GA 655.

flower like his mother; he also was conceived in the springtime, when blossoms first appear (March 25), and grew up in Nazareth, a city whose Hebrew name was said to mean "Flower." According to the *Golden Legend*, Frauenlob's likely source for this passage, "Nazareth means 'flower'; hence Bernard [of Clairvaux] says that the Flower willed to be born of a flower, in 'Flower,' in the season of flowers."[110]

The second part of 19b is an allegory of the seasons. Frauenlob turns months into verbs, as he will do with gemstones in 20b: Christ and Mary glow like a pair of youthful lovers, "marching, maying, springing" (19.25)—a line that sounds less peculiar in translation than it does in the original, since these are normal verbs in modern English but not in medieval German. As the year turns, Christ in his glory adorns himself with summer's dazzling hues (19.26–27) to banish the winter of Adam's curse (19.31–32). The most difficult season is fall: Mary says that her Son, wishing to make her his *herbest* (autumn/ harvest), "has pressed out in me the grapes that my father himself stooped down to pick for him" (19.28–29). The rather tortuous thought echoes 2b, where the Lady becomes pregnant by eating the sacred grapes that she then carries in her womb to become "mother of the Lamb and of the Dove" (2.16–17). While the "apple" represented as the fruit of Mary's womb in 8.9 evokes her role as New Eve, the grapes allude to the Eucharist. In 12b the Virgin is the Mystical Mill, and here she becomes the Mystical Winepress (Isa. 63:2–3).

Once again, Mary's total union with the Trinity results in what Frauenlob presents in deliberately scandalous language as an incestuous relationship: "thus my Child became my brother-in-law and my brother alike" (19.30). We have already learned that he is her "mother's father" (12.34) and, needless to say, he is also her lover. Medieval poets sometimes used the shock value of incest to stress the absolute, suprarational nature of the union between Mary and the Godhead, which subsumed and transcended all the possibilities of human relatedness.[111] Yet the strophe ends humbly, with the Virgin's promise of consolation and shelter to a generic "sinner." This line is addressed less to the visionary poet than to the devotee reading or listening to the *leich*.

Sources and analogues: In *Kreuzleich* 15, Frauenlob recounts the legend of the Cross more fully. The strophe begins "Adam biltsam vernam: er gram, / im quam ein siuche, die nicht lebenden zam: / durch trost, in helfes wise / den sun zum paradise / sante er nach einem rise" ("Adam came to an understanding by means of an image. He cried out in pain as a sickness came upon him, so that he could no longer live. For consolation, he sent his son on a journey to Paradise to seek help; it was from thence that the food of the eternal Fall had come. He died before the high, saving wood came to him, bearing rich help. Yet through his eating, the tree meant to him loss of salvation and lasting misery. Seth planted in the earth of Adam's grave the branch that later became the wood of the Cross. When the Sibyl [that is, the Queen of Sheba] made it known,

110. "The Annunciation of the Lord," in Jacobus de Voragine, *The Golden Legend: Readings on the Saints,* trans. William Granger Ryan, 2 vols. (Princeton: Princeton University Press, 1993): 1:197.

111. Newman, *God and the Goddesses,* 250–54, 282–83.

the will of Solomon, after an interval of silence, freely offered it due honor. Later it carried the door of all heavens. On it the Father shot the arrow of his soul").[112]

Strophe 20

In the final strophe of his *leich,* Frauenlob circles back to the twelve stones of the initial vision, now represented as Mary's heavenly jewels. It is in this context that he offers his most explicit theological statement of her double nature, its authority heightened by the Lady's first-person speech.

The opening lines are, even for Frauenlob, unusually dense. The strophe begins with another allusion to the Song, where the lover compares his bride's long, dancing locks to leaping goats: "your hair is like a flock of goats that have come up from Mount Gilead" (Cant. 4:1). Hair, according to Alan of Lille's *Elucidatio,* signifies thought because it adorns the head just as thoughts adorn the mind; and the Virgin's thoughts are subtle in contemplation and eminent in divine love. Hence in her thinking she mounts to the heights of contemplation, just as goats in their sharp-sighted agility scamper up mountains.[113] Thus Frauenlob's Lady proclaims that as "goats (*die geize*) climb up mountains seeking their nourishment (*nar*), [so] through my hair I may spring (*geleichen*) on high; I have climbed above the heights of heaven" (20.1−3)—either in her contemplation, as Alan declares, or more literally at her Assumption.[114] The allusiveness is enhanced by a buried Latin wordplay on *capellae* (goats) and *capilli* (hair).

From this abridged allegory, Frauenlob turns to Luke's Gospel, where Mary crosses the mountains of Judah to visit her cousin Elizabeth (Luke 1:39). This journey becomes the point of departure for a new allegory: as Queen of Heaven, the Virgin can still "come over the mountains" to the hard-hearted (20.5) and amend their sinful souls according to her lover's pleasure. In this way, after her own fashion, she harrows hell (20.7). Like Noah's ark, she is a sure refuge against the deadly flood of sin—a figure more often applied to the "ship" of the Church. Mary possesses this power because her humanity has been so thoroughly suffused (*durchswummen*) with divinity (20.4)—and here Frauenlob at last brings us to the heart of his Mariology. "Between humanity and God," she declares, "I stand on the borderline" (20.10−11). This assertion is not metaphorical; as the entire poem has demonstrated, the Lady of the *leich* is fully human, but she is also fully divine through her union with the Trinity. *Ich got, sie got, er got,* she proclaimed in 12.33, and in 20.28−31 she will offer a fuller if still enigmatic explanation.

Before reaching the doctrinal climax of his poem, however, Frauenlob provides a final complex image, which constitutes its exegetical climax. "I am the great City of God," the Lady had

112. *Kreuzleich* II.15.1−18; GA 314, 679−80; Kern, "*Heilvlies und selden holz,*" in *Festschrift Walter Haug und Burghart Wachinger,* 2:743−57. I have followed Kern's emendation of the GA's *heilvliez* ("stream of salvation") in II.15.10 to *heilvlies,* an abridged form of *heilverlies* ("loss of salvation"). Kern further claims an allusion to the secret of the mass (that is, the prayer "Te igitur") in the *stille* of 15.15. The last line alludes to Isaiah 49:2, "posuit me sicut sagittam electam, in pharetra sua abscondit me."

113. Alan of Lille, *Elucidatio* ad 4:1, PL 210:77d−78a.

114. Cf. Richard of St.-Laurent, *De laudibus beatae Mariae* 5.2.6, in *Alberti Magni Opera* 36:283: "The Virgin's hair, that is, her subtle, spiritual thoughts, sweetly clinging to Christ, her head, are compared to all these flocks, for with the eye of contemplation she penetrated the mysteries of the supreme Divinity more subtly than all the flocks of contemplatives."

asserted in 15.3. In the last strophe, she turns to John the Divine's vision of the New Jerusalem in Apocalypse 21, citing the twelve gems in its foundation (21:19–20) as the glittering adorn-ments of her beauty. This list of gemstones has a complicated history. It is loosely based on an ear-lier list in Exodus 28:17–20, where twelve jewels representing the twelve tribes of Israel are to be set in the breastplate of the high priest. Although the jewels in the two lists are not exactly the same, the passage in the Apocalypse is clearly meant to evoke and supersede the text of Exodus, indicating that the Church is the New Jerusalem and that the twelve apostles replace (or repre-sent) the twelve tribes.[115] Aside from this symbolic valence and their material worth, gemstones were also credited with healing properties (*virtutes*) in medieval medicine. Lapidaries, or hand-books on the properties of gems, tend to fuse their symbolic values with their medicinal ones.[116] In Frauenlob's list, the twelve gems and their meanings are ruby (martyrdom or Christ's Passion), emerald (chastity), sapphire (beauty), jasper (victory), beryl (true love), jacinth (inner fire), topaz (pure desire), chalcedony (modesty), amethyst (fertility), chrysolite (joy), garnet (gentleness), and chrysoprase (comfort). Some of these values are taken from lapidaries, while others appear to be the poet's own. The ruby of martyrdom is associated with Simeon's prophecy to the Virgin that "a sword shall pierce through your own soul also" at the sight of Christ's Passion (Luke 2:35).[117] Jasper, thought to have the medicinal property of staunching hemorrhages (20.19), here quenches the "flood of woe" (*die vlut des jamers*) resulting from Christ's death—but not before his blood has shattered the "diamond of the hard curse" (20.17). *Adamas* is a play on "adamant" (diamond) and "Adam": the curse of original sin has previously been described as rock (9.16), and it was believed that diamond, the hardest of all rocks, could only be cut by blood.[118] But 20.18 has another meaning as well: in overcoming the curse of sin, Christ also "preserved" (*gewerte*) his mother from it by means of her Immaculate Conception.

In 20.23–24, as earlier in 19.25, Frauenlob makes verbs out of nouns. In a final symbolic repre-sentation of her courtship with God, Mary declares, "his topazing came to me in pure desire; / then I chalcedoned in a way becoming to modesty." Why these strange locutions? Topaz often symbol-ized chastity, as in Chaucer's parodic *Tale of Sir Thopas*. But with his neologism *calcedonete*, Frauen-lob playfully calls attention to the central and most audacious doctrine of his poem. Chalcedony is a gemstone presumably named after the ancient Byzantine city of Chalcedon in Asia Minor.[119] But

115. A third list including nine gems is found in Ezekiel 28:13, describing the ornaments of Lucifer before his fall.

116. For a detailed compendium of Latin and German gem lore, see Salzer, *Die Sinnbilder*, 199–279.

117. Cf. Reinmar von Zweter, *Leich*, 204–8, p. 409: "Unz daz er si doch gewerte / mit dem Simeônes swerte / marter der si gerte: / diu marter, die si sehende leit, / in swertes wis ir herze sneit" (Mary concealed the depths of her love "until [Christ] granted her, with Simeon's sword, the martyrdom that she desired; the torment she suffered in seeing [the Passion] cut her heart like a sword").

118. The belief that a diamond can be softened by goat's blood is found in Pliny, *Naturalis historia* 37.15 (Stuttgart: Teubner,

1967), 5:406; Isidore of Seville, *Etymologiae* 16.13.2 (PL 82:577c); and Marbode of Rennes, *De lapidibus* 1, ed. John Riddle (Wiesbaden: Franz Steiner, 1977), 35–36. See also Friedrich Ohly, "Diamant und Bocksblut," in *Wolfram-Studien* 3 (1975): 72–188.

119. In modern mineralogy, chalcedony is a catchall term for a form of silicate, cryptocrystalline quartz. It comes in many colors with varieties including agate, bloodstone, carnelian, cat's eye, chrysoprase, flint, jasper, onyx, sard, and sardonyx. But contem-porary names for gemstones do not coincide with medieval usage, and it is seldom possible to determine precisely which stone the lapidary authors had in mind.

the Council of Chalcedon in 451 was, after Nicea, the most important of the seven ecumenical councils. It was there that the Church defined the dogma of Christ's double nature and single person against Monophysite and Nestorian heretics, declaring him to be "truly God and truly man, of a rational soul and body, consubstantial with the Father as regards his divinity, and consubstantial with us as regards his humanity."[120] According to Chalcedonian orthodoxy, the eternal Word of God did not cease to be divine at the moment of his incarnation in the Virgin, nor was he divided into two persons, one divine and one human. Rather, he united a complete and perfect human nature with his Godhead in such a way that he remained a single person yet subsisted thenceforth "in two natures, without confusion, without change, without division, without separation." Since his human nature could no longer be separated from his unique divine Person, Mary deserved to be called not only the mother of Jesus but also the mother of God (*Theotokos*)—a title that had been formally conferred on her twenty years earlier at the Council of Ephesus (431).

Frauenlob, who had dabbled in every art from alchemy to astronomy, surely knew enough theology and church history to be aware of these definitions, for, just a few lines after "I chalcedoned to him," we hear the Lady's declaration of her own dual nature: "Thus I, human, became divine, / indeed, divine and human—this he accomplished" (20.30–31). In a deliberate echo of the Chalcedonian formula, Frauenlob puts his own doctrinal statement into the mouth of Mary. Just as the divine Son became human at the moment of his incarnation, without ceasing to be God, so his mortal Mother became divine at the same moment, without ceasing to be human. This assertion is, strictly speaking, heterodox: the Church has never defined Mary as divine, and in the context of a Latin theological treatise such a statement would have merited censure or worse.[121] Nevertheless, the statement is in accord with the quasi-divine powers routinely ascribed to Mary in devotional literature and miracle stories, and with the sapiential Mariology of the Divine Office. From the twelfth century on, preexistence had been attributed to the Virgin because of her liturgical conflation with Sapientia, and from this high Mariology it was only a short step to the overt proclamation of her divinity.[122] As noted earlier, Frauenlob's near-contemporary, the beguine mystic Mechthild of Magdeburg (d. ca. 1282), had named the Virgin openly as "goddess" (*goettinne*).

Frauenlob's Lady is a goddess not in her own right but only in union with the Trinity. This union is asserted once more in the last of his allegories from the Song of Songs, a passage that also cements the prodigious formal unity of the poem. Just as the enumeration of the twelve gems in strophe 20 alludes back to strophe 1, where they were first mentioned (1.7), so the passage about the Virgin's "robbery" (20.28–29) echoes strophe 4b, where the "watchmen of the

---

120. "Sequentes igitur sanctos Patres, unum eundemque confiteri Filium Dominum nostrum Iesum Christum consonanter omnes docemus, eundem perfectum in deitate, eundem perfectum in humanitate, Deum vere et hominem vere, eundem ex anima rationali et corpore, consubstantialem Patri secundum deitatem et consubstantialem nobis eundem secundum humanitatem." "Definitio," in Heinrich Denzinger and Adolf Schönmetzer, *Enchiridion symbolorum, definitionum et declarationum de rebus fidei et morum,* 33rd ed. (Freiburg: Herder, 1965), 108.

121. On the relative immunity of vernacular poetry, see Newman, *God and the Goddesses,* 39–40, 304–9.

122. For the stages in this process, see ibid., chap. 5, esp. 194–206.

walls" seize the beloved Lady and steal her mantle. Both passages in turn allude to Canticle 5:7: "the watchmen who go about the city found me; they struck me, they wounded me; the watchmen of the walls took away my mantle." We have seen that Frauenlob's interpretation of this text follows the unusual exegesis of Alan of Lille, for whom the stolen mantle (*pallium*) represents the *velamen ignorantiae*, the "veil of ignorance" that has darkened human vision ever since the Fall. Thus the watchmen or "robbers" who steal the mantle are none other than the Father, Son, and Holy Spirit. In the Incarnation they have freed Mary from the "inborn cloud" (*angeborne nebel*, 20.27) so that now she can see God clearly and be united with him. Hence, as she says playfully, "the robbers will never again escape me" (20.29)—the three divine Persons will never depart from her. This assertion echoes 4.17–18, where the poet says that the "Trinity has sunk transformation deep in [her] wounds," and 12.30–31, where she identifies herself as "the throne the Godhead never left, since God slipped into me." Now we are finally in a position to understand why she claimed in the same passage, "I am God, they are God, he is God: this I will hide from none" (12.33).

After these climactic affirmations, the great poem comes at last to an end. Having fully declared herself, the Lady invites her devotees to "rejoice forever" in the healing and comfort she can offer them. With her saving help, the audience of the poem—or all believers—can become *des himels margariten*, "pearls of heaven" (20.36; Apoc. 21:21), the gems from which the twelve gates of the New Jerusalem are fashioned. It is interesting that the Middle English *Pearl*—the only medieval English text comparable to the *Marienleich* in its formal intricacy and virtuosity—ends with precisely the same allusion: after seeing a celestial Lady and the celestial City in his vision, the poet prays that he and all Christians may be transformed into "precious pearls to [God's] pleasure."[123] Frauenlob's pearls, like his diamond, stand apart from the twelve jewels that constitute the Lady's crown.

Even though the *Marienleich* is a vernacular poem meant for secular performance, its liturgical echoes are so strong that the scribe of one manuscript was moved to add a Latin colophon: *Amen. Expliciunt cantica canticorum vrowenlobiz.* "Here ends Frauenlob's Song of Songs."

Sources and analogues: Gemstones were often allegorized in lapidaries and other texts, but their meanings are far from consistent. Medical as well as devotional writers, not to mention Apocalypse commentators, assigned each gem a variety of virtues, often overlapping with others. Precious stones in general were thought to cure illness, repel demons, counteract poisons, and clarify the sight. The virtues they most commonly symbolize are wisdom and charity. Frauenlob's links between particular stones and their properties are to some extent arbitrary and, in all likelihood, derive from multiple sources. For example, Arnold of Saxony (ca. 1220) and Vincent of Beauvais both note that jasper has the ability to stop bleeding (20.19), an assertion first made by a twelfth-century commentator on the influential Marbode of Rennes.[124]

---

123. For a fuller comparison, see Newman, "The Artifice of Eternity."

124. Arnold of Saxony, *De virtutibus lapidum*, chap. 8, and Vincent of Beauvais, *Speculum naturale*, 8.77, both cited in Salzer, *Die Sinnbilder*, 237; Marbode, *De lapidibus* 4, pp. 40–41.

Marbode, following the late antique author Damigeron, was himself the source of an oft-cited belief that the wearing of beryl increases marital love; hence Frauenlob's *berillen warer minne* (20.21). Later authors, such as Ernest of Prague and Trithemius, extended this power to fostering love between the flesh and the spirit or God and the soul.[125] Hildegard of Bingen remarks that jacinth, held up to the sun, heats up quickly because it "remembers that it was born from fire" (cf. 20.22).[126] Lines 20.21–22 also recall a passage from Reinmar von Zweter's *leich,* though without the gems: "Diu Minne ist sô durchliuhtic gar, / daz nie sô trüebe ein herze wart, / sô dürre noch sô vlinsic hart, / wirt ir gewinket rehte dar, / si macht ez balde himelvar"[127] ("Love is so thoroughly luminous that never has any heart been so cloudy, so dry, or so flinty hard that, if she were rightly summoned, she could not soon make it clear and bright as heaven").

Frauenlob associates the "chrysolites of joy" with Mary's deliverance from original sin (20.26–27). Bernardino of Busti, writing in the late fifteenth century, would note that the chrysolite is a fitting gem for the Virgin's crown because, like her, it "expels melancholy from us and infuses joy and exultation into our souls."[128]

125. Marbode, *De lapidibus* 12, p. 50; Salzer, *Die Sinnbilder,* 207–9.

126. Hildegard of Bingen, *Physica* 4.2 (PL 197:1251a). According to Marbode, this stone's appearance changes with the weather: "nubilus obscuro, rutilans clarusque sereno" (*De lapidibus* 14, p. 52). See also 8.18.

127. *Leich,* 26–30, p. 402.

128. Bernardino of Busti, *Sermo 2 de coronatione Mariae,* cited in Salzer, *Die Sinnbilder,* 212.

GLOSSARY OF TECHNICAL TERMS

Abgesang. "Falling song"; the last of three metrical units comprising a strophe in minnesang or *Spruchdichtung*.

Anima mundi. World Soul, a term used in Plato's *Timaeus* for the divine emanation giving life to the universe; identified with the Holy Spirit by William of Conches and Peter Abelard.

Aufgesang. "Rising song"; the first two metrical units comprising a strophe in minnesang or *Spruchdichtung*.

Blumen. Rhetorical ornaments (*flores rhetorici*); figures of speech used especially to adorn a praise-poem.

Brautmystik. "Bridal mysticism"; erotic spirituality focused on the love affair between God and a generically feminine soul (*anima*); practiced widely but not exclusively by religious women.

Contrafactum. Text composed with the same metrical pattern as an earlier text, often in another language, so that it can be sung to the same melody.

Cursus. The cycle of eight modes or tonalities used in plainchant.

Dolce stil nuovo. "Sweet new style"; term coined by Dante for the introspective love lyrics of such poets as Guido Cavalcanti and Guido Guinicelli (*stilnovisti*).

Ewig-Weibliche. Eternal Feminine; a term coined by Goethe at the end of his *Faust* ("Das Ewig-Weibliche zieht uns hinan," "the Eternal Feminine draws us above").

Frau Werlt. "Lady World"; poetic and iconographic personification of the World as a temptation to be resisted, along with the Flesh and the Devil; imaged as a woman with a beautiful face and a worm-eaten back.

Geblümter Stil. "Flowery style"; a rhetorically ornate style favored by some late thirteenth- and fourteenth-century poets.

Heterometric. Poetry in which the lines in a stanza or strophe are of unequal length; opposite of "isometric."

Heterostrophic. A poetic form such as the sequence or *leich* in which the strophes are metrically dissimilar; opposite of "isostrophic."

Hohe Minne. "Exalted love"; the German equivalent of Provençal *fin' amors,* or English "courtly love."

Leich. An elaborate sung poem modeled on the Latin sequence form, composed of paired strophes with metrical and melodic repetition of selected units.

Marienlob. "Marian praise"; a genre of vernacular religious poetry.

Meistersingers. Professional poet-singers of the fifteenth through seventeenth centuries; organized in urban guilds; practiced a didactic art emphasizing complex form, rhetorical sophistication, and fidelity to the "tradition of the old masters."

Minne. Love, frequently personified as a lady or a goddess; may have either sacred or secular connotations, or both at once.

Minnelied. A strophic love song composed and performed by minnesingers, dealing with traditional lyric themes of love-longing, praise of ladies, and pleas for mercy.

Minnesingers. German poet-singers of the twelfth and thirteenth centuries, preoccupied with themes of courtly love; usually amateurs rather than professional poets, often of noble blood; parallel to the

Provençal *troubadours,* the northern French *trouvères,* and the Italian *stilnovisti.*

Modes. The eight musical scales or tonalities used in plainchant, characterized according to their "finals" (the last note of a melody in the given mode); an "authentic" and a "plagal" mode exist in the tonalities of D, E, F, and G.

Planctus Mariae. Devotional poem in which Mary laments at the foot of the Cross.

Praedicabilia. Aristotle's ten categories: substance, quality, quantity, relation, action, passion, time, place, position, and condition.

Praedicamenta. The five universals in Aristotelian logic: genus, species, specific difference, individual property, and accident.

Sängerkrieg. "Singers' war"; a real or fictional competition between rival poet-singers.

Sequence. Liturgical chant sung between the Alleluia and the Gospel at mass.

Shrine Madonna (*vierge ouvrante*). Sculptured Virgin whose front panels open to reveal the Trinity inside her body, normally God the Father holding a crucifix, with the Spirit in the form of a dove between the heads of the Father and the Son.

Singschule. "Singing school"; institution organized by the meistersingers, beginning in the fifteenth century, to promote the teaching of their art and to sponsor poetic competitions.

Spruchdichter. Professional poet-singers of the thirteenth and fourteenth centuries; traveled from court to court in the service of noble patrons; sometimes seen as representing a transitional stage between the minnesingers and the meistersingers.

Spruchdichtung (or **Sangspruchdichtung**). The repertoire of the *Spruchdichter;* sung strophic poetry on a range of political, religious, and moral themes.

Sprüche. "Sayings" or proverbs; the standard term for short, strophic, didactic poems.

Stollen. One of two metrically identical units comprising the *Aufgesang,* or "rising song," in a strophe of minnesang or *Spruchdichtung.*

Streitgedicht. Debate poem in which two or more characters or personifications argue which is superior.

Strophe. The basic metrical unit in minnesang and *Spruchdichtung,* generally tripartite, consisting of two *Stollen* plus an *Abgesang;* a strophe could be either an independent poem or one unit in a longer poem. In a *leich,* the strophe is bipartite and may consist of two metrically identical halves.

Tactus. A poetic foot or musical bar containing one stressed syllable.

Theotokos. "God-bearer"; Greek theological title for the Virgin Mary.

Ton (pl. **Töne**). "Tune"; a melodic and metrical template for the composition of strophic poems.

Vrouwe. "Lady" or "woman," especially as an object of literary praise; used idiosyncratically by Frauenlob in the sense of "mother." *Unsere Vrouwe,* "Our Lady," is a devotional title for the Virgin Mary.

Wip-vrouwe debate. A series of poems exchanged between Frauenlob and rival singers, arguing whether woman is more appropriately praised as *wip* ("woman") or *vrouwe* ("lady").

ABBREVIATIONS

MANUSCRIPTS

C   Manesse Codex: Heidelberg, Universitätsbibliothek Cod. pal. germ. 848.
E   Munich, Universitätsbibliothek 2° Cod. MS 731.
F   Weimar, Zentralbibliothek der deutschen Klassik Q 564.
J   Jena, Universitätsbibliothek MS El. f. 101.
L   Berlin, Stiftung Preussischer Kulturbesitz MS germ. oct. 403.
t   Colmar *Liederhandschrift*: Munich, Bayerische Staatsbibliothek Cod. germ. mon. 4997.
W   Vienna, Österreichische Nationalbibliothek Cod. Vind. 2701.

BOOKS AND SERIES

AH   *Analecta Hymnica Medii Aevi.* Edited by Clemens Blume and Guido Dreves, 55 vols. (Leipzig, 1866–1922; repr. New York: Johnson Reprint Corp., 1961).
CCCM   *Corpus christianorum: continuatio mediaevalis* (Turnhout: Brepols, 1966–).
CCSL   *Corpus christianorum: series latina* (Turnhout: Brepols, 1953–).
CSEL   *Corpus scriptorum ecclesiasticorum latinorum* (Vienna: C. Gerold, 1866–1974).
EETS   Early English Text Society.
GA   Göttingen Ausgabe: Frauenlob, *Leichs, Sangsprüche, Lieder.* Edited by Karl Stackmann and Karl Bertau, 2 vols. (Göttingen: Vandenhoeck & Ruprecht, 1981).
MGH.SS.   *Monumenta Germaniae historica, Scriptores.*
PL   J.-P. Migne, *Patrologiae cursus completus: series latina,* 221 vols. (Paris: Migne, 1844–64).

BIBLIOGRAPHY

PRIMARY SOURCES

Abelard, Peter. *Opera theologica*. Edited by Eligius Buy-
taert. CCCM 12. Turnhout: Brepols, 1969.
———. *Theologia "summi boni"* and *Theologia "scholar-
ium."* Edited by Eligius Buytaert and Constant
Mews. CCCM 13. Turnhout: Brepols, 1987.
Agrippa von Nettesheim, Heinrich Cornelius. *De nobili-
tate et praecellentia foeminei sexus: lateinischer Text und
deutsche Übersetzung in Prosa*, Edited and translated
by Otto Schönberger. Würzburg: Königshausen &
Neumann, 1997.
———. *Declamation on the Nobility and Preeminence of the
Female Sex*. Translated by Albert Rabil. Chicago:
University of Chicago Press, 1996.
Alan of Lille. *Anticlaudianus*. Edited by Robert Bossuat.
Paris: J. Vrin, 1955.
———. *Elucidatio in Cantica canticorum*. PL 210:51–110.
———. *Liber de planctu Naturae*. Edited by Nikolaus
Häring. *Studi Medievali, terza serie*, 19.2 (1978):
797–879.
———. "Rhythmus de Incarnatione Christi." PL 210:
577–80.
Albertus Magnus. *On Animals: A Medieval Summa Zoo-
logica*. Translated by Kenneth Kitchell Jr. and I. M.
Resnick. 2 vols. Baltimore: Johns Hopkins Univer-
sity Press, 1999.
Ambrose of Milan. *De incarnationis Dominicae sacramento*.
PL 16:817–46.
Analecta Hymnica Medii Aevi. Edited by Clemens Blume
and Guido Dreves. 55 vols. Leipzig, 1866–1922;
repr. New York: Johnson Reprint Corporation,
1961.

Augustine of Hippo. *The Trinity*. Translated by Stephen
McKenna. Washington, D.C.: Catholic University
of America Press, 1963.
Bach, Adolf, ed. *Das Rheinische Marienlob: Eine deutsche
Dichtung des 13. Jahrhunderts*. Leipzig: Hiersemann,
1934.
Bartsch, Karl, ed. *Meisterlieder der Kolmarer Handschrift*.
Stuttgart: Litterarischer Verein, 1862.
Batts, Michael, ed. *Bruder Hansens Marienlieder*. Tübin-
gen: Niemeyer, 1963.
Bede. *In Lucae Evangelium Expositio*. Edited by D. Hurst.
CCSL 120. Turnhout: Brepols, 1955.
Beheim, Michel. *Die Gedichte des Michel Beheim*. Edited by
Hans Gille and Ingeborg Spriewald. 3 vols.
Berlin: Akademie-Verlag, 1968–72.
Beleth, Jean. *Summa de ecclesiasticis officiis*. Edited by Her-
bert Douteil. CCCM 41–41a. Turnhout: Brepols,
1976.
Bernard of Clairvaux. *Sancti Bernardi Opera*. Edited by
Jean Leclercq, Henri Rochais, and C. H. Talbot. 5
vols. Rome: Editiones Cistercienses, 1957–77.
Bernardus Silvestris. *Cosmographia*. Edited by Peter
Dronke. Leiden: Brill, 1978.
———. *The "Cosmographia" of Bernardus Silvestris*. Trans-
lated by Winthrop Wetherbee. New York: Colum-
bia University Press, 1973.
Blank, Walter, and Günter and Gisela Kochendörfer,
eds. *Mittelhochdeutsche Spruchdichtung, früher Meis-
tersang: Der Codex Palatinus Germanicus 350 der
Universitätsbibliothek Heidelberg*. 3 vols. Wiesbaden:
Reichert, 1974.
Bonner, Anthony, ed. and trans. *Songs of the Troubadours*.
New York: Schocken Books, 1972.

Boppe. *Der Spruchdichter Boppe: Edition, Übersetzung, Kommentar.* Edited by Alex Heidrun. Tübingen: Niemeyer, 1998.

Conrad of Hirsau. *Speculum virginum.* Edited by Jutta Seyfarth. CCCM 5. Turnhout: Brepols, 1990.

Dante Alighieri. *Paradiso.* Edited and translated by John Sinclair. New York: Oxford University Press, 1961.

———. *Vita Nuova.* Translated by Mark Musa. Bloomington: Indiana University Press, 1973.

Denzinger, Heinrich, and Adolf Schönmetzer, eds. *Enchiridion symbolorum, definitionum et declarationum de rebus fidei et morum.* 33rd ed. Freiburg: Herder, 1965.

Durandus, William. *Rationale divinorum officiorum.* Edited by A. Davril and T. M. Thibodeau. CCCM 140–140b. Turnhout: Brepols, 1995–98.

Eckhart. *Meister Eckhart: Teacher and Preacher.* Edited and translated by Bernard McGinn. New York: Paulist, 1986.

Franko von Meschede. "Carmen magistrale de beata Maria Virgine." AH 29:185–204.

Frauenlob (Heinrich von Meissen). *Cantica Canticorum, or, The Lay of Our Lady.* Translated by A. E. Kroeger. St. Louis: Gray & Baker, 1877.

———. *Frauenlobs Marienleich.* Edited by Ludwig Pfannmüller. Strassburg: Karl Trübner, 1913.

———. *Heinrichs von Meissen des Frauenlobes Leiche, Sprüche, Streitgedichte und Lieder.* Edited by Ludwig Ettmüller. Leipzig, 1843; repr. Amsterdam: Rodopi, 1966.

———. *Leichs, Sangsprüche, Lieder.* Edited by Karl Stackmann and Karl Bertau. 2 vols. Göttingen: Vandenhoeck & Ruprecht, 1981.

Frawenlob, Johann. "Die lobwürdige Gesellschafft der gelehrten Weiber." In Elisabeth Gössmann, ed., *Eva, Gottes Meisterwerk,* 46–83. Munich: Iudicium, 1985.

Friedrich von Sonnenburg. *Die Sprüche Friedrichs von Sonnenburg.* Edited by Achim Masser. Tübingen: Niemeyer, 1979.

George, Stefan. *Sämtliche Werke.* 18 vols. Stuttgart: Klett-Cotta, 1982–2003.

Godfrey of Admont (?). *Homiliae festivales.* PL 174:633–1060.

Goethe, Johann Wolfgang von. *Sämtliche Werke.* 27 vols. Frankfurt am Main: Deutscher Klassiker Verlag, 1987–99.

Gottfried von Strassburg. *Tristan.* Edited by Reinhold Bechstein and Peter Ganz. 2 vols. Wiesbaden: Brockhaus, 1978.

Grosseteste, Robert. *Le Château d'Amour.* Edited by J. Murray. Paris: Champion, 1918.

Haustein, Jens, and Karl Stackmann, eds. *Sangsprüche in Tönen Frauenlobs: Supplement zur Göttinger Frauenlob-Ausgabe.* 2 vols. Göttingen: Vandenhoeck & Ruprecht, 2000.

Heinrich von Mügeln. *Die kleineren Dichtungen Heinrichs von Mügeln.* Edited by Karl Stackmann. 3 vols. Berlin: Akademie-Verlag, 1959.

———. *Der meide kranz.* Edited and translated by Annette Volfing, with commentary. Tübingen: Niemeyer, 1997.

Heinrich von Neustadt. *Apollonius von Tyrland, Gottes Zukunft, und Visio Philiberti.* Edited by Samuel Singer. Berlin: Weidmann, 1906.

Hildegard of Bingen. *Physica.* PL 197:1125–352.

———. *Symphonia armonie celestium revelationum.* Edited and translated by Barbara Newman. 2nd ed. Ithaca: Cornell University Press, 1998.

Hofmeister, Adolf, ed. *Die Chronik des Mathias von Neuenburg.* MGH.SS,, n.s. 4, fasc. 1. Berlin: Weidmann, 1924.

Hopkins, Gerard Manley. *The Poems of Gerard Manley Hopkins.* 4th ed. Edited by W. H. Gardner and N. H. MacKenzie. London: Oxford University Press, 1967.

Hours of the Divine Office in English and Latin. Collegeville, Minn.: Liturgical Press, 1964.

Hudry, Françoise, ed. *Alain de Lille (?): Lettres Familières (1167–1170).* Paris: J. Vrin, 2003.

Hugh of St. Victor. *Adnotationes elucidatoriae in quosdam Psalmos David.* PL 177:589–634.

———. *De laude charitatis.* PL 176:969–76.

Hugo von Trimberg. *Der Renner.* Edited by Gustav Ehrismann. 4 vols. Tübingen: Litterarischer Verein, 1908–11.

Hunt, Tony, ed. *Les Cantiques Salemon: The Song of Songs in MS Paris BNF fr. 14966.* Turnhout: Brepols, 2006.

Isidore of Seville. *Etymologiae.* PL 82.

Jacobus de Voragine. *The Golden Legend: Readings on the Saints.* Translated by William Granger Ryan. 2 vols. Princeton: Princeton University Press, 1993.

Jerome. *Adversus Jovinianum.* PL 23:211–352.

———. *Commentariorum in Matheum Libri.* Edited by D. Hurst and M. Adriaen. CCSL 77. Turnhout: Brepols, 1969.

————. *Epistulae*. Edited by Isidore Hilberg. CSEL 54–56. Vienna: Tempsky, 1910–18.

John of Hauville. *Architrenius*. Edited and translated by Winthrop Wetherbee. Cambridge: Cambridge University Press, 1994.

John of Neumarkt. *Briefe Johanns von Neumarkt*. Edited by Paul Piur. Berlin: Weidmann, 1937.

Julian of Norwich. *A Revelation of Love*. In Nicholas Watson and Jacqueline Jenkins, eds., *The Writings of Julian of Norwich*. University Park: The Pennsylvania State University Press, 2006.

Junker, Uwe, ed. *Das Buch der heiligen Dreifaltigkeit in seiner zweiten, alchemistischen Fassung (Kadolzburg, 1433)*. Cologne: F. Hansen, 1986.

Kiepe, Eva, and Hansjürgen Kiepe, eds. *Gedichte 1300–1500, nach Handschriften und Frühdrucken in zeitlicher Folge*. Vol. 2 of Walther Killy, ed., *Epochen der deutschen Lyrik*. Munich: Deutscher Taschenbuch, 1972.

Konrad von Würzburg. *Die goldene Schmiede*. Edited by Edward Schröder. Göttingen: Vandenhoeck & Ruprecht, 1926.

Kramer, Heinrich, and James Sprenger. *Malleus maleficarum*. Translated by Montague Summers. New York: Dover, 1971.

Lamprecht von Regensburg. *Sanct Francisken Leben und Tochter Syon*. Edited by Karl Weinhold. Paderborn: F. Schöningh, 1880.

Liber Usualis Missae et Officii. Edited by monks of Solesmes. Tournai, Belgium: Desclée, 1953.

Marbode of Rennes. *De lapidibus*. Edited by John Riddle. Wiesbaden: Franz Steiner, 1977.

Mechthild von Magdeburg. *Das fliessende Licht der Gottheit*. Edited by Gisela Vollmann-Profe. Frankfurt am Main: Deutscher Klassiker Verlag, 2003.

————. *The Flowing Light of the Godhead*. Translated by Frank Tobin. New York: Paulist, 1998.

Nagel, Bert, ed. *Meistersang: Meisterlieder und Singschulzeugnisse*. Stuttgart: Philipp Reclam, 1965.

Napier, Arthur S., ed. *History of the Holy Rood-Tree: A Twelfth-Century Version of the Cross-Legend*. EETS o.s. 103. London: K. Paul, Trench, Trübner & Co., 1894.

Neidhart von Reuental. *Die Lieder Neidharts*. Edited by Siegfried Beyschlag. Darmstadt: Wissenschaftliche Buchgesellschaft, 1975.

Notker of St.-Gall. *Notker der Dichter und seine geistige Welt*. Edited by Wolfram von den Steinen. 2 vols. Bern: A. Francke, 1948.

Ochsenbein, Peter, ed. "Das Compendium Anticlaudiani." *Zeitschrift für deutsches Altertum und deutsche Literatur* 98 (1969): 80–109.

Ohly, Friedrich, ed. *Das St. Trudperter Hohelied: Eine Lehre der liebenden Gotteserkenntnis*. Frankfurt am Main: Deutscher Klassiker Verlag, 1998.

Ottokar von Steiermark. *Österreichische Reimchronik*. Edited by Joseph Seemüller. MGH Script. vernac. 5. 2 vols. Hannover: Hahn, 1890–93.

Overgaard, Mariane, ed. *The History of the Cross-Tree Down to Christ's Passion: Icelandic Legend Versions*. Copenhagen: Munksgaard, 1968.

Peter von Zittau. *Chronicon Aulae Regiae: Fontes rerum bohemicarum* 4. Prague: Svoboda, 1976.

Pliny the Elder. *Naturalis historia*. 6 vols. Stuttgart: Teubner, 1967.

Pope, John C., ed. *Seven Old English Poems*. Indianapolis: Bobbs-Merrill, 1966.

Rabanus Maurus. *De universo*. PL 111:9–614.

Reinmar von Zweter. *Die Gedichte Reinmars von Zweter*. Edited by Gustav Roethe. Leipzig: Hirzel, 1887.

Richard of St.-Laurent. *De laudibus beatae Mariae*. In *Alberti Magni Opera omnia*. Edited by Auguste and Émile Borgnet. Vol. 36. Paris: Louis Vivès, 1898.

Richardson, Cyril, et al., ed. and trans. *Early Christian Fathers*. New York: Macmillan, 1970.

Rietsch, Heinrich, ed. *Gesänge von Frauenlob, Reinmar von Zweter und Alexander* (facsimile). Vienna, 1913; repr. Graz: Akademische Druck- und Verlagsanstalt, 1960.

Rossetti, Christina. *Complete Poems*. Edited by R. W. Crump. London: Penguin, 2001.

Rupert of Deutz. *Commentaria in Canticum canticorum*. Edited by Hraban Haacke. CCCM 26. Turnhout: Brepols, 1974.

Schröder, Edward, ed. *Die Kaiserchronik eines Regensburger Geistlichen*. MGH Script. vernac. 1. Hannover: Hahn, 1892.

Suchensinn. *Suchensinn und seine Dichtungen*. Edited by Emil Pflug. Hildesheim: Olms, 1908.

Tervooren, Helmut, and Ulrich Müller, eds. *Die Jenaer Liederhandschrift* (facsimile). Göppingen: A. Kümmerle, 1972.

Von der Hagen, Friedrich, ed. *Minnesinger: Deutsche Liederdichter des zwölften, dreizehnten und vierzehnten Jahrhunderts*. 5 vols. Leipzig: J. A. Barth, 1838–56.

Walther von der Vogelweide. *Leich, Lieder, Sangsprüche*. Edited by Christoph Cormeau. 14th ed. Berlin: Walter de Gruyter, 1996.

William of Conches. *Glosae super Boetium*. Edited by Lodi Nauta. CCCM 158. Turnhout: Brepols, 1999.

William of St.-Thierry. *Expositio altera super Cantica canticorum*. PL 180:473–546.

Wolfram von Eschenbach. *Parzival*. Edited by Karl Lachmann. 6th ed. Berlin: Walter de Gruyter, 1999.

STUDIES

d'Alverny, Marie-Thérèse. "Alain de Lille et la 'Theologia.'" In *L'Homme devant Dieu: Mélanges offerts au Père Henri de Lubac*, 2:111–28. Paris: Aubier, 1964.

Appelhans, Peter. *Untersuchungen zur spätmittelalterlichen Mariendichtung: Die rhythmischen mittelhochdeutschen Mariengrüsse*. Heidelberg: Carl Winter, 1970.

Astell, Ann. *The Song of Songs in the Middle Ages*. Ithaca: Cornell University Press, 1990.

Barber, Richard. *The Holy Grail: Imagination and Belief*. Cambridge: Harvard University Press, 2004.

Baumer, Christoph. "Die Schreinmadonna." *Marian Library Studies* 9 (1977): 239–72.

Beach, Alison. "Listening for the Voices of Admont's Twelfth-Century Nuns." In Linda Olson and Kathryn Kerby-Fulton, eds., *Voices in Dialogue: Reading Women in the Middle Ages*, 187–98. Notre Dame, Ind.: University of Notre Dame Press, 2005.

Beckers, Hartmut. "Die volkssprachige Literatur des Mittelalters am Niederrhein." *Digitale bibliotheek voor de Nederlandse letteren*. Online at http://www.dbnl.org.

Behr, Hans-Joachim. *Literatur als Machtlegitimation: Studien zur Funktion der deutschsprachigen Dichtung am böhmischen Königshof im 13. Jahrhundert*. Munich: Wilhelm Fink, 1989.

Bein, Thomas. "*Liep unde Lust*: Beobachtungen zu einem 'Minneprinzip' Frauenlobs unter besonderer Berücksichtigung von VII,38–40." In Schröder, ed., *Wolfram-Studien* 10:159–68.

———. "*Sus hup sich ganzer liebe vrevel*": *Studien zu Frauenlobs Minneleich*. Frankfurt am Main: Peter Lang, 1988.

Berg, Ludwig. "Die Mainzer Kirche und die heilige Hildegard." *Archiv für mittelrheinische Kirchengeschichte* 27 (1976): 49–70.

Bertau, Karl. "Über Themenanordnung und Bildung inhaltlicher Zusammenhänge in den religiösen Leichdichtungen des XIII. Jahrhunderts." *Zeitschrift für deutsche Philologie* 76 (1957): 129–49.

———. "Untersuchungen zur geistlichen Dichtung Frauenlobs." Dissertation, Göttingen 1954.

Blamires, Alcuin. *The Case for Women in Medieval Culture*. Oxford: Clarendon, 1997.

Brunner, Horst. "Die Spruchtöne Frauenlobs: Bemerkungen zur Form und zur formgeschichtlichen Stellung." In Haustein and Steinmetz, eds., *Studien zu Frauenlob und Heinrich von Mügeln*, 61–79.

———, ed. *Konrad von Würzburg: Seine Zeit, sein Werk, seine Wirkung. Tagung Würzburg 1987*. Marbach: Oswald von Wolkenstein-Gesellschaft, 1988.

Bühler, Harald. "Zur Gestaltung des lyrischen Ichs bei Cavalcanti und Frauenlob." In Werner Schröder, ed., *Wolfram-Studien* 10:179–89.

Bumke, Joachim. *Courtly Culture: Literature and Society in the High Middle Ages*. Translated by Thomas Dunlap. Berkeley and Los Angeles: University of California Press, 1991.

———. *Geschichte der deutschen Literatur im hohen Mittelalter*. Munich: Deutscher Taschenbuch, 1990.

———. *Mäzene im Mittelalter: Die Gönner und Auftraggeber der höfischen Literatur in Deutschland, 1150–1300*. Munich: Beck, 1979.

Bynum, Caroline Walker. *Holy Feast and Holy Fast: The Religious Significance of Food to Medieval Women*. Berkeley and Los Angeles: University of California Press, 1987.

Caputo, John. "Fundamental Themes of Meister Eckhart's Mysticism." *The Thomist* 42 (1978): 197–225.

Carruthers, Mary. *The Book of Memory: A Study of Memory in Medieval Culture*. Cambridge: Cambridge University Press, 1990.

Catta, Étienne. "*Sedes Sapientiae*." In Hubert du Manoir, ed., *Maria: Études sur la sainte Vierge*, 8 vols, 6:689–866. Paris: Beauchesne, 1949–71.

Classen, Albrecht, ed. *Women as Protagonists and Poets in the German Middle Ages: An Anthology of Feminist Approaches to Middle High German Literature*. Göppingen: Kümmerle, 1991.

Clooney, Francis X. *Divine Mother, Blessed Mother: Hindu Goddesses and the Virgin Mary*. New York: Oxford University Press, 2005.

Codex Manesse: Katalog zur Ausstellung vom 12. Juni bis 2. Oktober 1988, Universitätsbibliothek Heidelberg. Heidelberg: Edition Braus, 1988.

Condren, Edward. *The Numerical Universe of the "Gawain-Pearl" Poet: Beyond "Phi."* Gainesville: University Press of Florida, 2002.

Curtius, Ernst. *European Literature and the Latin Middle Ages.* Translated by Willard Trask. Princeton: Princeton University Press, 1953.

De Boor, Helmut. "Frauenlobs Streitgespräch zwischen Minne und Welt." *Beiträge zur Geschichte der deutschen Sprache und Literatur* 85 (1963): 383–409.

Delius, Walther. *Geschichte der Marienverehrung.* Munich: Ernst Reinhardt, 1963.

Derolez, Albert. "The Manuscript Transmission of Hildegard of Bingen's Writings: The State of the Problem." In Charles Burnett and Peter Dronke, eds., *Hildegard of Bingen: The Context of Her Thought and Art,* 17–27. London: Warburg Institute, 1998.

Diehl, Patrick. *The Medieval European Religious Lyric: An Ars Poetica.* Berkeley and Los Angeles: University of California Press, 1985.

Diehr, Achim. "Mediale Doppelgestalt: Text und Melodie in Frauenlobs Minneleich." *Jahrbuch der Oswald von Wolkenstein Gesellschaft* 10 (1998): 93–110.

Dobozy, Maria. "Konrad von Würzburg." *The Literary Encyclopedia,* 2003. Online at www.litencyc.com/php.

———. *Re-Membering the Present: The Medieval German Poet-Minstrel in Cultural Context.* Turnhout: Brepols, 2005.

Dronke, Peter. *Poetic Individuality in the Middle Ages: New Departures in Poetry, 1000–1150.* Oxford: Clarendon, 1970.

Edelmann-Ginkel, Alwine. *Das Loblied auf Maria im Meistersang.* Göppingen: Kümmerle, 1978.

Edwards, Cyril, Ernst Hellgardt, and Norbert Ott, eds. *Lied im deutschen Mittelalter: Überlieferung, Typen, Gebrauch. Chiemsee-Colloquium 1991.* Tübingen: Niemeyer, 1996.

"Eggenfelden: Pfarrkirche und Nebenkirchen." Pamphlet issued by the Katholisches Stadtpfarramt Eggenfelden, 2004.

Egidi, Margreth. *Höfische Liebe: Entwürfe der Sangspruchdichtung, Literarische Verfahrensweisen von Reinmar von Zweter bis Frauenlob.* Heidelberg: Carl Winter, 2002.

Ehrismann, Gustav. *Geschichte der deutschen Literatur bis zum Ausgang des Mittelalters.* Vol. 2. Munich: Beck, 1935.

Finckh, Ruth. *Minor Mundus Homo: Studien zur Mikrokosmos-Idee in der mittelalterlichen Literatur.* Göttingen: Vandenhoeck & Ruprecht, 1999.

Freytag, Hartmut. "Beobachtungen zu Konrads von Würzburg 'Goldener Schmiede' und Frauenlobs Marienleich." In Brunner, ed., *Konrad von Würzburg,* 181–93.

———. "Zu den Strophen 6 und 7 von Frauenlobs Marienleich." In Schröder, ed., *Wolfram-Studien* 10:71–79.

Fritsch-Starr, Susanne. "Bruder Hans: Spiegel spätmittelalterlicher Frauenlobrezeption am Niederrhein." *Jahrbuch der Oswald von Wolkenstein Gesellschaft* 10 (1998): 139–51.

Frühmorgen-Voss, Hella. "Bildtypen in der Manessischen Liederhandschrift." In Glier, ed., *Werk—Typ—Situation,* 184–216.

Fulton, Rachel. *From Judgment to Passion: Devotion to Christ and the Virgin Mary, 800–1200.* New York: Columbia University Press, 2002.

———. "Mimetic Devotion, Marian Exegesis, and the Historical Sense of the Song of Songs." *Viator* 27 (1996): 85–116.

———. "'Quae est ista quae ascendit sicut aurora consurgens?' The Song of Songs as the *Historia* for the Office of the Assumption." *Mediaeval Studies* 60 (1998): 55–122.

Gärtner, Kurt. "Franko von Meschede." *Verfasserlexikon,* 2nd ed., 2:829–34. Berlin: Walter de Gruyter, 1980.

———. "Das Hohelied in Frauenlobs Marienleich." In Schröder, ed., *Wolfram-Studien* 10:105–16.

Ganz, Peter. "'Nur eine schöne Kunstfigur': Zur 'Goldenen Schmiede' Konrads von Würzburg." *Germanisch-Romanische Monatsschrift* 29 (1979): 27–45.

Glier, Ingeborg. "Der Minneleich im späten 13. Jahrhundert." In *Werk—Typ—Situation,* 161–83.

———, ed. *Werk—Typ—Situation: Studien zu poetologischen Bedingungen in der älteren deutschen Literatur. Hugo Kuhn zum 60. Geburtstag.* Stuttgart: Metzler, 1969.

Graef, Hilda. *Mary: A History of Doctrine and Devotion.* 2 vols. New York: Sheed & Ward, 1963–65.

Guzzardo, John. *Dante: Numerological Studies.* New York: Peter Lang, 1987.

Harvey, Andrew, and Anne Baring. "Queen of Heaven." In *The Divine Feminine: Exploring the Feminine Face of God Around the World,* 102–19. Berkeley, Calif.: Conari Press, 1996.

Haustein, Jens, and Ralf-Henning Steinmetz, eds. *Studien zu Frauenlob und Heinrich von Mügeln: Festschrift für Karl Stackmann zum 80. Geburtstag.* Fribourg: Universitätsverlag, 2002.

Henkel, Nikolaus. *Studien zum Physiologus im Mittelalter.* Tübingen: Niemeyer, 1976.

———. "Die zwölf alten Meister: Beobachtungen zur Entstehung des Katalogs." *Beiträge zur Geschichte der deutschen Sprache und Literatur* 109 (1987): 375–89.

Hilpisch, Stephanus. "Der Kult der hl. Hildegard." *Pastor bonus* 45 (1934): 118–33.

Hinkel, Helmut. "St. Hildegards Verehrung im Bistum Mainz." In Anton Brück, ed., *Hildegard von Bingen, 1179–1979: Festschrift zum 800. Todestag der Heiligen,* 385–411. Mainz: Gesellschaft für Mittelrheinische Kirchengeschichte, 1979.

Hollywood, Amy. *The Soul as Virgin Wife: Mechthild of Magdeburg, Marguerite Porete, and Meister Eckhart.* Notre Dame, Ind.: University of Notre Dame Press, 1995.

Hopper, Vincent. *Medieval Number Symbolism: Its Sources, Meaning, and Influence on Thought and Expression.* New York: Columbia University Press, 1938.

Huber, Christoph. *Die Aufnahme und Verarbeitung des Alanus ab Insulis in mittelhochdeutschen Dichtungen.* Munich: Artemis, 1988.

———. "Frauenlob zum Minneprozess." In Schröder, ed., *Wolfram-Studien* 10:151–58.

———. "*Gepartiret und geschrenket:* Überlegungen zu Frauenlobs Bildsprache anhand des Minneleichs." In Haustein and Steinmetz, eds., *Studien zu Frauenlob und Heinrich von Mügeln,* 31–50.

Hübner, Gert. *Lobblumen: Studien zur Genese und Funktion der "Geblümten Rede."* Tübingen: A. Francke, 2000.

Jackson, Timothy R. "Erotic Imagery in Medieval Spiritual Poetry and the Hermeneutics of Metaphor." In Bernhard Debatin, Timothy R. Jackson, and Daniel Steuer, eds., *Metaphor and Rational Discourse,* 113–24. Tübingen: Niemeyer, 1997.

———. "Erotische Metaphorik und geistliche Dichtung: Bemerkungen zu Frauenlobs 'Marienleich.'" In Schröder, ed., *Wolfram-Studien* 10:80–86.

Jackson, William E. *Reinmar's Women: A Study of the Woman's Song ("Frauenlied" and "Frauenstrophe") of Reinmar der Alte.* Amsterdam: Benjamins, 1981.

Jaeger, C. Stephen. "Pessimism in the Twelfth-Century 'Renaissance.'" *Speculum* 78 (2003): 1151–83.

Jammers, Ewald. *Das Königliche Liederbuch des deutschen Minnesangs: Eine Einführung in die sogenannte Manessische Handschrift.* Heidelberg: Lambert Schneider, 1965.

Kästner, Hannes. "'Sermo Vulgaris' oder 'Hövischer Sanc': Der Wettstreit zwischen Mendikantenpredigern und Wanderdichtern um die Gunst des Laienpublikums und seine Folgen für die mittelhochdeutsche Sangspruchdichtung des 13. Jahrhunderts (Am Beispiel Bertholds von Regensburg und Friedrichs von Sonnenburg)." In Michael Schilling and Peter Strohschneider, eds., *Wechselspiele, Kommunikationsformen und Gattungsinterferenzen mittelhochdeutscher Lyrik,* 209–43. Heidelberg: Carl Winter, 1996.

Kasten, Ingrid, ed. *Frauenlieder des Mittelalters.* Stuttgart: Philipp Reclam, 1990.

Kautzsch, Rudolf, and Ernst Neeb. *Die Kunstdenkmäler der Stadt und des Kreises Mainz,* Bd. 2, Teil 1: *Der Dom zu Mainz.* Darmstadt: Hessische Staatsverlag, 1919.

Keller, Hildegard E. *My Secret Is Mine: Studies on Religion and Eros in the German Middle Ages.* Leuven: Peeters, 2000.

Kellner, Beate. "*Vindelse:* Konturen von Autorschaft in Frauenlob's 'Selbstrühmung' und im '*wip-vrowe*-Streit.'" In Elizabeth Andersen, Jens Haustein, Anne Simon, and Peter Strohschneider, eds., *Autor und Autorschaft im Mittelalter: Kolloquium Meissen 1995,* 255–76. Tübingen: Niemeyer, 1998.

Kemper, Tobias. "*Der smit von oberlande:* Zu Frauenlobs Marienleich 11.1f. und verwandten Stellen." *Beiträge zur Geschichte der deutschen Sprache und Literatur* 121 (1999): 201–13.

Kern, Peter. "*Heilvlies* und *selden holz:* Überlegungen zu Frauenlobs Kreuzleich." In Johannes Janota, ed., *Festschrift Walter Haug und Burghart Wachinger,* 2:743–57. Tübingen: Niemeyer, 1992.

———. *Trinität, Maria, Inkarnation: Studien zur Thematik der deutschen Dichtung des späteren Mittelalters.* Berlin: Erich Schmidt, 1971.

Kiepe-Willms, Eva. "'*Sus lêret Herman Dâmen*': Untersuchungen zu einem Sangspruchdichter des späten 13. Jahrhunderts." *Zeitschrift für deutsches Altertum und deutsche Literatur* 107 (1978): 33–49.

Kinsley, David. "Mary: Virgin, Mother, and Queen." In *The Goddesses' Mirror: Visions of the Divine from East and West*, 215–60. Albany: SUNY Press, 1989.

Köbele, Susanne. *Frauenlobs Lieder: Parameter einer literarhistorischen Standortbestimmung*. Tübingen: A. Francke, 2003.

———. "Umbesetzungen: Zur Liebessprache in Liedern Frauenlobs." In Christoph Huber, Burghart Wachinger, and Hans-Joachim Ziegeler, eds., *Geistliches in weltlicher und Weltliches in geistlicher Literatur des Mittelalters*, 213–35. Tübingen: Niemeyer, 2000.

Koschorreck, Walter, ed. *Minnesinger in Bildern der Manessischen Liederhandschrift mit Erläuterungen*. Frankfurt am Main: Insel, 1974.

Krasenbrink, Josef. "Die 'inoffizielle' Heilige: Zur Verehrung Hildegards diesseits und jenseits des Rheins." In Edeltraud Forster, ed., *Hildegard von Bingen, Prophetin durch die Zeiten: Zum 900. Geburtstag*, 496–513. Freiburg: Herder, 1997.

Krayer, Rudolf. *Frauenlob und die Natur-Allegorese: Motivgeschichtliche Untersuchungen*. Heidelberg: Carl Winter, 1960.

Krone und Schleier: Kunst aus mittelalterlichen Frauenklöstern. Bonn and Essen: Kunst- und Ausstellungshalle der Bundesrepublik Deutschland, Bonn, and Ruhrlandmuseum, Essen, 2005.

Kühne, Udo. "Deutsch und Latein als Sprachen der Lyrik in den 'Carmina Burana.'" *Beiträge zur Geschichte der deutschen Sprache und Literatur* 122 (2000): 57–73.

———. "*Latinum super cantica canticorum*: Die lateinische Übertragung von Frauenlobs Marienleich." In Haustein and Steinmetz, eds., *Studien zu Frauenlob und Heinrich von Mügeln*, 1–14.

Lochrie, Karma. *Covert Operations: The Medieval Uses of Secrecy*. Philadelphia: University of Pennsylvania Press, 1999.

März, Christoph. *Frauenlobs Marienleich: Untersuchungen zur spätmittelalterlichen Monodie*. Erlangen: Palm & Enke, 1987.

———. "Walthers Leich und das Carmen Buranum 60/60a: Überlegungen zu einer Kontrafaktur." In Edwards et al., eds., *Lied im deutschen Mittelalter*, 43–56.

Matter, E. Ann. "The Virgin Mary: A Goddess?" In Carl Olson, ed., *The Book of the Goddess, Past and Present*, 80–96. New York: Crossroad, 1983.

———. *The Voice of My Beloved: The Song of Songs in Western Medieval Christianity*. Philadelphia: University of Pennsylvania Press, 1990.

McDonald, William C. *Whose Bread I Eat: The Song-Poetry of Michel Beheim*. Göppingen: Kümmerle, 1981.

McGinn, Bernard. *The Flowering of Mysticism: Men and Women in the New Mysticism (1200–1350)*. New York: Crossroad, 1998.

———. *The Growth of Mysticism: Gregory the Great Through the Twelfth Century*. New York: Crossroad, 1994.

Meier, Christel. "Die Rezeption des *Anticlaudianus* Alans von Lille in Textkommentierung und Illustration." In Christel Meier and Uwe Ruberg, eds., *Text und Bild: Aspekte des Zusammenwirkens zweier Künste in Mittelalter und früher Neuzeit*, 408–549. Wiesbaden: Reichert, 1980.

Mews, Constant J. "The Council of Sens (1141): Abelard, Bernard, and the Fear of Social Upheaval." *Speculum* 77 (2002): 342–82.

———. "Religious Thinker: 'A Frail Human Being' on Fiery Life." In Newman, ed., *Voice of the Living Light*, 52–69.

Nagel, Bert, ed. *Der deutsche Meistersang*. Darmstadt: Wissenschaftliche Buchgesellschaft, 1967.

Newman, Barbara. "The Artifice of Eternity: Speaking of Heaven in Three Medieval Poems." *Religion and Literature* 37 (2005): 1–24.

———. *From Virile Woman to WomanChrist: Studies in Medieval Religion and Literature*. Philadelphia: University of Pennsylvania Press, 1995.

———. *God and the Goddesses: Vision, Poetry, and Belief in the Middle Ages*. Philadelphia: University of Pennsylvania Press, 2002.

———. "Love's Arrows: Christ as Cupid in Late Medieval Art and Devotion." In Anne-Marie Bouché and Jeffrey Hamburger, eds., *The Mind's Eye: Art and Theological Argument in the Medieval West*, 263–86. Princeton: Princeton University Press, 2005.

———. *Sister of Wisdom: St. Hildegard's Theology of the Feminine*. Berkeley and Los Angeles: University of California Press, 1987.

———. "What Did It Mean to Say 'I Saw'? The Clash Between Theory and Practice in Medieval Visionary Culture." *Speculum* 80 (2005): 1–43.

———, ed. *Voice of the Living Light: Hildegard of Bingen and Her World*. Berkeley and Los Angeles: University of California Press, 1998.

Ohly, Friedrich. "Diamant und Bocksblut." *Wolfram-Studien* 3 (1975): 72–188.

———. *Hohelied-Studien: Grundzüge einer Geschichte der Hohelied-Auslegung des Abendlandes bis um ca. 1200.* Wiesbaden: F. Steiner, 1958.

Otten, Willemien. *From Paradise to Paradigm: A Study of Twelfth-Century Humanism.* Leiden: Brill, 2004.

Palmer, Nigel. "Duzen und Ihrzen in Frauenlobs Marienleich und in der mittelhochdeutschen Mariendichtung." In Schröder, ed., *Wolfram-Studien* 10:87–104.

———. "Frauenlob and Meister Eckhart." In Helen Watanabe-O'Kelly, ed., *The Cambridge History of German Literature,* 82–85. Cambridge: Cambridge University Press, 1997.

Pelikan, Jaroslav. *Mary Through the Centuries: Her Place in the History of Culture.* New Haven: Yale University Press, 1996.

Peter, Brunhilde. *Die theologisch-philosophische Gedankenwelt des Heinrich Frauenlob.* Speyer: Jägersche Buchdruckerei, 1957.

Plate, Bernward. "Natura Parens Amoris: Beobachtungen zur Begründung der *minne* in mittelhochdeutschen und frühneuhochdeutschen Texten." *Euphorion* 67 (1973): 1–23.

Podrot, Michael. *Piero della Francesca's Legend of the True Cross.* Newcastle upon Tyne: University of Newcastle, 1974.

Poor, Sara S. *Mechthild of Magdeburg and Her Book: Gender and the Making of Textual Authority.* Philadelphia: University of Pennsylvania Press, 2004.

Rettelbach, Johannes. "Abgefeimte Kunst: Frauenlobs 'Selbstrühmung.'" In Edwards et al., eds., *Lied im deutschen Mittelalter,* 177–93.

Roob, Alexander. *The Hermetic Museum: Alchemy and Mysticism.* Translated by Shaun Whiteside. Cologne: Taschen, 1997.

Ruberg, Uwe. "Frauenlob-Gedenken: Das Begräbnis des Dichters im Mainzer Domkreuzgang." *Domblätter: Forum des Dombauvereins Mainz e.V.* 3 (2001): 77–83.

Ruh, Kurt. "Beginenmystik: Hadewijch, Mechthild von Magdeburg, Marguerite Porete." *Zeitschrift für deutsches Altertum* 106 (1977): 265–77.

———. "Textkritik zum Mystikerlied 'Granum Sinapis.'" In *Kleine Schriften.* Edited by Volker Mertens, 2:77–93. Berlin: Walter de Gruyter, 1984.

———. "Die trinitarische Spekulation in deutscher Mystik und Scholastik." *Zeitschrift für deutsche Philologie* 72 (1953): 24–53.

Salzer, Anselm. *Die Sinnbilder und Beiworte Mariens in der deutschen Literatur und lateinischen Hymnenpoesie des Mittelalters.* 1897; repr. Darmstadt: Wissenschaftliche Buchgesellschaft, 1967.

Sayce, Olive. *The Medieval German Lyric, 1150–1300: The Development of Its Themes and Forms in Their European Context.* Oxford: Clarendon, 1982.

Schäfer, Gerhard M. *Untersuchungen zur deutschsprachigen Marienlyrik des 12. und 13. Jahrhunderts.* Göppingen: Kümmerle, 1971.

Schäfer, Jörg. *Walther von der Vogelweide und Frauenlob: Beispiele klassischer und manieristischer Lyrik im Mittelalter.* Tübingen: Niemeyer, 1966.

Schanze, Frieder. *Meisterliche Liedkunst zwischen Heinrich von Mügeln und Hans Sachs.* 2 vols. Munich: Artemis, 1983.

Scheja, Georg. *The Isenheim Altarpiece.* Translated by Robert E. Wolf. New York: H. N. Abrams, 1969.

Schipflinger, Thomas. *Sophia—Maria: A Holistic Vision of Creation.* Translated by James Morgante. York Beach, Maine: Samuel Weiser, 1998.

Schmidt, Margot. "'Die spilende minnevluot': Der Eros als Sein und Wirkkraft in der Trinität bei Mechthild von Magdeburg." In Margot Schmidt and Dieter Bauer, eds., *"Eine Höhe, über die nichts geht": Spezielle Glaubenserfahrung in der Frauenmystik?* 71–133. Stuttgart-Bad Cannstatt: Frommann-Holzboog, 1986.

Schnyder, Mireille. "Eine Poetik des Marienlobs: Der Prolog zur *Goldenen Schmiede* Konrads von Würzburg." *Euphorion* 90 (1996): 41–61.

Schreiner, Klaus. *Maria: Jungfrau, Mutter, Herrscherin.* Munich: Carl Hanser, 1994.

Schröder, Werner, ed. *Wolfram-Studien* 10: *Cambridger "Frauenlob"-Kolloquium 1986.* Berlin: Erich Schmidt, 1988.

Seethaler, Paula. "Die Weisheitstexte in der Marienliturgie." *Benediktinische Monatschrift* 34 (1958): 111–20.

Shields, Michael. "Zum melodischen Aufbau des Marienleichs." In Schröder, ed., *Wolfram-Studien* 10:117–24.

Siebert, Johannes. "Die Astronomie in den Gedichten des Kanzlers und Frauenlobs." *Zeitschrift für deutsches Altertum* 75 (1938): 1–23.

Sittler, Lucien. *Der Isenheimer Altar des Meisters Mathis, genannt Grünewald*. Colmar: Alsatia, 1957.

Spitz, Hans-Jörg. "'*Ez ist sanc aller sange*': Das 'St. Trudperter Hohelied' zwischen Kommentar und Dichtung." In Volker Honemann and Tomas Tomasek, eds., *Germanistische Mediävistik*, 61–88. Münster: Lit, 1999.

Stackmann, Karl. "Bild und Bedeutung bei Frauenlob." *Frühmittelalterliche Studien* 6 (1972): 441–60.

———. "Frauenlob." *Die deutsche Literatur des Mittelalters: Verfasserlexikon*. 2nd ed., 2:865–77. Berlin: Walter de Gruyter, 1980.

———. "Frauenlob (Heinrich von Meissen)—eine Bilanz." In Stackmann and Haustein, eds., *Frauenlob, Heinrich von Mügeln und ihre Nachfolger*, 34–89.

———. "Frauenlob und Wolfram von Eschenbach." In Kurt Gärtner and Joachim Heinzle, eds., *Studien zu Wolfram von Eschenbach: Festschrift für Werner Schröder zum 75. Geburtstag*, 75–84. Tübingen: Niemeyer, 1989.

———. "Frauenlob, Verführer zu 'einer gränzenlosen Auslegung.'" In Schröder, ed., *Wolfram-Studien* 10:9–25.

———. "Magd und Königin." In Stackmann and Haustein, eds., *Frauenlob, Heinrich von Mügeln und ihre Nachfolger*, 9–33.

Stackmann, Karl, and Jens Haustein. *Wörterbuch zur Göttinger Frauenlob-Ausgabe*. Göttingen: Vandenhoeck & Ruprecht, 1990.

———, eds. *Frauenlob, Heinrich von Mügeln und ihre Nachfolger*. Göttingen: Wallstein, 2002.

The Stavelot Triptych: Mosan Art and the Legend of the True Cross. New York: Pierpont Morgan Library, 1980.

Steinmetz, Ralf-Henning. *Liebe als universales Prinzip bei Frauenlob: Ein volkssprachlicher Weltentwurf in der europäischen Dichtung um 1300*. Tübingen: Niemeyer, 1994.

Sticca, Sandro. *The "Planctus Mariae" in the Dramatic Tradition of the Middle Ages*. Translated by Joseph Berrigan. Athens: University of Georgia Press, 1988.

Stolz, Michael. "Maria und die Artes liberales: Aspekte einer mittelalterlichen Zuordnung." In Claudia Opitz, Hedwig Röckelein, Gabriela Signori, and Guy Marchal, eds., *Maria in der Welt: Marienverehrung im Kontext der Sozialgeschichte, 10.–18. Jahrhundert*, 95–120. Zurich: Chronos, 1993.

———. "*Tum*"-*Studien: Zur dichterischen Gestaltung im Marienpreis Heinrichs von Mügeln*. Tübingen: Francke, 1996.

Surles, Robert, ed. *Medieval Numerology: A Book of Essays*. New York: Garland, 1993.

Suydam, Mary. "Visionaries in the Public Eye: Beguine Literature as Performance." In Ellen Kittell and Mary Suydam, eds., *The Texture of Society: Medieval Women in the Southern Low Countries*, 131–52. New York: Palgrave Macmillan, 2004.

Suydam, Mary, and Joanna Ziegler, eds. *Performance and Transformation: New Approaches to Late Medieval Spirituality*. New York: St. Martin's, 1999.

Szövérffy, Joseph. *Marianische Motivik der Hymnen: Ein Beitrag zur Geschichte der marianischen Lyrik im Mittelalter*. Leiden: Classical Folia Editions, 1985.

Taylor, Archer. *The Literary History of Meistergesang*. London: Oxford, 1937.

Thoma, Herbert. "John of Neumarkt and Heinrich Frauenlob." In *Mediaeval German Studies Presented to Frederick Norman*, 247–54. London: University of London Institute of German Studies, 1965.

Trout, John. "Alan of Lille's Commentary on the Song of Songs: A Preliminary Study." *Cistercian Studies* 8 (1973): 25–36.

Turner, Denys. *Eros and Allegory: Medieval Exegesis of the Song of Songs*. Kalamazoo, Mich.: Cistercian Publications, 1995.

Wachinger, Burghart. "Frauenlobs Cantica canticorum." In Walter Haug and Burghart Wachinger, eds., *Literatur, Artes und Philosophie*, 23–43. Tübingen: Niemeyer, 1992.

———. "Hohe Minne um 1300: Zu den Liedern Frauenlobs und König Wenzels von Böhmen." In Schröder, ed., *Wolfram-Studien* 10:135–50.

———. *Sängerkrieg: Untersuchungen zur Spruchdichtung des 13. Jahrhunderts*. Munich: Beck, 1973.

Warner, Marina. *Alone of All Her Sex: The Myth and the Cult of the Virgin Mary*. New York: Knopf, 1976.

Watson, Nicholas. "Desire for the Past" and "Afterword." In Louise D'Arcens and Juanita Feros Ruys, eds., *Maistresse of My Wit: Medieval Women, Modern Scholars*, 149–88. Turnhout: Brepols, 2004.

Wehrli, Max. *Geschichte der deutschen Literatur vom frühen Mittelalter bis zum Ende des 16. Jahrhunderts*. Vol. 1. Stuttgart: Philipp Reclam, 1980.

Winston-Allen, Anne. *Stories of the Rose: The Making of the Rosary in the Middle Ages*. University Park: The Pennsylvania State University Press, 1997.

Wogan-Browne, Jocelyn, Nicholas Watson, Andrew Taylor, and Ruth Evans, eds. *The Idea of the Vernacular:*

*An Anthology of Middle English Literary Theory,
1280–1520.* University Park: The Pennsylvania
State University Press, 1999.

Ziolkowski, Jan. "Mastering Authority and Authorizing
Masters in the Long Twelfth Century." Paper
delivered at the 40th International Congress on
Medieval Studies, Kalamazoo, Michigan, May
2005.

INDEX OF MARIENLEICH CITATIONS

INDEX OF BIBLICAL CITATIONS

GENERAL INDEX

Colmar, 155, 165
Comtessa de Dia, 62
Conrad of Hirsau, 64 n. 3
Constance, Council of, 71
contrafacta, xv, 145
Crane, Hart, 91
Cuno, bishop of Regensburg, 94
Curtius, E. R., 133

Damen, Hermann, 62, 79, 143; as critic of Frauenlob, 52–54, 57–58, 60, 133
Damigeron, 218
Daniel, Arnaut, xv
Dante Alighieri, 43, 149, 174; *Commedia*, 65, 87–88, 125; *De vulgari eloquentia*, 134; *Vita Nuova*, 87, 211
Denifle, Heinrich, 173
Devotio Moderna, 153
dialectic. *See* Logic
Diana, 192
Diehl, Patrick, xi, 91, 100
Divine Office, 97–100, 185 n. 25, 197 n. 70, 216
Donatus, 145
double-coding, 190, 202, 211
double *cursus*, 124–25, 130, 201, 210
Dream of the Rood, 84

Eckhart, Meister, 43, 83 n. 52, 135, 173, 174, 198; on *gotheit* and *got*, 135, 194
Eggenfelden, retable of, 165–66
Ehrismann, Gustav, 173–74
Eleanor of Aquitaine, 62
Elisabeth of Schönau, 62 n. 53, 162
Elizabeth, cousin of Mary, 197, 214
Ephesus, Council of, 216
Epistle to Diognetus, 183 n. 18
Erik VIII, king of Denmark, 49, 61
Eriugena, John Scotus, 73–74
Ernest of Prague, 218
eroticism, in "crossover" poetry, 88, 120, 133, 190; in Heinrich von Mügeln, 152; in *Marienleich*, 180, 184–85, 190, 202; in Mechthild von Magdeburg, 116–19, 122; in Song of Songs, 92, 94–95, 110; objections to, 174, 190. *See also* sexuality
Esther, Queen, 68, 157
Eternal Feminine, 54, 62, 69, 170, 174
Ettmüller, Ludwig, ix, 170
Eucharist, 83–84, 177, 199; and Holy Grail, 192; and mystical mill, 194, 213; and priestly power, 161; Mary as mother of, 103, 161, 194, 198
Eve, 160, 191, 202; fall of, 66, 212; in Hildegard of Bingen, 102; in Mechthild of Magdeburg, 118; in *wip-vrouwe* poems, 66; renewed in Mary, 66, 102, 189, 211
Ewig-Weibliche. See Eternal Feminine
exegesis, x–xii, 64, 92–97, 114–17, 153. *See also* Index of Biblical Citations

felix culpa, 202
Finckh, Ruth, 72 n. 22, 73, 79

Four Daughters of God, 191
Franko von Meschede, 148–49, 151, 163
Frau Werlt, 73–74, 77
Frauenlob, biography of, 48–49, 62; critical reputation of, ix–x, 44, 46, 139, 156, 169–74; death and burial of, 43, 61, 170–71; editions of, ix, xv, 139, 170, 173, 175; elegy for Konrad von Würzburg, 56–57, 60; *Kreuzleich*, 79–85, 95, 121, 143, 195–96, 213–14; literary boast of, 52, 57–60; manuscripts of, 44–47, 140–47, 155–56; *Minne und Welt*, 62, 73–79, 121, 151, 155, 182, 208; *Minneleich*, 67–73, 121, 143, 197, 210; *Minnelieder*, 62, 87–89, 155; monuments to, 170; music of, xix–xx, 85–86, 124–25, 210; paintings of, 44–47; patrons of, 49, 61, 67, 98; satires against, 49–51, 59–61, 114–15; sobriquet of, 53, 66, 162; strophic songs of, 51–52, 61, 78, 85–86, 102, 126–27, 143, 155, 163–64, 184, 199, 203–4, 206, 209, 210; translations of, xv–xvii, 143–46, 149–50, 172, 182; *wip-vrouwe* poems, 63–67, 176. *See also* Index of *Marienleich* Citations
Frawenlob, Johann, 162
Freytag, Hartmut, 181
Friedrich, margrave of Brandenburg, 71
Friedrich von Husen, 155
Friedrich von Sonnenburg, 110, 113, 140, 143, 203
Fulton, Rachel, 93, 185 n. 26

Gärtner, Kurt, 92, 97
Geblümter Stil, ix, 55, 72, 132–37, 153–54, 212; critiques of, 133–35, 173–74
gemstones, 135–36, 184, 215, 217–18. *See also* images and symbols
Gentry, Francis, xxi
George, Stefan, 172–73
Gerhard von Hoya, Count, 49
Gertrude of Helfta, 62 n. 53
Gieselbrecht, archbishop of Bremen, 49, 98
Goethe, Johann Wolfgang von, 169–70
Golden Legend, 213
Gottfried von Strassburg, 113, 131, 186. See also *Tristan*
Grail, xiii, 121, 135, 186, 191–92
grammar, 135; and the Incarnation, 108, 148, 151, 205; and the Trinity, 81; archaic, 145
Granum sinapis, 88–89
Grosseteste, Robert, 104, 191
Grünewald, Matthias, 165–68
gynecology, 72

Hadewijch, 55
Hadlaub, Johannes, 140–41
harrowing of hell, 83, 200
Hartmann von Aue, 125, 131
Haustein, Jens, 156, 175
Heinrich, duke of Mecklenburg, 49
Heinrich IV, duke of Breslau, 49
Heinrich von Kärnten, Duke, 48–49
Heinrich von Meissen. *See* Frauenlob
Heinrich von Mügeln, 88, 125, 154, 156, 164–65, 173; *Der meide kranz*, 109, 150–52; *Tum*, 152–53
Heinrich von Neustadt, 147–48

Manesse Codex, 59–60, 160, 184 n. 21; illustrations in, 44–47, 142; poetic canon of, 140–41
Manesse, Rüdiger, 140
mannerism, xvii, 133, 153–54, 174
manuscripts, 44–47, 140–47, 155–56
Marbode of Rennes, 217–18
Marian Psalters, 100
Marian Te Deum, 165
Marie de Champagne, 62
Marie de France, x, 62
Marienleich. See Images and symbols; Index of *Marienleich* Citations
Marienlob, x, 92, 100, 110–13, 132, 178
Marner, 53, 141, 156
Martianus Capella, 106
Mary. *See* Virgin Mary
Mary Magdalene, 211
Marz, Christoph, 98, 126
Mathias von Neuenburg, 149
Mechthild of Hackeborn, 62 n. 53
Mechthild of Magdeburg, 54, 62, 88, 162, 179, 216; *Das fliessende Licht der Gottheit,* 110, 117–22, 136, 143, 165
Meissen, ix, 49, 51, 98
Meissner, 143
meisterschaft, 51, 134, 200–01
Meistersingers, ix, 44, 61, 139, 155–65
Melker Marienlied, 110
microcosm, 71–72, 74, 79
Milton, John, 91
Minne, 62, 87, 120, 147; in *Marienleich,* 74, 78, 105, 182, 208; in *Minne und Welt,* 73–79, 182, 208; in *Minneleich,* 68; in *Minnelieder,* 87; in Reinmar von Zweter, 54–55, 199, 218. *See also* Caritas; *Hohe Minne*
Minnemystik. See Brautmystik
Minnesingers, 48, 52, 140–41
modes, musical, 124–25, 130, 201, 210
Monk of Salzburg, 156, 163
music, 123–25, 184, 210; and scansion, 128–29; manuscripts of, 46 n. 8, 130 n. 16, 143; of Sequentia, xviii–xxi, 130 n. 16
Muskatblut, 53, 156
mystical mill, 194, 213
mystical winepress, 213
mysticism, 88–89. *See also Brautmystik*

Natura, xii, 62, 187; in Alan of Lille, 68–69, 78, 106–7, 150, 169, 183, 189; in Bernard Silvestris, 77 n. 36, 207; in Goethe, 169; in *Marienleich,* 78–79, 105–6, 206–8; in *Minne und Welt,* 75, 78, 182; in *Minneleich,* 68–69, 106, 210
Neidhart, 141, 153, 196 n. 67
neologisms, 136, 145, 195, 213, 215
Nequam, Alexander, 93
Notker of St. Gall, 83, 100, 123
numerology and numerical composition: in Dante, 125, 211; in *Kreuzleich,* 80; in *Marienleich,* 125–26, 135, 181–82, 210, 212; in *Minne und Welt,* 76; in *Minneleich,* 68; in music, 126

Otto II, count of Oldenburg, 49
Otto III, count of Ravensberg, 49

Ottokar von Steiermark, 49 n. 15

pagan gods, xii, 145, 187, 189, 192, 209
Palmer, Nigel, xxi
Parzival, 77–78, 159–60, 172, 186, 191, 197
Pearl, x, 125, 217
performance, 48–49, 98, 121–22
Peter, Brunhilde, 78 n. 38
Peter Lombard, 106
Peter von Aspelt, archbishop of Mainz, 49, 61
Peter von Reichenbach, 156
Peter von Zittau, 98
Petrarch, 44
Pfannmüller, Ludwig, ix–x, 83 n. 52, 186, 195 n. 61; as critic of Frauenlob, x, 133–34, 173
Philip of Harvengt, 93, 185
Physiologus, xiii, 113, 135, 192–94, 197
Planctus Mariae, 84–85, 110, 184, 186
Plate, Bernward, 72 n. 25
Plato, *Timaeus,* 77, 92, 105
Platonism, Christian, 51, 104–8, 204, 206–8; and German Romantics, 170
Pound, Ezra, xv
Prague, 49, 98; University of, 51, 150
Přemysl Ottokar II, king of Bohemia, 49
prosody, xvii, 86, 100, 127–32, 193
Puschmann, Adam, 93 n. 8

quaternity, 79, 162–66, 195
Queen of Sheba, 212–13
Querelle des femmes, 160, 162
Queste del saint Graal, 191

Regenbogen, 53, 155, 156; as critic of Frauenlob, 59–60, 65, 133–35, 141; in *Krieg von Würzburg,* 46, 159–61; in Manesse Codex, 46–47, 59, 141
Reinmar der Alte, 59, 87, 141
Reinmar von Zweter, 52, 110, 173, 174; Frauenlob's allusions to, 175, 190, 199, 203, 218; in Frauenlob's literary boast, 58–60; *Leich,* 54–55, 79, 113, 191, 215 n. 117, 218; manuscripts of, 141, 156
Rettelbach, Johannes, 57, 60–61
Rheinisches Marienlob, 110–11, 113, 121, 184
rhyme schemes, xvi–xvii, 86, 129–31
rhymed offices, 124
Richard of St.-Laurent, 186 n. 28, 188, 214 n. 114
rime riche, xvii, 60
Robert of Melun, 106
Roethe, Gustav, 173
Romantics, German, 169–70, 172
Rossetti, Christina, 127
Rostock, 61
Ruberg, Uwe, 149
Rubin, 143
Rudolf I, duke of Saxony, 143
Rudolf of Habsburg, 49, 61
Rumelant, 53, 61, 65, 143

INTRODUCTION

Frauenlob's lengthy praise-song to the Celestial Woman is a masterpiece of late medieval poetry, couched in the evocative and erudite language of *Minnedienst* (the service of courtly love) and of the Biblical visionaries. Although we do not know if this phenomenal work was created during Frauenlob's tenure at the royal court in Prague, or later during his final years in Mainz, its presence in two of the most famous fourteenth-century Minnesang collections (the Mannessische and the Würzburger Songbooks) as well as other, more fragmentary sources, attests to Frauenlob's widespread reputation in his own time. Although a fully contemporary poet, he nonetheless looked back to the twelfth century for inspiration in his poetical style, structure, and thematic devices.

As is usual in medieval manuscripts, there exist no indications of how this work is to be performed. Our realization of the Leich (which was created in the form of a lengthy sequence) begins with a single male voice accompanying himself on the harp (joined by other men and a second harp): the persona of "The Poet," whose vision of the Celestial Woman covers the first eight sections of the work (sections that ingeniously follow a formal structure progressing through the eight modes). He describes what he sees and feels standing before his vision, lending universal significance to his central experience. He speaks to the woman through the various modes of address that identify her as embodiments of characters found throughout Western literary tradition: principally, she is the Beloved of the Song of Songs, but is also the mother/maiden Maria, the Wisdom-like partner of the Creation, and the exalted Celestial Woman of the twelfth chapter of the Book of the Apocalypse. In the next five sections (which begin again the cycle of modes), various female soloists embody the woman of the vision, accompanied by the two harps. The woman speaks, introducing herself to the poet in a series of stunning images, revealing the qualities of her feminine nature. All of creation is essentially of this nature, and she puts it all into harmonious relationship with the creator. Gradually her recitations become more poignant and oriented toward the idea of incarnation, as other female figures come into the foreground. Sections 15–20 of the poem, while technically still spoken by the Celestial Woman, are a celebration of the myriad things of this world that we have seen come into being through the union of the male and female creative principles. These sections abound with references to medieval philosophical and religious tradition (Aristotle, Augustine, Porphyry), passages drawing on the lore of the seven *artes liberales*, the idea of heavenly and human Virtues, and the science of gemstones. One twelfth-century work that seems to have especially fascinated Frauenlob was the Commentary on the Song of Songs by the great religious poet Alain de Lille. His is also a theologically and poetically extravagant exploration of female images through the textual amplification of Marian themes. It is impossible to attempt a definitive interpretation of Frauenlob's work, yet we can sense the communicative genius behind his redefining for this time those venerable traditions that preceded him. While in the grip of an exuberantly fertile poetic muse, he writes like a man highly intoxicated with his perceptions and language. He presents to us the mythological precepts of his culture dressed, as it were, in adorning yet obscuring veils that are ever-swirling around the dancing figure herself, the contemplation of which pulls us into the very vortex of the dance and into the actual experience of the character or idea. He seems to be pushing his own involvement with tradition to the limits of expression in order that we awaken each of our senses to these experiences—experiences not just of textual significance but also of such various elements of presentation as mode, rhetoric, vocal tessitura, color, and accompaniment. At the same time that his language delights and stimulates the senses, it confounds them, transcends them. His explorations bring us to the threshold of the unfathomable world that produces myth and allows us to examine and to experience the truth of medieval archetypes.

In our work with medieval music over the years, we have been moved by the intensity with which medieval man lived out his imaginal life—in the immense proliferation of music and poetry at every level of society, in the world of liturgical practice, theater, and the visual arts. We hope—in our presentation of one of the highest medieval works of art—to remove any doubts that might remain as to whether or not the images, themes, and musical language of the Middle Ages can have meaning for our age.

Barbara Thornton (1987, revised 1994)

ABOUT THE SEQUENTIA FRAUENLOB PROJECT

In the history of Sequentia, important projects typically have demanded a long period of gestation and then have reemerged in various incarnations over the span of many years. Our initial contact with the *Frauenleich* was during 1985, when we included sections of the piece in a program called "The Apocalyptic Imagination." Subsequent intensive study of the piece led to a theatrical production, commissioned by the Alte Oper Frankfurt for the Frankfurt Feste in September 1987, and concert performances in the Utrecht Festival Oude Muziek and other festivals. During 1989–90 the work was completely reenvisioned for this recording, and it continued to be performed in concert as late as 1994. In this version, for instance, a larger mixed instrumental ensemble was replaced by two gothic harps, instruments that are most suitable for accompanying a piece that unfolds through all eight modes. This production was the last analog recording made by Sequentia for the Westdeutscher Rundfunk. Due to technical problems with the editing process and the analog tapes, its release was repeatedly delayed, until other projects (especially the Hildegard von Bingen complete works) began to take precedence. Finally, in 1995, after one final unsuccessful attempt to restore the tapes, Barbara Thornton and I decided to abandon the tapes and rerecord the work at a later date. In any case, we no longer agreed with some of the decisions we had made about the musical realization, and felt we could do a better job if given another chance. What musician has not known this feeling? But following Barbara's tragic death in 1998, I asked Deutsche Harmonia Mundi and the Westdeutscher Rundfunk to allow one more attempt at remastering the tapes, especially in light of new technical possibilities for digital restoration that did not exist before.

I feel it is important that this performance now be heard, especially considering the enormous amount of energy put into the Frauenlob project by the ensemble, and in honor of Barbara Thornton's own deeply personal involvement with the piece over a period of ten years—it was very much her personal creation—and finally as a record of her own vocal contributions that would have otherwise remained unheard forever. The release of *Frauenlob's Leich*, exactly ten years after its recording, is not only a major testimony to the genius of one of Germany's most innovative and profound poet-composers: this CD is also a "historical recording," the documentation of an important phase in the life of our ensemble, and a witness to the creative force of an artist whose voice was cruelly silenced in mid-career.

Benjamin Bagby (1999)

FRAUENLOB (HEINRICH VON MEISSEN, CA. 1260–1318)

In spite of the large number of his works that have survived, little is known about Heinrich von Meissen's background and personal life. He was clearly not of noble birth, but through the depth of his intellectual and poetic skill he was able to establish himself as a renowned guest at royal courts across northern and eastern Germany, where his voice was heard in the presence of King Wenceslas II of Bohemia, the Hapsburg King Rudolf I, Heinrich von Breslau, Margrave Waldemar of Brandenburg, the noble Minnesänger Wizlaw von Rügen, and Giselbert, the bishop of Bremen. At some point during these travels he acquired the name Frauenlob ("Praise of woman"), which may be linked to a famous poetic dispute he held with the Minnesänger Regenbogen ("Rainbow") on the relative merits of the words *vrouwe* (lady) and *wip* (woman) in courtly society and poetry. Of course, the term *vrouwe* also refers to the Virgin Mary and to the Celestial Woman, both of whom are celebrated in his works. The final years of his life were spent in the city of Mainz, where, according to legend, he established the first school for "Meistersänger," and where his tombstone is still visible today in the cathedral.

SEQUENTIA: ENSEMBLE FOR MEDIEVAL MUSIC

Founded in 1977 by Benjamin Bagby and Barbara Thornton, Sequentia is acknowledged to be an international leader in its field—an ensemble that combines vocal and instrumental virtuosity with innovative research and programming to reconstruct the living musical traditions of medieval Europe. Following the tragic death of Barbara Thornton in 1998, Sequentia continues under the direction of Benjamin Bagby as a multifaceted ensemble whose size and composition vary with the demands of the repertoire being performed. Sequentia is based in Cologne, Germany. Through international tours and more than twenty recordings with Deutsche Harmonia Mundi (available worldwide through BMG Classics) and major European radio networks, as well as films for television and independent filmmakers, Sequentia brings to life long-forgotten repertoires from the tenth to fourteenth centuries.

Sequentia performs extensively in Europe and North America, and since 1979 has undertaken numerous far-reaching tours under the auspices of the Goethe Institute, performing all over the world.

Sequentia has received prizes for several recordings, including the International CD Prize Frankfurt, the Netherlands' Edison Prize, the Innsbruck Radio Prize, a Grammy nomination (USA) and both the French Disque d'Or and Diapason d'Or, and has been awarded research grants for performance projects from the Siemens Foundation and the Volkswagen Foundation. In addition to their performing and recording activities, the members of the ensemble also teach medieval performance practice at special intensive courses held each year in Europe and North America.

After receiving the 1993 Deutsche Schallplattenpreis for their three-CD series of medieval Spanish music, *Vox Iberica*, Sequentia entered into a long-term relationship with BMG Classics/Deutsche Harmonia Mundi. This has resulted in a project to record the complete works of the German mystic and abbess Hildegard von Bingen (1098–1179); the third CD in this series, *Canticles of Ecstasy*, sold more than 400,000 copies worldwide. Other recordings span medieval repertoires from Iceland to Aquitania to Spain.